English
Literary Criticism:

THE

RENAISSANCE

GOLDENTREE BOOKS

R. C. BALD, SAMUEL H. BEER & WILLIAM C. DEVANE
Series Editors

THOMAS E. CONNOLLY, Editor
Joyce's "Portrait": Criticisms & Critiques

C. DAY LEWIS, Editor
English Lyric Poems, 1500–1900

O. B. HARDISON, JR., Editor
Modern Continental Literary Criticism

O. B. HARDISON, JR., Editor
English Literary Criticism: The Renaissance

SAMUEL HYNES, Editor
English Literary Criticism: Restoration and 18th Century

DANIEL G. HOFFMAN and SAMUEL HYNES, Editors
English Literary Criticism: Romantic and Victorian

KATHERINE LEVER
The Novel and the Reader

MILTON MARX
The Enjoyment of Drama, 2nd Edition

WILLIAM MATTHEWS, Editor
Later Medieval English Prose

HAROLD OREL, Editor
The World of Victorian Humor

ROBERT L. PETERS, Editor
Victorians on Literature & Art

EDWARD STONE, Editor
Henry James: Seven Stories and Studies

O. B. HARDISON, JR.

University of North Carolina

EDITOR

English Literary Criticism:
THE RENAISSANCE

New York

APPLETON-CENTURY-CROFTS

Division of Meredith Publishing Company

PREFACE

THE PERIOD COVERED by the present volume extends from Caxton's preface to Malory (1484) to Milton's preface to *Samson Agonistes* (1671). Some selection has been necessary, but the limited amount of formal criticism produced in England during this period makes it possible to present the major works and a generous sampling of the minor ones, including a portion of the best rhetorical text of the period, Wilson's *Arte of Rhetorique*. The result is a collection of essays which, it is hoped, represents the major critical trends of the age and accurately reflects the evolution of English criticism up to the age of Dryden.

With the exception of Caxton's prefaces, which have been modernized, the texts used are those of the standard Renaissance editions. The original spelling, capitalization, and use of italics have been followed except in the case of long *s*, which has regularly been changed to short *s*. Emendation has been kept to a minimum, and the temptation to indulge in profuse annotation has been resolutely resisted. Foreign-language quotations have been translated in the notes and their sources indicated when known; also a few obscure terms and allusions have been explained. References to classical works and authors listed in the standard handbooks have not been annotated. An appendix has been provided giving brief sketches of the Continental humanists referred to by English authors. Where possible, texts are presented uncut. Book-length works are necessarily represented by excerpts, but an effort has been made to reproduce the main line of each author's argument as well as his more striking conclusions.

The present volume is not a collaboration but is, in a sense, the product of a joint effort. It was originally conceived by Professor Daniel G. Hoffman of Swarthmore College, who had prepared a tentative table of contents and had gathered several texts when other obligations made it impossible for him to continue. At that time he generously suggested that the present editor complete the volume, giving him a free hand to modify the original plan should this seem desirable to him. The editor wishes

to express his sincere gratitude to Professor Hoffman both for
being asked to compile the anthology and for the many valuable
suggestions which he derived from Professor Hoffman's original
plan. The editor's modifications of this plan are the result of
ideas which occurred naturally during the work of compilation
and are intended to maximize the usefulness of the volume to
students of Renaissance criticism.

Among others who have offered advice and assistance, the
editor wishes particularly to thank Professors Walter Allen and
Albert Suskin of the University of North Carolina Department
of Classics; and Professors Richmond P. Bond, Albrecht Strauss,
Ernest Talbert, and William Wells of the University of North
Carolina Department of English. The encouragement and assistance of his wife has been, as always, too great for any expression
of gratitude to be adequate.

O.B.H.

Chapel Hill, North Carolina

CONTENTS

PART III: PRACTICAL CRITICISM

PART IV: SEVENTEENTH CENTURY CROSS CURRENTS

Contents

English

Literary Criticism:

THE

RENAISSANCE

Introduction

◦❖◦

ENGLISH RENAISSANCE CRITICISM is based on the classics as interpreted by the Italian scholars of the fifteenth and sixteenth centuries. Its native elements diminished in importance as the revival of learning created an international community of intellectuals with Latin as their universal language. The classical texts upon which criticism was based were originally established and annotated by the Italians, and the Italian influence remained strong even when the editions used were German or French. Moreover, the major critical issues had been explored by the Italians long before they were considered important in England. The debate over Latin versus the vernacular began in Italy in the fourteenth century with Dante Alighieri's *On Vernacular Eloquence* (*De Vulgari Eloquentia,* 1307), which attempted to establish the appropriate dialect and forms for serious poetry in Italian. The defense of poetry began with Books XIV and XV of Giovanni Boccaccio's *Genealogy of the Gods* (1363–64), which constitute a formal essay justifying poetry against its many opponents. Consciously Neoplatonic criticism emerged at the end of the fifteenth century in the work of the so-called Florentine Platonists—most notably, Angelo Politian and Pico della Mirandola. The revival of Aristotle's *Poetics,* the question of the relative merits of epic and romance, and the emergence of the Neoclassic 'rules' all occurred in Italy well before becoming important in England.

Many of the classical sources of English Renaissance criticism were works which could hardly be considered criticism today. Rhetoric may be defined as the formal study of techniques for composing and delivering orations, including working up the argument (invention), organization, style, delivery, and memory. It was a central element in the classical system of education and became so once again during the Renaissance. The most influential classical treatises on rhetoric were Cicero's *De Inventione*

1

ánd *De Oratore,* the anonymous *Rhetorica ad Herennium,* and
Quintilian's lengthy *Institute of Oratory,* followed, in approxi-
mate order of importance by Aristotle's *Rhetoric* and the exercise
books (*Progymnasmata*) of Hermogenes and Aphthonius. These
works and their Renaissance imitations formed the basis of the
standard critical discussions of *doctrina,* verisimilitude, decorum,
organization, and, above all, style. They were supplemented by
more specifically literary works. Horace's *Ars Poetica* 'explained'
by elaborate scholarly glosses was the most frequently cited of
these. The glosses themselves are instances of classical influence,
for they relied heavily on ancient commentaries—Servius and
Macrobius on Virgil, Donatus on Terence, Euanthius on comedy
and tragedy, Demetrius on style, and so forth.

Two other highly regarded classical treatments of poetry were
Cicero's spirited defense of a minor contemporary poet, *Pro
Archia Poeta,* and Plutarch's brief essay *On Reading the Poets.*
Greek works were read in Latin or cited second hand when
translations were not readily available. Plato was a pervasive influence, but most references are either from the commonplace
book or based on Marsilio Ficino's Latin translation, with commentaries, of the *Complete Works* (*Opera Omnia Divini Platonis*). Because Ficino missed the irony of the *Ion,* that dialogue
became a *locus classicus* for the idea of poetic inspiration.
Aristotle's *Poetics* was referred to in England during the 1550's,
but it did not have an important influence on criticism until the
last twenty years of the century, and at that time the references
are probably derived as often from Italian translations and commentaries as from first-hand knowledge of the Greek. For reasons
still imperfectly understood Longinus' *On the Sublime,* though
translated into Latin during the sixteenth century, had no appreciable influence on criticism—Italian, French, or English—until
the second half of the seventeenth century.

The Italian revival of learning to which the Elizabethans were
so heavily indebted began in the fourteenth century with Giovanni Boccaccio and Francis Petrarch. Boccaccio wrote on a
variety of literary matters in his *Comment on the Divine Comedy*
and his *Genealogy of the Gods,* but his influence was minor compared to that of Petrarch. As the author of the *Sonnets to Laura,*
Petrarch gained an international reputation which lasted through

out the seventeenth century. His other works, largely forgotten now, commanded equal respect during the Renaissance. In his verse epistles and letters he praised classical literature, criticized scholasticism, and described his constant efforts to recover manuscripts of classical works which were either lost or corrupt in his day. His Latin epic *Africa* was the first of numerous efforts, culminating in the work of Tasso, Spenser, and Milton, to rival Virgil's *Acneid*.

Petrarch's successors ably carried his work forward. By the end of the fifteenth century the way had been prepared for the Italian high Renaissance. The "Platonic Academy" of Florence was of particular importance in this work. An assembly of brilliant scholars subsidized by Cosimo and Lorenzo de' Medici and led by Marsilio Ficino, it directed its best efforts to editing, translating, and interpreting the works of Plato and the Neoplatonists. The result was Christian Platonism, a somewhat artificial synthesis of classical and Christian thought with broad implications for the arts.

During the sixteenth century Italian criticism passed through three distinct phases. The first was Platonic and rhetorical. The *Ars Poetica* was read by men like Politian in the light of the writings of Plato, Plotinus, Iamblichus, and the lesser Neoplatonists. In Politian's *Nutricia*—a verse essay on the early history of literature—poetry is the nurse of mankind, the source of religion, law, and science, and divinely inspired prophetic vision. Platonism encouraged didactic criticism, but its most characteristic contribution was its doctrine of *furor poeticus* and its corresponding encouragement of idealism, symbolism, and allegory. These elements were taken with sufficient seriousness by members of the Platonic Academy to arouse the indignation of Fra Girolamo Savonarola, who claimed that the humanists attributed to secular poetry an inspiration and depth of meaning found only in the Bible, and hence were guilty of blasphemy. Nevertheless, Platonic theories remained popular to the end of the sixteenth century in Italy, being apparent in the work of Girolamo Fracastoro (*Naugerius*, 1555) and Torquato Tasso (*Discorsi*, 1594).

Italian rhetorical criticism is illustrated by the *Dialogues* of Giovanni Pontanus, a Neapolitan critic, and the *Poetica* of Bernardino Daniello. Rhetoric had always been important in medieval poetic theory, but the rhetoric books used during the Middle Ages were elementary school texts—the *Ad Herennium,* the *De Inventione,* and the *Praeëxercitamenta* ("Exercises"). In these, technique—especially the use of the rhetorical figures—overshadows all other subjects. The rediscovery of works like Cicero's *De Oratore* and Quintilian's *Institute of Oratory* stimulated a new and much broader rhetoric emphasizing invention, logic, and arrangement as well as style, and involving consideration of philosophical and educational issues. The broadening of rhetoric led to a similar broadening of criticism. Pontanus' dialogue *Actius* (*c.* 1490) is a sophisticated attempt to distinguish between poet, orator, and historian, starting with the assumption that all use rhetoric but in different ways. Daniello's *Poetica* (1536) is restricted to poetry, but its organization, choice of topics, and— often—its language are strongly influenced by Cicero's *De Oratore.*

The second phase of Italian criticism was inaugurated in 1548 with Francis Robortello's *Explications of the Poetics of Aristotle,* containing the Greek text, Latin translation, and commentary. It was followed by several other commentaries and Aristotelian critical essays of which the most important was Lodovico Castelvetro's *Poetics of Aristotle in Italian* (1570). Although the *Poetics* was usually interpreted according to the Platonic and/or rhetorical prejudices of the commentators, it opened a whole new range of poetic topics including poetic unity, the nature of imitation, plot structure, catharsis, and dramatic conventions. Despite efforts by such critics as Sebastian Minturno and Torquato Tasso to assimilate Aristotle into the traditional Platonic-rhetorical frame of humanistic criticism, strains inevitably developed. The stricter Aristotelians tended to regard the *Poetics* as a prescriptive document, and attempted to formulate rules for each of the modes and genres of poetry. The doctrine of the three unities, usually traced to Castelvetro, is a case in point; but by far the most influential of the Aristotelians was Julius Caesar Scaliger, whose lengthy *Seven Books of Poetics* (*Poetices Libri Septem,* 1561) became the bible of the early Neoclassicists in France and England.

Toward the end of the sixteenth century Italian criticism entered a third phase. Clearly defined schools of criticism emerged whose differing points of view were aired in quarrels over such topics as the ancients versus the moderns, the relative merits of Homer and Virgil, the merits of the *Divine Comedy*, and the legitimacy of romance and tragi-comedy as literary forms. As a result of the pressures of controversy, criticism began to assume the characteristics associated with French Neoclassicism of the seventeenth and eighteenth centuries. The Accademia della Crusca—an Italian anticipation of the Académie française—undertook to purify the language; and Traiano Boccalini produced, in his *Reports from Parnassus* (1612) a form of satiric criticism which fascinated French and English Neoclassicists for the next hundred years. Contemporaneous with the rise of Neoclassicism was the emergence of a school of criticism which considered metaphor, conceit, and wit the essential elements of poetry. *Concettismo* is most clearly illustrated in the work of Emmanuele Tesauro (*The Aristotelian Telescope*, 1654) and is roughly equivalent to Spanish Gongorism, French mannerism, and English 'metaphysical' style.

A brief review of Italian achievements is necessary for a proper understanding of the development of English criticism during the Renaissance. At the end of the fifteenth century a few intrepid Englishmen like John Free and William Grocyn had traveled to Italy and become infected with the enthusiasms of the Italian humanists. When they returned, their work was cut out for them. A strong central government was emerging after the chaos of the War of the Roses. The language, though still uncertain, had passed through the most confusing stage of the transition from Middle to Modern English. The growth of English commerce had created new sources of wealth and an urban middle class with leisure and a desire for culture. Most important, the advent of the printing press in 1476 made it possible to publish books in large numbers and at a fraction of the cost of manuscripts. printer, helped to create awareness of England's literary heritage stabilize the literary language. William Caxton, England's first printer, helped to create awareness of England's literary heritage by his editions of Chaucer (1484), Gower (1483), and Malory (1484). The prefaces to these editions show the patriotic pride which he took in his work. In prefaces to works which he translated, he shows an awareness of the deficiencies of the English of his day and a desire to remedy them. Although Caxton did little to further the cause of the new learning, he published translations of classical works which had been medieval favorites— the *Aeneid,* Cicero's *On Friendship* and *On Old Age,* and Boethius' *Consolation of Philosophy,* among others. Despite Caxton's limitations, he deserves an honorable place in the history of English criticism. Wynkyn de Worde and Richard Pynson, his immediate successors, followed his lead without notable innovations. Greek type was not used in England before 1521, and Hebrew not before 1523.

By 1500 English intellectuals were consciously imitating the Italian humanists. William Grocyn and Thomas Linacre had sat at the feet of Guarino da Verona and Angelo Politian, and were eager to institute a thorough humanistic reform of English education. John Colet, Grocyn's disciple, founded St. Paul's School and so successfully guided its fortunes that it remained a bastion of humanism for the next century and a half, numbering William Camden and John Milton among its graduates. The visits of Erasmus to England and the work of Sir Thomas More and his circle greatly contributed to the prestige of Latin humanism, while English vernacular literature was revolutionized by the work of Wyatt, Surrey, Heywood, Bale, and many lesser figures. Yet for all its success the movement produced little formal criticism. Sir Thomas Elyot praised the classical poets in *The Book of The Governor* (1531), a work on the education of princes, but the important literary figures of the age remained silent. Their literary theory must be deduced from prefaces, digressions, casual remarks in tracts, letters, and the like.

Religious controversy occupied most English writers during the reign of Mary Tudor (1554–58). After the accession of Elizabeth in 1558, literary interests once again became fashionable. The period between 1558 and 1575 is analogous in the history of English criticism to the Italian fifteenth century. It is a period of preparation, and its major critical works are attempts to solve basic questions and establish objectives. The most obvious classicist of the period is Roger Ascham, whose critical ideas are a by-product of his educational program. In *The Schoolmaster* (1570), his central critical doctrine is "imitation." Although he recognizes the possibility of interpreting 'imitation' in the sense of *mimesis,* he uses it to mean 'following precedent,' as Virgil 'imitated' Homer, or Cicero, Demosthenes.

As Ascham's references to Erasmus, Melanchthon, Sturmius, and Politian indicate, the doctrine of imitation was typical of European humanism. The bad results of the doctrine are evident in the many slavish redactions of classical works produced by second-rate poets. The best writers, however, were able to 'imitate' creatively. Properly interpreted, 'imitation' is an attempt to reproduce in one's own age the greatness of the classics. It is not opposed to originality so much as to the idea that one can achieve literary excellence while ignoring the past. Its supreme justifications in English literature are *Paradise Lost* and *Samson Agonistes;* but it is justified endlessly in the jewel-like lyrics which Elizabethans 'imitated' from Horace, Catullus, Anacreon, and Petrarch; and in the great prose which the translators of the King James Bible 'imitated' from the Hebrew psalms, Hooker from Cicero, and Bacon from Seneca and Tacitus.

Like the Italians, Englishmen assigned rhetoric a central position in the system of the arts. Having diligently studied the endless lists of schemes, tropes, and figures inherited from classical rhetoric, they were sensitive to the use of language. Hence their puns, their balanced sentences and antitheses, and their delight in such a linguistic *tour de force* as John Lyly's *Euphues* (1578). Shakespeare's *Romeo and Juliet* and *Richard III* are fair samples of the influence of rhetoric on a young, extremely talented author. As Shakespeare matured, the obvious rhetorical flourishes disappeared, but the sensitivity to the resources of language which rhetoric encouraged continued to deepen.

A third important phase of the period of preparation is represented by George Gascoigne's *Certain Notes of Instruction* (1575). As a result of the work of the early Tudor poets, English prosody had become reasonably standardized. Gascoigne performed a useful service by codifying the basic rules in a straightforward, unpretentious manner. Unlike Ascham, Harvey, Stanyhurst, and other strict classicists, Gascoigne did not waste energy on an effort to devise an English quantitative system.

As the outlook for literature brightened during Elizabeth's reign, its opponents became more vocal. From Tertullian to Savonarola there had always been Christians who felt that secular literature was a threat to piety. The idea of poetic inspiration popularized by the Florentine Platonists, and their tendency to regard such pagans as Plato and Hermes Trismegistus as forerunners of Christianity, if not saints, was a challenge to the unique authority of Scriptural revelation. In England the theatres seemed particularly insidious. They were attacked as a market of bawdry and a diabolical papist plot to sap England's moral fibre. One of the standard sources of anti-literary invective was Cornelius Agrippa's *On the Vanity and Uncertainty of Human Learning* (1527; many later eds.), but the ancients were also summoned to testify. In the midst of the fogs of controversy three charges stand out. These are essentially the same charges made by Plato in the *Republic:* (1) that poetry is a tissue of lies; (2) that poetry encourages immorality; and (3) that even when unobjectionable, it is an imitation of an imitation and hence inherently trivial.

The great Italian and English sixteenth century defenses were written to refute these charges. Therefore they tended to follow a set pattern. Poetry was defended against the charge of lying by the assertion that the genres of epic, tragedy, ode, and hymn are 'true,' being based on history or theology. It was defended against the charge of immorality by the doctrine of example. Epic and lyric create exemplars of virtue which arouse admiration and, eventually, emulation. Tragedy, comedy, and satire create images of vice showing its disastrous results (tragedy) or its ridiculousness (comedy, satire). Tragic catharsis is the purging of the desire to commit the sin illustrated by the tragic protagonist. Emphasis on example led to the characteristic theory (usually attributed to Aristotle) that poetry is half way between history and moral philosophy. The historian chronicles the truth of particulars and often has to show evil triumphant over good. The philosopher deals with universals, and in the process puts most of his readers to sleep. The poet avoids both faults by treating historical figures according to the universal truths of philosophy. Poetry is thus a supreme synthesis. The theory neatly allows for modifications of history without admitting that these are 'lies.'

The defense of poetry against the charge of triviality involved two additional theories. Allegorical exegesis was used to show that poetry reveals truths so sacred that they must be hidden under the veil of fiction. The four levels of meaning attributed to Scripture were discovered in secular texts; or, alternately, the concealed truths of poetry were classified as mythic (i.e., theological), ethical, and natural (i.e., scientific). Neoplatonism encouraged a second—and to modern tastes more attractive—defense. Plato had called the artist an imitator of imitations. His Renaissance successors theorized that the inspired artist rises above the imperfect world of experience to imitate divine ideas. Thus poetry is truer than life. The artist reproducing his intuitions in all their radiant splendor offers men a glimpse of the golden world as it was before the Fall—the world purged of accidents, in which the Good is finally reconciled to the Beautiful and the True.

John Rainolds' Latin *Oration in Praise of the Art of Poetry* (c. 1572) is the first of the Elizabethan defenses. An academic oration, it relies heavily on the *Pro Archia Poeta* and various commonplaces culled from standard authors. Sidney's *Apologie* (or *Defence*) *for Poetrie* (1583) is the best of the group and still a moving document. George Puttenham's *Arte of English Poesie* (1589) is an English equivalent of such full-scale arts of poetry as Minturno's *De Poeta* and treats its subject systematically, beginning with a praise of poetry and continuing with chapters on the major genres, stanzaic forms and prosody, and style, ornament, and decorum. Many essays of the period are *ad hoc* justifications of specific forms. Spenser's *Letter to Raleigh* (wr. 1589) and Heywood's *Apology for Actors* (1612) are particularly interesting as testimony to the practical influence of Renaissance theory on significant creative artists.

While fighting to save poetry from her enemies, English critics also had to defend her from her friends. Many humanists were skeptical of the prospects of vernacular literature, and some, like George Buchanan, Walter Haddon, Thomas Campion, and John Milton wrote significant poetry in Latin. The possibility that Latin might replace English as a literary language was never, however, a serious issue. A much more real challenge was posed by the recurring argument that to equal the achievements of the ancients, English poets must employ the unrhymed quantitative forms of classical poetry. Spenser experimented briefly with a quantitative system devised by Thomas Drant; and the turn of the century witnessed the publication of Thomas Campion's *Art of English Poesy* (1602), the most attractive of the arguments for classical prosody. The merits of this work (there are many) have been obscured by the masterly reply by Samuel Daniel (1603?), which effectively settled the question in favor of accent and rhyme. On the other hand, the classical prosodists were not wholly ineffectual. Their influence on English poetry may be felt during most of the seventeenth century, most obviously in the blank verse of *Paradise Lost*.

By the beginning of the reign of King James (1603–25) the humanistic synthesis was showing signs of strain. Changes in the scientific, political, and social milieu called forth a variety of new responses. Neoclassicism is the most important of these, but it is extremely hard to define with precision. On the surface, Neoclassicists argued for the same principles defended by the humanists. There was, however, a marked difference. The quasi-religious fervor of humanistic criticism diminished, and rules became more important. The ideal of the *vates* was gradually replaced by that of the Man of Letters. Verisimilitude, decorum, and wit gained in popularity while allegory and symbolism lost favor. The earlier delight in ornament, digression, and fantasy, illustrated by Spenser's *Faerie Queene*, gave way to the ideal of precision and restraint, illustrated by Ben Jonson's *Epigrams* and *Forest*. The couplet became a major verse form, and French critics began to supplement the Italians as the major foreign source of critical theory, and finally replaced them.

Early Neoclassicism was closely associated with scientific rationalism. It is no coincidence that the English Neoclassic period is also called the Age of Reason. Bacon contributed a good deal to the critical tone of the period. Although he was prepared to accept literary fantasy and even (in *The Wisdom of the Ancients*, 1625) to believe that classical mythology was elaborate philosophical allegory, he suggested in *The Advancement of Learning* (1605) that most allegories were invented after the fact. To Bacon, poetry was a product of imagination, and imagination was, in turn, a fantasy-producing organ unless rigidly controlled by reason. Pure poetry is thus deceptive or, at best, trivial amusement. When controlled by reason, poetry can usefully make clear the lessons of the moral philosopher, but in such a case the work is a mixture of 'philosophy,' which gives it validity, and 'poetry,' which is merely pleasing decoration. The result of the Baconian view was to deprive poetry of much of the prestige which it enjoyed during the sixteenth century. Not until the imagination itself was redefined by Kant and Coleridge was the Baconian thesis effectively challenged. In the meanwhile, the genres of epic and tragedy became all but extinct, while such 'reasonable' poetic forms as verse essay, satire, and comedy flourished.

The alliance between rationalism and Neoclassicism persisted from Bacon through Hobbes and Davenant to Dryden. There were, however, defenders of the older tradition. Henry Reynolds' *Mythomystes* (1632) was an attack on Bacon heavily indebted to Ficino, Pico, and Politian. The seventeenth-century Spenserians and the Cambridge Neoplatonists attempted in their different ways—and without conspicuous success—to carry on the sixteenth-century tradition. The most impressive defender of the older values was, of course, John Milton, whose work subsumed the whole history of humanism in one grand restatement at the moment of its demise. Wherever Milton's political and religious sympathies lay, his literary allegiance was always to the Italy of Petrarch, Minturno, and Tasso, and to the England of Spenser. The difference between *Paradise Lost* and Pope's *Essay on Man*, or *Samson Agonistes* and Dryden's *All for Love* is a measure of the chasm separating humanistic from Neoclassic ideas of literature.

A final note is due concerning the omission, from the present anthology, of essays representing the metaphysical theory of poetry. The reason for this is simply that no such essays exist. Joel Spingarn believed Reynolds' *Mythomystes* to be 'metaphysical', but in the light of present-day knowledge, his reasons seem unsound. Emmanuele Tesauro's *Aristotelian Telescope* has no English equivalent. A good deal of metaphysical poetic theory can be garnered from occasional poems and digressive asides, but this material is too fragmentary to be included in an anthology of criticism.

The selections below are generally in chronological order, but this order has been modified to permit the grouping of selections in units illustrating the major phases of the period covered. Each selection is accompanied by a headnote and a brief bibliography. The following bibliography is intended to supplement the shorter ones. It is divided into four parts: I. Background; II. History of Criticism; III. Collections and Translations; IV. History of English Criticism. Certain special topics are dealt with in the bibliographies following the headnotes: Education, following Ascham; Rhetoric, following Wilson; The Attack on Poetry, following Gosson; Versification, following Spenser.

GENERAL BIBLIOGRAPHY

I. BACKGROUND: D. Bush, *English Literature in the Earlier Seventeenth Century* (1945); *The Renaissance and English Humanism* (1939); L. Einstein, *The Italian Renaissance in England* (1902); C. S. Lewis, *English Literature in the Sixteenth Century* (1954); J. Sandys, *A History of Classical Scholarship*, Vol. II (1908); M. Schoell, *Études sur l'humanisme continental en Angleterre* (1926); H. Taylor, *Thought and Expression in the Sixteenth Century*, 2 vols. (1910); H. White, *Plagiarism and Imitation During the English Renaissance* (1935).

II. HISTORY OF CRITICISM: L. Cooper and A. Gudeman, *A Bibliography of the Poetics of Aristotle* (1928); J. Cunningham, *Woe or Wonder* (1952); G. Giovannini, "Historical Realism and the Tragic Emotions in Renaissance Criticism," *PQ*, XXXIII (1953); V. Hall, *Renaissance Literary Criticism* (1945); O. Hardison, *The Enduring Monument: The Idea of Praise in Renaissance Literary Theory and Practice* (1962); B. Hathaway, *The Age of Criticism: The Late Renaissance in Italy* (1962); M. Herrick, *The Fusion of Horatian and Aristotelian Literary Criticism, 1531–1555* (1946); A. McMahon, *Seven Questions on Aristotelian Definitions of Tragedy and Comedy*, Harvard Studies in Classical Philology, XL (1929); G. Saintsbury, *A History of Criticism*, 3 vols. (1900–4); J. Spingarn, *A History of Literary Criticism in the Renaissance* (1899); C. Trabalza, *La Critica letteraria nel rinascimento* (1915); B. Weinberg, *A History of Literary Criticism in the Italian Renaissance*, 2 vols. (1961); W.

Wimsatt and C. Brooks, *Literary Criticism: A Short History* (1957).

III. COLLECTIONS AND TRANSLATIONS: Useful anthologies include: C. Gebert, *An Anthology of Elizabethan Dedications and Prefaces* (1933); A. Gilbert, *Literary Criticism: Plato to Dryden* (1940); G. Smith, *Elizabethan Critical Essays,* 2 vols. (1904); J. Spingarn, *Critical Essays of the Seventeenth Century,* 3 vols. (1909); B. Weinberg, *Critical Prefaces of the French Renaissance* (1939). The following translations are available of works or selections from works by Continental critics: Boccaccio, Bks. XIV and XV of *The Genealogy of the Gods,* tr. Osgood (1930); Castelvetro, *On the Poetics,* in A. Gilbert (see collections); Cinthio, *Discorses,* in A. Gilbert (collections); Dante, *Convivio,* tr. W. Jackson (1909); *Epistle to Can Grande,* in A. Gilbert (collections); Du Bellay, *Defense and Illustration of the French Language,* in Smith and Parks, *The Great Critics* (1939); Fracastoro, *Naugerius,* tr. R. Kelso (1924); Guarini, *Compendium of Tragicomic Poetry,* in A. Gilbert (collections); Lope de Vega, *The New Art of Making Comedies,* in A. Gilbert (collections); Mazzoni, *Defense of the Comedy of Dante,* in A. Gilbert (collections); Minturno, *The Art of Poetry,* in A. Gilbert (collections); Petrarch, selections in *Petrarch: The First Modern Scholar,* ed. J. Robinson and H. Rolfe (1914); Ronsard, *A Brief of the Art of French Poetry,* in Smith and Parks, *The Great Critics* (1939); Scaliger, *Select Translations,* tr. Padelford (1905); Tasso, *Discourses,* in A. Gilbert (collections); Trissino, *Poetics,* in A. Gilbert (collections); Vida, *Art of Poetry,* tr. A. Cook (1924).

IV. ON ENGLISH CRITICISM: J. Atkins, *English Literary Criticism: The Renascence* (1947); C. Baldwin, *Renaissance Literary Theory and Practice* (1939); T. Baldwin, *Shakespeare's Five-Act Structure* (1947); C. Baker, "Certain Religious Elements in the Doctrine of the Inspired Poet . . .," *ELH,* VI (1939); S. Bethell, "The Nature of Metaphysical Wit," in *Discussions of John Donne,* ed. F. Kermode (1962); E. Bloom, "The Allegorical Principle," *ELH,* XVIII (1951); M. Bundy, " 'Invention' and 'Imagination' in the Renaissance," *JEGP,* XXIX (1930); D. Clark, *Rhetoric and*

Poetry in the Renaissance (1922); W. Crane, *Wit and Rhetoric in the Renaissance* (1937); M. Doran, *Endeavors of Art* (1954); C. Green, *The Neoclassic Theory of Tragedy* (1934); H. Grierson, *Criticism and Creation* (1949); M. Herrick, *The Poetics of Aristotle in England* (1930); L. Jones, *The Divine Science* (1940); V. Rubel, *Poetic Diction in the English Renaissance* (1941); R. Sharp, *From Donne to Dryden* (1940); H. Swedenberg, *The Theory of Epic in England, 1650–1800* (1944); E. Sweeting, *Early Tudor Criticism* (1940); R. Tuve, *Elizabethan and Metaphysical Imagery* (1947); R. Wallerstein, *Seventeenth Century Poetic* (1950); B. Willey, *The Seventeenth Century Background* (1934); H. Wilson, "Some Meanings of 'Nature' in Renaissance Literary Theory," *JHI*, II (1941).

Part 1

THE PERIOD OF PREPARATION

William Caxton

[1421?–1491]

❦❦❦

A PROSPEROUS MERCER and governor of the Merchant Adventurers in
the Low Countries, 1463–69, Caxton learned the art of printing at
Cologne in 1471–72. His first book, which he translated from the
French, the *Recuyell of the Historyes of Troye,* was published at
Bruges in 1474. Returning to England in 1476, he set up his press at
Westminster. Among the more than eighty books which he published
in England are *The Dicts and Sayings of the Philosophers* (1477),
Boethius' *Consolation of Philosophy* (1479), Higden's *Polychronicon*
(1480), Cicero's *Of Old Age* and *Of Friendship* (1481), Gower's *Confessio Amantis* (1483), Aesop's *Fables* (1484), Malory's *Morte D'Arthur* (1484), Chaucer's *Canterbury Tales* (1484), Virgil's *Aeneid*
(1490), and Jerome's *Lives of the Fathers* (1495). As the list indicates, Caxton's publications form a five-foot shelf of what the age
considered literary classics. Although Caxton knew personally several
of the early English humanists, he was not greatly influenced by the
new learning. His major service—a great one—was to make the traditionally accepted classics available to the English reading public. His
editions of Chaucer, Gower, and Malory helped to re-establish the
continuity of English literary tradition after the cultural disruptions of
the mid-fifteenth century. Caxton's immediate successors, Wynkyn de
Worde and Richard Pynson, continued to publish medieval and popular works, but an increasing emphasis may be observed after 1520
on works representing the new learning.

Caxton's prefaces are the work of a straightforward, practical mind.
Their style is sometimes awkward and seldom learned by humanistic
standards, but considering the state of English prose at the end of the
fifteenth century they are a considerable achievement. The prefaces
to Chaucer and Malory merit attention as serious criticism. Chaucer
is praised as a great Englishman, a reformer of the language, and a
moral teacher. Caxton's remarks about the difficulty of obtaining a
correct manuscript of the *Canterbury Tales* show that he felt something like a scholar's obligation to his text. The Malory preface also

17

begins on a patriotic note: Arthur is a great English hero, one of the
nine worthies, and deserves more attention from his countrymen. Caxton's attempt to prove Arthur's historicity anticipates the Tudor campaign to use Arthur to buttress a shaky claim to the throne and
stimulate patriotism, a campaign which culminated in Spenser's *Faerie
Queene*.

The present text has been modernized for ease of comprehension.

BIBLIOGRAPHY. *The Prologues and Epilogues of William Caxton*, ed.
W. Crotch (EETS, 1928). For comment see: N. Aurner, *Caxton*
(1926); H. Bennett, "Caxton and his Public," *RES*, XIX (1943);
A. Byles, "Caxton as a Man of Letters," *Library*, XV (1934); H.
Plomer, *William Caxton* (1924); W. Roberts, *William Caxton, Writer
and Critic* (1930); D. Sands, "Caxton as a Literary Critic," *Papers of
the Bibliographical Society of America*, LI (1957); G. Winship, *William Caxton and his Work* (1937). On the early history and influence of
English printing, see: H. Bennett, *English Books and Readers, 1475–
1557* (1952); H. Lathrop, *Translations from the Classics into English,
1477–1620* (1933); H. Plomer, *Wynkyn de Worde and his Contemporaries* (1925).

Preface to

THE CANTERBURY TALES

[1484]

GREAT THANKS, LAUD, and honour ought to be given unto the
clerks, poets, and historiographs that have written many noble
books of wisdom of the lives, passions, and miracles of holy
saints, of histories of noble and famous acts and faites, and of
the chronicles since the beginning of the creation of the world
unto this present time, by which we be daily informed and have
knowledge of many things of whom we should not have known
if they had not left to us their monuments written. Among whom
and in especial before all others, we ought to give a singular laud
unto that noble and great philosopher Geoffrey Chaucer, the
which for his ornate writing in our tongue may well have the
name of a laureate poet. For to-fore that he by labour em-

bellished, ornated, and made fair our English, in this realm was
had rude speech and incongruous, as yet it appeareth by old
books, which at this day ought not to have place ne be compared
among, ne to, his beauteous volumes and ornate writings, of
whom he made many books and treatises of many a noble history,
as well in metre as in rhyme and prose; and them so craftily made
that he comprehended his matters in short, quick, and high sentences, eschewing prolixity, casting away the chaff of superfluity,
and shewing the picked grain of sentence uttered by crafty and
sugared eloquence; of whom among all others of his books I
purpose to print, by the grace of God, the book of the tales of
Canterbury, in which I find many a noble history of every state
and degree; first rehearsing the conditions and the array of each
of them as properly as possible is to be said. And after their tales
which be of nobleness, wisdom, gentleness, mirth, and also of
very holiness and virtue, wherein he finisheth this said book,
which book I have diligently overseen and duly examined, to
that end it be made according unto his own making. For I find
many of the said books which writers have abridged it, and many
things left out; and in some place have set certain verses that
he never made ne set in his book; of which books so incorrect
was one brought to me, 6 years past, which I supposed had been
very true and correct; and according to the same I did do imprint
a certain number of them, which anon were sold to many and
divers gentlemen, of whom one gentleman came to me and said
that this book was not according in many place unto the book
that Geoffrey Chaucer had made. To whom I answered that I
had made it according to my copy, and by me was nothing added
ne minished. Then he said he knew a book which his father had
and much loved, that was very true and according unto his own
first book by him made; and said more, if I would imprint it
again he would get me the same book for a copy, howbeit he
wist well that his father would not gladly depart from it. To
whom I said, in case that he could get me such a book, true
and correct, yet I would once endeavour me to imprint it again
for to satisfy the author, whereas before by ignorance I erred
in hurting and defaming his book in divers places, in setting in
some things that he never said ne made, and leaving out many
things that he made which be requisite to be set in it. And thus

we fell at accord, and he full gently got of his father the said
book and delivered it to me, by which I have corrected my book,
as hereafter, all along by the aid of Almighty God, shall follow;
whom I humbly beseech to give me grace and aid to achieve and
accomplish to his laud, honour, and glory; and that all ye that
shall in this book read or hear, will of your charity among your
deeds of mercy remember the soul of the said Geoffrey Chaucer,
first author and maker of this book. And also that all we that
shall see and read therein may so take and understand the good
and virtuous tales, that it may so profit unto the health of our
souls that after this short and transitory life we may come to
everlasting life in Heaven. Amen.

Preface to
MORTE D'ARTHUR
[1484]

AFTER THAT I had accomplished and finished divers histories, as
well of contemplation as of other historical and worldly acts of
great conquerors and princes, and also certain books of ensamples
and doctrine, many noble and divers gentlemen of this realm of
England came and demanded me many and oft times wherefore
that I have not done made and printed the noble history of the
Saint Graal, and of the most renowned Christian King, first and
chief of the three best Christian and worthy, Arthur, which
ought most to be remembered among us Englishmen before
all other Christian Kings. For it is notoyrly known through the
universal world that there be nine worthy and the best that
ever were; that is to wit three Paynims, three Jews, and three
Christian men. As for the Paynims, they were to-fore the Incarnation of Christ, which were named—the first, Hector of Troy,
of whom the history is come both in ballad and in prose—the
second, Alexander the Great; and the third, Julius Caesar, Emperor of Rome, of whom the histories be well known and had.
And as for the three Jews, which also were before the Incarnation of our Lord of whom the first was Duke Joshua, which

brought the children of Israel into the land of behest; the second, David, King of Jerusalem; and the third Judas Maccabæus; of these three the Bible rehearseth all their noble histories and acts. And since the said Incarnation have been three noble Christian men, installed and admitted through the universal world into the number of the nine best and worthy, of whom was first the noble Arthur, whose noble acts I purpose to write in this present book here following. The second was Charlemagne, or Charles the Great, of whom the history is had in many places both in French and English; and the third and last was Godfrey of Boulogne, of whose acts and life I made a book unto the excellent prince and king of noble memory, King Edward the Fourth. The said noble gentlemen instantly required me to print the history of the said noble king and conqueror, King Arthur, and of his knights, with the history of the Saint Graal, and of the death and ending of the said Arthur, affirming that I ought rather to print his acts and noble feats than of Godfrey of Boulogne or any of the other eight, considering that he was a man born within this realm, and king and emperor of the same; and that there be in French divers and many noble volumes of his acts, and also of his knights.[1] To whom I answered that divers men hold opinion that there was no such Arthur, and that all such books as be made of him be but feigned and fables, because that some chronicles make of him no mention, ne remember him nothing, ne of his knights; whereto they answered, and one in special said, that in him that should say or think that there was never such a king called Arthur, might well be aretted great folly and blindness; for he said that there were many evidences of the contrary. First ye may see his sepulchre in the monastery of Glastonbury; and also in 'Polychronicon,' in the fifth book, the sixth chapter, and in the seventh book, the twenty-third chapter,[2] where his body was buried, and after found and translated into the said monastery. Ye shall see also in the history of Boccaccio, in his book 'De casu principum,' part of his noble acts and also of his

[1] E.g., The *Lancelot, Yvain,* and *Perceval* of Chrétien de Troyes (fl. 1180).; however, several Arthurian romances in English are extant from the Middle Ages, most notably *Gawain and the Green Knight.*

[2] *Polychronicon* (c. 1350) is a survey of world history by Ranulf Higden (d. 1364), translated into English by John of Trevisa (1387), and printed by Caxton in 1480.

fall. Also Galfridus in his British book [3] recounteth his life, and in divers places of England many remembrances be yet of him, and shall remain perpetually, and also of his knights. First in the Abbey of Westminster at Saint Edward's shrine remaineth the print of his seal in red wax closed in beryl, in which is written 'Patricius Arthurus, Britanniae Galliae Germaniae Daciae Imperator.' [4] Item, in the castle of Dover ye may see Gawain's skull and Caradoc's mantle; at Winchester the round table; in other places Lancelot's sword, and many other things. Then all these things considered, there can no man reasonably gainsay but here was a king of this land named Arthur; for in all places, Christian and heathen, he is reputed and taken for one of the nine worthy, and the first of the three Christian men. And also he is more spoken of beyond the sea; more books made of his noble acts than there be in England, as well in Dutch, Italian, Spanish, and Greek as in French; and yet of record remain in witness of him in Wales in the town of Camelot the great stones and marvellous works of iron lying under the ground, and royal vaults, which divers now living hath seen. Wherefore it is a marvel why he is no more renowned in his own country, save only it accordeth to the word of God, which saith that no man is accepted for a prophet in his own country. Then all these things aforesaid alleged, I could not well deny but that there was such a noble king named Arthur, and reputed one of the nine worthy, and first and chief of the Christian men; and many noble volumes be made of him and of his noble knights in French, which I have seen and read beyond the sea, which be not had in our maternal tongue, but in Welsh be many, and also in French, and some in English, but nowhere nigh all. Wherefore such as have lately been drawn out briefly into English, I have, after the simple cunning that God hath sent to me, under the favour and correction of all noble lords and gentlemen, emprised to imprint a book of the noble histories of the said King Arthur and of certain of his knights, after a copy unto me delivered, which copy Sir Thomas Mallory did take out of certain books of French and reduced it into English. And I according to my copy have down

---

[3] Geoffrey of Monmouth, whose *History of the Kings of Britain* (1137) is the basic source of most later Arthurian material.

[4] "Noble Arthur, Ruler of Britain, Gaul, Germany, and Dacia."

set it in print, to the intent that noble men may see and learn the noble acts of chivalry, the gentle and virtuous deeds that some knights used in those days, by which they came to honour, and how they that were vicious were punished and oft put to shame and rebuke; humbly beseeching all noble lords and ladies and all other estates, of what estate or degree they be of, that shall see and read in this said book and work, that they take the good and honest acts in their remembrance and to follow the same, wherein they shall find many joyous and pleasant histories and noble and renowned acts of humanity, gentleness, and chivalry. For herein may be seen noble chivalry, courtesy, humanity, friendliness, hardyhood, love, friendship, cowardice, murder, hate, virtue, and sin. Do after the good and leave the evil, and it shall bring you to good fame and renown. And for to pass the time this book shall be pleasant to read in; but for to give faith and believe that all is true that is contained herein, ye be at your liberty. But all is written for our doctrine, and for to beware that we fall not to vice ne sin, but to exercise and follow virtue, by which we may come and attain to good fame and renown in this life, and after this short and transitory life to come unto everlasting bliss in heaven; the which He grant us that reigneth in Heaven, the Blessed Trinity. Amen.

Thomas Wilson

[1525–1581]

◆⧉◆

AFTER AN EDUCATION at Eton and Cambridge, where he came in contact with John Cheke, Roger Ascham, and Walter Haddon, Wilson embarked on a career as educator, author, and statesman. His *Rule of Reason,* a treatise on logic, appeared in 1551, followed by the *Arte of Rhetorique* in 1553 (later eds., 1560, 63, 67, etc.). After many tribulations during the reign of Queen Mary, he returned to England in 1559 and held a series of civic and political appointments, becoming Elizabeth's Secretary of State in 1579. Among his later works are *Three Orations of Demosthenes* (1570) and *A Discourse on Usury* (1572).

The *Arte of Rhetorique* is the best of a series of sixteenth century works on the subject. Others include Leonard Cox, *The Art or Craft of Rhetoric* (1524, 32); Richard Sherry, *A Treatise of the Figures of Grammar and Rhetoric* (1555); Richard Rainolde, *The Foundation of Rhetoric* (1563); Henry Peacham, *The Garden of Eloquence* (1577); and Abraham Fraunce, *The Arcadian Rhetoric* (1588). These and similar works are a reminder of the central importance of rhetoric during the sixteenth century. Contemptuous of what they felt to be the empty subtleties of scholasticism, Renaissance humanists made rhetoric the queen of the sciences. Being the science of persuasion, rhetoric would be the instrument for converting the social programs of the philosophers into practical realities. Inevitably, rhetoric tended to become an end in itself. Having laboriously memorized its rules and figures in school, Elizabethans used them in their writing and demanded them in what they read. The influence of rhetoric on prose can be seen from Lyly's *Euphues* and Sidney's *Apologie for Poetrie* to Milton's *Areopagitica* and beyond. Much of the linguistic exuberance of Elizabethan poetry can be traced to the delight in ornamental language which rhetoric encouraged.

Rhetoric may be considered a Renaissance equivalent of modern practical criticism, and the literature of the period cannot be understood fully without some knowledge of it. There were two popular types of rhetoric during the early Elizabethan period. The 'full-scale' rhetoric, exemplified by Wilson, treated invention (finding and developing the topic), disposition (organization), elocution (style, the figures), memory, and delivery. The second type of rhetoric concentrated on figures of speech (Sherry, Fraunce) or practical exercises in various forms of oration (Rainolde). The second type became more influential toward the end of the century as a result of the reforms advocated by the French philosopher Peter Ramus (1515–72).

The present text is based on the edition of 1560.

BIBLIOGRAHY. *The Arte of Rhetorique*, ed. G. Mair (1909). Several other Elizabethan rhetorics have been reprinted: e.g., Cox, ed. F. Carpenter; Rainolde, ed. F. Johnson; Peacham, ed. W. Crane; Fraunce, ed. F. Seaton; Hoskins, *Directions for Speech and Style*, ed. H. Hudson. For comment on Wilson see: A. Schmidt, "Thomas Wilson, Tudor Scholar-Statesman," *HLQ*, XX (1957); R. Wagner, "Thomas Wilson's Contributions to Rhetoric," in *Papers in Rhetoric*, ed. Bryant (1940); "Wilson and his Sources," *Quart. Journ. of Speech*, XV (1929). On the influence of rhetoric during the Renaissance, see: D. Clark, *Rhetoric and Poetry in the Renaissance* (1922); W. Crane, *Wit and Rhetoric in the Renaissance* (1937); W. Howell, *Rhetoric and Logic in England, 1500–1700* (1956); Sister Miriam Joseph, *Shakespeare's Use of the Arts of Language* (1947; an excellent introduction); R. Tuve, *Elizabethan and Metaphysical Imagery* (1947). For the extensive bibliography on Ramus and his influence, see: W. Howell (above) and W. Ong, S.J., *Ramus* (1958).

from

THE ARTE OF RHETORIQUE

[1560]

PREFACE

ELOQVENCE FIRST
giuen by God, and after lost
by man, and last repayred
by God againe.

MAN (IN WHOM IS POWRED the breath of life) was made at the first being an euerliuing creature, vnto the likenese of God, endued with reason, and appointed Lorde ouer all other thinges liuing. But after the fall of our first Father, sinne so crept in that our knowledge was much darkned, and by corruption of this our flesh, mans reason and entendement were both ouerwhelmed. At what time God being sore greeued with the follie of one man, pitied of his mere goodnesse the whole state and posteritie of Mankind. And therefore (whereas through the wicked suggestion of our ghostly enemie, the joyful fruition of Gods glorie was altogether lost:) it pleased our heauenly Father to repaire mankind of his free mercie, and to graunt an euerliuing enheritaunce, vnto all such as would by constaunt faith seeke earnestly hereafter. Long it was ere that man knewe himselfe being destitute of Gods grace, so that all thinges waxed sauage, the earth vntilled, societie neglected, Gods will not knowne, man against man, one against an other, and all against order. Some liued by spoyle: some like bruite beastes grased vpon the ground: some went naked: some roomed like Woodoses: none did any thing by reason, but most did what they could by manhood. None almost considered the euerliuing GOD, but all liued most commonly after their owne lust. By death they thought that all thinges ended: by life they looked for none other liuing. None remembred the true obseruation of Wedlocke: none tendered the educa-

tion of their children: Lawes were not regarded: true dealing
was not once vsed. For vertue, vice bare place: for right and
equitie, might vsed authoritie. And therefore, whereas man
through reason might haue vsed order: man through folie fell into
errour. And thus for lacke of skill, and for want of grace euill so
preuailed, that the deuil was most esteemed, and God either
almost vnknowne among them all, or els nothing feared among
so many. Therefore, euen now when man was thus past all hope
of amendement, God still tendering his owne workmanshippe stirring vp his faithfull and elect, to perswade with reason all men
to societie. And gaue his appointed Ministers knowledge both to
see the natures of men, and also graunted them the gift of vtteraunce, that they might with ease win folke at their will, and frame
them by reason to all good order. And therefore, whereas men
liued brutishly in open feeldes, hauing neither house to shroude
them in, nor attire to clothe their backes, nor yet any regard to
seeke their best auaile: these appointed of GOD called them together by vtteraunce of speech, and perswaded with them what
was good, what was bad, & what was gainful for mankind. And
although at first the rude could hardly learne, and either for the
straungenesse of the thing, would not gladly receiue the offer, or
els for lack of knowledge, could not perceiue the goodnesse: yet
being somewhat drawne, and delited with the pleasantnesse of
reason, and the sweetnesse of vtteraunce: after a certaine space
they became through Nurture and good aduisement, of wilde,
sober: of cruell, gentle: of fooles, wise: and of beastes, men:
such force hath the tongue, and such is the power of Eloquence
and reason, that most men are forced, euen to yeeld in that which
most standeth against their will. And therefore the Poets doe
feine, that *Hercules* beeing a man of great wisedome, had all men
lincked together by the eares in a chaine, to drawe them and
leade them euen as he lusted. For his witte was so great, his
tongue so eloquent, and his experience such, that no one man
was able to withstande his reason, but euery one was rather
driuen to doe that which he would, and to will that which he did:
agreeing to his aduise both in word and worke in all that euer
they were able. Neither can I see that men could haue beene
brought by any other meanes, to liue together in fellowship of
life, to maintaine Cities, to deale truely, and willingly obeye one

an other, if men at the first had not by art and eloquence, per-swaded that which they full oft found out by reason. For what man I pray you, beeing better able to maintaine himself by valiaunt courage, then by liuing in base subiection, would not rather looke to rule like a Lord, then to live like an vnderling: if by reason he were not perswaded, that it behoueth euery man to liue in his owne vocation: and not to seeke any higher roume, then whereunto he was at the first appointed? Who would digge and delue from Morne till Euening? Who would trauaile and toyle with ye sweat of his browes? Yea, who would for his Kings pleasure aduenture and hassarde his life, if witte had not so won men, that they thought nothing more needfull in this world, nor any thing whereunto they were more bounden: then here to liue in their duetie, and to traine their whole life according to their calling. Therefore, whereas men are in many thinges weake by Nature, and subiect to much infirmitie: I thinke in this one poinct they passe all other creatures liuing, that haue the gift of speech and reason. And among all other, I thinke him most worthie fame, and amongst all men to bee taken for halfe a GOD: that therein doth chiefly and aboue all other excell men, wherein men doe excell beastes. For he that is among the reasonable of al most reasonable, and among the wittie, of all most wittie, and among the eloquent, of all most eloquent: him thinke I among all men, not onely to be taken for a singuler man, but rather to be coumpted for halfe a God. For, in seeking the ex-cellencie hereof, the soner he draweth to perfection, the nyer he commeth to God, who is the cheefe wisedome, and therfore called God, because he is most wise, or rather wisedome it self.

Now then, seing that God giueth his heauenly grace, unto al such as call vnto him with stretched handes, and humble heart, neuer wanting to those, that want not to themselues: I purpose by his grace and especiall assistence, to set forth such precepts of eloquence, and to shewe what obseruation the wise have used, in handeling of their matters: that the vnlearned by seeing the practise of others, maie haue some knowledge themselues, and learne by their neighbours deuise, what is necessarie for them selues in their owne case.

Book I

What is Rhetorique.

Rhetorique is an Arte to set foorth by vtteraunce of words, matter at large, or (as *Cicero* doth say) it is a learned, or rather an artificiall declaration of the mynd, in the handling of any cause, called in contention, that may through reason largely be discussed.

¶ *The matter whereupon an*
Oratour must speake.

An Orator must be able to speake fully of al those questions, which by lawe & mans ordinance are enacted, and appointed for the vse and profite of man, such as are thought apt for the tongue to set forwarde. Nowe *Astronomie* is rather learned by demonstration, then taught by any great vtterance. *Arithmetique* smally needeth the vse of Eloquence, seeing it may be had wholy by nombring only. *Geometrie* rather asketh a good square, then a cleane flowing tongue to set out the art. Therefore an Orators profession, is to speake only of all such matters, as may largely be expounded for mans behoue, and may with much grace be set out, for all men to heare them.

¶ *Of questions.*

Every question or demaund in things, is of two sortes. Either it is an infinite question, & without end, or els it is definite, and comprehended within some ende.

Those questions are called infinite, which generally are propounded, without the comprehension of tyme, place, and persone, or any such like: that is to say, when no certaine thing is named, but onely words are generally spoken. As thus, whether it be best to marrie, or to liue single. Which is better, a courtiers life, or a Scholers life.

Those questions are called definite, which set forth a matter, with the appointment and naming of place, time, and person. As thus. Whether now it be best here in Englande, for a Priest to Marrie, or to liue single. Whether it were meete for the kings Maiestie that nowe is, to marrie with a stranger, or to marrie with one of his owne Subiects. Now the definite question (as

the which concerneth some one person) is most agreeing to the
purpose of an Orator, considering particuler matters in the law,
are euer debated betwixt certaine persons, the one affirming for
his parte, and the other denying as fast againe for his parte.

Thinges generally spoken without all circumstaunces, are more
proper vnto the *Logician,* who talketh of thinges vniuersally,
without respect of person, time, or place. And yet notwithstanding, *Tullie* doth say, that whosoeuer will talke of particuler matter
must remember, that within the same also is comprehended a
generall. As for example. If I shall aske this question, whether it
bee lawfull for William Conquerour to inuade England, and win
it by force of Armour, I must also consider this, whether it bee
lawfull for any man to vsurpe power, or it bee not lawful. That
if the greater cannot be borne withall, the lesse can not bee
neither. And in this respect, a generall question agreeth well to
an Orators profession, and ought well to bee knowne for the
better furtheraunce of his matter, notwithstanding the particuler
question is euer called in controuersie, and the generall only
thereupon considered to comprehend and compasse the same, as
the which is more generall.

¶ *The ende of Rhetorique.*

Three thinges are required of an Orator.

⎰ To teach.
⎱ To delight.
⎰ And to perswade.

First therefore, an Orator must labour to tell his tale, that the
hearers may well knowe what he meaneth, and vnderstand him
wholy, the which he shall with ease vse, if he vtter his minde in
plaine words, such as are vsually receiued, and tell it orderly,
without going about the bush. That if he doe not this, he shall
neuer doe the other. For what man can be delited, or yet be perswaded with the only hearing of those thinges, which he knoweth
not what they meane. The tongue is ordeined to expresse the
minde, that one may vnderstand an others meaning: now what
auaileth to speake, when none can tell what the speaker meaneth?
Therefore *Phauorinus* the Philosopher (as *Gellius* telleth the
tale) did hit a yong man ouer the Thumbes very handsomely, for
vsing ouer old, and ouer strange wordes. Sirha (quoth he) when
our olde great auncesters and Graundsires were aliue, they spake

plainly in their mothers tongue, and vsed olde language, such as was spoken then at the building of Roome. But you talke me such a Latine, as though you spake with them euen now, that were two or three thousand yeres agoe, and onely because you would hauc no man to vnderstand what you say. Now, were it not better for thee a thousande fold, (thou foolish fellowe) in seeking to haue thy desire, to holde thy peace, and speake nothing at all? For then by that meanes, fewe should knowe what were thy mcan-ing. But thou saiest, the olde antiquitie doth like thee best, because it is good, sober, and modest. Ah, live man, as they did before thee, and speake thy mind now as men doe at this day. And remember that which *Cæsar* saieth, beware as long as thou liuest of straunge wordes, as thou wouldest take heede and eschue great Rockes in the Sea.

The next part that he hath to play, is to chere his geastes, and to make them take pleasure, with hearing of thinges wittely deuised, and pleasauntly set foorth. Therefore euery Orator should earnestly labour to file his tongue, that his words may slide with ease, and that in his deliueraunce he may haue such grace, as the sound of a Lute, or any such Instrument doth giue. Then his sentences must be wel framed, and his words aptly vsed, through the whole discourse of his Oration.

Thirdly, such quicknesse of witte must bee shewed, and such pleasaunt sawes so well applied, that the eares may finde much delite, whereof I will speake largely, when I shall intreate of mouing laughter. And assuredly nothing is more needfull, then to quicken these heauie loden wittes of ours, and much to cherish these our lompish and vnweldie Natures, for except men finde delite, they will not long abide: delite them, and winne them: wearie them, and you lose them for euer. And that is the reason, that men commonly tarie the ende of a merie Play, and cannot abide the halfe hearing of a sower checking Sermon. Therefore euen these auncient Preachers, must now and then play the fooles in the pulpit, to serue the tickle eares of their fleting audience, or els they are like sometimes to preach to the bare walles, for though their spirite bee apt, and our will prone, yet our flesh is so heauie and humours so ouerwhelme vs, that we cannot without refresh-ing, long abide to heare any one thing. Thus we see that to delite is needfull, without the which weightie matters will not be heard

at all, and therefore him cunne I thanke, that both can and will
ever, mingle sweete among the sower, be he Preacher, Lawyer,
yea, or Cooke either hardly, when hee dresseth a good dish of
meate: now I need not to tell that scurrilitie, or ale-house, iesting,
would bee thought odious, or grosse mirth would be deemed
madnesse: considering that euen the meane witted do knowe that
alreadie, and as for other that haue no wit, they will neuer learne
it, therfore God speede them. Now when these two are done,
hee must perswade, and moue the affections of his hearers in
such wise, that they shalbe forced to yeeld vnto his saying,
whereof (because the matter is large, and may more aptly be
declared, when I shall speake of Amplification) I will surcease to
speake any thing thereof at this tyme.

¶ *By what meanes Eloquence*
is attained.

First needfull it is that hee, which desireth to excell in this gift
of Oratorie, and longeth to proue an eloquent man, must naturally haue a wit, and an aptnesse thereunto: then must he to his
Booke, and learne to bee well stored with knowledge, that he
may be able to minister matter for al causes necessarie. The
which when he hath got plentifully, he must vse much exercise,
both in writing, and also in speaking. For though hee haue a wit
and learning together, yet shall they both little auaile without
much practise. What maketh the Lawyer to haue such utter-
aunce? Practise. What maketh the Preacher to speake so roundly?
Practise. Yea, what maketh women goe so fast awaye with their
wordes? Mary practise I warrant you. Therefore in all faculties,
diligent practise, and earnest exercise, are the onely things that
make men proue excellent. Many men know the art very well,
and be in all points throughly grounded and acquainted with the
precepts, & yet it is not their hap to proue eloquent. And the
reason is, that eloquence it selfe, came not vp first by the art, but
the arte rather was gathered vpon eloquence. For wisemen seeing by much obseruation and diligent practise, the compasse of
diuers causes, compiled thereupon precepts and lessons, worthy
to be knowne and learned of all men. Therefore before arte was
inuented, eloquence was vsed, and through practise made perfect, the which in all things is a soueraigne meane, most highly
to excell.

Now, before we vse either to write, or speake eloquently, wee must dedicate our myndes wholy, to followe the most wise and learned men, and seeke to fashion as wel their speache and gesturing, as their witte or endyting. The which when we earnestly mynd to doe, we can not but in time appere somewhat like them. For if they that walke much in the Sunne, and thinke not of it, are yet for the most part Sunne burnt, it can not be but that they which wittingly and willingly trauayle to counterfeît other, must needes take some colour of them, and be like vnto them in some one thing or other, according to the Prouerbe, by companying with the wise, a man shall learne wisedome.

¶ *To what purpose this arte is set forthe.*

To this purpose and for this vse, is the arte compiled together, by the learned and wisemen, that those which are ignorant might judge of the learned, and labour (when time should require) to followe their woorkes accordingly. Againe, the arte helpeth well to dispose and order matters of our owne invention, the which wee may followe as well in speaking as in writing, for though many by nature without art, haue proued worthy men, yet is arte a surer guide then nature, considering we see as liuely by arte what we do, as though we read a thing in writing, where as Natures doings are not so open to all men. Againe, those that haue good wittes by Nature, shall better encrease them by arte, and the blunt also shall bee whetted through arte, that want Nature to helpe them forward.

¶ *Fiue things to be considered*
in an Oratour.

Any one that will largely handle any matter, must fasten his mynde first of all, vppon these fiue especiall pointes that followe, and learne them euery one.

  i. Inuention of matter.
  ii. Disposition of the same.
  iii. Elocution.
  iiii. Memorie.
  v. Utterance.

The finding out of apt matter, called otherwise Inuention, is a searching out of things true, or things likely, the which may reasonablie set forth a matter, and make it appeare probable. The places of *Logique*, giue good occasion to finde out plentifull

matter. And therefore, they that will proue any cause, and seeke
onely to teach thereby the trueth, must search out the places of
Logique, and no doubt they shall finde much plentie. But what
auaileth much treasure and apt matter, if man can not apply it
to his purpose. Therefore, in the second place is mentioned, the
setling or ordering of things inuented for this purpose, called in
Latine *Dispositio*, the which is nothing els but an apt bestowing,
and orderly placing of things, declaring where euery argument
shall be set, and in what maner euery reason shalbe applied for
confirmation of the purpose.

But yet what helpeth it though wee can finde good reasons,
and knowe how to place them, if wee haue not apt words and
picked Sentences, to commende the whole matter. Therefore,
this point must needes followe to beautifie the cause, the which
being called Elocution, is an applying of apt wordes and sentences to the matter, found out to confirme the cause. When all
these are had together it auaileth little, if man haue no Memorie
to containe them. The Memorie therefore must be cherished, the
which is a fast holding both of matter and words couched together, to confirme any cause.

Be it now that one haue all these fower, yet if he want the fift
all the other doe little profite. For though a man can finde out
good matter and good wordes, though hee can handsomely set
them together, and carie them very well awaie in his minde, yet
it is to no purpose if he haue no vtterance, when he should speake
his minde, and shewe men what he hath to saie. Vtterance therefore, is a framing of the voyce, countenaunce, and gesture after a
comely maner.

Thus we see, that euery one of these must goe together, to
make a perfite Oratour, and that the lack of one, is a hinderance
of the whole, and that as well all may be wanting as one, if wee
looke to haue an absolute Oratour.

There are seuen parts in every Oration.
  i. The Enterance or beginning.
  ii. The Narration.
  iii. The Proposition.
  iiii. The Deuision or seuerall parting of things.
  v. The confirmation.
  vi. The confutation.
  vii. The Conclusion.

The Entraunce or beginning is the former parte of the Oration, whereby the will of the standers by, or of the Iudge is sought for, and required to heare the matter.

The Narration is a plaine and manifest pointing of the matter, and an euident setting forth of all things that belong vnto the same, with a breefe rehersall grounded vpon some reason.

The proposition is a pithie sentence comprehended in a small roome, the somme of the whole matter.

The Deuision is an opening of things, wherein we agree and rest vpon, and wherein we sticke and stande in trauers, shewing what we haue to say in our owne behalfe.

The Confirmation is a declaration of our owne reasons, with assured and constant proofes.

The Confutation is a dissoluing, or wyping away of all such reasons as make against vs.

The Conclusion is a clarkly gathering of the matter spoken before, and a lapping vp of it altogether.

Now, because in euery one of these greate heede ought to bee had, and much arte must be vsed, to content and like all parties: I purpose in the second booke to set foorthe at large euery one of these, that both we may know in all partes what to followe, and what to eschue. And first, when time shalbe to talke of any matter I would aduise euery man to consider the nature of the cause it self, that the rather he might frame his whole Oration thereafter. . . .

¶ *There are three kindes of causes or Orations,*
which serue for euery matter.

Nothing can be handled by this arte, but the same is conteined within one of these three causes. Either the matter consisteth in praise, or dispraise of a thing or els in consulting, whether the cause be profitable, or vnprofitable: or lastly, whether the matter be right or wrong. And yet this one thing is to be learned, that in euery one of these three causes, these three seuerall endes, may euery one of them be conteined in any one of them. And therefore, he that shall haue cause to praise any one bodie, shall haue just cause to speake of Iustice, to entreate of profite, and ioyntly to talke of one thing with an other. But because these three causes, are commonly and for the most part seuerally parted, I will speake of them one after an other, as they are set forth by wise mens arguements, and particularly declare their properties all in order.

The Oration demonstratiue standeth either in praise, or dispraise of some one man, or of some one thing, or of some one deed doen.

¶ *The kind Demonstratiue, wherein*
cheefly it standeth.

There are diuers things which are praised and dispraised, as men, Countries, Cities, Places, Beastes, Hilles, Riuers, Houses, Castles, deedes doen by worthy men, and pollicies euented by great Warriors, but most commonly men are praised for diuers respectes, before any of the other things are taken in hande.

Now in praysing a noble personage, and in setting foorth at large his worthinesse: *Quintillian* giueth warning, to vse this threefold order.

Observe things.
- Before this life.
- In his life.
- After his death.

In a mans life, are considered these places.

- The Realme.
- The Sheire.
- The towne.
- The Parentes.
- The Auncesters.

In a mans life, praise must bee parted threefolde. That is to say, into the giftes of good things of the mynde, the body, and of fortune. Now the giftes of the body & of fortune, are not praise worthy of their owne nature: but euen as they are vsed, either to or fro, so they are either praised, or dispraised. Giftes of the mind deserue the whole trompe & sound commendation aboue all other, wherein we may use the rehearsal of vertues, as they are in order, and beginning at his infancie, tel all his doings till his last age.

¶ *The places whereof are these.*

- The birthe, and infancie.
- The childhood.

- Whether the persone be a man, or a woman.
- The brynging vp, the nurturing, and the behauour of his life.

{ The Striplyng age, or Spring-tide.	Whereunto are referred these.	{ To what study he taketh himself vnto, what company he useth, how he liueth.
{ The mannes state.		{ Prowesse doen, either abrode, or at home.
		{ His pollicies and wittie deuises, in behoufe of the publique weale.
{ The olde age. }		
{ The tyme of his departure, or death.		{ Things that haue happened about his death.

❀   ❀   ❀

¶ *An Oration deliberatiue.*

An Oration deliberatiue, is a meane, whereby we doe perswade, or disswade, entreate, or rebuke, exhorte, or dehort, commend, or comforte any man. In this kind of Oration, wee doe not purpose wholy to praise any bodie, nor yet to determine any matter in controuersie, but the whole compasse of this cause is, either to aduise our neighbour to that thing, which wee thinke most needefull for him, or els to call him backe from that follie, which hindereth much his estimation. As for example, if I would counsaile my friend to trauaile beyond the Seas, for knowledge of the tongues, and experience in forraine Countries: I might resort to this kinde of Oration, and finde matter to confirme my cause plentifully. And the reasons, which are commonly vsed to enlarge such matters, are these that followe.

{ The thing is honest. Profitable. Pleasaunt.	{ Saufe. Easie. Hard.

{ Lawfull and meete. Praise worthie. Necessarie.

❀   ❀   ❀

¶ *Of an Oration iudiciall.*

The whole burdein of weightie matters, and the earnest triall of all controuersies, rest onely vpon Iudgement. Therefore, when matters concerning land, goodes, or life, or any such thing of like weight are called in question, wee must euer haue recourse to this kinde of Oration, and after iust examining of our cause by the places thereof, looke for iudgement according to the lawe.

¶ *Oration iudiciall what it is.*

Oration Iudiciall, is an earnest debating in open assemblie, of some weightie matter before a Iudge, where the complainaunt commenseth his action, and the defendant thereupon aunswereth at his perill, to all such thinges as are laied to his charge. . . .

Book III
¶ *Of apt chusing and framing of words and*
sentences together, called Elocution.

And now we are come to that part of *Rhetorique*, the which aboue all other is most beautifull, wherby not onely words are aptly vsed, but also sentences are in right order framed. For whereas Inuention helpeth to finde matter, and Disposition serueth to place arguments: Elocution getteth words to set forth inuention, and with such beautie commendeth the matter, "that reason semeth to be clad in Purple, walking afore both bare and naked." Therefore *Tullie* saieth well, to finde out reason and aptly to frame it, is the part of a wiseman, but to commende it by wordes and with gorgious talke to tell our conceipt, that is onely proper to an Oratour. Many are wise, but fewe haue the gift to set forth their wisedome. . . .

¶ *Fower partes belonging to Elocution.*

i. Plainnesse.
ii. Aptnesse.
iii. Composition.
iiii. Exornation.

Among all other lessons this should first be learned, that wee neuer affect any straunge ynkehorne termes,[1] but we speake as is commonly receiued: neither seeking to be ouer fine, nor yet liuing ouer-carelesse using our speeche as most men doe, and ordering our wittes as the fewest haue done. Some seeke so far for outlandish English, that they forget altogether their mothers language. And I dare sweare this, if some of their mothers were aliue, thei were not able to tell what they say: and yet these fine English clerkes will say, they speake in their mother tongue, if a man should charge them for counterfeiting the Kings English.

---

[1] "Inkhorn terms." The phrase was used before Wilson but popularized by him. It refers to jargon, pedantic language, and neologisms and was used frequently in the literary feud between Harvey and Nashe.

Some farre iourneyed gentleman at their returne home, like as they loue to goe in forraine apparell, so thei wil pouder their talke with ouersea language. He that commeth lately out of Fraunce, will talke French English and neuer blush at the matter. An other chops in with English Italienated, and applieth the Italian phrase to our English speaking, the which is, as if an Oratour that professeth to vtter his mind in plaine Latine, would needes speake Poetrie, and farre fetched colours of straunge antiquitie. The Lawyer will store his stomacke with the prating of Pedlers. The Auditor in making his accompt and reckening, cometh in with *sise sould*, and *cater denere*, for vi.s. iiii.d.[2] The fine courtier wil talke nothing but *Chaucer*. The misticall wiseman and Poeticall Clerkes, will speake nothing but quaint Prouerbes, and blinde Allegories, delighting much in their owne darkenesse, especially, when none can tell what they doe say. The vnlearned or foolish phanaticall, that smelles but of learning (such fellowes as haue seen learned men in their daies) wil so Latin their tongues, that the simple can not but wonder at their talke, and thinke surely they speake by some reuelation. I know them that thinke *Rhetorique* to stande wholie vpon darke wordes, and hee that can catche an ynke horne terme by the tail, him they coumpt to be a fine Englishman, and a good *Rhetorician*. . . .

Now whereas wordes be receiued, aswell Greeke as Latine, to set forth our meaning in the English tongue, either for lacke of store, or els because we would enrich the language: it is well doen to vse them, and no man therein can be charged for any affectation, when all other are agreed to followe the same waie. There is no man agreeued when he heareth (Letters Patents) and yet Patentes is Latine, and signifieth open to all men. The Communion is a fellowship, or a comming together, rather Latin then English: the kings prerogatiue declareth his power roiall aboue al other, and yet I know no man greeued for these termes, being vsed in their place, nor yet any one suspected for affectation, when such generall wordes are spoken. The folie is espied, when either we will vse such wordes as fewe men doe vse, or vse them out of place, when an other might serue much better. Therefore to auoide such folly, we may learne of that most ex-

[2] Six shillings fourpence.

cellent Oratour *Tullie,* who in his third booke, where he speaketh
of a perfect Oratour, declareth vnder the name of *Crassus,* that
for the choise of words fower things should chiefly be obserued.
First that such words as we vse, should be proper vnto the
tongue wherein wee speake, againe, that they bee plaine for all
men to perceiue: thirdly, that they be apt and meete, most
properly to sette out the matter. Fourthly, that words translated
from one signification to an other (called of the Grecians *Tropes*)
be vsed to beautifie the sentence, as precious stones are set in a
ring to commende the gold.

¶ *Of Exornation.*

When wee haue learned apte wordes, and vsuall phrases to set
foorth our meaning, and can orderly place them without offence
to the Eare, wee may boldely commende and beautifie our talke
with diuers goodly colours, and delitefull translations, that our
speech may seeme as bright and precious as a rich stone is faire
and orient.

Exornation, is a gorgious beautifying of the tongue with borrowed wordes, and change of sentence or speech with much
varietie. First therefore (as *Tullie* saith) an oration is made to
seme right excellent by the kind selfe, by the colour and iuice of
speech. There are three maner of stiles or inditings, the great or
mightie kinde, when we vse great wordes, or vehement figures.

The small kinde, when wee moderate our heate by meaner
wordes, and vse not the most stirring sentences.

The lawe kinde, when we vse no *Metaphores* nor translated
words, nor yet vse any amplifications, but goe plainly to worke,
and speake altogether in common wordes. Now in al these three
kindes, the Oration is much commended, and appereth notable
when wee keepe vs still to that stile which we first professed,
and vse such wordes as seeme for that kinde of writing most
conuenient. Yea, if we minde to encrease or diminish: to be in a
heate, or to vse moderation. To speake pleasauntly or grauely:
To be sharpe or soft: to talke lordly, or to speak finely: to waxe
auncient or familiar (which all are comprehended vnder one of
the other three) we must euer make our wordes apt and agreeable
to the kinde of stile which we first began to vse. For as French
hoodes doe not become Lords: so Parliament robes are vnfitting

for Ladies. Comelinesse therefore must euer be vsed, and all
things obserued, that are most meete for euery cause, if we looke
by attemptes to haue our desire.

There is an other kind of Exornation, that is not egally sparpled
throughout the whole Oration, but is so disseuered and parted as
starres stande in the Firmament, or flowers in a garden, or pretie
deuised antiques in a cloth of Arras.

¶ *What a figure is.*

A figure is a certaine kinde, either of sentence, Oration, or
worde, vsed after some newe or straunge wise, much vnlike to
that which men commonly vse to speake.

¶ *The deuision of figures.*

There are three kindes of figures, the one is, when the nature
of wordes is chaunged from one signification to an other, called
a *Trope,* of the Grecians: The other serueth for words when they
are not chaunged by nature, but only altered by speaking, called
of the Grecians *Scheme.* The third is, when by diuersitie of inuention, a sentence is many wayes spoken, and also matters are
amplified by heaping examples, by dilating arguments, by comparing of things together, by similitudes, by contraries, and by
diuers other like, called by *Tullie* Exornation of sentences, or
colours of *Rhetorike.*

By all which figures euery Oration may be much beautified,
and without the same, not one can attaine to be coumpted an
Oratour, though his learning otherwise be neuer so great.

Of the first use of Tropes.

When learned and wisemen gan first to inlarge their tongue, and
sought with great vtterance of speech to commende causes: They
founde full oft much want of words to set out their meaning. And
therefore remembring thinges of like nature vnto those whereof
they speake: They vsed such wordes to express their mynde, as
were most like vnto other. As for example. If I should speake
against some notable Pharisey. I might vse translation of wordes
in this wise: Yonder man is of a crooked iudgement, his wittes
are cloudie, he liueth in deepe darknesse, dusked altogether with
blinde ignorance, and drowned in the raging sea of bottomlesse
Superstition. Thus is the ignorant set out by calling him crooked,
cloudie, darke, blinde, and drounde in Superstition. All which

wordes are not proper vnto ignorance, but borowed of other things that are of like nature vnto ignorance. For the vnskilfull man hath his witte set out of order, as a mans bodie is set out of ioynt, and thereupon it may be sayd to be crooked. . . .

And not onely doe men vse translation of words (called *Tropes*) for neede sake, when they can not finde other: but also when they may haue most apt words at hand, yet will they of a purpose vse translated wordes. And the reason is this. Men coumpt it a point of witte, to passe ouer such words as are at hand, and to vse such as are farre fetcht and translated: or els it is because the hearer is ledde by cogitation vppon rehearsall of a Metaphore, and thinketh more by remembraunce of a worde translated, then is there expressely spoken: or els because the whole matter seemeth by a similitude to be opened: or laste of all, because euery translation is commonly, and for the most part referred to the senses of the bodie, and especially to the sense of seeing, which is the sharpest and quickest aboue all other. For when I shall say that an angrie man fometh at the mouth, I am brought in remembrance by this translation to remember a Bore, that in fighting vseth much foming, the which is a foule and lothly sight. And I cause other to thinke that he brake pacience wonderfully, when I set out his rage comparable to a bores foming. . . .

¶ *A Trope.*

A *Trope* is an alteration of a worde or sentence, from the proper signification, to that which is not proper.

¶ *The deuision of Tropes.*

Tropes are either of a worde, or a long continued speeche or sentence.

¶ *Tropes of a worde are these.*

- A Metaphore or translation of wordes.
- A word making.
- Intellection.
- Abusion.
- Transmutation of a worde.
- Transumption.
- Chaunge of name.
- Circumlocution.

Tropes of a long continued speeche or sentences, are these.

- An Allegorie, or inuersion of wordes.
- Mounting.
- Resembling of things.
- Similitudes.
- Examples.

¶ *What is a Metaphore?*

A *Metaphore* is an alteration of a worde, from the proper and naturall meaning, to that which is not proper, and yet agreeth thereunto by some likenesse, that appereth to be in it.

An Oration is wounderfully enriched, when apte *Metaphores* are got, and applied to the matter. Neither can any one perswade effectuously, and winne men by weight of his Oration, without the helpe of wordes altered and translated.

¶ *The diuersitie of translations.*

First we alter a word from that which is in the mind, to that which is in the bodie. As when wee perceiue one that hath begiled vs, we vse to say. Ah sirrha, I am gladde I haue smelled you out. Becing greeued with a matter, wee say commonly wee cannot digest it. The lawier receiuing money more than needeth oftentimes, will say to his Client without any translation: I feele you wel, when the poore man thinketh that he doeth well vnderstande his cause, and will helpe hym to some good ende. For so commonly we say when we knowe a mans minde in any thing. This kinde of mutation is much vsed, when we talke earnestly of any matter.

¶ *From the creature without reason, to that which hath reason.*

The second kinde of translation is, when we goe from the creature without reason, to that which hath reason, or contrary from that which hath reason, to that which hath no reason. As if I should saie, such an vnreasonable brauler did nothing els but barke like a dog, or like a Fox. Women are said to chatter, churles to grunt, boyes to whine, & yongmen to yel. Contrariwise we call a foxe false, a Lion proude, and a dog flattryng.

¶ *From the liuing, to that which hath no life.*

From the liuing to the not liuing, wee vse many translations. As thus. You shall pray for all men, dispersed throughout the

face of the earth. The arme of a Tree. The side of a bancke. The
land crieth for vengeaunce. From the liuing to the not liuing.
Hatred buddeth among malicious men, his wordes flow out of his
mouth. I haue a whole world of businesse.

In obseruing the worke of Nature in all seuerall substances wee
may finde translations at will, then the which nothing is more
profitable for any one, that mindeth by his vtteraunce to stirre
the hartes of men, either one waie or other.

A woorde making called of the Grecians *Onomatapoia*, is when
wee make wordes of our owne minde, such as bee deriued from
the nature of things. As to call one Patche or Coulson, whom we
see to doe a thing foolishly, because these two in their tyme
were notable fooles. Or when one is lustie, to say Taratauntara,
declaring thereby that he is as lustie, as a Trumpette is delitefull
and stirring: or when one would seme galant, to crie hoigh,
whereby also is declared courage. Boyes being greeued will say
some one to another: sir, I will cap you, if you vse mee thus,
and withhold that from me which is mine owne: meaning that
he will take his cap from him. Again, when we see one gaie and
gallaunt, we vse to say, he courtes it. Quoth one that reasoneth
in Diuinitie with his fellowe, I like well to reason, but I cannot
chappe these textes in Scripture, if I should dye for it: meaning
that he could not tell in what Chapter thinges were conteined,
although he knewe full well, that there were such sayinges.

Intellection.

Intellection, called of the Grecians, *Synedoche*, is a Trope,
when we gather or iudge the whole by the part, or part by the
whole. As thus: The King is come to London, meaning therby
that other also be come with him. The French man is good to
keepe a Fort, or to skirmish on Horsbacke, whereby we declare
the French men generally. By the whole, the part thus. All
Cambridge sorrowed for the death of *Bucer*, meaning the most
part. All England reioyceth that Pilgrimage is banished, and
Idolatrie for euer abolished: and yet all England is not glad
but the most part.

The like phrases are in the Scripture, as when the *Magians*
came to *Hierusalem*, and asked where hee was that was borne
King of the Jewes. *Herode* start vp being greatly troubled, and
all the Citie of *Hierusalem* with him, and yet all the Citie was

not troubled, but the most part. By the signe wee vnderstand
the thing signified: as by an Iuie garland, we iudge there is wine
to sel. By the signe of a Beare, Bull, Lyon, or any such, we take
any house to be an Inne. By eating bread at the Communion,
we remember Christes death, and by faith receiue him spiritually.

Abusion.

Abusion, called of the Grecians *Catechresis,* is when for a
certaine proper worde, we vse that which is most nigh vnto it:
as in calling some water, a Fish Pond, though there be no Fish
in it at all. Or els when wee say, there is long talke, and small
matter. Which are spoken vnproperly, for wee cannot measure,
either talke, or matter by length, or breadth.

Transmutation of a worde.

Transmutation helpeth much for varietie, the which is, when
a word hath a proper signification of the owne, and being referred
to an other thing, hath an other meaning: the Grecians call it
Metonymia, the which is diuers waies vsed. When we vse the
author of a thing, for the thing self. As thus: Put vpon you the
Lord Jesus Christ, that is to say, be in liuing such a one as he
was. The Pope is banished England, that is to say, all his
Superstition and Hipocrisie, either is or should bee gone to the
Deuill, by the Kings expresse will and commaundement. Againe,
when that which doth conteine, is vsed for that which is conteined. As thus. I haue dronke an Hoggeshead this weeke: Heauen
may reioyce, and Hell may lament, when olde men are not
couetous. Contrariwise, when the thing conteined, is vsed for
the thing conteyning. As thus. I pray you come to me, that is to
say, come to my house. Fowerthly, when by the efficient cause,
the effect is streight gathered therevpon. As thus. The Sunne is
vp, that is to say, it is day. This fellowe is good with a long
Bowe, that is to say, he shooteth well.

Transumption.

Transumption is, when by degrees wee goe to that, which is
to be shewed. As thus. Such a one lieth in a dark Dungeon:
now in speaking of darkenesse, we vnderstand closenesse, by
closenesse, we gather blacknesse, & by blacknesse, we iudge
deepenesse.

Chaunge of name. [Autonomasia]

Chaunge of name, is when for the proper name, some name

of an Office, or other calling is vsed. As thus: The Prophet of
God saith: Blessed are they, whose sinnes bee not imputed vnto
them, meaning *Dauid*. The Poet saith: It is a vertue to eschue
vice: wherein I vnderstand *Horace*.

Circumlocution. [Periphrasis]

Circumlocution is a large description, either to set forth a
thing more gorgiously, or els to hide it, if the eares can not beare
the open speaking: or when with fewe words, we cannot open
our meaning to speake it more largely. Of the first thus. The
valiaunt courage of mightie *Scipio*, subdued the force of *Carthage*
and *Numantia*. Henry the fifth, the most puissaunt King of England, with seuen thousand men, tooke the French King prisoner
with al the flower of nobilitie in Fraunce. Of the second. When
Saule was easing himself vpon the ground, *Dauid* tooke a peece
of his garment, tooke his weapon that lay by him, and might
haue slaine him. Such a one defiled his bodie with such an euill
woman. For the third part, the large Commentaries written, and
the Paraphrasis of Erasmus Englished: are sufficient to shewe the
vse thereof.

¶ What is an Allegorie.

An Allegorie is none other thing, but a Metaphore, vsed
throughout a whole sentence, or Oration. As in speaking against
a wicked offendour, I might say thus. Oh Lord, his nature was
so euill, and his witte so wickedly bent, that he meant to bouge
the ship, where he himselfe sailed: meaning that he purposed the
destruction of his owne Countrey. It is euill putting strong Wine
into weake vessels, that is to say, it is euill trusting some women
with weightie matters. The English Prouerbes gathered by John
Heywood, helpe well in this behalfe, the which commonly are
nothing else but Allegories, and darke deuised sentences. Now
for the other fower figures, because I minde hereafter to speake
more largely of them, and *Quintilian* thinketh them more meete
to be placed among the figures of Exornation, I will not trouble
the Reader with double inculcation, and twise telling of one tale.

¶ Of Schemes, called otherwise sentences
of a worde and sentence.

I might tary long time, in declaring the nature of diuers
Schemes, which are wordes or sentences altered, either by speaking, or writing, contrarie to the vulgare custome of our speech,

without chaunging their nature at al: but because I knowe the
vse of the figures in worde, is not so great in this our tongue,
I will runne them ouer, with as much hast as I can.

The deuision of Schemes.

Straunge vsing of any worde or sentence, contrary to our
daielie wont, is either when we adde or take away a sillable, or
a worde, or encrease a sentence by chaunge of speech, contrary
to the common maner of speaking.

Figures of a worde.

Those be called figures of a word, when we change a word and
speake it contrary to our vulgare, and dayly speech. Of the
which sort, there are sixe in number.

- i. Addition at the first.
- ii. Abstraction from the first.
- iii. Interlacing in the middest.
- iiii. Cutting from the middest.
- v. Adding at the ende.
- vi. Cutting from the ende.

Of Addition. As thus: He did all to berattle him. Wherein
appeareth that a sillable is added to this word (rattle). Here
is good nale to sell, for good ale. *[Prosthesis]*

Of Abstraction from the first, thus. As I romed all alone, I
gan to thinke of matters great. In which sentence (gan) is vsed,
for began. *[Apheresis]*

Interlacing in the middest. As Relligion, for Religion. *[Epenthesis]*

Cutting from the middest. Idolatrie, for Idololatrie. *[Syncope]*

Adding at the end. Hasten your businesse, for Hast your businesse. *[Proparalepsis]*

Cutting from the ende. A faire maie, for maide. *[Apocope]*

Thus these figures are shortly set out, and as for the other
Schemes, which are vttered in whole sentences, and expressed
by varietie of speech: I will set them forth at large among the
colours and ornaments of Elocution, that followe.

¶ Of colours and ornaments, to commende and set forth an Oration.

Now, when we are able to frame a sentence handsomely
together, obseruing number, and keeping composition, such as
shall like best the eare, and doe knowe the vse of Tropes, and

can apply them to our purpose: then the ornaments are necessarie
in an Oration, and sentences would bee furnished with most
beautifull figures. Therefore, to the end that they may be knowne,
such as most commende and beautifie an Oration: I will set them
forth here in such wise, as I shall best be able, following the
order which *Tullie* hath vsed in his Booke, made of a perfect
Oratour.

¶ *Resting vpon a point [Commoration]*

When wee are earnest in a matter, and feele the weight of our
cause, we rest vpon some reason, which serueth best for our
purpose. Wherein this figure appeareth most, and helpeth much
to set forth our matter. For if we stil kepe vs to our strongest
hold, and make ofter recourse thither, though we be driuen
through by talke to goe from it now and then: we shall force them
at length, either to auoyd our strong defence, or els to yeeld
into our hands.

¶ *An euident, or plaine setting forth of a thing,*
as though it were presently done. [Illustris explanatio]

This figure is called a discription, or an euident declaration
of a thing, as though we saw it euen now done. An example: If
our enemies shal inuade, and by treason winne the victorie, we
shal all dye euery mothers sonne of vs, and our Citie shalbe
destroyed sticke and stone. I see our children made slaues, our
daughters rauished, our wiues caried away, the father forced
to kil his owne sonne, the mother her daughter, the sonne his
father, the sucking child slaine in the mothers bosome, one
standing to the knees in an others bloud, Churches spoyled,
houses pluckt downe, and al set in fire round about vs, euery
one cursing the day of their birth, children crying, women
wayling, and olde men passing for very thought, and euery one
thinking himselfe most happie that is rid out of this world, such
will the crueltie bee of our enemies, and with such horrible
hatred will they seeke to dispatch vs. Thus, where I might haue
said we shall all be destroyed, and say no more, I haue by
description set the euill foorth at large. It much auayleth to vse
this figure in diuers matters, the which whosoeuer can doe, with
any excellent gift, vndoubtedly he shal much delite the hearers.
The circumstances well considered in euery cause, giue much

matter, for the plaine opening of the thing. Also similitudes, examples, comparisons, from one thing to an other, apt translations, and heaping of Allegories, and all such figures as serue for amplifying, doe much commend the liuely setting forth of any matter. The miseries of the Courtiers life, might well bee described by this kind of figure. The commoditie of learning, the pleasure of Plowmen, and the care that a King hath. And not onely are matters set out by description, but men are painted out in their colours, yea, buildings are set foorth, Kingdomes and Realmes are portured, places and times are described. The Englishman for feeding and chaunging of apparell. The Dutchman for drinking. The Frenchman for pride & inconstance. The Spanyard for nimblenes of body, and much disdaine: the Italian for great wit and policie: the Scots for boldnesse, and the Boeme for stubbornesse.

Many people are described by their degree, as a man of good yeares, is coumpted sober, wise, and circumspect: a young man wilde and carelesse: a woman babling, inconstant, and readie to beleeue all that is tolde her.

By vocation of life, a Souldier is coumpted a great bragger, and a vaunter of himself: A Scholer simple: A Russet coate, sad, and sometimes craftie: a Courtier, flattering: a Citizen, gentle.

In describing of persons, there ought alwaies a comelinesse to bee vsed, so that nothing be spoken, which may bee thought is not in them. As if one shall describe Henry the sixth, he might cal him gentle, milde of nature, led by perswasion, and readie to forgiue, carelesse for wealth, suspecting none, mercifull to all, fearefull in aduersitie, and without forecast to espie his misfortune. Againe, for Richard the third, I might bring him in, cruel of heart, ambicious by nature, enuious of mind, a deepe dissembler, a close man for weightie matters, hardie to reuenge, and fearfull to lose his high estate, trustie to none, liberall for a purpose, casting still the worst, and hoping euer the best. By this figure also wee imagine a talke, for some one to speake, and according to his person, we frame the Oration. As if one should bring in noble Henrie the eight, of most famous memorie to enueigh against Rebelles, thus he might order his Oration. What if Henry the eight were a liue, and sawe such Rebellion in this

Realme, would not he say thus, and thus? Yea, me thinkes I heare him speake euen now. And so set forth such wordes, as we would haue him to say. . . .[3]

¶ *Example. [Exemplum]*

He that mindeth to perswade, must needes be well stored with examples. And therefore much are they to be commended, which searche Chronicles of all ages, and compare the state of our Elders with this present time. The Historie of Gods booke to the Christian is infallible, and therefore the rehearsall of such good things as are therein conteined, moue the faithfull to all vpright doing, and amendment of their life. The *Ethnicke* Authours stirre the hearers, being well applied to the purpose. For when it shalbe reported that thei which had no knowledge of God, liued in a brotherly loue one towards an other, detested iduoutry, banished periuries, hanged the vnthankful, kept the idle without meate till they laboured for their liuing: suffered none extortion, exempted bribes from bearing rule in the Common-weale, the Christians must needes bee ashamed of their euill behauiour, and studie much to passe those which are in calling much vnder them, and not suffer that the ignorant and Pagans life, shall counteruaile the taught children of God, and passe the Christians so much in good liuing, as the Christians passe them in good learning. Unegall examples commend much the matter. I call them vnegall when the weaker is brought in against the stronger, as if children be faithfull, much more ought men to be faithfull. If women be chast and vndefiled: men should much more be cleane and without fault. If an vnlearned man wil do no wrong, a learned man and a Preacher, must much more be vpright and liue without blame. If an Housholder will deale

[3] Omitted: "A stop" (*precisio*), "a close understanding" (*significatio*), "short sentences" (*brevitas*), "abating" (*extenuatio*), "iesting" (*illusio*), "digression" (*digressio*), "proposition" (*propositio*), "over passage" (*seiunctio*), "comming againe to the matter" (*redditus ad propositum*), "iterating" (*iteratio*), "conclusion" (*rationis conclusio*), "mounting above the trueth" (*veritas superlatio*), "asking other, and aunswering our selfe" (*rogatio*), "snappish asking" (*percontatio*), "dissembling" (*dissimulatio*), "distribution" (*distributio*), "correction" (*correctio*), "doubtfulnesse" (*dubitatio*), "a buttresse" (*premunitio*), "a familiar talke" (*communicatio*), "description of a mans nature or maners" (*descriptio*), "error" (*erroris inductio*), "mirth making" (*in hilaritatem impulsio*), "anticipation or prevention" (*ante occupatio*), "similitude" (*similitudo*).

iustly with his seruants: a King must much the rather deale iustly
with his subiects. Examples gathered out of histories, and vsed
in this sorte, helpe much towards perswasion. Yea, brute beastes
minister greate occasion of right good matter, considering many
of them haue shewed vnto vs, the paterns and Images of diuers
vertues. . . .

¶ *Of enlarging examples by copy.*

And now because examples enriched by copie, helpe much for
amplification: I will giue a taste howe these and such like histories
may bee encreased. And for the better handling of them, needfull
it is to marke well the circumstances: that being well obserued
and compared together on both partes, they may the rather bee
enlarged. As thus. That which brute beastes haue done, shalt
thou being a man, seeme not to haue done? They shewed themselues naturall, and wilt thou appeare vnnaturall? Naie, they
ouercame Nature, and wilt thou be ouercome of them? They
became of beastes in bodie, man in Nature, and wilt thou become
of a man in bodie, a beast in Nature? They beeing without reason,
declared the propertie of reasonable creatures, and wilt thou,
being a man endued with reason, appere in thy doings altogether
vnreasonable? Shall Dogges be thankfull: and men, yea, Christen
men want such a vertue? shall wormes shewe such kindnesse:
and men appeare gracelesse? It had bene no matter if they had
bene vnthankful: but man can neuer escape blame, seing God
hath commaunded, and Nature hath graffed this in al men: that
they should do to other, as they would be done vnto. Againe,
they for meate onely shewed themselues so kind: and shall man
for so many benefites recciued, and for such goodnesse shewed,
requite for good will euill deedes: for hartie loue deadly hatred:
for vertue vice: and for life giuen to him, yeeld death to other?
Nature hath parted man and beast: and shall man in Nature
bee no man? Shamed be that wretch that goeth against Nature,
that onely hath the shape of a man, and in Nature is worse then
a beast. Yea, worthy are all such rather to be torne with deuilles,
then to liue with men. Thus an example might most copiously
be augmented, but thus much for this time is sufficient.

The saying of Poetes and all their fables are not to be forgotten, for by them we may talke at large, and win men by
perswasion, if we declare before hand that these tales were not

fained of such wisemen without cause, neither yet continued vntill this time, and kept in memorie without good consideration, and therupon declare the true meaning of all such writing. For vndoubtedly there is no one tale among all the Poetes, but vnder the same is comprehended some thing that parteineth, either to the amendment of maners, to the knowledge of the trueth, to the setting forth of Natures work, or els the vnderstanding of some notable thing done. For what other is the painfull trauaile of *Vlisses*, described so largely by *Homer*, but a liuely picture of mans miserie in this life. And as *Plutarch* saieth: and likewise *Basilius Magnus*: in the *Iliades* are described strength, and valiantnesse of the bodie: In *Odissea* is set forth a liuely paterne of the minde. The Poetes were wisemen, and wished in hart the redresse of things, the which when for feare, they durst not openly rebuke, they did in colours painte them out, and tolde men by shadowes what they should doe in good sooth, or els because the wicked were vnworthie to heare the trueth, they spake so that none might vnderstande but those vnto whom they please to vtter their meaning, and knewe them to be men of honest conuersation.

We read of *Danae* the faire damosell, whom *Iupiter* tempted full oft, and could neuer haue his pleasure, till at length he made it raigne golde, and so as she sat in her Chimney, a great deale fell vpon her lappe, the which she tooke gladly and kept it there, within the which golde, *Iupiter* himselfe was comprehended, whereby is none other thing els signified, but that women haue bene, and will be ouercome with money.

Likewise *Iupiter* fansying the faire maide *Isis*, could not haue his will, till he turned himself into a faire white Bull, which signified that beautie may ouercome the best.

If a man could speake against couetous caitiues, can he better shew what they are, then by setting forth the straunge plague of *Tantalus*, who is reported to be in Hell, hauing Water comming still to his chin, and yet neuer able to drinke: And an Apple hanging before his mouth, and yet neuer able to eate?

Icarus would needes haue winges, and flie contrarie to Nature, whereupon when he had set them together with Waxe, and ioyned to his side, and mounted vp into the Ayre: But so sone as the Sunne had somewhat heated him, and his Waxe beganne

to melt, he fell downe into a greate Riuer, and was drowned
out of hand, the which water was euer after called by his name.
Nowe what other thing doeth this tale shewe vs, but that euery
man should not meddle with things aboue his compasse.

Midas desired that what soeuer he touched, the same might be
gold: whereupon when *Iupiter* had graunted him his bound: his
meate, drinke, and all other things turned into golde, and he
choked with his owne desire, as all couetous men lightly shalbe,
that can neuer be content when they haue enough.

What other things are the wonderfull labours of *Hercules*, but
that reason should withstand affection, and the spirit for euer
should fight against the flesh? Wee Christians had like Fables
heretofore of ioyly felowes, the Images whereof were set vp (in
Gods name) euen in our Churches. But is any man so madde to
think that euer there was such a one as Saint Christopher was
painted vnto vs? Mary God forbid. Assured that he liued vpon
earth there were other houses builded for him, then wee haue
at this time, and I thinke Tailers were much troubled to take
measure for him for making his garments. He might be of kinne
to Garganteo if he were as bigge as he is set forth in Antwerp.
But this was the meaning of our elders (and the name self doth
signifie none other) that euery man should beare Christ vpon
his backe, that is to say, he should loue his brother, as Christ loued
vs, and gaue his bodie for vs: he should trauaile through hunger,
cold, sorowe, sicknesse, death, and all daungers, with al sufferance
that might be. And whether should be trauaile? to the euerliuing
God. But how? In darknesse? No forsooth by the light of his
worde. And therfore S. Christopher beeing in the Sea, and not
wel able to get out (that is to say) being almost drowned in sinne,
(and not knowing which waie best to escape) an Eromite appeared vnto him with a Lanterne and a light therein, the which
doth signifie none other thing to the Christian, but the true worde
of God, which lighteneth the hearts of men, and giueth vnderstanding to the young lings (as the Prophet doth say). Againe,
S. George he is set on Horsebacke and killeth a Dragon with his
speare, which Dragon would haue deuoured a Virgine, whereby
is none other thing meant, but that a King and euery man, vnto
whom the execution of Iustice is committed, should defende the
innocent against the vngodly attempts of the wicked, and rather

kill such deuilles by Marciall lawe, then suffer the innocentes
to take any wrong. But who gaue our Cleargie any such authoritie
that those Monsters should be in Churches, as lay mens bookes?
God forbad by expresse worde, to make any grauen Image, and
shall wee bee so bold to breake Gods will for a good intent, and
call these Idolles laie mens bookes? I could talke largely of
examples, and heape a number here together, aswell of *Ethnik*
Authours, as of others here at home; but for feare I should be
tedious, these for this time shall suffice.

¶ *Of Fables.*

The feined Fables, such as are attributed vnto brute beastes,
would not be forgotten at any hande. For not onely they delite
the rude and ignorant, but also they helpe much for perswasion. . . .[4]

¶ *Of figures in sentences called Schemes.*

When any sentence vpon the placing or setting of wordes, is
sayd to be a figure: the said is alwaies called a Scheme, the
which words being altered or displaced, the figure straight doth
lose his name, and is called no more a Scheme. Of this sort
there is diuers, such as hereafter followe.

¶ *Doublets. [Geminatio verborum]*

Doublettes, is when we rehearse one and the same worde twise
together. Ah wretche, wretche, that I am. *Tullie* against *Catiline*,
enueighing sore against his traterous attempts, saieth after a long
rehearsed matter, and yet notwithstanding al this notorious
wickednesse: The man liueth still, liueth? Naie Marie, he cometh
into the counsaile house, which is more. An other. Darest thou
shew thy face, thou wretched theefe, thou theef, I say to thine
owne father, darest thou looke abroade? Thus the oft repeating
of one worde, doth much stirre the hearer, and makes the worde
seeme greater, as though a sworde were oft digged and thrust
twise, or thrise in one place of the body.

¶ *Altering part of a worde. [Paulum immutatum verbum]*

Altering parte of a worde, is when we take a letter or sillable
from some worde, or els adde a letter, or sillable to a worde. As
thus. William Somer seeing much adoe for accomptes making,

---

[4] Omitted: "Digestion" (*digestio*), "a wisht or warning to speake no more"
(*reticentia*), "contrarietie" (*contentio*), "freenesse of speeche" (*libera vox*),
"stomacke greefe" (*iracundia*).

and that the Kinges Maiestie of most worthie memorie Henrie
the eight wanted money, such as was due vnto him: and please
your grace (quoth he) you haue so many Frauditours, so many
Conueighers, and so many Deceiuers to get vp your money, that
they get all to themselues. Whether he sayd true or no, let God
iudge that, it was vnhappely spoken of a foole, and I thinke he
had some Schoolemaster: He should haue saide Auditours,
Surueighours, and Receiuers.

¶ *Repetition. [Repetitio a primo]*

Repetition, is when we beginne diuers sentences, one after an
other: with one and the same worde. As thus: when thou shalt
appeare at the terrible day of iudgement, before the high Maiestie
of God, where is then thy riches? Where is then thy daintie fare?
Where is then thy great band of men? Where are then thy faire
houses? Where are then thy Landes, Pastures, Parkes, and Forests? I might say thus of our soueraigne Lorde the Kings Maiestie,
that now is: King Edward hath ouerthrowen Idolatrie, King
Edward hath banished superstition: King Edward by Gods help,
hath brought vs to the true knowledge of our creation: King
Edward hath quieted our consciences, and laboured that all his
people should seeke health, by the death and passion of Christ
alone.

¶ *Conuersion. [Conversio]*

Conuersion, is an oft repeating of the last worde, and is contrary to that which went before. When iust dealing is not vsed:
wealth goeth awaie, frendship goeth awaie, trueth goeth awaie,
all goodnesse (to speake at a worde) goeth awaie. . . .[5]

¶ *Egall members. [Paria paribus relata]*

Egall members are such, when the one halfe of the sentence
answereth to the other, with iust proportion of number, not
that the Sillables of necessitie should bee of iust number, but
that the eare might iudge them to be so egall, that there may
appeare small difference. As thus. Law without mercie, is extreme power, yet men through foly deserue such Iustice. Learning
is daungerous, if an euill man haue it. The more noble a man is,
the more gentle he should bee. *Isocrates* passeth in this behalfe,

---

[5] Omitted: "Comprehension" (*conversio in eadem*), "progression" (*pro-
gressio*), "like ending, like falling" (*similiter desinens, similiter cadens*).

who is thought to write altogether in nomber, keeping iust proportion in framing of his sentence.

¶ *Like among themselues. [Similia inter se]*

Sentences are called like when contraries are set together, and the first taketh asmuch as the other following: and the other following taketh asmuch awaie, as that did which went before. As thus. Lust hath ouercome shamefastnesse, impudence hath ouercome feare, and madnesse hath ouercome reason. Or els sentences are said to be like among themselues, when euery part of one sentence is egall, and of like waight one with an other. As thus. Is it knowne, tried, proued, euident, open, and assured that I did such a deede? An other. Such riot, Dicing, Carding, picking, stealing, fighting, Ruffians, Queanes and Harlottes must needes bring him to naught.

Gradation. [Gradatio]

Gradation, is when we rehearse the word that goeth next before, and bring an other word thereupon that encreaseth the matter, as though one should goe vp a paire of stayres and not leaue till he come at the top. Or thus. Gradation is when a sentence is disseuered by degrees, so that the word which endeth the sentence going before doeth begin the next. Labour getteth learning, learning getteth fame, fame getteth honour, honour getteth blisse for euer. An other. Of sloth cometh pleasure, of pleasure cometh spending, of spending cometh whoring, of whoring cometh lack, of lacke cometh theft, of theft cometh hanging, and there an end for this worlde.

¶ *Regression. [Regressio]*

That is called regression, when we repeate a worde eftsone that hath bin spoken and rehersed before, whether the same be in the beginning, in the middest, or in the latter ende of a sentence. In the beginning, thus. Thou art ordeined to rule other, and not other to rule thee. In the middest, thus. He that hath money hath not giuen it, and he that hath giuen money, hath not his money still: and he that hath giuen thankes, hath thanks still, and he that hath them stil, hath giuen them notwithstanding. In the latter ende, thus. Man must not liue to eate, but eate to liue. Man is not made for the sabboth, but the sabboth is made for man. If man do any filthy thing, and take pleasure therein: the pleasure goeth away, but the shame tarieth stil. If man do any good thing with paine, the paines goe awaie, but the honestie abideth still.

¶ *Wordes loose. [Dissolutum]*

Wordes loose are such, which as are vttered without any addition of coniunctions, such as knitte words and sentences together. As thus. Obeye the King, feare his lawes, keepe thy vocation, doe right, seeke rest, like well a little, vse all men, as thou wouldest they should vse thee.

¶ *Outcrying. [Exclamatio]*

Out crying, is when with voyce we make an exclamation. Oh Lord, O God, O worlde, O life, O maners of men? O Death, where is thy sting? O Hell, where is thy victorie?

¶ *Oft vsing of one word in diuers places.*

Can he haue any mans harte in him, or deserueth hee the name of a man, that cruelly killeth a poore innocent man, who neuer thought him harme.

¶ *A cause giuen to a sentence—vttered.*

I feare not mine aduersarie, because I am not guiltie. I mistrust not the Iudges, because they are iust, the Quest will not cast me, the matter is so plaine.

¶ *A cause giuen to things contrary.*

Better it were to rule, then to serue. For, he that ruleth, liueth: because he is free. But he that serueth, cannot be said to liue. For where bondage is, there is no life properly. . . .[6]

---

[6] The list continues with "sufferaunce," "doubting," "reckening," "reasoning a matter with our selves" (*disputatio*), "resembling of things" (*imago*), "answering to our selfe," "order," and "briefe describing." Wilson concludes, like the classical rhetoricians, with brief discussions of "memory" and "pronunciation" (i.e., delivery).

Roger Ascham

[1515–1568]

◈

THE RISE OF HUMANISM is closely related to the success of humanistic educational reform. On the Continent such figures as Vittorino da Feltre, Guarino da Verona, Erasmus, Comenius, and Vives helped to create an educational system which made humanism self-perpetuating. Educational reform began in England with Thomas Linacre (1460–1524), William Grocyn (1446–1519), and John Colet (1467–1519). Their work was carried forward by Thomas Elyot, John Cheke, and Thomas Wilson (among others); and it was from Cheke that Ascham derived many of his basic ideas. *Toxophilus* (1545), a work in praise of the art of the long bow, reflects the ideal of *mens sana in corpore sano*. In 1548 Ascham became tutor to Queen (then Princess) Elizabeth, and later to Lady Jane Gray. Surprisingly, in view of his Protestantism, he served as Latin Secretary to Queen Mary. After Elizabeth's accession he became Greek preceptor at the Royal Court.

The Scholemaster (1570) testifies throughout to Ascham's dedication to education. His criticism of the severe punishments used in the grammar schools shows the human side of his character, which is somewhat less apparent in his invectives against medieval romances (including the *Morte D'Arthur*) and against the insidious lures of Italy. As a critic Ascham espouses the cause of English as a literary language but would like to see prosody reformed along classical lines. His remarks on 'imitation' are particularly important. Although he recognizes the existence of 'poetic imitation' (akin to Greek *mimesis*), he stresses imitation in the sense of 'following precedent.' An overwhelming majority of humanist educators would have agreed with him.

Schoolboys trained according to Ascham's precepts became intimately acquainted with the classics, dutifully imitated them in their own mature writings, and demanded imitation in authors who aspired to literary greatness. Not unnaturally, the line between imitation and plagiarism became extremely vague. The forms, tones, images, and very words of the ancients constantly recur in Elizabethan literature. When classical precedent was lacking, as in the case of a love sonnet

58

or romance, Elizabethans imitated Renaissance 'classics' such as Petrarch's *Canzoniere* or Ariosto's *Orlando Furioso*.

Imitation of Cicero is so important as to merit special note. Cicero's orations formed the core of grammar school education, and by the end of the fifteenth century in Italy, literary excellence was being equated with fidelity to the immortal Tully. During the sixteenth century a reaction set in. The Ciceronian purists were opposed by a group of anti-Ciceronians who were, in essence, defending the author's right to a measure of individuality. The *Ciceronianus* of Erasmus takes a moderate position. Later in the century the anti-Ciceronians became more dogmatic, opposing the style of Cicero to that of Seneca and Tacitus. Their arguments had an important effect on the development of English prose.

The present text of *The Scholemaster* is based on the 1570 edition.

BIBLIOGRAPHY. *The Scholemaster*, ed. E. Arber (1870). For comment on imitation, see: H. White, *Plagiarism and Imitation During the English Renaissance* (1935). For the background of educational theory and practice, see: J. Adamson, *The Reformation and English Education* (1931); D. Clark, *Milton at St. Paul's* (1948); F. Watson, *The English Grammar Schools to 1660* (1908); W. Woodward, *Vittorino da Feltre and Other Humanist Educators* (1897); *Studies in Education during the Age of the Renaissance* (1906). For Ciceronianism and anti-Ciceronianism, see: G. Williamson, *The Senecan Amble* (1954, includes additional refs.); H. Wilson and C. Forbes, "Gabriel Harvey's *Ciceronianus*," *University of Nebraska Studies in the Humanities*, IV (1945).

from

THE SCHOLEMASTER

[1570]

[i. IMITATION]

IMITATION IS A FACULTIE to expresse liuelie and perfitelie that example which ye go about to folow. And of it selfe it is large and wide: for all the workes of nature in a manner be examples for arte to folow.

But to our purpose: all languages, both learned and mother tonges, be gotten, and gotten onelie by *Imitation*. For as ye vse to heare, so ye learne to speake: if ye heare no other, ye speake not your selfe: and whome ye onelie heare, of them ye onelie learne.

And therefore, if ye would speake as the best and wisest do, ye must be conuersant where the best and wisest are: but if yow be borne or brought vp in a rude contrie, ye shall not chose but speake rudelie: the rudest man of all knoweth this to be trewe.

Yet neuerthelesse, the rudenes of common and mother tonges is no bar for wise speaking. For in the rudest contrie, and most barbarous mother language, many be found [that] can speake verie wiselie: but in the Greeke and Latin tong, the two onelie learned tonges, which be kept not in common taulke but in priuate bookes, we finde alwayes wisdome and eloquence, good matter and good vtterance, neuer or seldom asonder. For all soch Authors as be fullest of good matter and right iudgement in doctrine be likewise alwayes most proper in wordes, most apte in sentence, most plaine and pure in vttering the same.

And, contrariwise, in those two tonges, all writers, either in Religion or any sect of Philosophie, who so euer be founde fonde in iudgement of matter, be commonlie found as rude in vttering their mynde. For Stoickes, Anabaptistes, and Friers, with Epicures, Libertines, and Monkes, being most like in learning and life, are no fonder and pernicious in their opinions than they be rude and barbarous in their writinges. They be not wise therefore that say, 'What care I for a mans wordes and vtterance, if his matter and reasons be good.' Soch men say so, not so moch of ignorance, as eyther of some singular pride in themselues or some speciall malice or other, or for some priuate and parciall matter, either in Religion or other kinde of learning. For good and choice meates be no more requisite for helthie bodies than proper and apte wordes be for good matters, and also plaine and sensible vtterance for the best and depest reasons: in which two pointes standeth perfite eloquence, one of the fairest and rarest giftes that God doth geue to man.

Ye know not what hurt ye do to learning, that care not for wordes but for matter, and so make a deuorse betwixt the tong and the hart. For marke all aiges: looke vpon the whole course

of both the Greeke and Latin tonge, and ye shall surelie finde
that, when apte and good wordes began to be neglected, and
properties of those two tonges to be confounded, than also began
ill deedes to spring, strange maners to oppresse good orders,
newe and fond opinions to striue with olde and trewe doctrine,
first in Philosophie and after in Religion, right iudgement of all
thinges to be peruerted, and so vertue with learning is contemned,
and studie left of: of ill thoughtes cummeth peruerse iudgement,
of ill deedes springeth lewde taulke. Which fower misorders,
as they mar mans life, so destroy they good learning withall.

But behold the goodnesse of Gods prouidence for learning: all
olde authors and sectes of Philosophy, which were fondest in
opinion and rudest in vtterance, as Stoickes and Epicures, first
contemned of wise men and often forgotten of all men, be so
consumed by tymes, as they be now not onelie out of vse but
also out of memorie of man: which thing, I surelie thinke, will
shortlie chance to the whole doctrine and all the bookes of
phantasticall Anabaptistes and Friers, and of the beastlie Libertines and Monkes. . . .

But to returne to *Imitation* agayne: There be three kindes of
it in matters of learning.

The whole doctrine of Comedies and Tragedies is a perfite
imitation, or faire liuelie painted picture of the life of euerie degree of man. Of this *Imitation* writeth *Plato* at large in 3. *de Rep.,*
but it doth not moch belong at this time to our purpose.

The second kind of *Imitation* is to folow for learning of tonges
and sciences the best authors. Here riseth, emonges proude and
enuious wittes, a great controuersie, whether one or many are
to be folowed: and if one, who is that one; *Seneca* or *Cicero*;
Salust or *Cæsar*; and so forth in Greeke and Latin.

The third kinde of *Imitation* belongeth to the second: as, when
you be determined whether ye will folow one or mo, to know
perfitlie, and which way to folow, that one; in what place; by
what meane and order; by what tooles and instrumentes ye shall
do it; by what skill and iudgement ye shall trewelie discerne
whether ye folow rightlie or no.

This *Imitatio* is *dissimilis materiei similis tractatio* [1]; and, also,

---

[1] "unlike treatment of similar material"

similis materiei dissimilis tractatio,[2] as *Virgill* followed *Homer*: but the Argument to the one was *Vlysses*, to the other *Æneas*. *Tullie* persecuted *Antonie* with the same wepons of eloquence that *Demosthenes* vsed before against *Philippe*.

Horace foloweth *Pindar*, but either of them his owne Argument and Person; as the one, *Hiero* king of *Sicilie*, the other, *Augustus* the Emperor: and yet both for like respectes, that is, for their coragious stoutnes in warre and iust gouernment in peace.

One of the best examples for right *Imitation* we lacke, and that is *Menander*, whom our *Terence* (as the matter required), in like argument, in the same Persons, with equall eloquence, foote by foote did folow.

Som peeces remaine, like broken Iewelles, whereby men may rightlie esteme and iustlie lament the losse of the whole.

Erasmus, the ornament of learning in our tyme, doth wish that som man of learning and diligence would take the like paines in *Demosthenes* and *Tullie* that *Macrobius* hath done in *Homer* and *Virgill*, that is, to write out and ioyne together where the one doth imitate the other. *Erasmus* wishe is good, but surelie it is not good enough: for *Macrobius* gatherings for the *Æneados* out of *Homer*, and *Eobanus Hessus* more diligent gatherings for the *Bucolikes* out of *Theocritus*, as they be not fullie taken out of the whole heape, as they should be, but euen as though they had not sought for them of purpose but fownd them scatered here and there by chance in their way, euen so, onelie to point out and nakedlie to ioyne togither their sentences, with no farder declaring the maner and way how the one doth folow the other, were but a colde helpe to the encrease of learning.

But if a man would take his paine also, whan he hath layd two places of *Homer* and *Virgill* or of *Demosthenes* and *Tullie* togither, to teach plainlie withall, after this sort:

1. *Tullie* reteyneth thus moch of the matter, thies sentences, thies wordes:

2. This and that he leaueth out, which he doth wittelie to this end and purpose.

3. This he addeth here.

4. This he diminisheth there.

---

[2] "like treatment of unlike material"

5. This he ordereth thus, with placing that here, not there.

6. This he altereth and changeth, either in propertie of wordes, in forme of sentence, in substance of the matter, or in one or other conuenient circumstance of the authors present purpose.

In thies fewe rude English wordes are wrapt vp all the necessarie tooles and instrumentes, where with trewe *Imitation* is rightlie wrought withall in any tonge. Which tooles, I openlie confesse, be not of myne owne forging, but partlie left vnto me by the cunningest Master, and one of the worthiest Ientlemen that euer England bred, Syr *John Cheke*, partelie borowed by me out of the shoppe of the dearest frende I haue out of England, *Io. St*[urmius]. And therefore I am the bolder to borow of him, and here to leaue them to other, and namelie to my Children: which tooles, if it please God that an other day they may be able to vse rightlie, as I do wish and daylie pray they may do, I shal be more glad than if I were able to leaue them a great quantitie of land.

This foresaide order and doctrine of *Imitation* would bring forth more learning, and breed vp trewer iudgement, than any other exercise that can be vsed, but not for yong beginners, bicause they shall not be able to consider dulie therof. And, trewlie, it may be a shame to good studentes, who, hauing so faire examples to follow, as *Plato* and *Tullie*, do not vse so wise wayes in folowing them for the obteyning of wisdome and learning as rude ignorant Artificers do for gayning a small commoditie. For surelie the meanest painter vseth more witte, better arte, greater diligence, in hys shoppe, in folowing the Picture of any meane mans face, than commonlie the best studentes do, euen in the vniuersitie, for the atteining of learning it selfe.

Some ignorant, vnlearned, and idle student, or some busie looker vpon this litle poore booke, that hath neither will to do good him selfe, nor skill to iudge right of others, but can lustelie contemne, by pride and ignorance, all painfull diligence and right order in study, will perchance say that I am to precise, to curious, in marking and piteling thus about the imitation of others; and that the olde worthie Authors did neuer busie their heades and wittes in folowyng so preciselie, either the matter what other men wrote, or els the maner how other men wrote. They will say it were a plaine slauerie, and iniurie to, to shakkle and tye a good witte, and hinder the course of a mans good nature, with such bondes of seruitude, in folowyng other.

Except soch men thinke them selues wiser then *Cicero* for teaching of eloquence, they must be content to turne a new leafe. . . .

. . . *Ioan. Sturmius, de Nobilitate literata et de Amissa dicendi ratione,* [is] farre best of all, in myne opinion, that euer tooke this matter [of imitation] in hand. For all the rest declare chiefly this point, whether one, or many, or all are to be followed: but *Sturmius* onelie hath most learnedlie declared who is to be followed, what is to be followed, and, the best point of all, by what way and order trew Imitation is rightlie to be exercised. And although *Sturmius* herein doth farre passe all other, yet hath he not so fullie and perfitelie done it as I do wishe he had, and as I know he could. For though he hath done it perfitelie for precept, yet hath he not done it perfitelie enough for example: which he did, neither for lacke of skill, nor by negligence, but of purpose, contented with one or two examples, bicause he was mynded in those two bookes to write of it both shortlie, and also had to touch other matters.

Barthol. Riccius Ferrariensis also hath written learnedlie, diligentlie, and verie largelie of this matter, euen as hee did before verie well *de Apparatu linguae Lat.* He writeth the better in myne opinion, bicause his whole doctrine, iudgement, and order semeth to be borowed out of *Io. Stur.* bookes. He addeth also examples, the best kinde of teaching: wherein he doth well, but not well enough: in deede, he commiteth no faulte, but yet deserueth small praise. He is content with the meane, and followeth not the best: as a man that would feede vpon Acornes, whan he may eate as good cheape the finest wheat bread. He teacheth, for example, where and how two or three late *Italian* Poetes do follow *Virgil*; and how *Virgil* him selfe in the storie of *Dido* doth wholie imitate *Catullus* in the like matter of *Ariadna*: Wherein I like better his diligence and order of teaching than his iudgement in choice of examples for *Imitation*. But, if he had done thus, if he had declared where and how, how oft and how many wayes, *Virgil* doth folow *Homer*, as for example the comming of *Vlysses* to *Alcynous* and *Calypso*, with the comming of *Æneas* to *Cartage* and *Dido*; Likewise the games, running, wrestling, and shoting, that *Achilles* maketh in *Homer*, with the selfe same games that *Æneas* maketh in *Virgil*; The harnesse of *Achilles*, with the harnesse of *Æneas*, and the maner of making of them both by *Vulcane*; The notable combate betwixt *Achilles* and *Hector*, with as notable a combate betwixt *Æneas* and *Turnus*; The going downe to hell of *Vlysses* in *Homer*, with the going downe to hell of *Æneas* in *Virgil*; and other places infinite mo, as similitudes, narrations, messages, discriptions of persons, places, battels, tempestes, shipwrackes, and common places for diuerse purposes, which be as precisely taken out of *Homer* as euer did Painter in London follow the picture of any faire personage; And when thies places had bene gathered together by this way of diligence, than to haue conferred them together by this order of teaching, as diligently to marke what is kept and vsed in either author, in wordes, in sentences, in matter, what is added, what is left out, what ordered otherwise, either *praeponendo*, *interponendo*, or *postponendo*,[3] and what is altered for any respect, in word, phrase, sentence, figure, reason, argument, or by any way of circumstance: If *Riccius* had done this, he had not onely bene will liked for his diligence in teaching, but also iustlie commended for his right iudgement in right choice of examples for the best *Imitation*. . . .

In Tragedies (the goodliest Argument of all, and, for the vse either of a learned preacher or a Ciuill Ientleman, more profitable than *Homer*, *Pindar*, *Virgill*, and *Horace*, yea comparable in myne opinion with the doctrine of *Aristotle*, *Plato*, and *Xenophon*), the *Grecians Sophocles* and *Euripides* far ouer match our *Seneca* in Latin, namely in Οἰχονομίᾳ *et Decoro*,[4] although *Senecaes* elocution and verse be verie commendable for his tyme. And for the matters of *Hercules*, *Thebes*, *Hippolytus*, and *Troie*, his Imitation is to be gathered into the same booke, and to be tryed by the same touchstone, as is spoken before.

In histories, and namelie in *Liuie*, the like diligence of Imitation could bring excellent learning, and breede stayde iudgement, in taking any like matter in hand. Onely *Liuie* were a sufficient taske for one mans studie, to compare him, first with his fellow

[3] "by placement before, between, or after"
[4] "economy and decorum"

for all respectes, *Dion. Halicarnassaeus*; who both liued in one tyme, tooke both one historie in hande to write, deserued both like prayse of learnynge and eloquence: Than with *Polybius* that wise writer, whom *Liuie* professeth to follow; and, if he would denie it, yet it is plaine that the best part of the thyrd *Decade* in *Liuie* is in a maner translated out of the thyrd and rest of *Polibius*: Lastlie with *Thucydides*, to whose Imitation *Liuie* is curiouslie bent. . . .

And now to know what Author doth medle onelie with some one peece and member of eloquence, and who doth perfitelie make vp the whole bodie, I will declare, as I can call to remembrance the goodlie talke that I haue had oftentymes of the trew difference of Authors with that Ientleman of worthie memorie, my dearest frend, and teacher of all the litle poore learning I haue, Syr *John Cheke*.

The trew difference of Authors is best knowne *per diuersa genera dicendi* [5] that euerie one vsed. And therefore here I will deuide *genus dicendi*, not into these three, *Tenue, mediocre, et grande*, [6] but as the matter of euerie Author requireth, as

$$\text{in Genus} \begin{cases} \textit{Poeticum,} \\ \textit{Historicum,} \\ \textit{Philosophicum,} \\ \textit{Oratorium.} \end{cases}$$

These differre one from an other in choice of wordes, in framyng of Sentences, in handling of Argumentes, and vse of right forme, figure, and number, proper and fitte for euerie matter; and euerie one of these is diuerse also in it selfe, as the first,

$$\textit{Poeticum, in} \begin{cases} \textit{Comicum,} \\ \textit{Tragicum,} \\ \textit{Epicum,} \\ \textit{Melicum.} \end{cases}$$

And here, who soeuer hath bene diligent to read aduisedlie ouer *Terence, Seneca, Virgil, Horace*, or els *Aristophanes, Sophocles, Homer*, and *Pindar*, and shall diligently marke the difference they vse, in proprietie of wordes, in forme of sentence, in handlyng of their matter, he shall easelie perceiue what is fitte and

---

[5] "through the diverse kinds of expression"

[6] "Low, middle, and grand"—a reference to the 'three styles' of classical oratory. See Quintilian, *Inst. Orat.*, XII, 10; also, Puttenham, below, p. 176.

decorum in euerie one, to the trew vse of perfite Imitation. Whan
M. Watson in S. Iohns College at Cambrige wrote his excellent
Tragedie of *Absalon, M. Cheke,* he, and I, for that part of trew
Imitation, had many pleasant talkes togither, in comparing the
preceptes of *Aristotle* [7] and *Horace de Arte Poetica* with the examples of *Euripedes, Sophocles,* and *Seneca.* Few men, in writyng
of Tragedies in our dayes, haue shot at this marke. Some in
England, moe in *France, Germanie,* and *Italie* also, haue written
Tragedies in our tyme: of the which not one I am sure is able to
abyde the trew touch of *Aristotles* preceptes and *Euripides* examples, saue onely two that euer I saw, *M. Watsons Absalon* and
Georgius Buckananus Iephthe. One man in Cambrige, well
liked of many, but best liked of him selfe, was many tymes bold
and busie to bryng matters vpon stages, which he called Tragedies. In one, wherby he looked to wynne his spurres, and whereat
many ignorant felowes fast clapped their handes, he began the
Protasis with *Trochoeiis Octonariis* [8] which kinde of verse, as it
is but seldome and rare in Tragedies, so it is neuer vsed, saue
onelie *in Epitasi:* whan the Tragedie is hiest and hotest, and full
of greatest troubles. I remember ful well what *M. Watson* merelie
sayd vnto me of his blindnesse and boldnes in that behalfe, although otherwise there passed much frendship betwene them.
M. Watson had an other maner care of perfection, with a feare
and reuerence of the iudgement of the best learned: Who to this
day would neuer suffer yet his *Absalon* to go abroad, and that
onelie bicause, *in locis paribus,*[9] *Anapestus* is twise or thrise vsed
in stede of *Iambus:* A smal faulte, and such one as perchance
would neuer be marked, no neither in *Italie* nor *France.* This I
write, not so much to note the first, or praise the last, as to leaue
in memorie of writing, for good example to posteritie, what perfection, in any tyme, was most diligentlie sought for in like maner,
in all kinde of learnyng, in that most worthie College of S. Iohns
in Cambrige. . . .

[7] If the "preceptes" are from the *Poetics,* this is one of the earliest references to the work in English.

[8] The *protasis, epitasis* (mentioned below), and *catastasis* of classical
drama correspond to modern 'introduction', 'rising action', and 'falling action'.
Trochoeiis Octonariis refers to a line of eight trochaic feet, considered too
emotional for the relative calm of the *protasis.*

[9] "in like places"

[ii. LANGUAGE AND PROSODY]

The Latin tong, concerning any part of purenesse of it, from the spring to the decay of the same, did not endure moch longer than is the life of a well aged man, scarce one hundred yeares from the tyme of the last *Scipio Africanus* and *Laelius* to the Empire of *Augustus*. And it is notable that *Vellius Paterculus* writeth of *Tullie,* how that the perfection of eloquence did so remayne onelie in him and in his time, as before him were few which might moch delight a man, or after him any worthy admiration, but soch as *Tullie* might haue seene, and such as might haue seene *Tullie.* And good cause why: for no perfection is durable. Encrease hath a time, and decay likewise, but all perfit ripenesse remaineth but a moment: as is plainly seen in fruits, plummes, and cherries, but more sensibly in flowers, as Roses and such like; and yet as trewlie in all greater matters. For what naturallie can go no hier must naturallie yeld and stoupe againe.

Of this short tyme of any purenesse of the Latin tong, for the first fortie yeare of it, and all the tyme before, we haue no peece of learning left, saue *Plautus* and *Terence,* with a litle rude vnperfit pamflet of the elder *Cato.* And as for *Plautus,* except the scholemaster be able to make wise and ware choice, first in proprietie of wordes, than in framing of phrases and sentences, and chieflie in choice of honestie of matter, your scholer were better to play then learne all that is in him. But surelie, if iudgement for the tong, and direction for the maners, be wisely ioyned with the diligent reading of *Plautus,* than trewlie *Plautus* for that purenesse of the Latin tong in Rome, whan Rome did most florish in well doing, and so thereby in well speaking also, is soch a plentifull storeho[u]se for common eloquence, in meane matters, and all priuate mens affaires, as the Latin tong, for that respect, hath not the like agayne. Whan I remember the worthy tyme of Rome wherein *Plautus* did liue, I must nedes honor the talke of that tyme which we see *Plautus* doth vse.

Terence is also a storehouse of the same tong, for an other tyme, following soone after; and although he be not so full and plentiful as *Plautus* is, for multitude of matters and diuersitie of wordes, yet his wordes be chosen so purelie, placed so orderly, and all his stuffe so neetlie packed vp and wittely compassed in euerie place, as, by all wise mens iudgement, he is counted the cunninger workeman, and to haue his shop, for the rowme that is in it, more finely appointed and trimlier ordered than *Plautus* is.

Three thinges chiefly, both in *Plautus* and *Terence*, are to be specially considered: The matter, the vtterance, the words, the meter. The matter in both is altogether within the compasse of the meanest mens maners, and doth not stretch to any thing of any great weight at all, but standeth chiefly in vtteryng the thoughtes and conditions of hard fathers, foolish mothers, vn-thrifty yong men, craftie seruantes, sotle bawdes, and wilie harlots, and so is moch spent in finding out fine fetches and packing vp pelting matters, soch as in London commonlie cum to the hearing of the Masters of Bridewell. Here is base stuffe for that scholer that should becum hereafter either a good min-ister in Religion or a Ciuill Ientleman in seruice of his Prince and contrie (except the preacher do know soch matters to con-fute them), whan ignorance surelie in all soch thinges were better for a Ciuill Ientleman than knowledge. And thus, for matter, both *Plautus* and *Terence* be like meane painters, that worke by halfes, and be cunning onelie in making the worst part of the picture, as if one were skilfull in painting the bodie of a naked person from the nauell downward, but nothing else.

For word and speech *Plautus* is more plentifull, and *Terence* more pure and proper: And for one respect *Terence* is to be em-braced aboue all that euer wrote in hys kinde of argument: Bicause it is well known by good recorde of learning, and that by *Ciceroes* owne witnes, that some Comedies bearyng *Terence* name were written by worthy *Scipio* and wise *Laelius*, and namely *Heauton* and *Adelphi*. And therefore, as oft as I reade those Comedies, so oft doth sound in myne eare the pure fine talke of Rome, which was vsed by the floure of the worthiest nobilitie that euer Rome bred. Let the wisest man, and best learned that liueth, read aduisedlie ouer the first scene of *Heauton* and the first scene of *Adelphi*, and let him consideratlie iudge whether it is the talke of the seruile stranger borne, or rather euen that milde eloquent wise speach which *Cicero* in *Brutus* doth so liuely expresse in *Laelius*. And yet, neuertheless, in all this good proprietie of wordes and purenesse of phrases which

be in *Terence,* ye must not follow him alwayes in placing of
them, bicause for the meter sake some wordes in him somtyme
be driuen awrie, which require a straighter placing in plaine
prose, if ye will forme, as I would ye should do, your speach and
writing to that excellent perfitnesse which was onely in *Tullie,*
or onelie in *Tullies* tyme.

The meter and verse of *Plautus* and *Terence* be verie meane,
and not to be followed: which is not their reproch, but the fault
of the tyme wherein they wrote, whan no kinde of Poetrie in the
Latin tong was brought to perfection, as doth well appeare in
the fragmentes of *Ennius, Cecilius,* and others, and euidentlie in
Plautus and *Terence,* if thies in Latin be compared with right
skil with *Homer, Euripides, Aristophanes,* and other in Greeke
of like sort. *Cicero* him selfe doth complaine of this vnperfitnes,
but more plainly *Quintilian,* saying, in *Comoedia maxime claudi-
camus, et vix leuem consequimur umbram:* [10] and most earnestly
of all *Horace in Arte Poetica,* which he doth namely *propter
carmen Iambicum,* and referreth all good studentes herein to the
Imitation of the Greeke tong, saying,

> *Exemplaria Graeca*
> *nocturna versate manu, versate diurna.* [11]

This matter maketh me gladly remember my sweete tyme spent
at Cambrige, and the pleasant talke which I had oft with *M.
Cheke* and *M. Watson* of this fault, not onely in the olde Latin
Poets, but also in our new English Rymers at this day. They
wished as *Virgil* and *Horace* were not wedded to follow the
faultes of former fathers (a shrewd mariage in greater matters)
but by right *Imitation* of the perfit Grecians had brought Poetrie
to perfitnesse also in the Latin tong, that we Englishmen likewise
would acknowledge and vnderstand rightfully our rude beggerly
ryming, brought first into Italie by *Gothes* and *Hunnes,* whan all
good verses and all good learning to were destroyed by them, and
after caryed into France and Germanie, and at last receyued into
England by men of excellent wit in deede, but of small learning
and lesse iudgement in that behalfe.

---

[10] "We limp especially badly in comedy, and we scarcely gain a fleeting
shade." Quintilian, *Inst. Orat.,* X, 1.

[11] "Study the Greek examples night and day." Horace, *Ars Poetica,* 268–9.

But now, when men know the difference, and haue the examples, both of the best and of the worst, surelie to follow rather the *Gothes* in Ryming than the *Greekes* in trew versifiyng were euen to eate ackornes with swyne, when we may freely eate wheate bread emonges men. In deede, *Chauser, Th. Norton* of Bristow, my L. of Surrey, *M. Wiat, Th. Phaer,* and other Ientlemen, in translating *Ouide, Palingenius,* and *Seneca,* haue gonne as farre to their great praise as the copie they followed could cary them; but, if soch good wittes and forward diligence had bene directed to follow the best examples, and not haue bene caryed by tyme and custome to content themselues with that barbarous and rude Ryming, emonges their other worthy praises, which they hauc iustly deserued, this had not bene the least, to be counted emonges men of learning and skill more like vnto the Grecians than vnto the Gothians in handling of their verse.

In deed, our English tong, hauing in vse chiefly wordes of one syllable which commonly be long, doth not well receiue the nature of *Carmen Herotcum,* bicause *dactylus,* the aptest footc for that verse, conteining one long and two short, is seldom therefore found in English; and doth also rather stumble than stand vpon *Monasyllabis. Quintilian,* in hys learned Chapiter *de Compositione,*[12] geueth this lesson *de Monasyllabis* before me; and in the same placc doth iustlie inuey against all Ryming; that if there be any who be angrie with me for misliking of Ryming may be angry for company to with *Quintilian* also for the same thing. And yet *Quintilian* had not so iust cause to mislike of it than as men haue at this day. . . .

This mislikyng of Ryming beginneth not now of any newfangle singularitie, but hath bene long misliked of many, and that of men of greatest learnyng and deepest iudgment. And soch that defend it do so, either for lacke of knowledge what is best, or els of verie enuie that any should performe that in learnyng, whereunto they, as I sayd before, either for ignorance can not, or for idlenes will not, labor to attaine vnto.

And you that prayse this Ryming, bicause ye neither haue reason why to like it nor can shew learning to defend it, yet I will helpe you with the authoritie of the oldest and learnedst tyme.

[12] *Inst. Orat.,* IX, 3.

In *Grece,* whan Poetrie was euen as the hiest pitch of perfitnes, one *Simmias Rhodius* of a certaine singularitie wrote a booke in ryming *Greke* verses, naming it ὠόν,[13] conteyning the fable how *Iupiter* in likenes of a swan gat that egge vpon *Leda,* whereof came *Castor, Pollux,* and faire [*H*]*elena.* This booke was so liked that it had few to read it, but none to folow it: But was presentlie contemned: and, sone after, both Author and booke so forgotten by men, and consumed by tyme, as scarse the name of either is kept in memorie of learnyng. And the like folie was neuer folowed of any many hondred yeares after, vntil the *Hunnes* and *Gothians* and other barbarous nations of ignorance and rude singularitie did reuiue the same folie agayne.

The noble Lord *Th.* Earle of Surrey, first of all English men in translating the fourth booke of *Virgill,* and *Consaluo Periz,* that excellent learned man, and Secretarie to kyng *Philip of Spaine,* in translating the *Vlisses* of *Homer* out of *Greke* into *Spanish,* haue both, by good iudgement, auoyded the fault of Ryming, yet neither of them hath fullie hit[t]e perfite and trew versifying. In deede, they obserue iust number, and euen feete: but here is the fault, that their feete be feete without ioyntes, that is to say, not distinct by trew quantitie of sillabes: And so soch feete be but numme feete, and be euen as vnfitte for a verse to turne and runne roundly withall as feete of brasse or wood be unweeldie to go well withall. And as a foote of wood is a plaine shew of a manifest maime, euen so feete in our English versifying without quantitie and ioyntes be sure signes that the verse is either borne deformed, vnnaturall, and lame, and so verie vnseemlie to looke vpon, except to men that be gogle eyed them selues.

The spying of this fault now is not the curiositie of English eyes, but euen the good iudgement also of the best that write in these dayes in *Italie*: and namelie of that worthie *Senese Felice Figliucci,* who, writyng vpon *Aristotles Ethickes* so excellentlie in *Italian,* as neuer did yet any one in myne opinion either in *Greke* or *Latin,* amongst other thynges doth most earnestlie inuey agaynst the rude ryming of verses in that tong: And whan soeuer he expresseth *Aristotles* preceptes with any example out of *Homer* or *Euripides,* he translateth them, not after the Rymes

[13] "The Egg" The work is not in rhyme as Ascham believes, but in shaped stanzas.

of *Petrarke*, but into soch kinde of perfite verse, with like feete
and quantitie of sillabes, as he found them before in the *Greke*
tonge; exhortyng earnestlie all the *Italian* nation to leaue of their
rude barbariousnesse in ryming, and folow diligently the excellent *Greke* and *Latin* examples in trew versifiyng.

And you that be able to vnderstand no more then ye finde in
the *Italian* tong, and neuer went farder than the schole of
Petrarke and *Ariostus* abroad, or els of *Chaucer* at home, though
you haue pleasure to wander blindlie still in your foule wrong
way, enuie not others that seeke, as wise men haue done before
them, the fairest and rightest way; or els, beside the iust reproch
of malice, wisemen shall trewlie iudge that you do so, as I haue
sayd and say yet agayne vnto you, bicause either for idlenes ye
will not, or for ignorance ye can not, cum by no better your selfe.

And therfore, euen as *Virgill* and *Horace* deserue most worthie
prayse, that they, spying the vnperfitnes in *Ennius* and *Plautus*,
by trew Imitation of *Homer* and *Euripides* brought Poetrie to
the same perfitnes in *Latin* as it was in *Greke*, euen so those that
by the same way would benefite their tong and contrey deserue
rather thankes than dispraise in that behalfe.

And I reioyce that euen poore England preuented *Italie*, first
in spying out, than in seekyng to amend this fault in learnyng.

George Gascoigne

[1525?–1577]

❧

GASCOIGNE WAS A MEMBER of Parliament, a soldier of fortune, a dramatist, and a critic. His *Supposes* (1566) is a translation from Ariosto and the first true prose comedy in English; and his *Jocasta* (1566) is a Senecan blank-verse tragedy in the vein of *Gorboduc*. *The Steel Glass* (1576) establishes his claim to prominence among the rather mediocre poets of the pre-1580 era. *Certayne Notes of Instruction* (1575) was in part anticipated by Ascham, but deserves credit as the first formal treatise in English on prosody. Unlike Ascham and such later Elizabethans as Harvey, Stanyhurst, and Campion, Gascoigne accepts the standard accentual prosody of his day. His discussion is unsophisticated and direct, and for that reason it doubtless performed a useful service for the general reader, although Gabriel Harvey tempered his enthusiasm with several criticisms.

The present text is based on the 1575 edition of *The Posies of George Gascoigne*.

BIBLIOGRAPHY. *Complete Works,* ed. J. Cunliffe, 2 vols. (1907, 10); *Certayne Notes of Instruction* is reprinted by G. Smith, *Elizabethan Critical Essays*, I, 46–57. Smith's notes (I, 358–62) include the comments made by Gabriel Harvey in his copy of the 1575 edition. For comment see: C. Prouty, *Gascoigne* (1942); F. Schelling, *The Life and Writings of George Gascoigne* (1889).

CERTAYNE NOTES OF INSTRUCTION CONCERNING THE MAKING OF VERSE OR RYME IN ENGLISH

[1575]

SIGNOR EDOUARDO, SINCE PROMISE is debt, and you (by the lawe of friendship) do burden me with a promise that I shoulde lende

you instructions towards the making of English verse or ryme, I
will assaye to discharge the same, though not so perfectly as I
would, yet as readily as I may: and therwithall I pray you consider that *Quot homines, tot Sententiae,*[1] especially in Poetrie,
wherein (neuerthelesse) I dare not challenge any degree, and
yet will I at your request aduenture to set downe my simple skill
in such simple manner as I haue vsed, referring the same hereafter to the correction of the *Laureate*. And you shall haue it in
these few poynts followyng.

The first and most necessarie poynt that euer I founde meete to
be considered in making of a delectable poeme is this, to grounde
it upon some fine inuention. For it is not inough to roll in pleasant
woordes, nor yet to thunder in *Rym, Ram, Ruff* [2] by letter (quoth
my master *Chaucer*), nor yet to abounde in apt vocables or
epythetes, vnlesse the Inuention haue in it also *aliquid salis*. By
this *aliquid salis* I meane some good and fine deuise, shewing the
quicke capacitie of a writer: and where I say some *good and fine
inuention* I meane that I would haue it both fine and good. For
many inuentions arc so superfine that they are *Vix good*. And,
againe, many Inuentions are good, and yet not finely handled.
And for a general forwarning: what Theame soeuer you do take
in hande, if you do handle it but *tanquam in oratione perpetua,*[3]
and neuer studie for some depth of deuise in the Inuention, and
some figures also in the handlyng thereof, it will appeare to the
skilfull Reader but a tale of a tubbe. To deliuer vnto you generall
examples it were almoste vnpossible, sithence the occasions of
Inuentions are (as it were) infinite; neuerthelesse, take in worth
mine opinion, and perceyue my furder meanyng in these few
poynts. If I should vndertake to wryte in prayse of a gentle-
woman, I would neither praise hir christal eye, nor hir cherrie
lippe, etc. For these things are *trita et obuia*. But I would either
finde some supernaturall cause wherby my penne might walke
in the superlatiue degree, or els I would vndertake to aunswere
for any imperfection that shee hath, and therevpon rayse the
prayse of hir commendacion. Likewise, if I should disclose my

---

[1] "So many men, so many opinions."
[2] The phrase used by Chaucer's Parson, in the Prologue to his tale, to
describe the crude alliterative verse of his day.
[3] "as though in endless speech"

pretence in loue, I would eyther make a strange discourse of some intollerable passion, or finde occasion to pleade by the example of some historie, or discouer my disquiet in shadowes *per Allegoriam,* or vse the couertest meane that I could to auoyde the vncomely customes of common writers. Thus much I aduenture to deliuer vnto you (my freend) vpon the rule of Inuention, which of all other rules is most to be marked, and hardest to be prescribed in certayne and infallible rules; neuerthelesse, to conclude therein, I would haue you stand most vpon the excellencie of your Inuention, and sticke not to studie deepely for some fine deuise. For, that beyng founde, pleasant woordes will follow well inough and fast inough.

2. Your Inuention being once deuised, take heede that neither pleasure of rime nor varietie of deuise do carie you from it: for as to vse obscure and darke phrases in a pleasant Sonet is nothing delectable, so to entermingle merie iests in a serious matter is an *Indecorum.*

3. I will next aduise you that you hold the iust measure wherewith you begin your verse. I will not denie but this may seeme a preposterous ordre; but, bycause I couet rather to satisfie you particularly than to vndertake a generall tradition, I will not somuch stand vpon the manner as the matter of my precepts. I say then, remember to holde the same measure wherwith you begin, whether it be in a verse of sixe syllables, eight, ten, twelue, etc.: and though this precept might seeme ridiculous vnto you, since euery yong scholler can conceiue that he ought to continue in the same measure wherewith he beginneth, yet do I see and read many mens Poems now adayes, whiche beginning with the measure of xij. in the first line, and xiiij. in the second (which is the common kinde of verse),[4] they wil yet (by that time they haue passed ouer a few verses) fal into xiiij. and fourtene, *et sic de similibus,* the which is either forgetfulnes or carelesnes.

4. And in your verses remember to place euery worde in his natural *Emphasis* or sound, that is to say, in such wise, and with such length or shortnesse, eleuation or depression of sillables, as it is commonly pronounced or vsed. To expresse the same we haue three maner of accents, *grauis, leuis, et circumflexa,* the

---

[4] I.e., "poulter's measure." See p. 82.

whiche I would english thus, the long accent, the short accent, and that whiche is indifferent: the graue accent is marked by this caracter\ , the light accent is noted thus /, and the circumflexe or indifferent is thus signified ⁓ : The graue accent is drawen out or eleuate, and maketh that sillable long wherevpon it is placed; the light accent is depressed or snatched vp, and maketh that sillable short vpon the which it lighteth; the circumflexe accent is indifferent, sometimes short, sometimes long, sometimes depressed and sometimes eleuate. For example of th' emphasis or natural sound of words, this word *Treasure* hath the graue accent vpon the first sillable; whereas if it should be written in this sorte *Treasúre,* nowe were the second sillable long, and that were cleane contrarie to the common vse wherwith it is pronounced. For furder explanation hereof, note you that commonly now a dayes in English rimes (for I dare not cal them English verses) we vse none other order but a foote of two sillables, wherof the first is depressed or made short, and the second is eleuate or made long; and that sound or scanning continueth throughout the verse. We haue vsed in times past other kindes of Meeters, as for example this following:

No wight in this world, that wealth can attayne,

Vnlésse hè bèléue thàt áll ìs bùt váyne.

Also our father *Chaucer* hath vsed the same libertie in feete and measures that the Latinists do vse: and who so euer do peruse and well consider his workes, he shall finde that although his lines are not alwayes of one selfe same number of Syllables, yet, beyng redde by one that hath vnderstanding, the longest verse, and that which hath most Syllables in it, will fall (to the eare) correspondent vnto that whiche hath fewest sillables in it: and like wise that whiche hath in it fewest syllables shalbe founde yet to consist of woordes that haue suche naturall sounde, as may seeme equall in length to a verse which hath many moe sillables of lighter accentes. And surely I can lament that wee are fallen into suche a playne and simple manner of wryting, that there is none other foote vsed but one; wherby our Poemes may iustly be

called Rithmes, and cannot by any right challenge the name of
a Verse. But, since it is so, let vs take the forde as we finde it,
and lette me set down vnto you suche rules or precepts that euen
in this playne foote of two syllables you wreste no woorde from
his natural and vsuall sounde. I do not meane hereby that you
may vse none other wordes but of twoo sillables, for therein you
may vse discretion according to occasion of matter, but my meaning is, that all the wordes in your verse be so placed as the first
sillable may sound short or be depressed, the second long or
eleuate, the third shorte, the fourth long, the fifth shorte, etc. For
example of my meaning in this point marke these two verses:

I vnderstand your meanying by your eye.
Your meaning I vnderstand by your eye.

In these two verses there seemeth no difference at all, since the
one hath the very selfe same woordes that the other hath, and
yet the latter verse is neyther true nor pleasant, and the first verse
may passe the musters. The fault of the latter verse is that this
worde *vnderstand* is therein so placed as the graue accent falleth
upon *der,* and therby maketh *der* in this worde *vnderstand* to be
eleuated; which is contrarie to the naturall or vsual pronunciation, for we say *vnderstand,* and not *vnderstand.*

5. Here by the way I thinke it not amisse to forewarne
you that you thrust as few wordes of many sillables into your
verse as may be: and herevnto I might alledge many reasons.
First, the most auncient English wordes are of one sillable, so
that the more monasyllables that you vse the truer Englishman
you shall seeme, and the lesse you shall smell of the Inkehorne:
Also wordes of many syllables do cloye a verse and make it
vnpleasant, whereas woordes of one syllable will more easily fall
to be shorte or long as occasion requireth, or will be adapted to
become circumflexe or of an indifferent sounde.

6. I would exhorte you also to beware of rime without reason:
my meaning is hereby that your rime leade you not from your
firste Inuention, for many wryters, when they haue layed the
platforme of their inuention, are yet drawen sometimes (by

ryme) to forget it or at least to alter it, as when they cannot
readily finde out a worde whiche maye rime to the first (and yet
continue their determinate Inuention) they do then eyther botche
it vp with a worde that will ryme (howe small reason soeuer it
carie with it), or els they alter their first worde and so percase
decline or trouble their former Inuention: But do you alwayes
hold your first determined Inuention, and do rather searche the
bottome of your braynes for apte wordes than chaunge good
reason for rumbling rime.

7. To help you a little with ryme (which is also a plaine yong
schollers lesson), worke thus: when you haue set downe your
first verse, take the last worde thereof and coumpt ouer all the
wordes of the selfe same sounde by order of the Alphabete: As,
for example, the laste woorde of your first line is *care*, to ryme
therwith you haue *bare*, *clare*, *dare*, *fare*, *gare*, *hare*, and *share*,
mare, *snare*, *rare*, *stare*, and *ware*, &c. Of all these take that which
best may serue your purpose, carying reason with rime: and if
none of them will serue so, then alter the laste worde of your
former verse, but yet do not willingly alter the meanyng of your
Inuention.

8. You may vse the same Figures or Tropes in verse which
are vsed in prose, and in my iudgment they serue more aptly and
haue greater grace in verse than they haue in prose: but yet
therein remembre this old adage, *Ne quid nimis,* as many wryters
which do not know the vse of any other figure than that whiche
is expressed in repeticion of sundrie wordes beginning all with
one letter, the whiche (beyng modestly vsed) lendeth good
grace to a verse, but they do so hunte a letter to death that they
make it *Crambe,* and *Crambe bis positum mors est*: therefore
Ne quid nimis.[5]

9. Also, asmuche as may be, eschew straunge words, or
obsoleta et inusitata, vnlesse the Theame do giue iust occasion:
marie, in some places a straunge worde doth drawe attentiue
reading, but yet I woulde haue you therein to vse discretion.

10. And asmuch as you may, frame your stile to *perspicuity*

---

[5] *Crambe* is a kind of cabbage. "Crambe repetita" is used by Juvenal
(*Satires*, VII, 154) to mean "stale repetitions." Hence the proverb, quoted
by Gascoigne, "Crambe served twice is death." *Ne quid nimis*: "Nothing
too much."

and to be sensible, for the haughty obscure verse doth not much delight, and the verse that is to easie is like a tale of a rosted horse; but let your Poeme be such as may both delight and draw attentiue readyng, and therewithal may deliuer such matter as be worth the marking.

11. You shall do very well to vse your verse after thenglishe phrase, and not after the maner of other languages. The Latinists do commonly set the adiectiue after the Substantiue: As, for example, *Femina pulchra, aedes altae, &c.*; but if we should say in English a woman fayre, a house high, etc. it would haue but small grace, for we say a good man, and not a man good, etc. And yet I will not altogether forbidde it you, for in some places it may be borne, but not so hardly as some vse it which wryte thus:

> *Now let vs go to Temple ours.*
> *I will go visit mother myne* &c.

Surely I smile at the simplicitie of such deuisers which might aswell haue sayde it in playne Englishe phrase, and yet haue better pleased all eares, than they satisfie their owne fancies by suche *superfinesse*. Therefore euen as I haue aduised you to place all wordes in their naturall or most common and vsuall pronunciation, so would I wishe you to frame all sentences in their mother phrase and proper *Idióma*; and yet sometimes (as I haue sayd before) the contrarie may be borne, but that is rather where rime enforceth, or *per licentian Poëticam*, than it is otherwise lawfull or commendable.

12. This poeticall licence is a shrewde fellow, and couereth many faults in a verse; it maketh wordes longer, shorter, of mo sillables, of fewer, newer, older, truer, falser; and, to conclude, it turkeneth all things at pleasure, for example, *ydone* for *done*, *adowne* for *downe*, *orecome* for *ouercome*, *tane* for *taken*, *power* for *powre*, *heauen* for *heaun*, *thewes* for good partes or good qualities, and a numbre of other, whiche were but tedious and needlesse to rehearse, since your owne iudgement and readying will soone make you espie such aduauntages.

13. There are also certayne pauses or restes in a verse, whiche may be called *Ceasures*, whereof I woulde be lothe to stande long, since it is at discretion of the wryter, and they haue bene first deuised (as should seeme) by the Musicians: but yet thus

much I will aduenture to wryte, that in mine opinion in a verse of eight sillables the pause will stand best in the middest; in a verse of tenne it will best be placed at the ende of the first foure sillables; in a verse of twelue, in the midst; in verses of twelue in the firste and fouretene in the seconde wee place the pause commonly in the midst of the first, and at the ende of the first eight sillables in the second. In Rithme royall it is at the wryters discretion, and forceth not where the pause be untill the ende of the line.

14. And here, bycause I haue named Rithme royall, I will tell you also mine opinion aswell of that as of the names which other rymes haue commonly borne heretofore. Rythme royall is a verse of tenne sillables; and seuen such verses make a staffe, whereof of the first and thirde lines do aunswer (acrosse) in like terminations and rime, the second, fourth, and fifth do likewise answere eche other in terminations, and the two last do combine and shut vp the Sentence: this hath bene called Rithme royall, and surely it is a royall kinde of verse, seruing best for graue discourses. There is also another kinde, called Ballade, and thereof are saundrie sortes: for a man may write a ballade in a staffe of six lines, euery line conteyning eighte or six sillables, whereof the firste and third, second and fourth do rime acrosse, and the fifth and sixth do rime togither in conclusion. You may write also your ballad of tenne sillables, rimyng as before is declared; but these two were wont to be most commonly vsed in ballade, which propre name was (I thinke) deriued of this worde in Italian *Ballare*, whiche signifieth to daunce. And in deed those kinds of rimes serue beste for daunces or light matters. Then haue you also a rondlette, the which doth alwayes end with one self same foote or repeticion, and was thereof (in my judgement) called a rondelet. This may consist of such measures as best liketh the wryter. Then haue you Sonnets: some thinke that all Poemes (being short) may be called Sonets, as in deede it is a diminutiue worde deriued of *Sonare*, but yet I can beste allowe to call those Sonnets whiche are of fourtene lynes, euery line conteyning tenne syllables. The firste twelue do ryme in staues of foure lines by crosse meetre, and the last two ryming togither do conclude the whole. There are Dyzaynes, and Syxaines, which are of ten lines, and of sixe lines, commonly vsed by the French, which

some English writers do also terme by the name of Sonettes. Then is there an old kinde of Rithme called Ver layes, deriued (as I haue redde) of this worde *Verd,* whiche betokeneth Greene, and *Laye,* which betokeneth a Song, as if you would say greene Songes: but I muste tell you by the way that I neuer redde any verse which I saw by aucthoritie called *Verlay* but one, and that was a long discourse in verses of tenne sillables, whereof the foure first did ryme acrosse, and the fifth did aunswere to the firste and thirde, breaking off there, and so going on to another termination. Of this I could shewe example of imitation in mine own verses written to the right honorable the Lord *Grey* of *Wilton* upon my journey into *Holland,* etc. There are also certaine Poemes deuised of tenne syllables, whereof the first aunswereth in termination with the fourth, and the second and thirde answere eche other: these are more vsed by other nations than by vs, neyther can I tell readily what name to giue them. And the commonest sort of verse which we vse now adayes (*vis.* the long verse of twelue and fourtene sillables) I know not certainly howe to name it, vnlesse I should say that it doth consist of Poulters measure, which giueth xii. for one dozen and xiiij. for another. But let this suffise (if it be not to much) for the sundrie sortes of verses which we vse now adayes.

15. In all these sortes of verses, when soeuer you vndertake to write, auoyde prolixitie and tediousnesse, and euer, as neare as you can, do finish the sentence and meaning at the end of euery staffe where you wright staues, and at the end of euery two lines where you write by cooples or poulters measure: for I see many writers which draw their sentences in length, and make an ende at latter Lammas: for, commonly, before they end, the Reader hath forgotten where he begon. But do you (if you wil follow my aduise) eschue prolixitie and knit vp your sentences as compendiously as you may, since breuitie (so that it be not drowned in obscuritie) is most commendable.

16. I had forgotten a notable kinde of ryme, called ryding rime, and that is suche as our Mayster and Father *Chaucer* vsed in his Canterburie tales, and in diuers other delectable and light enterprises; but, though it come to my remembrance somewhat out of order, it shall not yet come altogether out of time, for I will nowe tell you a conceipt whiche I had before forgotten to wryte: you

may see (by the way) that I holde a preposterous order in my traditions but, as I sayde before, I wryte moued by good wil, and not to shewe my skill. Then to returne too my matter, as this riding rime serueth most aptly to write a merie tale, so Rythme royall is fittest for a graue discourse. Ballades are beste of matters of loue, and rondlettes moste apt for the beating or handlyng of an adage or common prouerbe: Sonets serue aswell in matters of loue as of discourse: Dizaynes and Sixaines for shorte Fantazies: Verlayes for an effectual proposition, although by the name you might otherwise iudge of Verlayes; and the long verse of twelue and fouretene sillables, although it be now adayes vsed in all Theames, yet in my iudgement it would serue best for Psalmes and Himpnes.

I woulde stande longer in these traditions, were it not that I doubt mine owne ignoraunce; but, as I sayde before, I know that I write to my freende, and, affying my selfe therevpon, I make an ende.

Part II

THE DEFENSE OF POETRY

Stephen Gosson

[1555–1624]

֎

DURING THE 1570's Stephen Gosson was known to his contemporaries as a dramatist-poet of some promise. His plays (which later caused him acute embarrassment) include *Catiline's Conspiracy, Captain Mario,* and *Praise at Parting.* When Gosson turned from literature to morality he did so with a vengeance. While he was a student at Oxford, the London stage had already provoked attack in the form of a Parliamentary Act against "Rogues, Vacabounds, and Sturdye Beggers" (1573), and the theaters were expelled from London proper in 1575. In 1577 the attack gained momentum with Wilcock's Paul's Cross sermon condemning "sumptuous Theatrehouses," and the publication of John Northbrook's *A treatise wherein Dicing, Dauncing, Vaine playes or Enterludes . . . are reproved by the authoritie of the worde of God and auncient writers.*

The Schoole of Abuse was entered in the Stationer's Register in August, 1579, and dedicated without authorization to Sir Philip Sidney. According to a letter from Spenser to Harvey (Oct. 16, 1579), Gosson was "for hys labor scorned"; but Sidney never replied directly. Other critics were less tactful. The lost *Strange News out of Affrick* (1579) was apparently the first reply, followed almost immediately by Thomas Lodge's *Defence of Poetry* (1579). The controversy was intensified by the publication of Gosson's *Short Apologie of the Schoole of Abuse* (also dedicated to Sidney!). In rapid succession there followed Henry Denham's *A Second and third blast of retrait from plaies and Theatres* (1580), Gosson's *Playes confuted in five Actions* (1582), Stubbes' *Anatomie of Abuses* (1583), and William Rankins' *Mirror of Monsters.* William Prynne's *Histrio-Mastix* (1633) and Jeremy Collier's *Short View of the Prophaneness and Immorality of the English Stage* (1698) show that hostility to drama persisted throughout the seventeenth century.

Gosson is less important as a critic than as a representative of the attitudes against which Renaissance poetry had to be defended. The earliest formal defense is John Rainolds' *Oratio in Laudem Artis*

Poeticae (*c.* 1572), an academic oration. Rainolds' enthusiasm is ironic in view of his later (1599) denunciation of the theatres. The important defenses in the period include Lodge's *Defence*, Sidney's *Defence* (or *Apologie*) (1583), Webbe's *Discourse of English Poetrie* (1586), Puttenham's *Arte of English Poesie* (1589), and Harington's *Preface, or rather a Briefe Apologie of Poetrie* (1591). To these large-scale works must be added the numerous prefaces, apologies, inductions, and 'letters to readers' which proclaim the social and moral utility of specific works.

The present text is based on the 1579 edition.

BIBLIOGRAPHY. *The Schoole of Abuse,* ed. Arber (1868). For comment see: W. Orwen, "Spenser and Gosson," *MLN*, LII (1937); W. Ringler, "The First Phase of the Elizabethan Attack on the Stage, 1558–79," *HLQ*, V (1942); *Stephen Gosson* (1942); W. Ringler and W. Allen, intr. and tr., *John Rainolds' Oratio in Laudem Artis Poeticae* (1940); E. Thompson, *The Controversy Between the Puritans and the Stage* (1903).

from

THE SCHOOLE OF ABUSE

[1579]

THE SYRACUSANS USED such varietie of dishes in their banquets, that when they were set, and their bordes furnished, they were many times in doubt which they should touch first, or taste last. And in my opinion the worlde geveth every writer so large a fielde to walke in, that before he set penne to the booke, he shall find him selfe feasted at Syracusa, uncertayne where to begin, or when to end: this caused Pindarus to question with his Muse, whether he were better with his art to discifer the life of Nimpe Melia, or Cadmus encounter with the dragon, or the warres of Hercules at the walles of Thebes, or Bacchus cuppes, or Venus jugling? [1] He saw so many turnings layde open to his feete, that hee knew not which way to bende his pace.

[1] The reference is vague. Probably Gosson is thinking of the eleventh Pythian ode.

Therefore, as I cannot but commend his wisdom which in ban-quetting feedes most uppon that that doth nourishe best, so must I dispraise his methode in writing which, following the course of amarous poets, dwelleth longest on those points that profit least, and like a wanton whelpe leaveth the game to runne riot. The scarabe flies over many a sweet flower, and lightes in a cowsherd. It is the custome of the flie to leave the sound places of the horse, and sucke at the botch: the nature of colloquintida to draw the worst humors to it selfe: the manner of swine to for-sake the fayre fields and wallowe in the myre; and the whole practise of poets, either with fables to shewe their abuses, or with playne tearmes to unfolde their mischeefe, discover their shame, discredite themselves, and disperse their poison through the world. Virgil sweats in describing his gnatte; Ovid bestirreth him to paint out his flea: the one shewes his art in the lust of Dido; the other his cunning in the incest of Myrrha, and that trumpet of bawdrie, the Craft of Love.

I must confesse that poets are the whetstones of wit, notwith-standing that wit is dearely bought: where honie and gall are mixt, it will be hard to sever the one from the other. The deceit-full phisition geveth sweete syrroppes to make his poyson goe downe the smoother: the jugler casteth a myst to work the closer: the Syrens songue is the saylers wracke; the fowlers whistle the birdes death; the wholesome baite the fishes bane. The Harpies have virgin faces, and vultures talents: Hyena speakes like a friend, and devours like a foe: the calmest seas hide dangerous rockes: the woolfe jets in weathers felles. Manie good sentences are spoken by Davus to shadowe his knaverie, and written by poets as ornamentes to beautifie their woorkes, and sette their trumperie to sale without suspect.

But if you looke well to Epæus horse, you shall finde in his bowels the destruction of Troy: open the sepulchre of Semyramis, whose title promiseth suche wealth to the kynges of Persia, you shall see nothing but dead bones: rip up the golden ball that Nero consecrated to Jupiter Capitollinus, you shall [find] it stuffed with the shavinges of his bearde: pul off the visard that poets maske in, you shall disclose their reproch, bewray their vanitie, loth their wantonnesse, lament their folly, and perceive their sharpe sayinges to be placed as pearles in dunghils, fresh

pictures on rotten walles, chaste matrons apparel on common
curtesans. These are the cuppes of Circes, that turne reasonable
creatures into brute beastes; the balles of Hippomenes, that
hinder the course of Atalanta, and the blocks of the Devil, that
are cast in our wayes to cut of the race of toward wittes. No
marveyle though Plato shut them out of his schoole, and banished them quite from his common wealth, as effeminate writers,
unprofitable members, and utter enimies to vertue.

The Romans were very desirous to imitate the Greekes, and
yet very loth to receive their poets; insomuch that Cato layeth it
in the dishe of Marcus, the noble, as a foule reproche, that in
the time of his Consulshippe he brought Ennius, the poet, into
his province. Tully accustomed to read them with great diligence
in his youth, but when he waxed graver in studie, elder in yeers,
ryper in judgement, hee accompted them the fathers of lyes, pipes
of vanitie, and Schooles of Abuse.[2] Maximus Tyrius taketh uppon
him to defend the discipline of these doctors under the name of
Homer, wresting the rashness of Ajax to valour, the cowardice
of Ulisses to policie, the dotage of Nestor to grave counsell, and
the battaile of Troy to the woonderfull conflicte of the foure ele-
mentes; where Juno, which is counted the ayre, settes in her
foote to take up the strife, and steps boldly betwixt them to part
the fray.[3] It is a pageant woorth the sighte to beholde how he
labors with mountaines to bring forth mice; much like to some of
those Players, that come to the scaffold with drumme and trumpet
to profer skirmishe, and when they have sounded Allarme, off goe
the peeces to encounter a shadow, or conquere a paper monster.
You will smile, I am sure, if you reade it, to see how this morall
philosopher toyles to draw the lions skinne upon Æsops asse,
Hercules shoes on a childes feet; amplifying that which, the more
it is stirred, the more it stinkes, the lesser it is talked of the better
it is liked; and as waiwarde children, the more they bee flattered
the woorse they are, or as curste sores with often touching waxe
angry, and run the longer without healing. Hee attributeth the
beginning of vertue to Minerva, of friendshippe to Venus, and
the roote of all handy crafts to Vulcan; but if he had broke his

2 *Tusculan Disputations*, I, 2.
3 *Dissertations*, XV.

arme aswel as his legge, when he fell out of heaven into Lemnos, either Apollo must have plaied the bone setter, or every occupation beene layde in water.

Plato, when he saw the doctrine of these teachers neither for profit necessary, nor to bee wished for pleasure, gave them all Drummes entertainment, not suffering them once to shew their faces in a reformed common wealth.[4] And the same Tyrius, that layes such a foundation for poets in the name of Homer, overthrowes his whole building in the person of Mithecus, which was an excellent cooke among the Greekes, and asmuche honoured for his confections, as Phidias for his carving. But when he came to Sparta, thinking there for his cunning to be accompted a god, the good lawes of Licurgus, and custome of the countrey were too hot for his diet. The Governors banished him and his art, and al the inhabitants, folowing the steppes of their predecessors, used not with dainties to provoke appetite, but with labour and travell to whette their stomackes to their meate. I may well liken Homer to Mithecus, and poets to cookes: the pleasures of the one winnes the body from labour, and conquereth the sense: the allurement of the other drawes the minde from vertue, and confoundeth wit. As in every perfect common wealth there ought to be good lawes established, right mainteined, wrong repressed, vertue rewarded, vice punished, and all manner of abuses thoroughly purged, so ought there such schooles for the furtherance of the same to be advaunced, that young men may be taught that in greene yeeres, that becomes them to practise in gray hayres.

Anarcharsis being demaunded of a Greeke, whether they had not instrumentes of musicke or schooles of poetrie in Scythia? aunsweared, yes, and that without vice; as though it were eyther impossible, or incredible that no abuse should be learned where such lessons are taught, and such schooles mainteined.

Salust in describing the nurture of Sempronia commendeth her witte, in that shee coulde frame her selfe to all companies, to talke discretly with wyse men, and vaynely with wantons, takyng a quip ere it came to grounde, and returning it backe without a

[4] *Republic*, X, 605. This banishment was never far from the minds of either the enemies or the defenders of poetry.

faulte. She was taught (saith he) both Greek and Latine; she
could versifie, sing and daunce better then became an honest
woman. Sappho was skilful in poetrie and sung wel, but she was
whorish. I set not this downe to condemne the giftes of versifying,
daunsing or singing in women, so they bee used with meane and
exercised in due time; but to shew you that, as by Anacharsis
report the Scythians did it without offence, so one swallow brings
not summer, nor one particular example is sufficient proofe for a
generall precept. White silver drawes a black lyne; fyre is as
hurtfull as healthie; water is as daungerous as it is commodious,
and these qualities as harde to be wel used when we have them,
as they are to be learned before wee get them. He that goes to
sea must smel of the ship, and that which sayles into ports wil
savour of pitch.

C. Marius in the assembly of the whole Senate of Rome, in a
solemne oration, giveth an account of his bringing up: he sheweth
that he hath beene taught to lye on the ground, to suffer all
weathers, to leade men, to strike his fo, to feare nothing but an
evill name; and chalengeth praise unto himself in that he never
learned the Greeke tounge, neither ment to be instructed in it
hereafter, either that he thought it too farre a jorney to fetch
learning beyonde the fielde, or because he doubted the abuses of
those schooles where poets were ever the head maisters. Tiberius,
the emperour, sawe somewhat when he judged Scaurus to death
for writing a tragedy; Augustus when hee banished Ovid, and
Nero when he charged Lucan to put up his pipes, to stay his
penne, and write no more. Burrus and Seneca, the schoolemaisters
of Nero, are flowted and hated of the people for teaching their
scholer the song of Attis: for Dion saith, that he hearing thereof
wrounge laughter and teares from most of those that were then
about him. Whereby I judge that they scorned the folly of the
teachers, and lamented the frenzy of the scholer, who being emperour of Rome, and bearing the weight of the whole common
wealth uppon his shoulders, was easier to bee drawen to vanitie
by wanton poets, then to good government by the fatherly counsel
of grave senators. They were condemned to dye by the lawes of
the Heathens whiche inchaunted the graine in other mens
grounds; and are not they accursed, thinke you, by the mouth of
God, which having the government of young Princes, with

poetical fantasies draw them to the schooles of their own abuses, bewitching the graine in the greene blade, that was sowed for the sustenance of many thousands, and poysoning the spring with their amorous layes, whence the whole common wealth should fetch water? But to leave the scepter to Jupiter, and instructing of Princes to Plutarch and Xenophon, I wil beare a lowe saile, and rowe neere the shore, least I chaunce to bee carried beyonde my reache, or runne a grounde in those coasts which I never knewe. My onely indevour shalbe to shew you that in a rough cast which I see in a cloude, loking through my fingers.

And because I have matriculated my self in the schoole where so many abuses florish, I wil imitate the dogs of Ægypt, which comming to the bancks of Nylus to quench theyr thirste, syp and away, drinke running, lest they be snapt short for a pray to crocodiles. I shoulde tell tales out of schoole and bee ferruled for my fault, or hyssed at for a blab, yf I layde all the orders open before your eyes. You are no soner entred but libertie looseth the reynes and geves you head, placing you with poetrie in the lowest forme, when his skill is showne too make his scholer as good as ever twangde: he preferres you to pyping, from pyping to playing, from play to pleasure, from pleasure to slouth, from slouth to sleepe, from sleepe to sinne, from sinne to death, from death too the Divel, if you take your learning apace, and passe through every forme without revolting. Looke not to have me discourse these at large: the crocodile watcheth to take me tardie: whichesoever of them I touche is a byle: tryppe and goe, for I dare not tarry.

Heraclides accounteth Amphion the ringleader of poets and pipers: Delphus Philammones penned the birth of Latona, Diana and Apollo in verse, and taught the people to pype and daunce rounde aboute the Temple of Delphos. Hesiodus was as cunning in pipyng as in poetrye: so was Terpandrus, and after hym Clonas. Apollo, whiche is honoured of poets as the God of their art, had at the one syde of his idoll in Delos a bowe, and at the other the three Graces with sundrie instrumentes; and some writers doe affirme that he piped himself nowe and then.

Poetrie and piping have alwayes been so united togither, that til the time of Melanippides pipers were poets hyerlings. But marke, I pray you, how they are now both abused.

The right use of auncient poetrie was to have the notable ex-
ploytes of worthy captaines, the holesome councels of good
fathers and vertuous lives of predecessors set downe in numbers,
and sung to the instrument at solemne feastes, that the sound of
the one might draw the hearers from kissing the cup too often,
the sense of the other put them in minde of things past, and
chaulke out the way to do the like. After this manner were the
Bæotians trained from rudenesse to civilitie, the Lacedæmonians
instructed by Tyrtæus verse, the Argives by the melody of Tele-
silla, and the Lesbians by Alcæus odes. . . .

For as poetrie and piping are cosen germaines, so piping and
playing are of great affinitye, and all three chayned in linkes of
abuse.

Plutarch complayneth that ignorant men, not knowing the
majestie of auncient musike, abuse both the eares of the people,
and the arte it self, with bringing sweet comfortes into Theaters,
which rather effeminate the minde as prickes unto vice, then
procure amendment of maners as spurres to vertue. Ovid, the
high Martial of Venus feeld, planteth his mayn battell in publike
assemblies, sendeth out his scoutes to Theaters to descrye the
enimie, and in steede of vaunte curriers, with instruments of
musick, playing, singing and dauncing gives the first charge.
Maximus Tyrius holdeth it for a maxime, that the bringing of
instrumentes to Theaters and playes was the first cuppe that
poysoned the common wealth. They that are borne in Seriphos
and cockered continually in those islandes, where they see nothing but foxes and hares, will never be persuaded that there are
huger beasts. They that never went out of the champion in
Brabant will hardly conceive what rocks are in Germany; and
they that never goe out of their houses, for regarde of their
credite, nor steppe from the university for love of knowledge,
seeing but slender offences and smal abuses within their own
walles, wil never beleeve that such rocks are abrode, nor such
horrible monsters in playing places. But as (I speake the one to
my comforte, the other to my shame, and remember both with a
sorowful heart) I was first instructed in the University, after
drawn like a novice to these abuses, so will I shew you what I
see, and informe you what I reade of such affaires. Ovid saith
that Romulus builte his theater as a horsfaire for hoores, made

triumphes and set out playes to gather the faire women together, that every one of his souldiers might take where hee liked a snatch for his share: whereupon the amarous schoolmaister bursteth out in these wordes:—

> *Romule, militibus solus dare præmia nosti:*
> *Hæc mihi si dederis commoda, miles ero.*[5]

Thou, Romulus, alone knowest how thy souldiers to reward:
Graunt me the like, my selfe will be attendant on thy gard.

It should seeme that the abuse of such places was so great, that for any chaste liver to haunt them was a black swan, and a white crow. Dion so streightly forbiddeth the ancient families of Rome, and gentlewomen that tender their name and honor, to come to Theaters, and rebuks them so sharply when he takes them napping, that if they be but once seene there, hee judgeth it sufficient cause to speake ill of them and thinke worse. The shadow of a knave hurts an honest man; the sent of the stewes a sober matron; and the shew of Theaters a simple gaser. Clitomachus the wrestler, geven altogether to manly exercise, if hee had hearde any talke of love, in what company soever he had ben, would forsake his seat and bid them adue.

Lacon, when hee sawe the Athenians studie so much to set out playes, sayde they were madde. If men for good exercise, and women for their credite, be shut from Theaters, whom shall we suffer to goe thither? Little children? Plutarche with a caveat keepeth them out, not so muche as admitting the litle crackhalter, that carrieth his masters pantables, to set foote within those doores; and allegeth this reason—that those wanton spectacles of light huswives drawing gods from the heavens, and young men from themselves to shipwracke of honesty, wil hurt them more then if at the epicures table they had burst their guts with over feeding. For if the bodie be overcharged, it may bee holpe, but the surfite of the soule is hardely cured. Here, I doubt not, but some archeplayer or other that hath read a little, or stumbled by chance upon Plautus comedies, will cast me a bone or two to pick, saying that whatsoever these ancient writers have spoken against plaies is to be applied to the abuses in olde comedies,

[5] Ovid, *Ars Amatoria*, I, 131–2. Misquoted.

where gods are brought in as prisoners to beautie, ravishers of virgines, and servantes by love to earthly creatures.[6] But the comedies that are exercised in our dayes are better sifted: they shewe no such branne. The first smelt of Plautus; these tast of Menander: the leudenes of the gods is altred and chaunged to the love of young men; force to friendshippe; rapes to mariage; woing allowed by assurance of wedding; privie meetings of bachelours and maidens on the stage, not as murderers that devour the good name ech of other in their mindes, but as those that desire to bee made one in hearte. Nowe are the abuses of the worlde revealed: every man in a playe may see his owne faultes, and learne by this glasse to amende his manners. Curculio may chatte till his heart ake, ere any bee offended with his girdes. Deformities are checked in jeast, and mated in earnest. The sweetenesse of musicke, and pleasure of sportes temper the bitternes of rebukes, and mittigate the tartnes of every taunt according to this:—

Omne vafer vitium ridenti Flaccus amico
Narrat, et admissus circum precordia ludit.[7]

Flaccus among his friends, with fawning muse,
Doth nippe him neere that fostreth foule abuse.

Therefore, they are either so blinde that they cannot, or so blunt that they will not see why this exercise shoulde not be suffered as a profitable recreation. For my part, I am neither so fonde a phisition, nor so bad a cooke, but I can allowe my patient a cuppe of wine to meales, althoughe it be hotte and pleasant sawces to drive downe his meate, if his stomacke be queasie. Notwithstanding, if people will bee instructed (God bee thanked) wee have divines enough to discharge that, and moe by a great many then are well harkened to: yet sith these abuses are growne to heade, and sinne so ripe, the number is lesse then I would it were. . . .

. . . In our assemblies at playes in London, you shall see suche

---

[6] "Old comedy" (*comoedia vetus*) is the type of comedy written by Aristophanes and was contrasted to the more restrained and instructive "new comedy" (*comoedia nova*) written by Menander, Plautus, and Terence.
[7] Persius, *Satires*, I, 116–7. Misquoted.

heaving and shooving, suche ytching and shouldering to sytte by women; suche care for their garments that they be not trode on; suche eyes to their lappes that no chippes lighte in them; such pillowes to their backes that they take no hurte; suche masking in their eares, I know not what; suche geving them pippins to passe the time; suche playing at foote saunt without cardes; such ticking, such toying, such smiling, such winking, and such manning them home when the sportes are ended, that it is a right comedie to marke their behaviour, to watch their conceates, as the catte for the mouse, and as good as a course at the game it selfe, to dogge them a little, or follow aloofe by the printe of their feete, and so discover by slotte where the deare taketh soyle.

If this were as well noted as il seene, or as openly punished as secretly practised, I have no doubt but the cause woulde be seared to drye up the effect, and these prettie rabbets verye cunningly ferretted from their borrowes. For they that lacke customers all the weeke, either because their haunt is unknowen, or the constables and officers of their parish watch them so narrowly that they dare not queatche, to celebrate the Sabboth flocke too theaters, and there keepe a generall market of bawdrie. Not that anye filthinesse, in deede, is committed within the compasse of that ground, as was once done in Rome, but that every wanton and [his] paramour, everye man and his mistresse, every John and his Joane, every knave and his queane are there first acquainted, and cheapen the marchandise in that place, which they pay for else where, as they can agree. These wormes, when they dare not nestle in the pescod at home, find refuge abrode and ar hidde in the eares of other mens corne. . . .

. . . How often hath her Majestie, with the grave advice of her whole Councel, set downe the limits of apparel to every degree, and how soone againe hath the pride of our harts overflowen the chanel? Howe many times hath accesse to theaters beene restrained, and howe boldely againe have we reentred? overlashing in apparel is so common a fault, that the verye hyerlings of some of our plaiers, which stand at reversion of vi^s by the weeke, jet under gentlemens noses in sutes of silke, exercising them selves to prating on the stage, and common scoffing when they come abrode, where they looke askance over the shoulder at every man of whom the Sunday before they begged an almes. I speake not this as though every one that professeth the qualitie so abused him selfe, for it is wel knowen that some of them are sober, discreete, properly learned, honest housholders, and citizens well thought on amonge their neighbours at home, though the pride of their shadowes (I meane those hangbyes whome they succour with stipend) cause them to bee somewhat il talked of abrode.

And as some of the players are farre from abuse, so some of their playes are without rebuke, which are easily remembered, as quickly reckoned. The two prose bookes played at the Belsavage, where you shall finde never a woorde without witte, never a line without pith, never a letter placed in vaine. The Jew, and Ptolome, showne at the Bull; the one representing the greedinesse of worldly chusers, and bloody mindes of usurers; the other very lively describing howe seditious estates with their owne devises, false friendes with their owne swoords, and rebellious commons in their owne snares are overthrowne; neither with amorous gesture wounding the eye, nor with slovenly talke hurting the eares of the chast hearers. The Black Smiths Daughter, and Catilins Conspiracies, usually brought in at the Theater: the firste containing the trechery of Turks, the honourable bountye of a noble mind, the shining of vertue in distresse. The last because it is knowen to be a pig of mine owne Sowe, I will speake the lesse of it; onely giving you to understand that the whole mark which I shot at in that woorke was to showe the rewarde of traytors in Catiline, and the necessary government of learned men in the person of Cicero, which forsees every danger that is likely to happen, and forstalles it continually ere it take effect. Therefore I give these playes the commendation that Maximus Tyrius gave to Homers works—καλὰ μὲν γὰρ τὰ Ὁμήρου ἔπη, καὶ ἔπων τὰ κάλλιστα, καὶ φανώτατα, καὶ ἄδεσθαι μουσαῖς πρέποντα ἀλλα οὐ πᾶσι καλὰ, οὐδὲ ἀεὶ καλά.[8]

These playes are good playes and sweete playes, and of all playes the best playes, and most to be liked, woorthy to be soung of the Muses, or set out with the cunning of Roscius him self, yet are they not fit for every mans dyet: neither ought they com-

[8] "The verses of Homer are beautiful, and the most excellent of verses, and the most famous, and fitted for the Muses to sing; but they are not beautiful to all, nor always beautiful." *Dissertations,* III.

monly to be showen. Now, if any man aske me why my selfe have penned comedyes in time past, and inveigh so egerly against them here, let him knowe that *Semel insanivimus omnes:* [9] I have sinned, and am sorry for my fault: he runnes far that never turnes: better late then never. . . .

[9] "At one time or another we have all been mad."

Sir Philip Sidney

[1554–1586]

❧❧

POET, SCHOLAR, COURTIER, soldier, critic—Sir Philip Sidney was recognized during his lifetime as an incarnation of the Renaissance ideal of the *uomo universale*. Yet he carried his accomplishments lightly, affecting the *sprezzatura*—the offhand excellence—deemed essential to the true gentleman. Sidney's sonnet cycle *Astrophel and Stella* (pr. 1591) and his epic novel *Arcadia* (pr. 1593) insure his place in the history of literature. His most unique contribution is his brilliant *Apologie for* (or *Defence of*) *Poetrie* (wr. 1583; publ. 1595). The immediate occasion for its composition was probably the unauthorized dedication to Sidney of Gosson's *Schoole of Abuse* (1579), for it is clearly designed to answer the major Puritan objections to poetry. In form, content, and tone (if not in length) it resembles the Italian defenses of the middle sixteenth century. Sebastian Minturno (*De Poeta*, 1559; *L'Arte Poetica*, 1564) is usually cited as an important source. There are also echoes of Daniello, Trissino, Scaliger, and others. The problem of sources is complicated by the fact that many of Sidney's ideas are commonplaces repeated with variations from critic to critic. Sidney was obviously influenced by the 'new criticism' stemming from the rediscovery of Aristotle's *Poetics* by the Italian critics around 1550, but, like Minturno, he assimilated Aristotle into a system which remained essentially Platonic.

Sidney's essay follows the organization of the classical oration. For convenience, the major sections, adopted with modifications from K. Myrick (see bibliography), are indicated by roman numerals: I. Introduction; II. The antiquity of Poetry; III. The ancient regard for poetry as indicated by the terms *Areytos, Vates,* and *Maker;* IV. Poetry as *mimesis;* V. Superiority of poetry in this sense to philosophy and history; VI. The 'kinds' of poetry and their effects; VII. Answers to objections; VIII. English poetry—history and potential; IX. Conclusion.

The present text is from Olney's edition of 1595.

BIBLIOGRAPHY. *Works,* ed. Feuillerat (4 vols., 1912–26). For comment see: C. Dowlin, "Sidney's Two Definitions of Poetry," *MLQ,* III (1942); "Sidney and Other Men's Thoughts," *RES,* XVI (1940); K. Myrick, *Sir Philip Sidney as a Literary Craftsman* (1935); I. Samuel, "The Influence of Plato on Sir Philip Sidney's *Defence of Poesie,*" *MLQ,* I (1940); J. Thorne, "A Ramistical Commentary on Sidney's *An Apologie for Poetrie,*" *MP,* LIV (1955). See also the excellent notes in G. Smith, *Elizabethan Critical Essays,* I, 382–403.

AN APOLOGIE FOR POETRIE

[1583]

[I.] WHEN THE RIGHT VERTUOUS *Edward Wotton* and I were at the Emperors Court together, wee gaue our selues to learne horse-manship of *Iohn Pietro Pugliano,* one that with great commenda-tion had the place of an Esquire in his stable. And hee, according to the fertilnes of the Italian wit, did not onely afoord vs the demonstration of his practise, but sought to enrich our mindes with the contemplations therein which hee thought most precious. But with none I remember mine eares were at any time more loden, then when (either angred with slowe paiment, or mooued with our learner-like admiration) he exercised his speech in the prayse of his facultie. Hee sayd, Souldiours were the noblest estate of mankinde, and horsemen the noblest of Souldiours. Hee sayde they were the Maisters of warre, and ornaments of peace; speedy goers, and strong abiders; triumphers both in Camps and Courts. Nay, to so vnbeleeued a poynt hee proceeded, as that no earthly thing bred such wonder to a Prince as to be a good horseman. Skill of gouernment was but a Pedanteria in comparison. Then would hee adde certaine prayses, by telling what a peerlesse beast a horse was; the onely seruiceable Courtier without flattery, the beast of most beutie, faithfulnes, courage, and such more, that if I had not beene a peece of a Logician before I came to him, I think he would haue perswaded mee to haue wished my selfe a horse. But thus much at least with his no fewe words hee draue into me, that selfe-loue is better then any guilding to make that seeme gorgious wherein our selues are parties. Wherein, if

Pugliano his strong affection and weake arguments will not satisfie
you, I wil giue you a neerer example of my selfe, who (I knowe not
by what mischance) in these my not old yeres and idelest times,
hauing slipt into the title of a Poet, am prouoked to say somthing
vnto you in the defence of that my vnelected vocation, which if
I handle with more good will then good reasons, beare with me,
sith the scholler is to be pardoned that foloweth the steppes of
his Maister. And yet I must say that as I haue iust cause to make
a pittiful defence of poore Poetry, which from almost the highest
estimation of learning is fallen to be the laughing-stocke of children; so haue I need to bring some more auaileable proofes: sith
the former is by no man barred of his deserued credite, the silly
latter hath had euen the names of Philosophers vsed to the de-
facing of it, with great danger of ciuill war among the Muses.

[II.] And first, truly to al them that professing learning inueigh
against Poetry, may iustly be obiected, that they goe very neer
to vngratfulnes, to seek to deface that which, in the noblest nations and languages that are knowne, hath been the first light-
giuer to ignorance, and first Nurse, whose milk by little and little
enabled them to feed afterwards of tougher knowledges: and
will they now play the Hedgehog that, being receiued into the den,
draue out his host? or rather the Vipers, that with theyr birth
kill their Parents? Let learned Greece in any of her manifold
Sciences be able to shew me one booke before *Musæus, Homer,*
and *Hesiodus,* all three nothing els but Poets. Nay, let any historie be brought that can say any Writers were there before them,
if they were not men of the same skil, as *Orpheus, Linus,* and
some other are named: who, hauing beene the first of that Country
that made pens deliuerers of their knowledge to their posterity,
may iustly chalenge to bee called their Fathers in learning: for
not only in time they had this priority (although in its self antiquity be venerable) but went before them, as causes to drawe
with their charming sweetnes the wild vntamed wits to an admiration of knowledge. So as *Amphion* was sayde to moue stones
with his Poetrie to build Thebes; and *Orpheus* to be listened to by
beastes, indeed stony and beastly people. So among the Romans
were *Liuius, Andronicus,* and *Ennius.* So in the Italian language
the first that made it aspire to be a Treasure-house of Science

were the Poets *Dante, Boccace,* and *Petrarch.* So in our English
were *Gower* and *Chawcer.*

After whom, encouraged and delighted with theyr excellent
fore-going, others haue followed, to beautifie our mother tongue,
as wel in the same kinde as in other Arts. This did so notably
shewe it selfe, that the Phylosophers of Greece durst not a long
time appeare to the worlde but vnder the masks of Poets. So
Thales, Empedocles, and *Parmenides* sange their naturall Phylosophie in verses: so did *Pythagoras* and *Phocilides* their morrall
counsells: so did *Tirteus* in war matters, and *Solon* in matters of
policie: or rather, they, being Poets, dyd exercise their delightful
vaine in those points of highest knowledge, which before them
lay hid to the world. For that wise *Solon* was directly a Poet it
is manifest, hauing written in verse the notable fable of the
Atlantick Iland, which was continued by *Plato.*

And truely, euen *Plato,* whosoeuer well considereth, shall find
that in the body of his work, though the inside and strength were
Philosophy, the skinne as it were and beautie depended most of
Poetrie: for all standeth vpon Dialogues, wherein he faineth many
honest Burgesses of Athens to speake of such matters, that, if
they had been sette on the racke, they would neuer haue con-
fessed them. Besides, his poetical describing the circumstances
of their meetings, as the well ordering of a banquet, the delicacie
of a walke, with enterlacing meere tales, as *Giges* Ring, and
others, which who knoweth not to be flowers of Poetrie did neuer
walke into *Apollos* Garden.

And even Historiographers (although theyr lippes sounde of
things doone, and veritie be written in theyr fore-heads) haue
been glad to borrow both fashion and perchance weight of Poets.
So *Herodotus* entituled his Historie by the name of the nine
Muses: and both he and all the rest that followed him either
stole or vsurped of Poetrie their passionate describing of passions,
the many particularities of battailes, which no man could affirme,
or, if that be denied me, long Orations put in the mouthes of
great Kings and Captaines, which it is certaine they neuer pronounced. So that, truely, neyther Phylosopher nor Historiographer
coulde at the first haue entred into the gates of populer iudgements, if they had not taken a great passport of Poetry, which in

all Nations at this day, wher learning florisheth not, is plaine to
be seene: in all which they haue some feeling of Poetry.

[III.*a*.] In Turky, besides their lawe-giuing Diuines, they haue
no other Writers but Poets. In our neighbour Countrey Ireland,
where truelie learning goeth very bare, yet are theyr Poets held
in a deuoute reuerence. Euen among the most barbarous and
simple Indians where no writing is, yet haue they their Poets, who
make and sing songs, which they call *Areytos,* both of theyr
Auncestors deedes and praises of theyr Gods: a sufficient probabilitie that if euer learning come among them, it must be by
hauing theyr hard dull wits softned and sharpened with the
sweete delights of Poetrie. For vntill they find a pleasure in the
exercises of the minde, great promises of much knowledge will
little perswade them that knowe not the fruites of knowledge.
In Wales, the true remnant of the auncient Brittons, as there
are good authorities to shewe the long time they had Poets, which
they called *Bardes,* so through all the conquests of Romaines,
Saxons, Danes, and Normans, some of whom did seeke to ruine
all memory of learning from among them, yet doo their Poets,
euen to this day, last; so as it is not more notable in soone beginning then in long continuing. But since the Authors of most
of our Sciences were the Romans, and before them the Greekes,
let vs a little stand vppon their authorities, but euen so farre as
to see what names they haue giuen vnto this now scorned skill.

[*b*.] Among the Romans a Poet was called *Vates,* which is as
much as a Diuiner, Fore-seer, or Prophet, as by his conioyned
wordes *Vaticinium* and *Vaticinari* is manifest: so heauenly a title
did that excellent people bestow vpon this hart-rauishing knowledge. And so farre were they carried into the admiration thereof,
that they thought in the chaunceable hitting vppon any such
verses great foretokens of their following fortunes were placed.
Whereupon grew the worde of *Sortes Virgilianae,* when, by
suddaine opening *Virgils* booke, they lighted vpon any verse of
hys making: whereof the histories of the Emperors liues are full;
as of *Albinus,* the Gouernour of our Iland, who in his childehoode
mette with this verse,

Arma amens capio nec sat rationis in armis; [1]

[1] "Maddened I seize arms; yet little purpose is there in arms." *Aeneid,*
II, 314.

and in his age performed it: which although it were a very vaine
and godles superstition, as also it was to think that spirits were
commaunded by such verses—whereupon this word charmes,
deriued of *Carmina*, commeth—so yet serueth it to shew the great
reuerence those wits were helde in. And altogether not without
ground, since both the Oracles of *Delphos* and *Sibillas* prophecies
were wholy deliuered in verses. For that same exquisite obseruing
of numbers and measures in words, and that high flying liberty
of conceit proper to the Poet, did seeme to haue some dyuine
force in it.

And may not I presume a little further, to shew the reason-
ablenes of this worde *Vates*? And say that the holy *Dauids* Psalmes
are a diuine Poem? If I doo, I shall not do it without the testimonie of great learned men, both auncient and moderne: but
euen the name Psalmes will speake for mee, which, being interpreted, is nothing but songes. Then that it is fully written in
meeter, as all learned Hebricians agree, although the rules be not
yet fully found. Lastly and principally, his handeling his prophecy,
which is meerely poetical. For what els is the awaking his
musicall instruments; the often and free changing of persons; his
notable *Prosopopeias*,[2] when he maketh you, as it were, see God
comming in his Maiestie; his telling of the Beastes ioyfulnes, and
hills leaping, but a heauenlie poesie, wherein almost hee sheweth
himselfe a passionate louer of that vnspeakable and euerlasting
beautie to be seene by the eyes of the minde, onely cleered by
fayth? But truely nowe hauing named him, I feare mee I seeme
to prophane that holy name, applying it to Poetrie, which is among
vs throwne downe to so ridiculous an estimation: but they that
with quiet iudgement will looke a little deeper into it, shall finde
the end and working of it such, as beeing rightly applyed, deserueth not to bee scourged out of the Church of God.

[c.] But now, let vs see how the Greekes named it, and howe
they deemed of it. The Greekes called him a Poet, which name
hath, as the most excellent, gone thorough other Languages. It
commeth of this word *Poiein*, which is to make: wherein I know
not, whether by lucke or wisedome, wee Englishmen haue mette
with the Greekes in calling him a maker: which name, how high

[2] *Prosopopeia*. The rhetorical figure for introducing into an oration or
poem a speech by someone not actually present. A type of personification.

and incomparable a title it is, I had rather were knowne by
marking the scope of other Sciences then by my partiall allegation.

There is no Arte deliuered to mankinde that hath not the
workes of Nature for his principall obiect, without which they
could not consist, and on which they so depend, as they become
Actors and Players, as it were, of what Nature will haue set
foorth. So doth the Astronomer looke vpon the starres, and, by
that he seeth, setteth downe what order Nature hath taken
therein. So doe the Geometrician and Arithmetician in their
diuerse sorts of quantities. So doth the Musitian in times tel you
which by nature agree, which not. The naturall Philosopher
thereon hath his name, and the Morrall Philosopher standeth
vpon the naturall vertues, vices, and passions of man; and
'followe Nature' (saith hee) 'therein, and thou shalt not erre.'
The Lawyer sayth what men haue determined. The Historian
what men haue done. The Grammarian speaketh onely of the
rules of speech; and the Rethorician and Logitian, considering
what in Nature will soonest proue and perswade, thereon giue
artificiall rules, which still are compassed within the circle of a
question, according to the proposed matter. The Phisition
waigheth the nature of a mans bodie, and the nature of things
helpeful or hurtefull vnto it. And the Metaphisick, though it
be in the seconde and abstract notions, and therefore be counted
supernaturall, yet doth hee indeede builde vpon the depth of
Nature. Onely the Poet, disdayning to be tied to any such subiection, lifted vp with the vigor of his owne inuention, dooth
growe in effect another nature, in making things either better
then Nature bringeth forth, or, quite a newe, formes such as
neuer were in Nature, as the *Heroes, Demigods, Cyclops,
Chimeras, Furies,* and such like: so as hee goeth hand in hand
with Nature, not inclosed within the narrow warrant of her
guifts, but freely ranging onely within the Zodiack of his owne
wit.

Nature neuer set forth the earth in so rich tapistry as diuers
Poets haue done, neither with plesant riuers, fruitful trees, sweet
smelling flowers, nor whatsoeuer els may make the too much
loued earth more louely. Her world is brasen, the Poets only
deliuer a golden. But let those things alone and goe to man, for
whom as the other things are, so it seemeth in him her vttermost

cunning is imployed, and knowe whether shee haue brought foorth so true a louer as *Theagines*, so constant a friende as *Pilades*, so variant a man as *Orlando*, so right a Prince as *Xenophons Cyrus*, so excellent a man euery way as *Virgils Aeneas*: neither let this be iestingly conceiued, because the works of the one be essentiall, the other, in imitation or fiction; for any vnderstanding knoweth the skil of the Artificer standeth in that *Idea* or fore-conceite of the work, and not in the work it selfe. And that the Poet hath that *Idea* is manifest, by deliuering them forth in such excellencie as hee hath imagined them. Which deliuering forth also is not wholie imaginatiue, as we are wont to say by them that build Castles in the ayre: but so farre substantially it worketh, not onely to make a *Cyrus*, which had been but a particuler excellencie, as Nature might haue done, but to bestow a *Cyrus* vpon the worlde, to make many *Cyrus's*, if they wil learne aright why and how that Maker made him.

Neyther let it be deemed too sawcie a comparison to ballance the highest poynt of mans wit with the efficacie of Nature: but rather giue right honor to the heauenly Maker of that maker, who, hauing made man to his owne likenes, set him beyond and ouer all the workes of that second nature, which in nothing hee sheweth so much as in Poetrie, when with the force of a diuine breath he bringeth things forth far surpassing her dooings, with no small argument to the incredulous of that first accursed fall of *Adam*: sith our erected wit maketh vs know what perfection is, and yet our infected will keepeth vs from reaching vnto it. But these arguments wil by fewe be vnderstood, and by fewer granted. Thus much (I hope) will be giuen me, that the Greekes with some probabilitie of reason gaue him the name aboue all names of learning. Now let vs goe to a more ordinary opening of him, that the trueth may be more palpable: and so I hope, though we get not so vnmatched a praise as the Etimologie of his names wil grant, yet his very description, which no man will denie, shall not iustly be barred from a principall commendation.

[IV.] Poesie therefore is an arte of imitation, for so *Aristotle* termeth it in his word *Mimesis*, that is to say, a representing, counterfetting, or figuring foorth: to speake metaphorically, a speaking picture: with this end, to teach and delight. Of this haue beene three seuerall kindes.

The chiefe both in antiquitie and excellencie were they that did imitate the inconceiuable excellencies of GOD. Such were *Dauid* in his Psalmes, *Salomon* in his song of Songs, in his Ecclesiastes, and Prouerbs, *Moses* and *Debora* in theyr Hymnes, and the writer of *Iob*; which, beside other, the learned *Emanuell Tremelius* and *Franciscus Iunius* doe entitle the poeticall part of the Scripture. Against these none will speake that hath the holie Ghost in due holy reuerence. In this kinde, though in a full wrong diuinitie, were *Orpheus, Amphion, Homer* in his hymnes, and many other, both Greekes and Romaines: and this Poesie must be vsed, by whosoeuer will follow S. *Iames* his counsell, in singing Psalmes when they are merry: and I knowe is vsed with the fruite of comfort by some, when, in sorrowfull pangs of their death-bringing sinnes, they find the consolation of the neuer-leauing goodnesse.

The second kinde is of them that deale with matters Philosophicall; eyther morrall, as *Tirteus, Phocilides,* and *Cato*; or naturall, as *Lucretius* and *Virgils Georgicks*; or Astronomicall, as *Manilius* and *Pontanus*; or historical, as *Lucan*: which who mislike, the faulte is in their iudgements quite out of taste, and not in the sweet foode of sweetly vttered knowledge.

But because thys second sorte is wrapped within the folde of the proposed subiect, and takes not the course of his owne inuention, whether they properly be Poets or no let Gramarians dispute: and goe to the thyrd, indeed right Poets, of whom chiefly this question ariseth; betwixt whom and these second is such a kinde of difference as betwixt the meaner sort of Painters (who counterfet onely such faces as are sette before them) and the more excellent, who, hauing no law but wit, bestow that in collours vpon you which is fittest for the eye to see: as the constant though lamenting looke of *Lucrecia,* when she punished in her selfe an others fault; wherein he painteth not *Lucrecia* whom he neuer sawe, but painteth the outwarde beauty of such a vertue. For these third be they which most properly do imitate to teach and delight, and to imitate borrow nothing of what is, hath been, or shall be: but range, onely rayned with learned discretion, into the diuine consideration of what may be, and should be. These bee they that, as the first and most noble sorte, may iustly bee termed *Vates,* so these are waited on in the excellen[te]st languages and best vnderstandings, with the fore described name of Poets: for these indeede doo meerely make to imitate, and imitate both to delight and teach, and delight to moue men to take that goodnes in hande, which without delight they would flye as from a stranger; and teach, to make them know that goodnes whereunto they are mooued, which being the noblest scope to which euer any learning was directed, yet want there not idle tongues to barke at them.

These be subdiuided into sundry more speciall denominations. The most notable bee the *Heroick, Lirick, Tragick, Comick, Satirick, Iambick, Elegiack, Pastorall,* and certaine others, some of these being termed according to the matter they deale with, some by the sorts of verses they liked best to write in, for indeede the greatest part of Poets have apparelled their poeticall inuentions in that numbrous kinde of writing which is called verse: indeed but apparelled, verse being but an ornament and no cause to Poetry, sith there haue beene many most excellent Poets that neuer versified, and now swarme many versifiers that neede neuer aunswere to the name of Poets. For *Xenophon,* who did imitate so excellently as to giue vs *effigiem iusti imperii,* the portraiture of a iust Empire vnder the name of *Cyrus* (as *Cicero* sayth of him), made therein an absolute heroicall Poem; so did *Heliodorus* in his sugred inuention of that picture of loue in *Theagines* and *Cariclea;* and yet both these writ in Prose: which I speak to shew that it is not riming and versing that maketh a Poet, no more then a long gowne maketh an Aduocate, who though he pleaded in armor should be an Aduocate and no Souldier. But it is that fayning notable images of vertues, vices, or what els, with that delightfull teaching, which must be the right describing note to know a Poet by: although indeed the Senate of Poets hath chosen verse as their fittest rayment, meaning, as in matter they passed all in all, so in maner to goe beyond them: not speaking (table talke fashion or like men in a dreame) words as they chanceably fall from the mouth, but peyzing each sillable of each worde by iust proportion according to the dignitie of the subiect.

[V.*a.*] Nowe therefore it shall not bee amisse first to waigh this latter sort of Poetrie by his works, and then by his partes; and if in neyther of these Anatomies hee be condemnable, I

hope wee shall obtaine a more fauourable sentence. This purifing
of wit, this enritching of memory, enabling of iudgment, and enlarging of conceyt, which commonly we call learning, vnder
what name soeuer it com forth, or to what immediat end soeuer
it be directed, the final end is to lead and draw vs to as high a
perfection as our degenerate soules, made worse by theyr clayey
lodgings, can be capable of. This, according to the inclination of
the man, bred many formed impressions. For some that thought
this felicity principally to be gotten by knowledge, and no knowledge to be so high and heauenly as acquaintance with the starres,
gaue themselues to Astronomie; others, perswading themselues to
be *Demigods* if they knewe the causes of things, became naturall
and supernaturall Philosophers; some an admirable delight drew
to Musicke; and some the certainty of demonstration to the Mathe-
matickes: But all, one and other, hauing this scope—to knowe, and
by knowledge to lift vp the mind from the dungeon of the body to
the enioying his owne diuine essence. But when by the ballance of
experience it was found that the Astronomer looking to the starres
might fall into a ditch, that the enquiring Philosopher might be
blinde in himselfe, and the Mathematician might draw foorth a
straight line with a crooked hart; then loe, did proofe, the ouer
ruler of opinions, make manifest that all these are but seruing
Sciences, which as they haue each a priuate end in themselues, so
yet are they all directed to the highest end of the mistress Knowledge, by the Greekes called *Arkitecktonike*, which stands, (as I
thinke) in the knowledge of a mans selfe, in the Ethicke and politick consideration, with the end of well dooing and not of well
knowing onely; euen as the Sadlers next end is to make a good
saddle, but his farther end to serue a nobler facultie, which is
horsemanship; so the horsemans to souldiery, and the Souldier not
onely to haue the skill, but to performe the practise of a Souldier:
so that, the ending end of all earthly learning being vertuous
action, those skilles that most serue to bring forth that haue a
most iust title to bee Princes ouer all the rest. Wherein if wee
can shewe the Poets noblenes, by setting him before his other
Competitors, among whom as principall challengers step forth
the morrall Philosophers, whom, me thinketh, I see comming
towards mee with a sullen grauity, as though they could not

abide vice by day light, rudely clothed for to witnes outwardly
their contempt of outward things, with bookes in their hands
agaynst glory, where to they sette theyr names, sophistically
speaking against subtility, and angry with any man in whom they
see the foule fault of anger: these men casting larges as they goe
of Definitions, Diuisions, and Distinctions, with a scornefull in-
terogatiue doe soberly aske whether it bee possible to finde any
path so ready to leade a man to vertue as that which teacheth
what vertue is? and teacheth it not onely by deliuering forth
his very being, his causes, and effects; but also by making known
his enemie vice, which must be destroyed, and his combersome
seruant Passion, which must be maistered; by shewing the
generalities that contayneth it, and the specialities that are deriued from it; lastly, by playne setting downe, how it extendeth
it selfe out of the limits of a mans own little world to the
gouernment of families, and maintayning of publique societies.

[*b.*] The Historian scarcely giueth leysure to the Moralist to
say so much, but that he, loden with old Mouse-eaten records,
authorising himselfe (for the most part) vpon other histories,
whose greatest authorities are built vpon the notable foundation
of Heare-say, hauing much a-doe to accord differing Writers and
to pick trueth out of partiality, better acquainted with a thousande yeeres a goe then with the present age, and yet better
knowing how this world goeth then how his owne wit runneth,
curious for antiquities and inquisitiue of nouelties, a wonder to
young folkes and a tyrant in table talke, denieth, in a great chafe,
that any man for teaching of vertue, and vertuous actions, is
comparable to him. I am *Lux vitae, Temporum magistra, Vita
memoriae, Nuncia vetustatis, &c.*[3]

'The Phylosopher' (sayth hee) 'teacheth a disputatiue vertue,
but I doe an actiue: his vertue is excellent in the dangerlesse
Academie of *Plato,* but mine sheweth foorth her honorable face
in the battailes of *Marathon, Pharsalia, Poitiers,* and *Agincourt.*
Hee teacheth vertue by certaine abstract considerations, but I
onely bid you follow the footing of them that haue gone before
you. Olde-aged experience goeth beyond the fine-witted Phy-

[3] "The light of life, the teacher of the ages, the life of memory, the mes-
senger of antiquity." Inaccurately quoted from Cicero, *De Oratore,* II, 9.

losopher, but I giue the experience of many ages. Lastly, if he make the Song-booke, I put the learners hande to the Lute: and if hee be the guide, I am the light.'

Then woulde hee alledge you innumerable examples, conferring storie by storie, how much the wisest Senatours and Princes haue beene directed by the credite of history, as *Brutus*, *Alphonsus* of *Aragon*, and who not, if need bee? At length long lyne of theyr disputation maketh a poynt in thys, that the one giueth the precept, and the other the example.

Nowe, whom shall wee finde (sith the question standeth for the highest forme in the Schoole of learning) to bee Moderator? Trulie, as mee seemeth, the Poet; and if not a Moderator, euen the man that ought to carrie the title from them both, and much more from all other seruing Sciences. Therefore compare we the Poet with the Historian, and with the Morrall Phylosopher, and, if hee goe beyond them both, no other humaine skill can match him. For as for the Diuine, with all reuerence it is euer to be excepted, not only for hauing his scope as far beyonde any of these as eternitie exceedeth a moment, but euen for passing each of these in themselues. And for the Lawyer, though *Ius* bee the Daughter of Iustice, and Iustice the chiefe of Vertues, yet because hee seeketh to make men good rather *Formidine poenae* then *Virtutis amore*,[4] or, to say righter, dooth not indeuour to make men good, but that their euill hurt not others, hauing no care, so hee be a good Cittizen, how bad a man he be: Therefore, as our wickednesse maketh him necessarie, and necessitie maketh him honorable, so is hee not in the deepest trueth to stande in rancke with these who all indeuour to take naughtines away, and plant goodness euen in the secretest cabinet of our soules. And these foure are all that any way deale in that consideration of mens manners, which beeing the supreme knowledge, they that best breed it deserue the best commendation.

The Philosopher therfore and the Historian are they which would win the gole, the one by precept, the other by example. But both not hauing both, doe both halte. For the Philosopher, setting down with thorny argument the bare rule, is so hard of vtterance, and so mistie to bee conceiued, that one that hath no

---

[4] "By fear of punishment" (rather than) "by love of virtue,"

other guide but him shall wade in him till hee be olde before he shall finde sufficient cause to bee honest: for his knowledge standeth so vpon the abstract and generall, that happie is that man who may vnderstande him, and more happie that can applye what hee dooth vnderstand. On the other side, the Historian, wanting the precept, is so tyed, not to what shoulde bee but to what is, to the particuler truth of things and not to the general reason of things, that hys example draweth no necessary consequence, and therefore a lesse fruitfull doctrine.

[*c.*] Nowe dooth the peerelesse Poet performe both: for whatsoeuer the Philosopher sayth shoulde be doone, hee giueth a perfect picture of it in some one, by whom hee presupposeth it was doone. So as hee coupleth the generall notion with the particuler example. A perfect picture I say, for hee yeeldeth to the powers of the minde an image of that whereof the Philosopher bestoweth but a woordish description: which dooth neyther strike, pierce, nor possesse the sight of the soule so much as that other dooth.

For as in outward things, to a man that had neuer seene an Elephant or a Rinoceros, who should tell him most exquisitely all theyr shapes, cullour, bignesse, and perticular markes, or of a gorgeous Pallace the Architecture, with declaring the full beauties, might well make the hearer able to repeate, as it were by rote, all hee had heard, yet should neuer satisfie his inward conceits with being witnes to it selfe of a true liuely knowledge: but the same man, as soone as hee might see those beasts well painted, or the house wel in moddel, should straightwaies grow, without need of any description, to iudicial comprehending of them: so no doubt the Philosopher with his learned definition, bee it of vertue, vices, matters of publick policie or priuat gouernment, replenisheth the memory with many infallible grounds of wisdom, which, notwithstanding, lye darke before the imaginatiue and iudging powre, if they bee not illuminated or figured foorth by the speaking picture of Poesie.

Tullie taketh much paynes, and many times not without poeticall helpes, to make vs knowe the force loue of our Countrey hath in vs. Let vs but heare old *Anchises* speaking in the middest of Troyes flames, or see *Vlisses* in the fulnes of all *Calipso's* delights bewayle his absence from barraine and beggerly *Ithaca*.

Anger, the *Stoicks* say, was a short madnes: let but *Sophocles* bring you *Aiax* on a stage, killing and whipping Sheepe and Oxen, thinking them the Army of Greeks, with theyr Chiefetaines *Agamemnon* and *Menelaus*, and tell mee if you haue not a more familiar insight into anger then finding in the Schoolemen his *Genus* and difference. See whether wisdome and temperance in *Vlisses* and *Diomedes*, valure in *Achilles*, friendship in *Nisus* and *Eurialus*, euen to an ignoraunt man carry not an apparent shyning: and, contrarily, the remorse of conscience in *Oedipus*, the soone repenting pride of *Agamemnon*, the selfe-deuouring crueltie in his Father *Atreus*, the violence of ambition in the two *Theban* brothers, the sowre-sweetnes of reuenge in *Medæa*, and, to fall lower, the *Terentian Gnato* and our *Chaucers Pandar* so exprest that we now vse their names to signifie their trades: and finally, all vertues, vices, and passions so in their own naturall seates layd to the viewe, that wee seeme not to heare of them, but cleerely to see through them. But euen in the most excellent determination of goodnes, what Philosophers counsell can so redily direct a Prince, as the fayned *Cyrus* in *Xenophon*? or a vertuous man in all fortunes, as *Aeneas* in *Virgill*? or a whole Common-wealth, as the way of Sir *Thomas Moores Eutopia*? I say the way, because where Sir *Thomas Moore* erred, it was the fault of the man and not of the Poet, for that way of patterning a Common-wealth was most absolute, though hee perchaunce hath not so absolutely perfourmed it: for the question is, whether the fayned image of Poesie or the regular instruction of Philosophy hath the more force in teaching: wherein if the Philosophers haue more rightly shewed themselues Philosophers then the Poets haue obtained to the high top of their profession, as in truth,

> *Mediocribus esse poetis,*
> *Non Di, non homines, non concessere Columnae,* [5]

it is, I say againe, not the fault of the Art, but that by fewe men that Arte can bee accomplished. Certainly, euen our Sauiour Christ could as well haue giuen the morrall common places of vncharitablenes and humblenes as the diuine narration of *Diues* and *Lazarus*; or of disobedience and mercy, as that heauenly

[5] "Not gods or men or booksellers permit poets to be mediocre." Horace, *Ars Poetica*, 372–3.

discourse of the lost Child and the gratious Father; but that hys through-searching wisdom knewe the estate of *Diues* burning in hell, and of *Lazarus* being in *Abrahams* bosome, would more constantly (as it were) inhabit both the memory and iudgment. Truly, for my selfe, mee seemes I see before my eyes the lost Childes disdainefull prodigality, turned to enuie a Swines dinner: which by the learned Diuines are thought not historicall acts, but instructing Parables. For conclusion, I say the Philosopher teacheth, but he teacheth obscurely, so as the learned onely can vnderstande him, that is to say, he teacheth them that are already taught; but the Poet is the foode for the tenderest stomacks, the Poet is indeed the right Popular Philosopher, whereof *Esops* tales giue good proofe: whose pretty Allegories, stealing vnder the formall tales of Beastes, make many, more beastly then Beasts, begin to heare the sound of vertue from these dumbe speakers.

But now may it be alledged that if this imagining of matters be so fitte for the imagination, then must the Historian needs surpasse, who bringeth you images of true matters, such as indeede were doone, and not such as fantastically or falsely may be suggested to haue been doone. Truely, *Aristotle* himselfe, in his discourse of Poesie, plainely determineth this question, saying that Poetry is *Philosophoteron* and *Spoudaioteron*, that is to say, it is more Philosophicall and more studiously serious then history.[6] His reason is, because Poesie dealeth with *Katholou*, that is to say, with the vniuersall consideration; and the history with *Kathekaston*, the perticuler: 'nowe,' sayth he, 'the vniuersall wayes what is fit to bee sayd or done, eyther in likelihood or necessity, (which the Poesie considereth in his imposed names), and the perticuler onely marks whether *Alcibiades* did, or suffered, this or that.' Thus farre *Aristotle*: which reason of his (as all his) is most full of reason. For indeed, if the question were whether it were better to haue a perticular acte truly or falsely set down, there is no doubt which is to be chosen, no more then whether you had rather haue *Vespasians* picture right as hee was, or at the Painters pleasure nothing resembling. But if the question be for your owne vse and learning, whether it be better to haue

[6] *Poetics,* IX.

it set downe as it should be, or as it was, then certainely is more doctrinable the fained *Cirus* in *Xenophon* then the true *Cyrus* in *Iustine,* and the fayned *Aeneas* in *Virgil* then the right *Aeneas* in *Dares Phrigius.* As to a Lady that desired to fashion her countenance to the best grace, a Painter should more benefite her to portraite a most sweet face, wryting *Canidia* vpon it, then to paynt *Canidia* as she was, who, *Horace* sweareth, was foule and ill fauoured.

If the Poet doe his part a-right, he will shew you in *Tantalus, Atreus,* and such like, nothing that is not to be shunned; in *Cyrus, Aeneas, Vlisses,* each thing to be followed; where the Historian, bound to tell things as things were, cannot be liberall (without hee will be poeticall) of a perfect patterne, but, as in *Alexander* or *Scipio* himselfe, shew dooings, some to be liked, some to be misliked. And then how will you discerne what to followe but by your owne discretion, which you had without reading *Quintus Curtius*? And whereas a man may say, though in vniuersall consideration of doctrine the Poet preuaileth, yet that the historie, in his saying such a thing was doone, doth warrant a man more in that hee shall follow, the aunswere is manifest, that if hee stande vpon that was—as if hee should argue, because it rayned yesterday, therefore it shoulde rayne to day—then indeede it hath some aduantage to a grose conceite; but if he know an example onlie informes a coniectured likelihood, and so goe by reason, the Poet dooth so farre exceede him, as hee is to frame his example to that which is most reasonable, be it in warlike, politick, or priuate matters, where the Historian in his bare *Was* hath many times that which wee call fortune to ouer-rule the best wisedome. Manie times he must tell euents whereof he can yeelde no cause: or, if hee doe, it must be poeticall.

For that a fayned example hath asmuch force to teach as a true example (for as for to mooue, it is cleere, sith the fayned may bee tuned to the highest key of passion), let vs take one example wherein a Poet and a Historian doe concur. *Herodotus* and *Iustine* do both testifie that *Zopirus,* King *Darius* faithfull seruaunt, seeing his Maister long resisted by the rebellious *Babilonians,* fayned himselfe in extreame disgrace of his King: for verifying of which, he caused his own nose and eares to be cut off: and so flying to the *Babylonians,* was receiued, and for his knowne valour so far credited, that hee did finde meanes to deliuer them ouer to *Darius.* Much like matter doth *Liuie* record of *Tarquinius* and his sonne. *Xenophon* excellently faineth such another strategeme, performed by *Abradates* in *Cyrus* behalfe. Now would I fayne know, if occasion bee presented vnto you to serue your Prince in such an honest dissimulation, why you doe not as well learne it of *Xenophons* fiction as of the others verity: and truely so much the better, as you shall saue your nose by the bargaine; for *Abradates* did not counterfet so far. So then the best of the Historian is subiect to the Poet; for whatsoeuer action, or faction, whatsoeuer counsell, pollicy, or warre stratagem the Historian is bound to recite, that may the Poet (if he list) with his imitation make his own; beautifying it both for further teaching, and more delighting, as it pleaseth him: hauing all, from *Dante* his heauen to hys hell, vnder the authoritie of his penne. Which if I be asked what Poets haue done so, as I might well name some, yet say I, and say againe, I speak of the Arte, and not of the Artificer.

Nowe, to that which commonly is attributed to the prayse of histories, in respect of the notable learning is gotten by marking the successe, as though therein a man should see vertue exalted and vice punished. Truely that commendation is peculiar to Poetrie, and faare of from History. For indeede Poetrie euer setteth vertue so out in her best cullours, making Fortune her wel-wayting hand-mayd, that one must needs be enamored of her. Well may you see *Vlisses* in a storme, and in other hard plights; but they are but exercises of patience and magnanimitie, to make them shine the more in the neere-following prosperitie. And of the contrarie part, if euill men come to the stage, they euer goe out (as the Tragedie Writer answered to one that misliked the shew of such persons) so manacled as they little animate folkes to followe them. But the Historian, beeing captiued to the trueth of a foolish world, is many times a terror from well dooing, and an incouragement to vnbrideled wickednes.

For see wee not valiant *Milciades* rot in his fetters? The iust *Phocion* and the accomplished *Socrates* put to death like Traytors? The cruell *Seuerus* liue prosperously? The excellent *Seuerus* miserably murthered? *Sylla* and *Marius* dying in theyr beddes?

Pompey and *Cicero* slaine then when they would haue thought
exile a happinesse? See wee not vertuous *Cato* driuen to kyll
himselfe? and rebell *Cæsar* so aduaunced that his name yet, after
1600 yeares, lasteth in the highest honor? And marke but euen
Cæsars own words of the fore-named *Sylla* (who in that onely
did honestly, to put downe his dishonest tyrannie), *Literas
nesciuit*,[7] as if want of learning caused him to doe well. Hee
meant it not by Poetrie, which, not content with earthly plagues,
deuiseth new punishments in hel for Tyrants: nor yet by Philosophie, which teacheth *Occidendos esse*;[8] but no doubt by skill in
Historie, for that indeede can affoord your *Cipselus, Periander,
Phalaris, Dionisius,* and I know not how many more of the same
kennell, that speede well enough in theyr abhominable vniustice
or vsurpation. I conclude, therefore, that hee excelleth Historie,
not onely in furnishing the minde with knowledge, but in setting
it forward to that which deserueth to be called and accounted
good: which setting forward, and moouing to well dooing, indeed setteth the Lawrell crowne vpon the Poet as victorious,
not onely of the Historian, but ouer the Phylosopher, howsoeuer
in teaching it may bee questionable.

For suppose it be granted (that which I suppose with great
reason may be denied) that the Philosopher, in respect of his
methodical proceeding, doth teach more perfectly then the Poet,
yet do I thinke that no man is so much *Philophilosophos* as to
compare the Philosopher, in moouing, with the Poet.

And that moouing is of a higher degree than teaching, it may
by this appeare, that it is wel nigh the cause and the effect of
teaching. For who will be taught, if hee bee not mooued with
desire to be taught? and what so much good doth that teaching
bring forth (I speak still of morrall doctrine) as that it mooueth
one to doe that which it dooth teach? for, as *Aristotle* sayth, it is
not *Gnosis* but *Praxis*[9] must be the fruit. And howe *Praxis* cannot
be, without being mooued to practise, it is no hard matter to
consider.

The Philosopher sheweth you the way, hee informeth you of
the particularities, as well of the tediousnes of the way, as of

[7] "He was ignorant of letters." Suetonius, *Julius Caesar*, LXXVII.
[8] "They should be slain."
[9] "Not knowledge but action." Aristotle, *Nichomachean Ethics*, I, 3.

the pleasant lodging you shall haue when your iourney is ended, as of the many by-turnings that may diuert you from your way. But this is to no man but to him that will read him, and read him with attentiue studious painfulnes. Which constant desire, who soeuer hath in him, hath already past halfe the hardnes of the way, and therefore is beholding to the Philosopher but for the other halfe. Nay truely, learned men haue learnedly thought that, where once reason hath so much ouer-mastred passion as that the minde hath a free desire to doe well, the inward light each minde hath in it selfe is as good as a Philosophers booke; seeing in nature we know it is wel to doe well, and what is well and what is euill, although not in the words of Arte which Philosophers bestowe vpon vs. For out of naturall conceit the Philosophers drew it, but to be moued to doe that which we know, or to be mooued with desire to knowe, *Hoc opus, hic labor est*.[10]

Nowe therein of all Sciences (I speak still of humane, and according to the humaine conceits) is our Poet the Monarch. For he dooth not only show the way, but giueth so sweete a prospect into the way, as will intice any man to enter into it. Nay, he dooth, as if your iourney should lye through a fayre Vineyard, at the first giue you a cluster of Grapes, that, full of that taste, you may long to passe further. He beginneth not with obscure definitions, which must blur the margent with interpretations, and load the memory with doubtfulnesse; but hee commeth to you with words sent in delightfull proportion, either accompanied with, or prepared for, the well inchaunting skill of Musicke; and with a tale forsooth he commeth vnto you, with a tale which holdeth children from play, and old men from the chimney corner. And, pretending no more, doth intende the winning of the mind from wickednesse to vertue: euen as the childe is often brought to take most wholsom things by hiding them in such other as haue a pleasant tast: which, if one should beginne to tell them the nature of *Aloes* or *Rubarb* they shoulde receiue, woulde sooner take their Phisicke at their eares then at their mouth. So is it in men (most of which are childish in the best things, till they bee cradled in their graues): glad they will

[10] "This is the work, this the labor." *Aeneid*, VI, 129.

be to heare the tales of *Hercules, Achilles, Cyrus,* and *Aeneas;*
and, hearing them, must needs heare the right description of
wisdom, valure, and iustice; which, if they had been barely, that
is to say Philosophically, set out, they would sweare they bee
brought to schoole againe.

That imitation, whereof Poetry is, hath the most conueniency to
Nature of all other, in somuch that, as *Aristotle* sayth, those things
which in themselues are horrible, as cruell battailes, vnnaturall
Monsters, are made in poeticall imitation delightfull.[11] Truely,
I haue knowen men, that euen with reading *Amadis de Gaule*
(which God knoweth wanteth much of a perfect Poesie) haue
found their harts mooued to the exercise of courtesie, liberalitie,
and especially courage. Who readeth *Aeneas* carrying olde
Anchises on his back, that wisheth not it were his fortune to
perfourme so excellent an acte? Whom doe not the words of
Turnus mooue? (the tale of *Turnus* hauing planted his image
in the imagination)

> *Fugientem haec terra videbit?*
> *Vsque adeone mori miserum est?* [12]

Where the Philosophers, as they scorne to delight, so must they
bee content little to mooue, sauing wrangling whether Vertue
bee the chiefe or the onely good, whether the contemplatiue
or the actiue life doe excell: which *Plato* and *Boetius* well knew,
and therefore made Mistres Philosophy very often borrow the
masking rayment of Poesie. For euen those harde harted euill
men who thinke vertue a schoole name, and knowe no other
good but *indulgere genio,*[13] and therefore despise the austere
admonitions of the Philosopher, and feele not the inward reason
they stand vpon, yet will be content to be delighted, which is
al the good felow Poet seemeth to promise; and so steale to see
the forme of goodnes (which seene they cannot but loue) ere
themselues be aware, as if they tooke a medicine of Cherries.
Infinite proofes of the strange effects of this poeticall inuention

[11] *Poetics,* IV.
[12] "Shall this land see [Turnus] fleeing? And is it so miserable to die?"
Aeneid, XII, 645–6.
[13] "To indulge one's nature." A reversal of Persius' advice (*Satires,* V,
151), *indulge genio*—"give free reign to your nature [for tomorrow you
will die]."

might be alledged; onely two shall serue, which are so often remembred, as I thinke all men knowe them.

The one of *Menenius Agrippa*, who, when the whole people of Rome had resolutely deuided themselues from the Senate, with apparent shew of vtter ruine, though hee were (for that time) an excellent Oratour, came not among them vpon trust of figuratiue speeches or cunning insinuations; and much lesse with farre fet *Maximes* of Phylosophie, which (especially if they were *Platonick*) they must haue learned Geometrie before they could well haue conceiued; but forsooth he behaues himselfe like a homely and familiar Poet. Hee telleth them a tale, that there was a time when all the parts of the body made a mutinous conspiracie against the belly, which they thought deuoured the fruits of each others labour: they concluded they would let so vnprofitable a spender starue. In the end, to be short, (for the tale is notorious, and as notorious that it was a tale) with punishing the belly they plagued themselues. This applied by him wrought such effect in the people, as I neuer read that euer words brought forth but then so suddaine and so good an alteration; for vpon reasonable conditions a perfect reconcilement ensued. The other is of *Nathan* the Prophet, who when the holie *Dauid* had so far forsaken God as to confirme adulterie with murther, when hee was to doe the tenderest office of a friende, in laying his owne shame before his eyes, sent by God to call againe so chosen a seruant, how doth he it but by telling of a man whose beloued Lambe was vngratefullie taken from his bosome? the applycation most diuinely true, but the discourse it selfe fayned; which made *Dauid* (I speake of the second and instrumentall cause) as in a glasse to see his own filthines, as that heauenly Psalme of mercie wel testifieth.

By these, therefore, examples and reasons, I think it may be manifest that the Poet, with that same hand of delight, doth draw the mind more effectually then any other Arte dooth: and so a conclusion not vnfitlie ensueth, that as vertue is the most excellent resting place for all worldlie learning to make his end of, so Poetrie, beeing the most familiar to teach it, and most princelie to moue towards it, in the most excellent work is the most excellent workman.

[VI.] But I am content not onely to decipher him by his

workes (although works in commendation or disprayse must euer holde an high authority), but more narrowly will examine his parts: so that (as in a man) though al together may carry a presence ful of maiestie and beautie, perchance in some one defectious peece we may find a blemish. Now in his parts, kindes, or *Species* (as you list to terme them), it is to be noted that some Poesies haue coupled together two or three kindes, as Tragicall and Comicall, wher-vpon is risen the Tragicomicall. Some in the like manner haue mingled Prose and Verse, as *Sanazzar* and *Boetius*. Some haue mingled matters Heroicall and Pastorall. But that commeth all to one in this question, for, if seuered they be good, the coniunction cannot be hurtfull. Therefore perchaunce forgetting some, and leauing some as needlesse to be remembred, it shall not be amisse in a worde to cite the speciall kindes, to see what faults may be found in the right vse of them.

[*a.*] Is it then the Pastorall Poem which is misliked? (for perchance, where the hedge is lowest they will soonest leape ouer). Is the poore pype disdained, which sometimes out of *Melibeus* mouth can shewe the miserie of people vnder hard Lords or rauening Souldiours? and again, by *Titirus*, what blessednes is deriued to them that lye lowest from the goodnesse of them that sit highest? sometimes, vnder the prettie tales of Wolues and Sheepe, can include the whole considerations of wrong dooing and patience; sometimes shew that contention for trifles can get but a trifling victorie. Where perchaunce a man may see that euen *Alexander* and *Darius*, when they straue who should be Cocke of thys worlds dunghill, the benefit they got was that the after-liuers may say,

> *Haec memini et victum frustra contendere Thirsin:*
> *Ex illo Coridon, Coridon est tempore nobis.*[14]

[*b.*] Or is it the lamenting Elegiack, which in a kinde hart would mooue rather pitty then blame, who bewailes with the great Philosopher *Heraclitus* the weakenes of mankind and the wretchednes of the world: who surely is to be praysed, either for compassionate accompanying iust causes of lamentation, or for rightly paynting out how weake be the passions of woful-

---

[14] "I remember all this, and that vanquished Thirsis competed in vain. From that time it has been Croydon—only Croydon—with us." Virgil, *Eclogues*, VII, 69–70.

nesse? Is it the bitter but wholsome Iambick, which rubs the galled minde, in making shame the trumpet of villanie with bolde and open crying out against naughtines? Or the Satirick, who

Omne vafer vitium ridenti tangit amico? [15]

who sportingly neuer leaueth vntil hee make a man laugh at folly, and, at length ashamed, to laugh at himselfe; which he cannot auoyd, without auoyding the follie; who, while

circum praecordia ludit, [16]

giueth vs to feele how many head-aches a passionate life bringeth vs to—how, when all is done,

Est Vlubris, animus si nos non deficit aequus? [17]

[c.] No, perchance it is the Comick, whom naughtie Playmakers and Stage-keepers haue iustly made odious. To the argument of abuse I will answer after. Onely thus much now is to be said, that the Comedy is an imitation of the common errors of our life, which he representeth in the most ridiculous and scornefull sort that may be; so as it is impossible that any beholder can be content to be such a one.

Now, as in Geometry the oblique must bee knowne as wel as the right, and in Arithmetick the odde as well as the euen, so in the actions of our life who seeth not the filthines of euil wanteth a great foile to perceiue the beauty of vertue. This doth the Comedy handle so in our priuate and domestical matters, as with hearing it we get as it were an experience, what is to be looked for of a nigardly *Demea*, of a crafty *Dauus*, of a flattering *Gnato*, of a vaine glorious *Thraso*, and not onely to know what effects are to be expected, but to know who be such, by the signifying badge giuen them by the Comedian. And little reason hath any man to say that men learne euill by seeing it so set out: sith, as I sayd before, there is no man liuing but, by the

---

[15] "The rogue touches every vice while making his friend laugh." Persius, *Satires*, I, 116–7. The "rogue" is Horace.

[16] "Touches the heart." From the same passage in Persius.

[17] "What we seek can be found at Ulubrae [a notoriously boring place] if we keep a balanced mind." Horace, *Epistles*, I, 11, 30.

force trueth hath in nature, no sooner seeth these men play their parts, but wisheth them in *Pistrinum*: although perchance the sack of his owne faults lye so behinde hys back that he seeth not himselfe daunce the same measure; whereto yet nothing can more open his eyes then to finde his own actions contemptibly set forth.

[d.] So that the right vse of Comedy will (I thinke) by no body be blamed, and much lesse of the high and excellent Tragedy, that openeth the greatest wounds, and sheweth forth the Vlcers that are couered with Tissue; that maketh Kinges feare to be Tyrants, and Tyrants manifest their tirannicall humors; that, with sturring the affects of admiration and commiseration, teacheth the vncertainety of this world, and vpon how weake foundations guilden roofes are builded; that maketh vs knowe,

> *Qui sceptra saeuus duro imperio regit,*
> *Timet timentes, metus in auctorem redit.*[18]

But how much it can mooue, *Plutarch* yeeldeth a notable testimonie of the abhominable Tyrant *Alexander Pheraeus*; from whose eyes a Tragedy, wel made and represented, drewe abounbance of teares, who, without all pitty, had murthered infinite nombers, and some of his owne blood. So as he, that was not ashamed to make matters for Tragedies, yet coulde not resist the sweet violence of a Tragedie. And if it wrought no further good in him, it was that he, in despight of himselfe, withdrewe himselfe from harkening to that which might mollifie his hardened heart.

[e.] But it is not the Tragedy they doe mislike: For it were too absurd to cast out so excellent a representation of whatsoeuer is most worthy to be learned. Is it the Liricke that most displeaseth, who with his tuned Lyre and wel accorded voyce, giueth praise, the reward of vertue, to vertuous acts? who giues morrall precepts, and naturall Problemes, who sometimes rayseth vp his voice to the height of the heauens, in singing the laudes of the immortall God. Certainly I must confesse my own barbarousnes: I neuer heard the olde song of *Percy* and *Duglas* that I found not my heart mooued more then with a Trumpet; and

---

[18] "The cruel tyrant who rules with an iron hand fears his cowed [subjects]; fear returns to its source." Seneca, *Oedipus*, 705–6.

yet is it sung but by some blinde Crouder, with no rougher voyce then rude stile; which being so euill apparrelled in the dust and cobwebbes of that vnciuill age, what would it worke trymmed in the gorgeous eloquence of *Pindar?* In *Hungary* I haue scene it the manner at all Feasts, and other such meetings, to haue songes of their Auncestours valour; which that right Souldier-like Nation thinck the chiefest kindlers of braue courage. The incomparable *Lacedemonians* did not only carry that kinde of Musicke euer with them to the field, but euen at home, as such songs were made, so were they all content to bee the singers of them, when the lusty men were to tell what they dyd, the olde men what they had done, and the young men what they wold doe. And where a man may say that *Pindar* many times prayseth highly victories of small moment, matters rather of sport then vertue; as it may be aunswered, it was the fault of the Poet, and not of the Poetry; so indeede the chiefe fault was in the tyme and custome of the Greckes, who set those toyes at so high a price that *Phillip* of *Macedon* reckoned a horse-race wonne at *Olimpus* among hys three fearefull felicities. But as the vnimitable *Pindar* often did, so is that kinde most capable and most fit to awake the thoughts from the sleep of idlenes, to imbrace honorable enterprises.

[*f.*] There rests the Heroicall, whose very name (I thinke) should daunt all back-biters; for by what conceit can a tongue be directed to speake euill of that which draweth with it no lesse Champions then *Achilles, Cyrus, Aeneas, Turnus, Tideus,* and *Rinaldo?* who doth not onely teach and moue to a truth, but teacheth and mooueth to the most high and excellent truth; who maketh magnanimity and iustice shine throughout all misty fearefulnes and foggy desires; who, if the saying of *Plato* and *Tullie* bee true, that who could see Vertue would be wonderfully rauished with the loue of her beauty: this man sets her out to make her more louely in her holyday apparell, to the eye of any that will daine not to disdaine vntill they vnderstand. But if any thing be already sayd in the defence of sweete Poetry, all concurreth to the maintaining the Heroicall, which is not onely a kinde, but the best and most accomplished kinde of Poetry. For as the image of each action styrreth and instructeth the mind, so the loftie image of such Worthies most inflameth

the mind with desire to be worthy, and informes with counsel
how to be worthy. Only let *Aeneas* be worne in the tablet of
your memory; how he gouerneth himselfe in the ruine of his
Country; in the preseruing his old Father, and carrying away
his religious ceremonies; in obeying the Gods commandement to
leaue *Dido*, though not onely all passionate kindenes, but euen
the humane consideration of vertuous gratefulnes, would haue
craued other of him; how in storms, howe in sports, howe in
warre, howe in peace, how a fugitiue, how victorious, how
besiedged, how besiedging, howe to strangers, howe to allyes,
how to enemies, howe to his owne; lastly, how in his inward
selfe, and how in his outward gouernment; and I thinke, in a
minde not preiudiced with a preiudicating humor, hee will be
found in excellencie fruitefull, yea, euen as *Horace* sayth,

Melius Chrisippo et Crantore.[19]

But truely I imagine it falleth out with these Poet-whyppers,
as with some good women, who often are sicke, but in fayth they
cannot tel where. So the name of Poetrie is odious to them, but
neither his cause nor effects, neither the sum that containes
him nor the particularities descending from him, giue any fast
handle to their carping disprayse.

[g.] Sith then Poetrie is of all humane learning the most
auncient and of most fatherly antiquitie, as from whence other
learnings haue taken theyr beginnings; sith it is so vniuersall
that no learned Nation dooth despise it, nor no barbarous Nation
is without it; sith both Roman and Greek gaue diuine names
vnto it, the one of prophecying, the other of making; and that
indeede that name of making is fit for him, considering that
where as other Arts retaine themselues within their subiect, and
receiue, as it were, their beeing from it, the Poet onely bringeth
his owne stuffe, and dooth not learne a conceite out of a matter,
but maketh matter for a conceite; Sith neither his description
nor his ende contayneth any euill, the thing described cannot be
euill; Sith his effects be so good as to teach goodnes and to
delight the learners; Sith therein (namely in morrall doctrine,
the chiefe of all knowledges) hee dooth not onely farre passe

---

[19] "Better than [the philosophers] Chrisippus and Crantor." Horace,
Epistles, I, 2, 4.

the Historian, but, for instructing, is well nigh comparable to the Philosopher, and, for mouing, leaues him behind him; Sith the holy scripture (wherein there is no vncleannes) hath whole parts in it poeticall, and that euen our Sauiour Christ vouchsafed to vse the flowers of it; Sith all his kindes are not onlie in their vnited formes but in their seuered dissections fully commendable: I think (and think I thinke rightly) the Lawrell crowne appointed for tryumphing Captaines does worthilie (of al other learnings) honor the Poets tryumph.

[VII.] But because wee haue eares aswell as tongues, and that the lightest reasons that may be will seeme to weigh greatly, if nothing be put in the counter-ballance, let vs heare, and aswell as wee can ponder, what obiections may bee made against this Arte, which may be worthy eyther of yeelding or answering.

First, truely I note not onely in these *Mysomousoi,* Poet-haters, but in all that kinde of people who seek a prayse by dispraysing others, that they doe prodigally spend a great many wandering wordes in quips and scoffes, carping and taunting at each thing, which, by styrring the Spleene, may stay the braine from a thorough beholding the worthines of the subiect.

[*a.*] Those kinde of obiections, as they are full of very idle easines, sith there is nothing of so sacred a maiestie but that an itching tongue may rubbe it selfe vpon it, so deserue they no other answer, but, in steed of laughing at the iest, to laugh at the iester. Wee know a playing wit can prayse the discretion of an Asse, the comfortablenes of being in debt, and the iolly commoditie of beeing sick of the plague. So of the contrary side, if we will turne *Ouids* verse,

Vt lateat virtus proximitate mali,[20]

that good lye hid in neerenesse of the euill, *Agrippa* will be as merry in shewing the vanitie of Science as *Erasmus* was in commending the follie. Neyther shall any man or matter escape some touch of these smyling raylers. But for *Erasmus* and *Agrippa,* they had another foundation than the superficiall part would promise. Mary, these other pleasant Fault-finders, who wil correct the Verbe before they vnderstande the Noune, and confute others

[20] Ovid, *Ars Amatoria,* II, 662. Sidney translates the passage.

knowledge before they confirme theyr owne, I would haue them
onely remember that scoffing commeth not of wisedom. So as the
best title in true English they gette with their merriments is to be
called good fooles, for so haue our graue Fore-fathers euer termed
that humorous kinde of iesters. But that which gyueth greatest
scope to their scorning humors is ryming and versing. It is already
sayde (and, as I think, trulie sayde) it is not ryming and versing
that maketh Poesie. One may bee a Poet without versing, and a
versifyer without Poetry. But yet presuppose it were inseparable
(as indeede it seemeth *Scaliger* iudgeth) [21] truelie it were an inseparable commendation. For if *Oratio* next to *Ratio*, Speech next
to Reason, bee the greatest gyft bestowed vpon mortalitie, that
can not be praiselesse which dooth most pollish that blessing of
speech, which considers each word, not only (as a man may say)
by his forcible qualitie but by his best measured quantitie, carrying euen in themselues a Harmonie (without, perchaunce, Number, Measure, Order, Proportion be in our time growne odious).
But lay a side the iust prayse it hath, by beeing the onely fit
speech for Musick (Musick I say, the most diuine striker of the
sences), thus much is vndoubtedly true, that if reading bee foolish
without remembring, memorie being the onely treasurer of knowl-
ed[g]e, those words which are fittest for memory are likewise
most conuenient for knowledge.

Now, that Verse farre exceedeth Prose in the knitting vp of the
memory, the reason is manifest; the words (besides theyr delight,
which hath a great affinitie to memory) beeing so set as one word
cannot be lost but the whole worke failes: which accuseth it selfe,
calleth the remembrance backe to it selfe, and so most strongly
confirmeth it; besides, one word so, as it were, begetting another,
as, be it in ryme or measured verse, by the former a man shall
haue a neere gesse to the follower: lastly, euen they that haue
taught the Art of memory haue shewed nothing so apt for it as a
certaine roome deuided into many places well and thoroughly
knowne. Now, that hath the verse in effect perfectly, euery word
hauing his naturall seate, which seate must needes make the words
remembred. But what needeth more in a thing so knowne to all
men? who is it that euer was a scholler that doth not carry away

[21] *Poetices libri septem*, I, 2.

some verses of *Virgill, Horace,* or *Cato,* which in his youth he learned, and euen to his old age serue him for howrely lessons? But the fitnes it hath for memory is notably proued by all deliuery of Arts: wherein for the most part, from Grammer to Logick, Mathematick, Phisick, and the rest, the rules chiefely necessary to bee borne away are compiled in verses. So that, verse being in it selfe sweete and orderly, and beeing best for memory, the onely handle of knowledge, it must be in iest that any man can speake against it.

[*b.*] Nowe then goe wee to the most important imputations laid to the poore Poets: for ought I can yet learne, they are these. First, that there beeing many other more fruitefull knowledges, a man might better spend his tyme in them then in this. Secondly, that it is the mother of lyes. Thirdly, that it is the Nurse of abuse, infecting vs with many pestilent desires; with a Syrens sweetnes, drawing the mind to the Serpents tayle of sinfull fancy. And heerein, especially, Comedies giue the largest field to erre, as *Chaucer* sayth: howe both in other Nations and in ours, before Poets did soften vs, we were full of courage, giuen to martiall exercises, the pillers of manlyke liberty, and not lulled a sleepe in shady idlenes with Poets pastimes. And lastly, and chiefely, they cry out with an open mouth, as if they out shot *Robin Hood,* that *Plato* banished them out of hys Common-wealth. Truely, this is much, if there be much truth in it. First to the first: that a man might better spend his tyme is a reason indeed: but it doth (as they say) but *Petere principium:* [22] for if it be, as I affirme, that no learning is so good as that which teacheth and mooueth to vertue, and that none can both teach and moue thereto so much as Poetry, then is the conclusion manifest that Incke and Paper cannot be to a more profitable purpose employed. And certainly, though a man should graunt their first assumption, it should followe (me thinkes) very vnwillingly, that good is not good because better is better. But I still and vtterly denye that there is sprong out of earth a more fruitefull knowledge. To the second therefore, that they should be the principall lyars, I aunswere paradoxically, but, truely, I thinke truely, that of all Writers vnder the sunne the Poet is the least lier, and, though he would, as a

---

[22] A logical expression roughly equivalent to "beg the question."

Poet can scarcely be a lyer. The Astronomer, with his cosen the Geometrician, can hardly escape, when they take vpon them to measure the height of the starres. How often, thinke you, doe the Phisitians lye, when they auer things good for sicknesses, which afterwards send *Charon* a great nomber of soules drownd in a potion before they come to his Ferry? And no lesse of the rest, which take vpon them to affirme. Now, for the Poet, he nothing affirmes, and therefore neuer lyeth. For, as I take it, to lye is to affirme that to be true which is false. So as the other Artists, and especially the Historian, affirming many things, can, in the cloudy knowledge of mankinde, hardly escape from many lyes. But the Poet (as I sayd before) neuer affirmeth. The Poet neuer maketh any circles about your imagination, to coniure you to beleeue for true what he writes. Hee citeth not authorities of other Histories, but euen for hys entry calleth the sweete Muses to inspire into him a good inuention; in troth, not labouring to tell you what is, or is not, but what should or should not be: and therefore, though he recount things not true, yet because hee telleth them not for true, he lyeth not, without we will say that *Nathan* lyed in his speech, before alledged, to *Dauid*. Which as a wicked man durst scarce say, so think I none so simple would say that *Esope* lyed in the tales of his beasts: for who thinks that *Esope* writ it for actually true were well worthy to haue his name cronicled among the beastes hee writeth of. What childe is there that, comming to a Play, and seeing *Thebes* written in great Letters vpon an olde doore, doth beleeue that it is *Thebes?* If then a man can ariue, at that childs age, to know that the Poets persons and dooings are but pictures what should be, and not stories that haue beene, they will neuer giue the lye to things not affirmatiuely but allegorically and figuratiuelie written. And therefore, as in Historie, looking for trueth, they goe away full fraught with falsehood, so in Poesie, looking for fiction, they shal vse the narration but as an imaginatiue groundplot of a profitable inuention.

But heereto is replyed, that the Poets gyue names to men they write of, which argueth a conceite of an actuall truth, and so, not being true, prooues a falshood. And doth the Lawyer lye then, when vnder the names of *Iohn a stile* and *Iohn a noakes* hee puts his case? But that is easily answered. Theyr naming of men is but to make theyr picture the more liuely, and not to builde any historie; paynting men, they cannot leaue men namelesse. We see we cannot play at Chesse but that wee must giue names to our Chesse-men; and yet, mee thinks, hee were a very partiall Champion of truth that would say we lyed for giuing a peece of wood the reuerend title of a Bishop. The Poet nameth *Cyrus* or *Aeneas* no other way then to shewe what men of theyr fames, fortunes, and estates should doe.

[*c.*] Their third is, how much it abuseth mens wit, trayning it to wanton sinfulnes and lustfull loue: for indeed that is the principall, if not the onely abuse I can heare alledged. They say the Comedies rather teach then reprehend amorous conceits. They say the Lirick is larded with passionate Sonnets: The Elegiack weepes the want of his mistresse: And that euen to the Heroical *Cupid* hath ambitiously climed. Alas, Loue, I would thou couldest as well defende thy selfe as thou canst offende others. I would those, on whom thou doost attend, could eyther put thee away, or yeelde good reason why they keepe thee. But grant loue of beautie to be a beastlie fault (although it be very hard, sith onely man, and no beast, hath that gyft to discerne beauty). Grant that louely name of Loue to deserue all hatefull reproches (although euen some of my Maisters the Phylosophers spent a good deale of theyr Lamp-oyle in setting foorth the excellencie of it). Grant, I say, what soeuer they wil haue granted; that not onely loue, but lust, but vanitie, but (if they list) scurrilitie, possesseth many leaues of the Poets bookes: yet thinke I, when this is granted, they will finde theyr sentence may with good manners put the last words foremost, and not say that Poetrie abuseth mans wit, but that mans wit abuseth Poetrie.

For I will not denie but that mans wit may make Poesie (which should be *Eikastike*, which some learned haue defined, figuring foorth good things) to be *Phantastike*: [23] which doth, contrariwise, infect the fancie with vnworthy obiects. As the Painter, that shoulde giue to the eye eyther some excellent perspectiue, or some fine picture, fit for building or fortification, or contayning

[23] The distinction between *eikastic* and *phantastic* was debated in Italy by Mazzoni and Tasso. Mazzoni believed that poetry was *phantastic*—fictional and hence related to sophistic, the branch of logic dealing with falsehood made to seem like truth. Tasso, like Sidney, felt that poetry was *eikastic*—based upon probabilities and related to dialectic.

in it some notable example, as *Abraham* sacrificing his Sonne *Isaack*, *Iudith* killing *Holofernes*, *Dauid* fighting with *Goliath*, may leaue those, and please an ill-pleased eye with wanton shewes of better hidden matters. But what, shall the abuse of a thing make the right vse odious? Nay truely, though I yeeld that Poesie may not onely be abused, but that beeing abused, by the reason of his sweete charming force, it can doe more hurt then any other Armie of words, yet shall it be so far from concluding that the abuse should giue reproch to the abused, that contrari-wise it is a good reason, that whatsoeuer, being abused, dooth most harme, beeing rightly vsed (and vpon the right vse each thing conceiueth his title), doth most good.

Doe wee not see the skill of Phisick (the best rampire to our often-assaulted bodies) beeing abused, teach poyson, the most violent destroyer? Dooth not knowledge of Law, whose end is to euen and right all things being abused, grow the crooked fosterer of horrible iniuries? Doth not (to goe to the highest) Gods word abused breed heresie? and his Name abused become blasphemie? Truely, a needle cannot doe much hurt, and as truely (with leaue of Ladies be it spoken) it cannot doe much good. With a sword thou maist kill thy Father, and with a sword thou maist defende thy Prince and Country. So that, as in their calling Poets the Fathers of lyes they say nothing, so in this theyr argument of abuse they prooue the commendation.

They alledge heere-with, that before Poets beganne to be in price our Nation hath set their harts delight vpon action, and not vpon imagination: rather doing things worthy to bee written, then writing things fitte to be done. What that before tyme was, I thinke scarcely *Sphinx* can tell: Sith no memory is so auncient that hath the precedence of Poetrie. And certaine it is that, in our plainest homelines, yet neuer was the *Albion* Nation without Poetrie. Mary, thys argument, though it bee leaueld against Poetrie, yet is it indeed a chaine-shot against all learning, or bookishnes, as they commonly tearme it. Of such minde were certaine *Gothes*, of whom it is written that, hauing in the spoile of a famous Citie taken a fayre librarie, one hangman (bee like fitte to execute the fruites of their wits), who had murthered a great number of bodies, would haue set fire on it: 'no,' sayde another very grauely, 'take heede what you doe, for whyle they are busie about these toyes, wee shall with more leysure conquer their Countries.'

This indeede is the ordinary doctrine of ignorance, and many wordes sometymes I haue heard spent in it: but because this reason is generally against all learning, aswell as Poetrie, or rather, all learning but Poetry; because it were too large a digression to handle, or at least to superfluous (sith it is manifest that all gouernment of action is to be gotten by knowledg, and knowledge best by gathering many knowledges, which is reading), I onely, with *Horace,* to him that is of that opinion,

Iubeo stultum esse libenter: [24]

for as for Poetrie it selfe, it is the freest from thys obiection. For Poetrie is the companion of the Campes.

I dare vndertake, *Orlando Furioso,* or honest King *Arthur,* will neuer displease a Souldier: but the quiddity of *Ens* and *Prima materia* will hardely agree with a Corslet: and therefore, as I said in the beginning, euen Turks and Tartares are delighted with Poets. *Homer,* a Greek, florished before Greece florished. And if to a slight coniecture a coniecture may be opposed, truly it may seeme, that as by him their learned men tooke almost their first light of knowledge, so their actiue men receiued their first motions of courage. Onlie *Alexanders* example may serue, who by *Plutarch* is accounted of such vertue, that Fortune was not his guide but his foote-stoole: whose acts speake for him, though *Plutarch* did not; indeede the Phœnix of warlike Princes. This *Alexander* left his Schoolemaister, liuing *Aristotle,* bchinde him, but tooke deade *Homer* with him: he put the Philosopher *Calisthenes* to death for his seeming philosophicall, indeed mutinous, stubburnnes; but the chiefe thing he euer was heard to wish for was that *Homer* had been aliue. He well found he receiued more brauerie of minde bye the patterne of *Achilles* then by hearing the definition of Fortitude: and therefore, if *Cato* misliked *Fuluius* for carying *Ennius* with him to the fielde, it may be aunswered that, if *Cato* misliked it, the noble *Fuluius* liked it, or els he had not doone it: for it was not the excellent *Cato Vticensis* (whose authority I would much more haue reuerenced), but it was the

[24] "I bid him be stupid to his heart's content." Intentionally misquoted from Horace, *Satires,* I, 1, 65.

former, in truth a bitter punisher of faults, but else a man that had neuer wel sacrificed to the Graces. Hee misliked and cryed out vpon all Greeke learning, and yet, being 80 yeeres olde, began to learne it; be-like fearing that *Pluto* vnderstood not Latine. Indeede, the Romaine lawes allowed no person to be carried to the warres but hee that was in the Souldiers role: and therefore, though *Cato* misliked his vnmustered person, hee misliked not his worke. And if hee had, *Scipio Nasica*, iudged by common consent the best Romaine, loued him. Both the other *Scipio* Brothers, who had by their vertues no lesse surnames then of *Asia* and *Affrick*, so loued him that they caused his body to be buried in their Sepulcher. So as *Cato* his authoritie being put against his person, and that aunswered with so farre greater then himselfe, is heerein of no validitie.

[*d.*] But now indeede my burthen is great; now *Plato* his name is layde vpon mee, whom, I must confesse, of all Philosophers I haue euer esteemed most worthy of reuerence, and with great reason, sith of all Philosophers he is the most poeticall. Yet if he will defile the Fountaine out of which his flowing streames haue proceeded, let vs boldly examine with what reasons hee did it. First truly, a man might maliciously obiect that *Plato*, being a Philosopher, was a naturall enemie of Poets: for indeede, after the Philosophers had picked out of the sweete misteries of Poetrie the right discerning true points of knowledge, they forthwith, putting it in method, and making a Schoole-arte of that which the Poets did onely teach by a diuine delightfulnes, beginning to spurne at their guides, like vngratefull Prentises, were not content to set vp shops for themselues, but sought by all meanes to discredit their Maisters. Which by the force of delight beeing barred them, the lesse they could ouerthrow them, the more they hated them. For indeede, they found for *Homer* seauen Cities stroue who should haue him for their Citizen; where many Citties banished Philosophers as not fitte members to liue among them. For onely repeating certaine of *Euripides* verses, many *Athenians* had their lyues saued of the *Siracusians*; when the *Athenians* themselues thought many Philosophers vnwoorthie to liue. Certaine Poets, as *Simonides* and *Pindarus*, had so preuailed with *Hiero* the first, that of a Tirant they made him a iust King, where *Plato* could do so little with *Dionisius*, that he himselfe of a Philosopher was made a slaue. But who should doe thus, I confesse, should requite the obiections made against Poets with like cauillation against Philosophers, as likewise one should doe that should bid one read *Phædrus* or *Symposium* in *Plato*, or the discourse of loue in *Plutarch*, and see whether any Poet doe authorize abhominable filthines, as they doe. Againe, a man might aske out of what Common-wealth *Plato* did banish them? insooth, thence where he himselfe alloweth communitie of women. So as belike this banishment grewe not for effeminate wantonnes, sith little should poeticall Sonnets be hurtfull when a man might haue what woman he listed. But I honor philosophicall instructions, and blesse the wits which bred them: so as they be not abused, which is likewise stretched to Poetrie.

S. *Paule* himselfe, who (yet for the credite of Poets) alledgeth twise two Poets, and one of them by the name of a Prophet, setteth a watch-word vpon Philosophy, indeede vpon the abuse. So dooth *Plato* vpon the abuse, not vpon Poetrie. *Plato* found fault that the Poets of his time filled the worlde with wrong opinions of the Gods, making light tales of that vnspotted essence; and, therefore, would not haue the youth depraued with such opinions. Heerin may much be said: let this suffice: the Poets did not induce such opinions, but dyd imitate those opinions already induced. For all the Greek stories can well testifie that the very religion of that time stoode vpon many, and many-fashioned, Gods, not taught so by the Poets, but followed according to their nature of imitation. Who list may reade in *Plutarch* the discourses of *Isis* and *Osiris*, of the cause why Oracles ceased, of the diuine prouidence, and see whether the Theologie of that nation stood not vpon such dreames which the Poets indeed supersticiously obserued, and truly (sith they had not the light of Christ) did much better in it then the Philosophers, who, shaking off superstition, brought in Atheisme. *Plato* therefore (whose authoritie I had much rather iustly conster then vniustly resist) meant not in general of Poets, in those words of which *Iulius* Scaliger saith, *Qua authoritate barbari quidam atque hispidi abuti velint ad Poetas e republica exigendos;* [25] but only meant

---

[25] "This authority certain barbaric and crude people wish to use to expell poets from the state." *Poetices libri septem,* I, 2.

to driue out those wrong opinions of the Deitie (whereof now, without further law, Christianity hath taken away all the hurtful beliefe), perchance (as he thought) norished by the then esteemed Poets. And a man need goe no further then to *Plato* himselfe to know his meaning: who, in his Dialogue called *Ion,* giueth high and rightly diuine commendation to Poetrie.[26] So as *Plato,* banishing the abuse, not the thing, not banishing it, but giuing due honor vnto it, shall be our Patron and not our aduersarie. For indeed I had much rather (sith truly I may doe it) shew theyr mistaking of *Plato* (vnder whose Lyons skin they would make an Asse-like braying against Poesie) then goe about to ouerthrow his authority, whom the wiser a man is the more iust cause he shall find to haue in admiration; especially sith he attributeth vnto Poesie more then my selfe doe, namely, to be a very inspiring of a diuine force, farre aboue mans wit, as in the afore-named Dialogue is apparant.

Of the other side, who wold shew the honors haue been by the best sort of iudgements granted them, a whole Sea of examples woulde present themselues: *Alexanders, Cæsars, Scipios,* al fauorers of Poets; *Lelius,* called the Romane *Socrates,* him selfe a Poet, so as part of *Heautontimorumenos* in *Terence* was supposed to be made by him. And euen the Greek *Socrates,* whom *Apollo* confirmed to be the onely wise man, is sayde to haue spent part of his old tyme in putting *Esops* fables into verses. And therefore, full euill should it become his scholler *Plato* to put such words in his Maisters mouth against Poets. But what need more? *Aristotle* writes the Arte of Poesie: and why, if it should not be written? *Plutarch* teacheth the vse to be gathered of them, and how, if they should not be read? And who reades *Plutarchs* eyther historie or philosophy shall finde hee trymmeth both theyr garments with gards of Poesie.

[*e.*] But I list not to defend Poesie with the helpe of her vnderling Historiography. Let it suffise that it is a fit soyle for prayse to dwell vpon; and what dispraise may set vpon it, is eyther easily ouer-come, or transformed into iust commendation. So that, sith the excellencies of it may be so easily and so iustly

---

[26] Sidney probably read the *Ion* in the light of Marsilio Ficino's enthusiastic but somewhat uncritical preface to his Latin translation of the dialogue.

confirmed, and the low-creeping obiections so soone troden
downe; it not being an Art of lyes, but of true doctrine; not of
effeminatenes, but of notable stirring of courage; not of abusing
mans witte, but of strengthning mans wit; not banished, but
honored by *Plato*; let vs rather plant more Laurels for to en-
garland our Poets heads (which honor of beeing laureat, as
besides them onely tryumphant Captaines weare, is a sufficient
authority to shewe the price they ought to be had in) then suffer
the ill-fauouring breath of such wrong-speakers once to blowe
vpon the cleere springs of Poesie.

[VIII.] But sith I haue runne so long a careere in this matter,
me thinks, before I giue my penne a fulle stop, it shalbe but a little
more lost time to inquire why England (the Mother of excellent
mindes) should bee growne so hard a step-mother to Poets, who
certainly in wit ought to passe all other; sith all onely proceedeth
from their wit, being indeede makers of themselues, not takers
of others. How can I but exclaime,

Musa mihi causas memora, quo numine laeso.[27]

Sweete Poesie, that hath aunciently had Kings, Emperors, Sen-
ators, great Captaines, such as, besides a thousand others, *Dauid,
Adrian, Sophocles, Germanicus,* not onely to favour Poets, but to
be Poets. And of our neerer times can present for her Patrons a
Robert, king of Sicil, the great king *Francis* of France, King *Iames*
of Scotland. Such Cardinals as *Bembus* and *Bibiena.* Such famous
Preachers and Teachers as *Beza* and *Melancthon.* So learned
Philosophers as *Fracastorius* and *Scaliger.* So great Orators as
Pontanus and *Muretus.* So piercing wits as *George Buchanan.*
So graue Counsellors as, besides many, but before all, that *Hos-
pitall* of Fraunce, then whom (I thinke) that Realme neuer
brought forth a more accomplished iudgement, more firmely
builded vpon vertue. I say these, with numbers of others, not
onely to read others Poesies, but to Poetise for others reading.
That Poesie, thus embraced in all other places, should onely finde
in our time a hard welcome in England, I thinke the very earth
lamenteth it, and therfore decketh our Soyle with fewer Laurels

[27] "O muse recall the causes; what godhead was offended. . . ." *Aeneid,*
I, 8.

then it was accustomed. For heertofore Poets haue in England also florished; and, which is to be noted, euen in those times when the trumpet of *Mars* did sounde loudest. And now that an ouer-faint quietnes should seeme to strew the house for Poets, they are almost in as good reputation as the *Mountibancks* at *Venice.* Truly euen that, as of the one side it giueth great praise to Poesie, which like *Venus* (but to better purpose) hath rather be troubled in the net with *Mars* then enioy the homelie quiet of *Vulcan;* so serues it for a peece of a reason why they are lesse gratefull to idle England, which nowe can scarce endure the payne of a pen. Vpon this necessarily followeth, that base men with seruile wits vndertake it: who think it inough if they can be rewarded of the Printer. And so as *Epaminondas* is sayd, with the honor of his vertue, to haue made an office, by his exercising it, which before was contemptible, to become highly respected; so these, no more but setting their names to it, by their owne disgracefulnes disgrace the most gracefull Poesie. For now, as if all the Muses were gotte with childe, to bring foorth bastard Poets, without any commission they doe poste ouer the banckes of *Helicon,* tyll they make the readers more weary then Post-horses; while, in the mean tyme, they,

Queis meliore luto finxit praecordia Titan,[28]

are better content to suppresse the out-flowing of their wit, then by publishing them to bee accounted Knights of the same order. But I that, before euer I durst aspire vnto the dignitie, am ad-mitted into the company of the Paper-blurrers, doe finde the very true cause of our wanting estimation is want of desert; taking vpon vs to be Poets in despight of *Pallas.* Nowe, wherein we want desert were a thanke-worthy labour to expresse: but if I knew, I should haue mended my selfe. But I, as I neuer desired the title, so haue I neglected the meanes to come by it. Onely, ouer-mastred by some thoughts, I yeelded an inckie tribute vnto them. Mary, they that delight in Poesie it selfe should seeke to knowe what they doe, and how they doe; and, especially, looke them-selues in an vnflattering Glasse of reason, if they bee inclinable vnto it. For Poesie must not be drawne by the eares; it must bee

---

[28] "Whose hearts Titan made with finer earth." Juvenal, *Satires,* XIV, 34–5.

gently led, or rather it must lead. Which was partly the cause
that made the auncient-learned affirme it was a diuine gift, and no
humaine skill: sith all other knowledges lie ready for any that
hath strength of witte: A Poet no industrie can make, if his owne
Genius bee not carried vnto it: and therefore is it an old Prouerbe,
Orator fit, Poeta nascitur.[29] Yet confesse I alwayes that as the
firtilest ground must bee manured, so must the highest flying wit
haue a *Dedalus* to guide him. That *Dedalus,* they say, both in this
and in other, hath three wings to beare it selfe vp into the ayre
of due commendation: that is, Arte, Imitation, and Exercise. But
these, neyther artificiall rules nor imitatiue patternes, we much
cumber our selues withall. Exercise indeede wee doe, but that very
fore-backwardly: for where we should exercise to know, wee
exercise as hauing knowne: and so is oure braine deliuered of
much matter which neuer was begotten by knowledge. For, there
being two principal parts, matter to be expressed by wordes and
words to expresse the matter, in neyther wee vse Arte or Imitation rightly. Our matter is *Quodlibet* indeed, though wrongly
perfourming *Ouids* verse

Quicquid conabar dicere versus erit: [30]

neuer marshalling it into an assured rancke, that almost the
readers cannot tell where to finde themsclucs.

Chaucer, vndoubtedly, did excellently in hys *Troylus* and *Cres-
seid*; of whom, truly, I know not whether to meruaile more, either
that he in that mistie time could see so clearely, or that wee in
this cleare age walke so stumblingly after him. Yet had he great
wants, fitte to be forgiuen in so reuerent antiquity. I account the
Mirrour of Magistrates meetely furnished of beautiful parts; and
in the Earle of Surries *Liricks* many things tasting of a noble
birth, and worthy of a noble minde. The *Sheapheards Kalender*
hath much Poetrie in his Eglogues: indeede worthy the reading,
if I be not deceiued. That same framing of his stile to an old
rustick language I dare not alowe, sith neyther *Theocritus* in
Greeke, *Virgill* in Latine, nor *Sanazar* in Italian did affect it. Besides these, doe I not remember to haue seene but fewe (to
speake boldely) printed, that haue poeticall sinnewes in them:

[29] "The orator is made; the poet is born."
[30] "Whatever I shall try to say, it will be verse." Ovid, *Tristia,* IV, 10, 26.

for proofe whereof, let but most of the verses bee put in Prose,
and then aske the meaning; and it will be found that one verse
did but beget another, without ordering at the first what should
be at the last; which becomes a confused masse of words, with
a tingling sound of ryme, barely accompanied with reason.

Our Tragedies and Comedies (not without cause cried out
against), obseruing rules neyther of honest ciuilitie nor of skilfull
Poetrie, excepting *Gorboduck* (againe, I say, of those that I haue
seene), which notwithstanding, as it is full of stately speeches and
well sounding Phrases, clyming to the height of *Seneca* his stile,
and as full of notable moralitie, which it doth most delightfully
teach, and so obtayne the very end of Poesie, yet in troth it is
very defectious in the circumstaunces, which greeueth mee, because it might not remaine as an exact model of all Tragedies.
For it is faulty both in place and time, the two necessary companions of all corporall actions. For where the stage should
alwaies represent but one place, and the vttermost time presup-
posed in it should be, both by *Aristotles* precept and common
reason, but one day, there is both many dayes, and many places,
inartificially imagined. But if it be so in *Gorboduck*, how much
more in al the rest? where you shal haue *Asia* of the one side,
and *Affrick* of the other, and so many other vnder-kingdoms, that
the Player, when he commeth in, must euer begin with telling
where he is, or els the tale wil not be conceiued. Now ye shal
haue three Ladies walke to gather flowers, and then we must
beleeue the stage to be a Garden. By and by, we heare newes of
shipwracke in the same place, and then wee are to blame if we
accept it not for a Rock. Vpon the backe of that, comcs out a
hidious Monster, with fire and smoke, and then the miserable
beholders are bounde to take it for a Caue. While in the meantime
two Armies flye in, represented with foure swords and bucklers,
and then what harde heart will not receiue it for a pitched fielde?
Now, of time they are much more liberall, for ordinary it is that
two young Princes fall in loue. After many trauerces, she is got
with childe, deliuered of a faire boy; he is lost, groweth a man,
falls in loue, and is ready to get another child; and all this in
two hours space: which how absurd it is in sence euen sence may
imagine, and Arte hath taught, and all auncient examples iustified,
and, at this day, the ordinary Players in Italie wil not erre in. Yet

wil some bring in an example of *Eunuchus* in *Terence,* that
containeth matter of two dayes, yet far short of twenty yeeres.
True it is, and so was it to be playd in two daies, and so fitted
to the time it set forth. And though *Plautus* hath in one place
done amisse, let vs hit with him, and not misse with him. But
they wil say, how then shal we set forth a story, which containeth
both many places and many times? And doe they not knowe
that a Tragedie is tied to the lawes of Poesie, and not of Historie?
not bound to follow the storie, but, hauing liberty, either to faine
a quite newe matter, or to frame the history to the most tragicall
conuenicncie. Againe, many things may be told which cannot be
shewed, if they knowe the differcnce betwixt reporting and representing. As, for example, I may speake (though I am heere) of
Peru, and in speech digresse from that to the description of
Calicut; but in action I cannot represent it without *Pacolets* horse:
and so was the manner the Aunciuents tooke, by some *Nuncius,*
to recount thinges done in former time or other place. Lastly, if
they wil reprcsent an history, they must not (as *Horace* saith)
beginne *Ab ouo,* but they must come to the principall poynt of
that one action which they wil represent. By example this wil be
best exprcsscd. I haue a story of young *Polidorus,* deliuered for
safeties sake, with great riches, by his Father *Priamus* to *Polim-
nestor,* king of *Thrace,* in the Troyan war time. Hee after some
yeeres, hearing the ouer-throwe of *Priamus,* for to make the
treasure his owne, murthereth the child; the body of the child is
taken vp by *Hecuba;* shee the same day findeth a slight to bee
reuenged most cruelly of the Tyrant: where nowe would one of
our Tragedy writers begin, but with the deliuery of the childe?
Then should he sayle ouer into *Thrace,* and so spend I know not
how many yeeres, and trauaile numbers of places. But where
dooth *Euripides?* Euen with the finding of the body, leauing the
rest to be tolde by the spirit of *Polidorus.* This need no further to
be inlarged; the dullest wit may conceiue it.

But besides these grosse absurdities, how all theyr Playes be
neither right Tragedies, nor right Comedies; mingling Kings and
Clownes, not because the matter so carrieth it, but thrust in
Clownes by head and shoulders, to play a part in maiesticall
matters, with neither decencie nor discretion: So as neither the
admiration and commiseration, nor the right sportfulnes, is by

their mungrell Tragy-comedie obtained. I know *Apuleius* did some-what so, but that is a thing recounted with space of time, not represented in one moment: and I knowe the Auncients haue one or two examples of Tragy-comedies, as *Plautus* hath *Amphitrio*. But, if we marke them well, we shall find, that they neuer, or very daintily, match Horn-pypes and Funeralls. So falleth it out that, hauing indeed no right Comedy, in that comicall part of our Tragedy we haue nothing but scurrility, vnwoorthy of any chast eares, or some extreame shew of doltishness, indeed fit to lift vp a loude laughter, and nothing els: where the whole tract of a Comedy shoulde be full of delight, as the Tragedy shoulde be still maintained in a well raised admiration. But our Comedians thinke there is no delight without laughter; which is very wrong, for though laughter may come with delight, yet commeth it not of delight, as though delight should be the cause of laughter; but well may one thing breed both together: nay, rather in themselues they haue, as it were, a kind of contrarietie: for delight we scarcely doe but in things that haue a conueniencie to our selues or to the generall nature: laughter almost euer commeth of things most disproportioned to our selues and nature. Delight hath a ioy in it, either permanent or present. Laughter hath onely a scornful tickling. For example, we are rauished with delight to see a faire woman, and yet are far from being moued to laughter. We laugh at deformed creatures, wherein certainely we cannot delight. We delight in good chaunces, we laugh at mischaunces; we delight to heare the happines of our friends, or Country, at which he were worthy to be laughed at that would laugh; wee shall, contrarily, laugh sometimes to finde a matter quite mistaken and goe downe the hill agaynst the byas, in the mouth of some such men, as for the respect of them one shalbe hartely sorry, yet he cannot chuse but laugh; and so is rather pained then delighted with laughter. Yet deny I not but that they may goe well together; for as in *Alexanders* picture well set out wee delight without laughter, and in twenty mad Anticks we laugh without delight, so in *Hercules,* painted with his great beard and furious countenance, in womans attire, spinning at *Omphales* commaundment, it breedeth both delight and laughter. For the representing of so strange a power in loue procureth delight: and the scornefulnes of the action stirreth laughter. But I speake to this purpose, that all the end of the comicall part bee not vpon such scornefull matters as stirreth laughter onely, but, mixt with it, that delightful teaching which is the end of Poesie. And the great fault euen in that point of laughter, and forbidden plainely by *Aristotle,* is that they styrre laughter in sinfull things, which are rather execrable then ridiculous: or in miserable, which are rather to be pittied then scorned. For what is it to make folkes gape at a wretched Begger, or a beggerly Clowne? or, against lawe of hospitality, to iest at straungers, because they speake not English so well as wee doe? what do we learne? sith it is certaine

> *Nil habet infelix paupertas durius in se,*
> *Quam quod ridiculos homines facit.*[31]

But rather a busy louing Courtier, a hartles threatening *Thraso,* a selfe-wise-seeming schoolemaster, a awry-transformed Traueller: These if wee sawe walke in stage names, which wee play naturally, therein were delightfull laughter, and teaching delightfulnes: as in the other, the Tragedies of *Buchanan* doe iustly bring forth a diuine admiration. But I haue lauished out too many wordes of this play matter. I doe it because as they are excelling parts of Poesie, so is there none so much vsed in England, and none can be more pittifully abused. Which like an vnmannerly Daughter, shewing a bad education, causeth her mother Poesies honesty to bee called in question.

Other sorts of Poetry almost haue we none, but that Lyricall kind of Songs and Sonnets: which, Lord, if he gaue vs so good mindes, how well it might be imployed, and with howe heauenly fruite, both priuate and publique, in singing the prayses of the immortall beauty, the immortall goodnes of that God who gyueth vs hands to write and wits to conceiue; of which we might well want words, but neuer matter; of which we could turne our eies to nothing, but we should euer haue new budding occasions. But truely many of such writings as come vnder the banner of vnresistable loue, if I were a Mistres, would neuer perswade mee they were in loue; so coldely they apply fiery speeches, as men that had rather red Louers writings, and so caught vp certaine swelling phrases, which hang together like a man which once tolde mee

---

[31] "Harsh poverty has nothing worse than this—that it makes men ridiculous." Juvenal, *Satires,* III, 152–3.

the winde was at North West, and by South, because he would
be sure to name windes enowe,—then that in truth they feele
those passions, which easily (as I think) may be bewrayed by
that same forciblenes, or *Energia* (as the Greekes cal it), of the
writer. But let this bee a sufficient though short note, that wee
misse the right vse of the materiall point of Poesie.

Now, for the out-side of it, which is words, or (as I may tearme
it) *Diction*, it is euen well worse. So is that honny-flowing Matron
Eloquence apparelled, or rather disguised, in a Curtizan-like
painted affectation: one time with so farre fette words, they may
seeme Monsters, but must seeme straungers to any poore English
man; another tyme, with coursing of a Letter, as if they were
bound to followe the method of a Dictionary; an other tyme, with
figures and flowers, extreamelie winter-starued. But I would this
fault were only peculier to Versifiers, and had not as large possession among Prose-printers, and (which is to be meruailed)
among many Schollers, and (which is to be pittied) among some
Preachers. Truly I could wish, if at least I might be so bold to
wish in a thing beyond the reach of my capacity, the diligent
imitators of *Tullie* and *Demosthenes* (most worthy to be imitated) did not so much keep *Nizolian* Paper-bookes [32] of their
figures and phrases, as by attentiue translation (as it were)
deuoure them whole, and make them wholly theirs. For nowe
they cast Sugar and Spice vpon euery dish that is serued to the
table; like those Indians, not content to weare eare-rings at the fit
and naturall place of the eares, but they will thrust Iewels through
their nose and lippes, because they will be sure to be fine. *Tullie*,
when he was to driue out *Catiline*, as it were with a Thunder-bolt
of eloquence, often vsed that figure of repitition, *Viuit. viuit? imo
in Senatum venit &c.* [33] Indeed, inflamed with a well-grounded
rage, hee would haue his words (as it were) double out of his
mouth; and so doe that artificially which we see men doe in
choller naturally. And wee, hauing noted the grace of those words,

[32] *Nizolian* Paper-bookes. An allusion to the notorious *Thesaurus Ciceronianus* of Marius Nizolius (1498?–1576), a low point in servile imitation of
Cicero.

[33] "He lives. He lives? Indeed, and comes to the senate." Based on
Cicero, *In Catalinum*, I, 2.

hale them in sometime to a familier Epistle, when it were too much choller to be chollerick.

Now for similitudes, in certaine printed discourses, I thinke all Herbarists, all stories of Beasts, Foules, and Fishes are rifled vp, that they come in multitudes to waite vpon any of our conceits; which certainly is as absurd a surfet to the eares as is possible: for the force of a similitude not being to prooue anything to a contrary Disputer but onely to explane to a willing hearer, when that is done, the rest is a most tedious pratling, rather ouer-swaying the memory from the purpose whereto they were applyed then any whit informing the iudgement, already eyther satisfied, or by similitudes not to be satisfied. For my part, I doe not doubt, when *Antonius* and *Crassus*, the great forefathers of *Cicero* in eloquence, the one (as *Cicero* testifieth of them) pretended not to know Arte, the other not to set by it, because with a playne sensiblenes they might win credit of popular eares; which credit is the neerest step to perswasion; which perswasion is the chiefe marke of Oratory;—I doe not doubt (I say) but that they vsed these tracks very sparingly, which who doth generally vse any man may see doth daunce to his owne musick; and so be noted by the audience more careful to speake curiously then to speake truly.

Vndoubtedly (at least to my opinion vndoubtedly) I haue found in diuers smally learned Courtiers a more sounde stile then in some professors of learning: of which I can gesse no other cause, but that the Courtier, following that which by practise hee findeth fittest to nature, therein (though he know it not) doth according to Art, though not by Art: where the other, vsing Art to shew Art, and not to hide Art (as in these cases he should doe), flyeth from nature, and indeede abuseth Art.

But what? me thinkes I deserue to be pounded for straying from Poetrie to Oratorie: but both haue such an affinity in this wordish consideration, that I thinke this digression will make my meaning receiue the fuller vnderstanding: which is not to take vpon me to teach Poets howe they should doe, but onely, finding my selfe sick among the rest, to shewe some one or two spots of the common infection growne among the most part of Writers: that, acknowledging our selues somewhat awry, we may bend to the

right use both of matter and manner; whereto our language
gyueth vs great occasion, beeing indeed capable of any excellent
exercising of it. I know some will say it is a mingled language.
And why not so much the better, taking the best of both the
other? Another will say it wanteth Grammer. Nay truly, it hath
that prayse, that it wanteth not Grammer: for Grammer it might
haue, but it needes it not; beeing so easie of it selfe, and so
voyd of those cumbersome differences of Cases, Genders, Moodes,
and Tenses, which I thinke was a peece of the Tower of *Babilons*
curse, that a man should be put to schoole and learne his mother-
tongue. But for the vttering sweetly and properly the conceits
of the minde, which is the end of speech, that hath it equally
with any other tongue in the world: and is particulerly happy in
compositions of two or three words together, neere the Greeke,
far beyond the Latine: which is one of the greatest beauties can
be in a language.

Now, of versifying ther are two sorts, the one Auncient, the
other Moderne: the Auncient marked the quantitie of each silable,
and according to that framed his verse; the Moderne obseruing
onely number (with some regarde of the accent), the chiefe life
of it standeth in that lyke sounding of the words, which wee call
Ryme. Whether of these be the most excellent, would beare many
speeches. The Auncient (no doubt) more fit for Musick, both
words and tune obseruing quantity, and more fit liuely to expresse
diuers passions, by the low and lofty sounde of the well-weyed
silable. The latter likewise, with hys Ryme, striketh a certaine
musick to the eare: and, in fine, sith it dooth delight, though by
another way, it obtaines the same purpose: there beeing in eyther
sweetnes, and wanting in neither maiestie. Truely the English,
before any other vulgar language I know, is fit for both sorts:
for, for the Ancient, the Italian is so full of Vowels that it must
euer be cumbred with *Elisions*; the Dutch so, of the other side,
with Consonants, that they cannot yeeld the sweet slyding fit for
a Verse; the French, in his whole language, hath not one word
that hath his accent in the last silable, sauing two, called
Antepenultima; and little more hath the Spanish: and, therefore,
very gracelesly may they vse *Dactiles*. The English is subject to
none of these defects.

Nowe, for the ryme, though wee doe not obserue quantity, yet wee obserue the accent very precisely: which other languages eyther cannot doe or will not doe so absolutely. That *Cæsura*, or breathing place in the middest of the verse, neither Italian nor Spanish haue, the French, and we, neuer almost fayle of. Lastly, euen the very ryme it selfe the Italian cannot put in the last silable, by the French named the Masculine ryme, but still in the next to the last, which the French call the Female, or the next before that, which the Italians terme *Sdrucciola.* The example of the former is *Buono, Suono,* of the *Sdrucciola, Femina, Semina.* The French, of the other side, hath both the Male, as *Bon, Son,* and the Female, as *Plaise, Taise.* But the *Sdrucciola* hee hath not: where the English hath all three, as *Due, True, Father, Rather, Motion, Potion*; with much more which might be sayd, but that I finde already the triflingnes of this discourse is much too much enlarged.

[IX.] So that sith the euer-praise-worthy Poesie is full of vertue-breeding delightfulnes, and voyde of no gyfte that ought to be in the noble name of learning: sith the blames laid against it are either false or feeble; sith the cause why it is not esteemed in Englande is the fault of Poet-apes, not Poets; sith, lastly, our tongue is most fit to honor Poesie, and to bee honored by Poesie; I coniure you all that haue had the euill lucke to reade this inckewasting toy of mine, euen in the name of nyne Muses, no more to scorne the sacred misteries of Poesie, no more to laugh at the name of Poets, as though they were next inheritours to Fooles, no more to iest at the reuerent title of a Rymer; but to beleeue, with *Aristotle,* that they were the auncient Treasurers of the Græcians Diuinity. To beleeue, with *Bembus,* that they were first bringers in of all ciuilitie. To beleeue, with Scaliger, that no Philosophers precepts can sooner make you an honest man then the reading of *Virgill.* To beleeue, with *Clauserus,* the Translator of *Cornutus,* that it pleased the heauenly Deitie, by *Hesiod* and *Homer,* vnder the vayle of fables, to giue vs all knowledge, Logick, Rethorick, Philosophy, naturall and morall; and *Quid non?* To beleeue, with me, that there are many misteries contained in Poetrie, which of purpose were written darkely, least by prophane wits it should bee abused. To beleeue, with *Landin,* that they are so beloued of the Gods that whatsoeuer they write proceeds of a diuine fury. Lastly, to beleeue themselues, when they tell you they will make you immortall by their verses.

Thus doing, your name shal florish in the Printers shoppes; thus doing, you shall bee of kinne to many a poeticall Preface; thus doing, you shall be most fayre, most ritch, most wise, most all; you shall dwell vpon Superlatiues. Thus dooing, though you be *Libertino patre natus,* you shall suddenly grow *Herculea proles,*[34]

Si quid mea carmina possunt.[35]

Thus doing, your soule shal be placed with *Dantes Beatrix,* or *Virgils Anchises.* But if (fie of such a but) you be borne so neere the dull making *Cataphract* of *Nilus* that you cannot heare the Plannet-like Musick of Poetrie, if you haue so earth-creeping a mind that it cannot lift it selfe vp to looke to the sky of Poetry, or rather, by a certaine rusticall disdaine, will become such a Mome as to be a *Momus* of Poetry; then, though I will not wish vnto you the Asses eares of *Midas,* nor to bee driuen by a Poets verses (as *Bubonax* was) to hang himselfe, nor to be rimed to death, as is sayd to be doone in Ireland; yet thus much curse I must send you, in the behalfe of all Poets, that while you liue, you liue in loue, and neuer get fauor for lacking skill of a *Sonnet*; and when you die, your memory die from the earth for want of an *Epitaph.*

[34] ". . . though you be the son of a freedman, you shall suddenly grow [i.e., become] a child of Hercules."
[35] "If my songs are of any avail." Virgil, *Aeneid,* IX, 446.

George Puttenham

[1532?–1590]

❧⭓❧

THE *Arte of English Poesie*, ascribed to George Puttenham, appeared in 1589. It is in three books. Book I ("Of Poets and Poesie") treats the history, purpose, and kinds of poetry; Book II ("Of Proportion"), stanzaic forms and prosody; Book III ("Of Ornament"), style and decorum. The organization reflects the influence of rhetoric books like Cicero's *De Oratore* as adapted to criticism by such Italian writers as Bernardino Daniello (*La Poetica*, 1536). The *Arte of English Poesie* is the fullest and most characteristic of the Elizabethan arts of poetry. It appears to have been influenced by Sidney's *Apologie*, which circulated widely in manuscript before publication; otherwise, its sources are classical rhetoric, Horace, and minor late classical critics. The author was well-read in ancient and contemporary literature but seems to have been less interested than Sidney in the Italian revival of Aristotle. The ascription of the work to George Puttenham is based on statements by Richard Carew (in Camden's *Remains*, 1614) and Edmund Bolton (*Hypercritica*, 1618?), but has occasionally been challenged.

The present selections, based on the edition of 1589, cover the main topics of Books I and III. Book II is of less general interest than the other two. Its most important feature is its vacillation between the claims of quantitative and accentual prosody. Chapter XIII wistfully suggests that "if all maner of sodaine innovations were not very scandalous . . . . the use of the Greeke and Latine feete might be brought into our vulgar poesie, and with good grace inough."

BIBLIOGRAPHY. *The Arte of English Poesie by George Puttenham*, ed. G. Willcock and A. Walker (1936).

from

THE ARTE OF ENGLISH POESIE

[1589]

THE FIRST BOOKE
OF POETS AND POESIE

CHAP. I.

WHAT A POET AND POESIE IS, AND WHO MAY BE WORTHILY
SAYD THE MOST EXCELLENT POET OF OUR TIME.

A POET IS AS MUCH to say as a maker. And our English name well
conformes with the Greeke word, for of ποιεῖν, to make, they call
a maker *Poeta*. Such as (by way of resemblance and reuerently)
we may say of God; who without any trauell to his diuine imagination made all the world of nought, nor also by any paterne or
mould, as the Platonicks with their Idees do phantastically suppose. Euen so the very Poet makes and contriues out of his owne
braine both the verse and matter of his poeme, and not by any
foreine copie or example, as doth the translator, who therefore
may well be sayd a versifier, but not a Poet. The premises considered, it giueth to the name and profession no smal dignitie
and preheminence, aboue all other artificers, Scientificke or Mechanicall. And neuerthelesse, without any repugnancie at all, a
Poet may in some sort be said a follower or imitator, because he
can express the true and liuely [image] of euery thing is set before
him, and which he taketh in hand to describe: and so in that respect is both a maker and a counterfaitor: and Poesie an art not
only of making, but also of imitation. And this science in his perfection can not grow but by some diuine instinct—the Platonicks
call it *furor*; or by excellencie of nature and complexion; or by
great subtiltie of the spirits & wit; or by much experience and observation of the world, and course of kinde; or peraduenture, by all
or most part of them. Otherwise, how was it possible that *Homer,*

being but a poore priuate man, and, as some say, in his later age
blind, should so exactly set foorth and describe, as if he had bene
a most excellent Captaine or Generall, the order and array of
battels, the conduct of whole armies, the sieges and assaults of
cities and townes? or, as some great Princes maiordome and perfect Surueyour in Court, the order, sumptuousnesse, and magnificence of royal bankets, feasts, weddings, and enteruewes? or,
as a Polititian very prudent and much inured with the priuat and
publique affaires, so grauely examine the lawes and ordinances
Ciuill, or so profoundly discourse in matters of estate and formes
of all politique regiment? Finally, how could he so naturally
paint out the speeches, countenance, and maners of Princely
persons and priuate, to wit, the wrath of *Achilles*, the magnanimitie of *Agamemnon*, the prudence of *Menelaus*, the prowesse
of *Hector*, the maiestie of king *Priamus*, the grauitie of *Nestor*,
the pollicies and eloquence of *Vlysses*, the calamities of the dis-
tressed *Queenes*, and valiance of all the Captaines and aduenturous knights in those lamentable warres of Troy? It is therefore
of Poets thus to be conceiued, that if they be able to deuise and
make all these things of them selues, without any subiect of
veritie, that they be (by maner of speech) as creating gods. If
they do it by instinct diuine or naturall, then surely much fauoured from aboue; if by their experience, then no doubt very
wise men; if by any president or paterne layd before them, then
truly the most excellent imitators & counterfaitors of all others.
But you (Madame) [1] my most Honored and Gracious, if I should
seeme to offer you this my deuise for a discipline and not a delight, I might well be reputed of all others the most arrogant and
iniurious, your selfe being alreadie, of any that I know in our
time, the most excellent Poet; forsooth by your Princely purse,
fauours, and countenance, making in maner what ye list, the poore
man rich, the lewd well learned, the coward couragious, and vile
both noble and valiant: then for imitation no lesse, your person
as a most cunning counterfaitor liuely representing *Venus* in
countenance, in life *Diana*, *Pallas* for gouernement, and *Iuno* in
all honour and regall magnificence.

---

[1] The work is dedicated to Queen Elizabeth.

CHAP. II.

THAT THERE MAY BE AN ART OF OUR ENGLISH POESIE, ASWELL AS THERE IS OF THE LATINE AND GREEKE.

Then as there was no art in the world till by experience found out, so if Poesie be now an Art, & of al antiquitie hath bene among the Greeks and Latines, & yet were none vntill by studious persons fashioned and reduced into a method of rules and precepts, then no doubt may there be the like with vs. And if th'art of Poesie be but a skill appertaining to vtterance, why may not the same be with vs aswel as with them, our language being no less copious, pithie, and significatiue then theirs, our conceipts the same, and our wits no less apt to deuise and imitate then theirs were? If againe Art be but a certaine order of rules prescribed by reason, and gathered by experience, why should not Poesie be a vulgar Art with vs aswell as with the Greeks and Latines, our language admitting no fewer rules and nice diuersities then theirs? but peraduenture moe by a peculiar [ity], which our speech hath in many things differing from theirs; and yet, in the generall points of that Art, allowed to go in common with them: so as if one point perchance, which is their feete whereupon their measures stand, and in deede is all the beautie of their Poesie, and which feete we haue not, nor as yet neuer went about to frame (the nature of our language and wordes not permitting it), we haue in stead thereof twentie other curious points in that skill more then they euer had, by reason of our rime and tunable concords or simphonie, which they neuer obserued. Poesie therefore may be an Art in our vulgar, and that verie methodicall and commendable.

CHAP. III.

HOW POETS WERE THE FIRST PRIESTS, THE FIRST PROPHETS, THE FIRST LEGISLATORS AND POLITITIANS IN THE WORLD.

The profession and vse of Poesie is most ancient from the beginning, and not, as manie erroniously suppose, after, but before, any ciuil society was among men. For it is written that Poesie was th'originall cause and occasion of their first assemblies, when before the people remained in the woods and mountains, vagrant and dispersed like the wild beasts, lawlesse and naked, or verie ill clad, and of all good and necessarie prouision for harbour or sustenance vtterly vnfurnished, so as they litle diffred for their maner of life from the very brute beasts of the field. Whereupon it is fayned that *Amphion* and *Orpheus,* two Poets of the first ages, one of them, to wit *Amphion,* builded vp cities, and reared walles with the stones that came in heapes to the sound of his harpe, figuring thereby the mollifying of hard and stonie hearts by his sweete and eloquent perswasion. And *Orpheus* assembled the wilde beasts to come in heards to harken to his musicke, and by that meanes made them tame, implying thereby, how by his discreete and wholesome lesons vttered in harmonie and with melodious instruments he brought the rude and sauage people to a more ciuill and orderly life, nothing, as it seemeth, more preuailing or fit to redresse and edifie the cruell and sturdie courage of man then it. And as these two poets, and *Linus* before them, and *Museus* also and *Hesiodus* in Greece and Archadia, so by all likelihood had mo Poets done in other places and in other ages before them, though there be no remembrance left of them, by reason of the Recordes by some accident of time perished and failing. Poets therefore are of great antiquitie. Then forasmuch as they were the first that entended to the obseruation of nature and her works, and specially of the Celestiall courses, by reason of the continuall motion of the heauens, searching after the first mouer, and from thence by degrees comming to know and consider of the substances separate & abstract, which we call the diuine intelligences or good Angels (*Demones*), they were the first that instituted sacrifices of placation, with inuocations and worship to them, as to Gods; and inuented and stablished all the rest of the obseruances and ceremonies of religion, and so were the first Priests and ministers of the holy misteries. And because for the better execution of that high charge and function it behoued them to liue chast, and in all holines of life, and in continual studie and contemplation, they came by instinct diuine, and by deepe meditation, and much abstinence (the same assubtiling and refining their spirits) to be made apt to receaue visions, both waking and sleeping, which made them vtter prophesies and foretell things to come. So also were they the first Prophetes or seears, *Videntes,* for so the Scripture tearmeth them in Latine after the Hebrue word, and all the oracles and answers of the gods were giuen in meeter or verse, and published to the people by their direction. And for that they were aged and graue men, and of much wisedome and experience in th'affaires of the world, they were the first lawmakers to the people, and the first polititiens, deuising all expedient meanes for th'establishment of Common wealth, to hold and containe the people in order and duety by force and vertue of good and wholesome lawes, made for the preseruation of the publique peace and tranquillitie: the same peraduenture not purposely intended, but greatly furthered by the aw of their gods and such scruple of conscience as the terrors of their late inuented religion had led them into.

CHAP. IV.

HOW POETS WERE THE FIRST PHILOSOPHERS, THE FIRST ASTRONOMERS AND HISTORIOGRAPHERS AND ORATOURS AND MUSITIENS OF THE WORLD.

Vtterance also and language is giuen by nature to man for per-swasion of others and aide of them selues, I meane the first abilite to speake. For speech it selfe is artificiall and made by man, and the more pleasing it is, the more it preuaileth to such purpose as it is intended for: but speech by meeter is a kind of vtterance more cleanly couched and more delicate to the eare then prose is, because it is more currant and slipper vpon the tongue, and withal tunable and melodious, as a kind of Musicke, and therfore may be tearmed a musicall speech or vtterance, which cannot but please the hearer very well. Another cause is, for that is briefer & more compendious, and easier to beare away and be retained in memorie, then that which is contained in multitude of words and full of tedious ambage and long periods. It is beside a maner of vtterance more eloquent and rethoricall then the or-dinarie prose which we vse in our daily talke, because it is decked and set out with all maner of fresh colours and figures, which maketh that it sooner inuegleth the iudgement of man, and carieth his opinion this way and that, whither soeuer the heart by impression of the eare shalbe most affectionatly bent and di-rected. The vtterance in prose is not of so great efficacie, because

not only it is dayly vsed, and by that occasion the eare is ouer-
glutted with it, but is also not so voluble and slipper vpon the
tongue, being wide and lose, and nothing numerous, nor con-
triued into measures and sounded with so gallant and harmonical
accents, nor, in fine, alowed that figuratiue conueyance nor so
great license in choise of words and phrases as meeter is. So as
the Poets were also from the beginning the best perswaders, and
their eloquence the first Rethoricke of the world, euen so it became that the high mysteries of the gods should be reuealed &
taught by a maner of vtterance and language of extraordinarie
phrase, and briefe and compendious, and aboue al others sweet
and ciuill as the Metricall is. The same also was meetest to register
the liues and noble gests of Princes, and of the great Monarkes
of the world, and all other the memorable accidents of time: so
as the Poet was also the first historiographer. Then forasmuch as
they were the first obseruers of all naturall causes & effects in the
things generable and corruptible, and from thence mounted vp
to search after the celestiall courses and influences, & yet pene-
trated further to know the diuine essences and substances separate, as is sayd before, they were the first Astronomers and Philos-
ophists and Metaphisicks. Finally, because they did altogether
endeuor them selues to reduce the life of man to a certaine
method of good maners, and made the first differences betweene
vertue and vice, and then tempered all these knowledges and
skilles with the exercise of a delectable Musicke by melodious instruments, which withall serued them to delight their hearers, &
to call the people together by admiration to a plausible and vertuous conuersation, therefore were they the first Philosophers
Ethick, & the first artificial Musicians of the world. Such was
Linus, Orpheus, Amphion, & *Museus,* the most ancient Poets and
Philosophers of whom there is left any memorie by the prophane
writers. King *Dauid* also & *Salomon* his sonne and many other of
the holy Prophets wrate in meeters, and vsed to sing them to the
harpe, although to many of vs, ignorant of the Hebrue language
and phrase, and not obseruing it, the same seeme but a prose. It
can not bee therefore that anie scorne or indignitie should iustly
be offred to so noble, profitable, ancient, and diuine a science as
Poesie is.

CHAP. V.

And the Greeke and Latine Poesie was by verse numerous and metricall, running vpon pleasant feete, sometimes swift, sometime slow (their words very aptly seruing that purpose) but without any rime or tunable concord in th'end of their verses, as we and all other nations now vse. But the Hebrues & Chaldees, who were more ancient then the Greekes, did not only vse a metricall Poesie, but also with the same a maner of rime, as hath bene of late obserued by learned men. Wherby it appeareth that our vulgar running Poesie was common to all the nations of the world besides, whom the Latines and Greekes in speciall called barbarous. So as it was, notwithstanding, the first and most ancient Poesie, and the most vniuersall; which two points do otherwise giue to all humane inuentions and affaires no small credit. This is proued by certificate of marchants and trauellers, who by late nauigations haue surueyed the whole world, and discouered large countries and strange peoples wild and sauage, affirming that the American, the Perusine, and the very Canniball do sing and also say their highest and holiest matters in certaine riming versicles, and not in prose, which proues also that our maner of vulgar Poesie is more ancient then the artificiall of the Greeks and Latines, ours comming by instinct of nature, which was before Art or obseruation, and vsed with the sauage and unciuill, who were before all science or ciuilitie, euen as the naked by prioritie of time is before the clothed, and the ignorant before the learned. The naturall Poesie therefore, being aided and amended by Art, and not vtterly altered or obscured, but some signe left of it (as the Greekes and Latines haue left none), is no lesse to be allowed and commended then theirs.

CHAP. VI.

But it came to passe, when fortune fled farre from the Greekes and Latines, & that their townes florished no more in traficke, nor their Vniuersities in learning as they had done continuing those Monarchies, the barbarous conquerers inuading them with innumerable swarmes of strange nations, the Poesie metricall of the Grecians and Latines came to be much corrupted and altered, in so much as there were times that the very Greekes and Latines themselues tooke pleasure in Riming verses, and vsed it as a rare and gallant thing. Yea, their Oratours proses nor the Doctors Sermons were acceptable to Princes nor yet to the common people, vnlesse it went in manner of tunable rime or metricall sentences, as appeares by many of the auncient writers about that time and since. And the great Princes, and Popes, and Sultans would one salute and greet an other sometime in friendship and sport, sometime in earnest and enmitie, by ryming verses, & nothing seemed clerkly done, but must be done in ryme. Whereof we finde diuers examples from the time of th'Emperours Gracian & Valentinian downwardes: For then aboutes began the declination of the Romain Empire, by the notable inundations of the *Hunnes* and *Vandalles* in Europe, vnder the conduict of *Totila* & *Atila* and other their generalles. This brought the ryming Poesie in grace, and made it preuaile in Italic and Greece (their owne long time cast aside, and almost neglected), till after many yeares that the peace of Italie and of th'Empire Occidentall reuiued new clerkes, who, recouering and perusing the bookes and studies of the ciuiler ages, restored all maner of arts, and that of the Greeke and Latine Poesie withall, into their former puritie and netnes. Which neuerthelesse did not so preuaile but that the ryming Poesie of the Barbarians remained still in his reputation, that one in the schole, this other in Courts of Princes more ordinary and allowable.

CHAP. VIII

[POETRY AND PHANTASY]

. . . in these dayes, although some learned Princes may take delight in them [poets], yet vniuersally it is not so. For as well Poets as Poesie are despised, & the name become of honorable infamous, subiect to scorne and derision, and rather a reproch than a prayse to any that vseth it: for commonly who so is studious in th'Arte or shewes him selfe excellent in it, they call him in disdayne a *phantasticall*; and a light headed or phantasticall man (by conuersion) they call a Poet. And this proceedes through the barbarous ignoraunce of the time, and pride of many Gentlemen and others, whose grosse heads not being brought vp or acquainted with any excellent Arte, nor able to contriue or in manner conceiue any matter of subtiltie in any businesse or science, they doe deride and scorne it in all others as superfluous knowledges and vayne sciences, and whatsoeuer deuise be of rare inuention they terme it *phantasticall*, construing it to the worst side: and among men such as be modest and graue, & of litle conuersation, nor delighted in the busie life and vayne ridiculous actions of the popular, they call him in scorne a *Philosopher* or *Poet*, as much to say as a phantasticall man, very iniuriously (God wot), and to the manifestation of their own ignoraunce, not making difference betwixt termes. For as the euill and vicious disposition of the braine hinders the sounde iudgement and discourse of man with busie & disordered phantasies, for which cause the Greekes call him φανταστικός, so is that part, being well affected, not onely nothing disorderly or confused with any monstruous imaginations or conceits, but very formall, and in his much multiformitie *vniforme*, that is well proportioned, and so passing cleare, that by it, as by a glasse or mirrour, are represented vnto the soule all maner of bewtifull visions, whereby the inuentiue parte of the mynde is so much holpen as without it no man could deuise any new or rare thing: and where it is not excellent in his kind, there could be no politique Captaine, nor any witty enginer or cunning artificer, nor yet any law maker or counsellor of deepe discourse, yea, the Prince of Philosophers stickes not to say *animam non intelligere absque phantasmate*; [2] which text to another purpose *Alexander Aphrodis[i]ens[is]* well noteth, as learned men know. And this phantasie may be resembled to a glasse, as hath bene sayd, whereof there be many tempers and manner of makinges, as the *perspectiues* doe acknowledge, for some be false glasses and shew thinges otherwise than they be in deede, and others right as they be in deede, neither fairer nor fouler, nor greater nor smaller. There be againe of these glasses that shew thinges exceeding faire and comely; others that shew figures very monstruous & illfauored. Euen so is the phantasticall

[2] "The soul cannot know without phantasms." Aristotle, *De Anima*, III, 7.

part of man (if it be not disordered) a representer of the best, most comely, and bewtifull images or apparances of thinges to the soule and according to their very truth. If otherwise, then doth it breede *Chimeres* & monsters in mans imaginations, & not onely in his imaginations, but also in his ordinarie actions and life which ensues. Wherefore such persons as be illuminated with the brightest irradiations of knowledge and of the veritie and due proportion of things, they are called by the learned men not *phantastici* but *euphantasioti*, and of this sorte of phantasie are all good Poets, notable Captaines stratagematique, all cunning artificers and enginers, all Legislators, Polititiens, & Counsellours of estate, in whose exercises the inuentiue part is most employed, and is to the sound and true iudgement of man most needful. This diuersitie in the termes perchance euery man hath not noted, & thus much be said in defence of the Poets honour, to the end no noble and generous minde be discomforted in the studie thereof. . . .

CHAP. X.

THE SUBIECT OR MATTER OF POESIE.

Hauing sufficiently sayd of the dignitie of Poets and Poesie, now it is tyme to speake of the matter or subiect of Poesie, which to myne intent is what soeuer wittie and delicate conceit of man meet or worthy to be put in written verse, for any necessary vse of the present time, or good instruction of the posteritie. But the chief and principal is the laud, honour, & glory of the immortall gods (I speake now in phrase of the Gentiles): secondly, the worthy gests of noble Princes, the memoriall and registry of all great fortunes, the praise of vertue & reproofe of vice, the instruction of morall doctrines, the reuealing of sciences naturall & other profitable Arts, the redresse of boistrous & sturdie courages by perswasion, the consolation and repose of temperate myndes: finally, the common solace of mankind in all his trauails and cares of this transitorie life; and in this last sort, being vsed for recreation onely, may allowably beare matter not alwayes of the grauest or of any great commoditie or profit, but rather in some sort vaine, dissolute, or wanton, so it be not very scandalous & of euill example. But as our intent is to make this Art vulgar for all English mens vse, & therefore are of necessitie to set downe the principal rules therein to be obserued, so in mine opinion it is no lesse expedient to touch briefly all the chief points of this auncient Poesie of the Greeks and Latines, so far forth as it conformeth with ours. So as it may be knowen what we hold of them as borrowed, and what as of our owne peculiar. Wherefore, now that we haue said what is the matter of Poesie, we will declare the manner and formes of poemes vsed by the auncients.

CHAP. XI.

OF POEMS AND THEIR SUNDRY FORMES, AND HOW THEREBY THE AUNCIENT POETS RECEAUED SURNAMES.

As the matter of Poesie is diuers, so was the forme of their poemes & maner of writing, for all of them wrote not in one sort, euen as all of them wrote not vpon one matter. Neither was euery Poet alike cunning in all, as in some one kinde of Poesie, nor vttered with like felicitie. But wherein any one most excelled, thereof he tooke a surname, as to be called a Poet *Heroick, Lyrick, Elegiack, Epigrammatist,* or otherwise. Such therefore as gaue themselues to write long histories of the noble gests of kings & great Princes entermedling the dealings of the gods, halfe gods, or *Heroes* of the gentiles, & the great & waighty consequences of peace and warre, they called Poets *Heroick,* whereof *Homer* was chief and most auncient among the Greeks, *Virgill* among the Latines: Others who more delighted to write songs or ballads of pleasure, to be song with the voice, and to the harpe, lute, or citheron, & such other musical instruments, they were called melodious Poets (*melici*), or, by a more common name, *Lirique* Poets: of which sort was *Pindarus, Anacreon,* and *Callimachus,* with others among the Greeks, *Horace* and *Catullus* among the Latines. There were an other sort, who sought the fauor of faire Ladies, and coueted to bemone their estates at large & the perplexities of loue in a certain pitious verse called *Elegie,* and thence were called *Elegiack*: such among the Latines were *Ouid, Tibullus,* & *Propertius.* There were also Poets that wrote onely for the stage, I meane playes and interludes, to recreate the people with matters of disporte, and to that intent did set forth

in shewes [&] pageants, accompanied with speach, the common
behauiours and maner of life of priuate persons, and such as were
the meaner sort of men, and they were called *Comicall* Poets: of
whom among the Greekes *Menander* and *Aristophanes* were most
excellent, with the Latines *Terence* and *Plautus*. Besides those
Poets *Comick* there were other who serued also the stage, but
medled not with so base matters, for they set forth the dolefull
falles of infortunate & afflicted Princes, & were called Poets
Tragicall: such were *Euripides* and *Sophocles* with the Greeks,
Seneca among the Latines. There were yet others who mounted
nothing so high as any of them both, but, in base and humble
stile by maner of Dialogue, vttered the priuate and familiar talke
of the meanest sort of men, as shepheards, heywards, and such
like: such was among the Greekes *Theocritus*, and *Virgill* among
the Latines; their poems were named *Eglogues* or shepheardly
talke. There was yet another kind of Poet, who intended to taxe
the common abuses and vice of the people in rough and bitter
speaches, and their inuectiues were called *Satyres*, and them
selues *Satyricques*: such were *Lucilius, Iuuenall,* and *Persius*
among the Latines, & with vs he that wrote the booke called Piers
plowman. Others of a more fine and pleasant head were giuen
wholly to taunting and scoffing at vndecent things, and in short
poemes vttered pretie merry conceits, and these men were called
Epigrammatistes. There were others that for the peoples good
instruction, and triall of their owne witts, vsed in places of great
assembly to say by rote nombers of short and sententious meetres,
very pithie and of good edification, and thereupon were called
Poets *Mimistes*, as who would say, imitable and meet to be followed for their wise and graue lessons. There was another kind
of poeme, inuented onely to make sport & to refresh the company
with a maner of buffonry or counterfaiting of merry speaches,
conuerting all that which they had hard spoken before to a certaine derision by a quite contrary sence, and this was done when
Comedies or *Tragedies* were a playing, & that betweene the actes
when the players went to make ready for another, there was great
silence, and the people waxt weary, then came in these maner of
conterfait vices; they were called *Pantomimi,* and all that had
before bene sayd, or great part of it, they gaue a crosse construc-

tion to it very ridiculously. Thus haue you how the names of the
Poets were giuen them by the formes of their poemes and maner
of writing.

CHAP. XII.

IN WHAT FORME OF POESIE THE GODS OF THE GENTILES WERE PRAYSED AND HONORED.

The gods of the Gentiles were honoured by their Poetes in
hymnes, which is an extraordinarie and diuine praise, extolling
and magnifying them for their great powers and excellencie of
nature in the highest degree of laude; and yet therein their Poets
were after a sort restrained, so as they could not with their credit
vntruly praise their owne gods, or vse in their lauds any maner
of grosse adulation or vnueritable report. For in any writer
vntruth and flatterie are counted most great reproches. Wherfore
to praise the gods of the Gentiles, for that by authoritie of their
owne fabulous records they had fathers and mothers, and kindred
and allies, and wiues and concubines, the Poets first commended
them by their genealogies or pedegrees, their mariages and
aliances, their notable exploits in the world for the behoofe of
mankind, and yet, as I sayd before, none otherwise then the truth
of their owne memorials might beare, and in such sort as it might
be well auouched by their old written reports, though in very
deede they were not from the beginning all historically true, and
many of them verie fictions, and such of them as were true were
grounded vpon some part of an historie or matter of veritie, the
rest altogether figuratiue & misticall, couertly applied to some
morall or natural sense, as *Cicero* setteth it foorth in his bookes
de natura deorum. For to say that *Iupiter* was sonne to *Saturne*,
and that he maried his owne sister *Iuno*, might be true, for such
was the guise of all great Princes in the Orientall part of the
world both at those dayes and now is. Againe, that he loued
Danae, Europa, Leda, Cal[l]isto, & other faire Ladies, daughters
to kings, besides many meaner women, it is likely enough, because he was reported to be a very incontinent person and giuen
ouer to his lustes, as are for the most part all the greatest Princes;
but that he should be the highest god in heauen, or that he should
thunder and lighten, and do manie other things very vnnaturally

and absurdly, also that *Saturnus* should geld his father *Coelus,* to th'intent to make him vnable to get any moe children, and other such matters as are reported by them, it seemeth to be some wittie deuise and fiction made for a purpose, or a very no[ta]ble and impudent lye, which could not be reasonably suspected by the Poets, who were otherwise discreete and graue men, and teachers of wisedome to others. Therefore either to transgresse the rules of their primitiue records or to seeke to giue their gods honour by belying them (otherwise then in that sence which I haue alledged) had bene a signe not onely of an vnskilfull Poet but also of a very impudent and leude man. . . .

. . . And these hymnes to the gods was the first forme of Poesie and the highest & the stateliest, & they were song by the Poets as priests, and by the people or whole congregation, as we sing in our Churches the Psalmes of *Dauid,* but they did it commonly in some shadie groues of tall tymber trees: In which places they reared aulters of green turfe, and bestrewed them all ouer with flowers, and vpon them offred their oblations and made their bloudy sacrifices (for no kinde of gift can be dearer then life) of such quick cattaille, as euery god was in their conceit most delighted in, or in some other respect most fit for the misterie: temples or churches or other chappels then these they had none at those dayes.

CHAP. XIII.

IN WHAT FORME OF POESIE VICE AND THE COMMON ABUSES OF MANS LIFE WAS REPREHENDED.

Some perchance would thinke that next after the praise and honoring of their gods should commence the worshippings and praise of good men, and specially of great Princes and gouernours of the earth in soueraignety and function next vnto the gods. But it is not so, for before that came to passe the Poets or holy Priests chiefly studied the rebuke of vice, and to carpe at the common abuses, such as were most offensiue to the publique and priuate, for as yet for lacke of good ciuility and wholesome doctrines there was greater store of lewde lourdaines then of wise and learned Lords or of noble and vertuous Princes and gouernours. So as next after the honours exhibited to their gods, the Poets, finding in

man generally much to reproue & litle to praise, made certaine
poems in plaine meetres, more like to sermons or preachings
then otherwise, and when the people were assembled togither
in those hallowed places dedicate to their gods, because they had
yet no large halles or places of conuenticle, nor had any other
correction of their faults, but such as rested onely in rebukes of
wise and graue men, such as at these dayes make the people
ashamed rather then afeard, the said aunctient Poets vsed for that
purpose three kinds of poems reprehensiue, to wit, the *Satyre,*
the *Comedie,* and the *Tragedie.* And the first and most bitter
inuectiue against vice and vicious men was the *Satyre*: which,
to th'intent their bitternesse should breede none ill will, either to
the Poets, or to the recitours (which could not haue bene chosen
if they had bene openly knowen), and besides to make their
admonitions and reproofs seme grauer and of more efficacie, they
made wise as if the gods of the woods, whom they called *Satyres*
or *Siluanes,* should appeare and recite those verses of rebuke,
whereas in deede they were but disguised persons vnder the
shape of *Satyres,* as who would say, these terrene and base gods,
being conuersant with mans affaires, and spiers out of all their
secret faults, had some great care ouer man, & desired by good
admonitions to reforme the euill of their life, and to bring the
bad to amendment by those kinde of preachings; whereupon the
Poets inuentours of the deuise were called *Satyristes.*

CHAP. XIV.

HOW VICE WAS AFTERWARD REPROUVED BY TWO OTHER MANER OF POEMS, BETTER REFORMED THEN THE SATYRE, WHEREOF THE FIRST WAS COMEDY, THE SECOND TRAGEDIE.

But when these maner of solitary speaches and recitals of rebuke, vttered by the rurall gods out of bushes and briers, seemed
not to the finer heads sufficiently perswasiue, nor so popular
as if it were reduced into action of many persons, or by many
voyces liuely represented to the eare and eye, so as a man might
thinke it were euen now a doing, the Poets deuised to haue
many parts played at once by two or three or foure persons, that
debated the matters of the world, sometimes of their owne priuate
affaires, sometimes of their neighbours, but neuer medling with

any Princes matters nor such high personages, but commonly of marchants, souldiers, artificers, good honest housholders, and also of vnthrifty youthes, yong damsels, old nurses, bawds, brokers, ruffians, and parasites, with such like, in whose behauiors lyeth in effect the whole course and trade of mans life, and therefore tended altogither to the good amendment of many by discipline and example. It was also much for the solace & recreation of the common people by reason of the pageants and shewes. And this kind of poeme was called *Comedy*, and followed next after the *Satyre*, & by that occasion was somewhat sharpe and bitter after the nature of the *Satyre*, openly & by expresse names taxing men more maliciously and impudently then became, so as they were enforced for feare of quarrel & blame to disguise their players with strange apparell, and by colouring their faces and carying halts & capps of diuerse fashions to make them selues lesse knowen. But as time & experience do reforme euery thing that is amisse, so, this bitter poeme called the old *Comedy* being disused and taken away, the new *Comedy* came in place, more ciuill and pleasant a great deale, and not touching any man by name, but in a certaine generalitie glancing at euery abuse, so as from thenceforth fearing none illwill or enmitie at any bodies hands they left aside their disguisings and playcd bare face, till one *Roscius Gallus*, the most excellent player among the Romaines, brought vp these vizards which we see at this day vsed, partly to supply the want of players, when there were moe parts than there were persons, or that it was not thought meet to trouble & pester princes chambers with too many folkes. Now by the chaunge of a vizard one man might play the king and the carter, the old nurse & the yong damsell, the marchant and the souldier, or any other part he listed very conueniently. There be that say *Roscius* did it for another purpose, for being him selfe the best *Histrien* or buffon that was in his dayes to be found, insomuch as *Cicero* said *Roscius* contended with him by varietie of liuely gestures to surmount the copy of his speach, yet because he was squint eyed and had a very vnpleasant countenance, and lookes which made him ridiculous or rather odious to the presence, he deuised these vizards to hide his owne ilfauored face. And thus much touching the *Comedy*.

CHAP. XV.

But because in those days when the Poets first taxed by *Satyre* and *Comedy* there was no great store of Kings or Emperors or such high estats (al men being yet for the most part rude, & in a maner popularly egall), they could not say of them or of their behauiours any thing to the purpose, which cases of Princes are sithens taken for the highest and greatest matters of all. But after that some men among the moe became mighty and famous in the world, soueraignetie and dominion hauing learned them all maner of lusts and licentiousnes of life, by which occasions also their high estates and felicities fell many times into most lowe and lamentable fortunes: whereas before in their great prosperities they were both feared and reuerenced in the highest degree, after their deathes, when the posteritie stood no more in dread of them, their infamous life and tyrannies were layd open to all the world, their wickednes reproched, their follies and extreme insolencies derided, and their miserable ends painted out in playes and pageants, to shew the mutabilitie of fortune, and the iust punishment of God in reuenge of a vicious and evill life. These matters were also handled by the Poets, and represented by action as that of the *Comedies*: but because the matter was higher then that of the *Comedies*, the Poets stile was also higher and more loftie, the prouision greater, the place more magnificent; for which purpose also the players garments were made more rich & costly and solemne, and euery other thing apperteining, according to that rate: So as where the *Satyre* was pronounced by rusticall and naked *Syluanes* speaking out of a bush, & the common players of interludes called *Planipedes* played barefoote vpon the floore, the later *Comedies* vpon scaffolds, and by men well and cleanely hosed and shod. These matters of great Princes were played vpon lofty stages, & the actors thereof ware vpon their legges buskins of leather called *Cothurni*, and other solemne habits, & for a speciall preheminence did walke vpon those high corked shoes or pantofles, which now they call in Spaine and Italy *Shoppini*. And because those buskins and high shoes were commonly made of goats skinnes very finely tanned, and dyed into colours, or for that, as some say, the best players reward was a goate to be giuen him, or for that, as other thinke, a goate was the peculiar sacrifice of the god *Pan,* king of all the gods of the woodes—forasmuch as a goate in Greeke is called *Tragos,* therfore these stately playes were called *Tragedies.* And thus haue ye foure sundry formes of Poesie *Drammatick* reprehensiue, & put in cxccution by the feate and dexteritie of mans body, to wit, the *Satyre,* old *Comedie,* new *Comedie,* and *Tragedie,* whereas all other kinde of poems, except *Eglogue,* whereof shalbe entreated hereafter, were onely recited by mouth or song with the voyce to some melodious instrument.

CHAP. XVI.

IN WHAT FORME OF POESIE THE GREAT PRINCES AND DOMINATORS OF THE WORLD WERE HONORED.

But as the bad and illawdable parts of all estates and degrees were taxed by the Poets in one sort or an other, and those of great Princes by Tragedie in especial, & not till after their deaths, as hath bene before remembred, to th'intent that such exemplifying (as it were) of their blames and aduersities, being now dead, might worke for a secret reprehension to others that were aliue, liuing in the same or like abuses: so was it great reason that all good and vertuous persons should for their well doings be rewarded with commendation, and the great Princes aboue all others with honors and praises, [it] being for many respects of greater moment to haue them good & vertuous then any inferior sort of men. Wherfore the Poets, being in deede the trumpetters of all praise and also of slaunder (not slaunder, but well deserued reproch), were in conscience & credit bound next after the diuine praises of the immortall gods to yeeld a like ratable honour to all such amongst men as most resembled the gods by excellencie of function, and had a certaine affinitie with them, by more then humane and ordinarie vertues shewed in their actions here vpon earth. They were therfore praised by a second degree of laude: shewing their high estates, their Princely genealogies and pedegrees, mariages, aliances, and such noble exploites, as they had done in th'affaires of peace & of warre to the benefit of their people and countries, by inuention of any noble science or profitable Art, or by making wholesome lawes or enlarging of their dominions by honorable and iust conquests, and many other wayes. Such personages among the Gentiles were *Bacchus, Ceres, Perseus, Hercules, Theseus,* and many other, who thereby came to be accompted gods and halfe gods or goddesses (*Heroes*), & had their commendations giuen by Hymne accordingly, or by such other poems as their memorie was therby made famous to the posteritie for euer after, as shal be more at large sayd in place conuenient. But first we will speake somewhat of the playing places, and prouisions which were made for their pageants & pomps representatiue before remembred.

CHAP. XVIII.

OF THE SHEPHEARDS OR PASTORALL POESIE CALLED EGLOGUE, AND TO WHAT PURPOSE IT WAS FIRST INUENTED AND VSED.

Some be of opinion, and the chiefe of those who haue written in this Art among the Latines, that the pastorall Poesie which we commonly call by the name of *Eglogue* and *Bucolick,* a tearme brought in by the Sicilian Poets, should be the first of any other, and before the *Satyre, Comedie,* or *Tragedie,* because, say they, the shepheards and haywards assemblies & meetings when they kept their cattell and heards in the common fields and forests was the first familiar conuersation, and their babble and talk vnder bushes and shadie trees the first disputation and contentious reasoning, and their fleshly heates growing of ease the first idle wooings, and their songs made to their mates or paramours either vpon sorrow or iolity of courage the first amorous musicks; sometime also they sang and played on their pipes for wagers, striuing who should get the best game and be counted cunningest. All this I do agree vnto, for no doubt the shepheards life was the first example of honest felowship, their trade the first art of lawfull acquisition or purchase, for at those daies robbery was a manner of purchase. So saith *Aristotle* in his bookes of the Politiques; and that pasturage was before tillage, or fishing, or fowling, or any other predatory art or cheuisance. And all this may be true, for before there was a shepheard keeper of his owne or of some other bodies flocke, there was none owner in the world, quick cattel being the first property of any forreine possession. I say forreine, because alway men claimed property in their apparell and armour, and other like things made by their owne trauel and industry, nor thereby was there yet any good towne, or city, or Kings palace, where pageants and pompes might be shewed by Comedies or Tragedies. But for all this, I do deny that the *Eglogue* should be the first and most auncient forme of artificiall Poesie, being perswaded that the Poet deuised the *Eglogue* long after the other *dramatick* poems, not of purpose to counterfait or represent the rusticall manner of loues and communication, but vnder the vaile of homely persons and in rude speeches to insinuate and glaunce at greater matters, and such as perchance had not bene safe to haue beene disclosed in any other sort, which may be perceiued by the Eglogues of *Virgill*, in which are treated by figure matters of greater importance then the loues of *Titirus* and *Corydon*. These Eglogues came after to containe and enforme morall discipline, for the amendment of mans behauiour, as be those of *Mantuan* and other moderne Poets.

CHAP. XIX.

OF HISTORICALL POESIE, BY WHICH THE FAMOUS ACTS OF PRINCES AND THE VERTUOUS AND WORTHY LIUES OF OUR FOREFATHERS WERE REPORTED.

There is nothing in man of all the potential parts of his mind (reason and will except) more noble or more necessary to the actiue life than memory; because it maketh most to a sound iudgement and perfect worldly wisedome, examining and comparing the times past with the present, and, by them both considering the time to come, concludeth with a stedfast resolution what is the best course to be taken in all his actions and aduices in this world. It came, vpon this reason, experience to be so highly commended in all consultations of importance, and preferred before any learning or science, and yet experience is no more than a masse of memories assembled, that is, such trials as man hath made in time before. Right so no kinde of argument in all the Oratorie craft doth better perswade and more vniuersally satisfie then example, which is but the representation of old

memories, and like successes happened in times past. For these
regards the Poesie historicall is of all other next the diuine most
honorable and worthy, as well for the common benefit as for the
speciall comfort euery man receiueth by it: no one thing in the
world with more delectation reuiuing our spirits then to behold
as it were in a glasse the liuely image of our deare forefathers,
their noble and vertuous maner of life, with other things auten-
tike, which because we are not able otherwise to attaine to the
knowledge of by any of our sences, we apprehend them by
memory, whereas the present time and things so swiftly passe
away, as they giue vs no leasure almost to looke into them, and
much lesse to know & consider of them throughly. The things
future, being also euents very vncertaine, and such as can not
possibly be knowne because they be not yet, can not be used for
example nor for delight otherwise then by hope; though many
promise the contrary, by vaine and deceitfull arts taking vpon
them to reueale the truth of accidents to come, which, if it were
so as they surmise, are yet but sciences meerely coniecturall, and
not of any benefit to man or to the common wealth where they
be vsed or professed. Therefore the good and exemplarie things
and actions of the former ages were reserued only to the historicall reportes of wise and graue men: those of the present time
left to the fruition and iudgement of our sences: the future, as
hazards and incertaine euentes vtterly neglected and layd aside
for Magicians and mockers to get their liuings by, such manner
of men as by negligence of Magistrates and remiss[n]es of lawes
euery countrie breedeth great store of. These historical men
neuerthelesse vsed not the matter so precisely to wish that al they
wrote should be accounted true, for that was not needeful nor
expedient to the purpose, namely to be vsed either for example
or for pleasure: considering that many times it is seene a fained
matter or altogether fabulous, besides that it maketh more mirth
than any other, works no less good conclusions for example then
the most true and veritable, but often times more, because the
Poet hath the handling of them to fashion at his pleasure, but
not so of th'other, which must go according to their veritie, and
none otherwise, without the writers great blame. Againe, as ye
know, mo and more excellent examples may be fained in one day
by a good wit then many ages through mans frailtie are able to
put in vse; which made the learned and wittie men of those times

to deuise many historical matters of no veritie at all, but with purpose to do good and no hurt, as vsing them for a maner of discipline and president of commendable life. Such was the common wealth of *Plato*, and Sir *Thomas Moores Vtopia*, resting all in deuise, but neuer put in execution, and easier to be wished then to be performed. And you shall perceiue that histories were of three sortes, wholly true, and wholly false, and a third holding part of either, but for honest recreation and good example they were all of them. And this may be apparent to vs not onely by the Poeticall histories but also by those that be written in prose: for as *Homer* wrate a fabulous or mixt report of the siege of Troy and another of *Ulisses* errors or wandrings, so did *Museus* compile a true treatise of the life & loues of *Leander* and *Hero*, both of them *Heroick*, and to none ill edification. Also, as *Theucidides* wrate a worthy and veritable historie of the warres betwixt the *Athenians* and the *Peloponeses*, so did *Zenophon*, a most graue Philosopher and well trained courtier and counsellour, make another (but fained and vntrue) of the childhood of *Cyrus*, king of *Persia*; neuertheless both to one effect, that is for example and good information of the posteritie. Now because the actions of meane & base personages tend in very few cases to any great good example; for who passeth to follow the steps and maner of life of a craftes man, shepheard, or sailer, though he were his father or dearest frend? yea how almost is it possible that such maner of men should be of any vertue other then their profession requireth? therefore was nothing committed to historie but matters of great and excellent persons & things, that the same by irritation of good courages (such as emulation causeth) might worke more effectually, which occasioned the story writer to chuse an higher stile fit for his subiect, the Prosaicke in prose, the Poet in meetre, and the Poets was by verse exameter for his grauitie and statelinesse most allowable: neither would they intermingle him with any other shorter measure, vnlesse it were in matters of such qualitie as became best to be song with the voyce and to some musicall instrument, as were with the Greeks all your Hymnes & *Encomia* of *Pindarus* & *Callimachus*, not very histories, but a maner of historical reportes; in which cases they made those poemes in variable measures, & coupled a short verse with a long to serue that purpose the better. And we our selues who compiled this treatise haue written for pleasure a litle brief *Romance* or historicall ditty in the English tong, of the Isle of great *Britaine*, in short and long meetres, and by breaches or diuisions to be more commodiously song to the harpe in places of assembly, where the company shalbe desirous to heare of old aduentures & valiaunces of noble knights in times past, as are those of king *Arthur* and his knights of the round table, Sir *Beuys* of *Southampton, Guy of Warwicke,* and others like. Such as haue not premonition hereof, and consideration of the causes alledged, would peraduenture reproue and disgrace euery *Romance* or short historicall ditty for that they be not written in long meeters or verses *Alexandrins,* according to the nature and stile of large histories; wherin they should do wrong, for they be sundry formes of poems, and not all one.

CHAP. XXI.

THE FORME WHEREIN HONEST AND PROFITABLE ARTES AND SCIENCES WERE TREATED.

The profitable sciences were no lesse meete to be imported to the greater number of ciuill men for instruction of the people and increase of knowledge then to be reserued and kept for clerkes and great men onely. So as next vnto the things historicall such doctrines and arts as the common wealth fared the better by were esteemed and allowed. And the same were treated by Poets in verse *Exameter* sauouring the *Heroicall,* and for the grauitie and comelinesse of the meetre most vsed with the Greekes and Latines to sad purposes. Such were the Philosophicall works of *Lucretius Carus* among the Romaines, the Astronnomicall of *Aratus* and *Manilius,* one Greeke, th'other Latine, the Medicinall of *Nicander,* and that of *Oppianus* of hunting and fishes, and many moe that were too long to recite in this place.

CHAP. XXII.

IN WHAT FORME OF POESIE THE AMOROUS AFFECTIONS AND ALLUREMENTS WERE VTTERED.

The first founder of all good affections is honest loue, as the mother of all the vicious is hatred. It was not therefore without reason that so commendable, yea honourable, a thing as loue well meant, were it in Princely estate or priuate, might in all ciuil common wealths be vttered in good forme and order as other laudable things are. And because loue is of all other humane affections the most puissant and passionate, and most generall to all sortes and ages of men and women, so as whether it be of the yong or old, or wise or holy, or high estate or low, none euer could truly bragge of any exemption in that case: it requireth a forme of Poesie variable, inconstant, affected, curious, and most witty of any others, whereof the ioyes were to be vttered in one sorte, the sorrowes in an other, and, by the many formes of Poesie, the many moodes and pangs of louers thoroughly to be discouered; the poore soules sometimes praying, beseeching, sometimes honouring, auancing, praising, an other while railing, reuiling, and cursing, then sorrowing, weeping, lamenting, in the ende laughing, reioysing, & solacing the beloued againe, with a thousand delicate deuises, odes, songs, elegies, ballads, sonets, and other ditties, moouing one way and another to great compassion.

CHAP. XXIII.

THE FORME OF POETICALL REIOYSINGS.

Pleasure is the chiefe parte of mans felicity in this world, and also (as our Theologians say) in the world to come. Therefore, while we may (yet alwaies if it coulde be), to reioyce and take our pleasures in vertuous and honest sort, it is not only allowable but also necessary and very naturall to man. And many be the ioyes and consolations of the hart, but none greater than such as he may vtter and discouer by some convenient meanes: euen as to suppresse and hide a mans mirth, and not to haue therein a partaker, or at least wise a witnes, is no little griefe and infelicity. Therfore nature and ciuility haue ordained (besides the priuate solaces) publike reioisings for the comfort and recreation of many. And they be of diuerse sorts and vpon diuerse occasions growne. One & the chiefe was for the publike peace of a countrie, the greatest of any other ciuill good; and wherein your Maiestie (my most gracious Soueraigne) haue shewed your selfe to all the world, for this one and thirty yeares

space of your glorious raigne, aboue all other Princes of Christendome, not onely fortunate, but also most sufficient, vertuous,
and worthy of Empire. An other is for iust & honourable victory
atchieued against the forraine enemy. A third at solemne feasts
and pompes of coronations and enstallments of honourable orders. An other for iollity at weddings and marriages. An other
at the births of Princes children. An other for priuate entertain-
ments in Court, or other secret disports in chamber, and such
solitary places. And as these reioysings tend to diuers effects,
so do they also carry diuerse formes and nominations; for those
of victorie and peace are called *Triumphall,* whereof we our
selues haue heretofore giuen some example by our *Triumphals,*
written in honour of her Maiesties long peace. And they were
vsed by the auncients in like manner as we do our generall
processions or Letanies, with bankets and bonefires and all
manner of ioyes. Those that were to honour the persons of great
Princes or to solemnise the pompes of any installment were
called *Encomia*; we may call them carols of honour. Those to
celebrate marriages were called songs nuptiall or *Epithalamies,*
but in certaine misticall sense, as shall be said hereafter. Others
for magnificence at the natiuities of Princes children, or by
custome vsed yearely vpon the same dayes, are called songs
natall, or *Genethliaca.* Others for secret recreation and pastime
in chambers with company or alone were the ordinary Musickes
amorous, such as might be song with voice or to the Lute,
Citheron, or Harpe, or daunced by measures, as the Italian
Pauan and galliard are at these daies in Princes Courts and other
places of honourable or ciuill assembly; and of all these we will
speake in order and very briefly.

CHAP. XXIV.

THE FORME OF POETICALL LAMENTATIONS.

Lamenting is altogether contrary to reioising; euery man saith
so, and yet it is a peece of ioy to be able to lament with ease,
and freely to poure forth a mans inward sorrowes and the greefs
wherewith his minde is surcharged. This was a very necessary
deuise of the Poet and a fine, besides his poetrie to play also
the Phisitian, and not onely by applying a medicine to the or-

dinary sicknes of mankind, but by making the very greef it selfe
(in part) cure of the disease. Nowe are the causes of mans
sorrowes many: the death of his parents, frends, allies, and
children (though many of the barbarous nations do reioyce at
their burials and sorrow at their birthes), the ouerthrowes and
discomforts in battell, the subuersions of townes and cities, the
desolations of countreis, the losse of goods and worldly promo-
tions, honour and good renowne, finally, the trauails and torments
of loue forlorne or ill bestowed, either by disgrace, deniall,
delay, and twenty other wayes, that well experienced louers
could recite. . . .

CHAP. XXX.

OF SHORT EPIGRAMES CALLED POSIES.

There be also other like Epigrammes that were sent vsually
for new yeares giftes, or to be Printed or put vpon their
banketting dishes or sugar plate or of march paines, & such other
dainty meates as by the curtesie & custome euery gest might
carry from a common feast home with him to his owne house,
& were made for the nonce. They were called *Nenia* or *apo-
phoreta*, and neuer contained aboue one verse, or two at the
most, but the shorter the better; we call them Posies, and do
paint them now a dayes vpon the backe sides of our fruite
trenchers of wood, or vse them as deuises in rings and armes
and about such courtly purposes.

So haue we remembred and set forth to your Maiestie very
briefly all the commended fourmes of the auncient Poesie, which
we in our vulgare makings do imitate and vse vnder these
common names: enterlude, song, ballade, carroll, and ditty;
borrowing them also from the French, al sauing this word 'song'
which is our naturall Saxon English word: the rest, such as
time and vsurpation by custome haue allowed vs out of the
primitiue Greeke & Latine, as Comedie, Tragedie, Ode, Epi-
taphe, Elegie, Epigramme, and other moe. And we haue purposely ommitted all nice or scholasticall curiosities not meete for
your Maiesties contemplation in this our vulgare arte, and what
we haue written of the auncient formes of Poemes we haue
taken from the best clerks writing in the same arte. The part

that next followeth, to wit of proportion, because the Greeks nor
Latines neuer had it in vse nor made any obseruation, no more
then we doe of their feete, we may truly affirme to haue bene
the first deuisers thereof our selues, as αὐτοδίδακτοι, and not to
haue borrowed it of any other by learning or imitation, and
thereby trusting to be holden the more excusable if any thing
in this our labours happen either to mislike or to come short of
th'authors purpose, because commonly the first attempt in any
arte or engine artificiall is amendable, & in time by often ex-
periences reformed. And so no doubt may this deuise of ours be,
by others that shall take the penne in hand after vs.

THE THIRD BOOKE
OF ORNAMENT
CHAP. I.

OF ORNAMENT POETICALL.

AS NO DOUBT THE good proportion of any thing doth gretly adorne
and commend it, and right so our late remembred proportions
doe to our vulgar Poesie, so is there yet requisite to the perfection of this arte another maner of exornation, which resteth in
the fashioning of our makers language and stile, to such purpose
as it may delight and allure as well the mynde as the eare of the
hearers with a certaine noueltie and strange maner of conueyance,
disguising it no litle from the ordinary and accustomed; neuerthelesse making it nothing the more vnseemely or misbecomming,
but rather decenter and more agreable to any ciuill eare and
vnderstanding. And as we see in these great Madames of honour,
be they for personage or otherwise neuer so comely and bewtifull,
yet if they want their courtly habillements or at leastwise such
other apparell as custome and ciuilitie haue ordained to couer
their naked bodies, would be halfe ashamed or greatly out of
countenaunce to be seen in that sort, and perchance do then
thinke themselues more amiable in euery mans eye when they
be in their richest attire, suppose of silkes or tyssewes & costly
embroderies, then when they go in cloth or in any other plaine
and simple apparell; euen so cannot our vulgar Poesie shew it
selfe either gallant or gorgious, if any lymme be left naked and

bare and not clad in his kindly clothes and colours, such as may
conuey them somwhat out of sight, that is from the common
course of ordinary speach and capacitie of the vulgar iudgement,
and yet being artificially handled must needes yeld it much more
bewtie and commendation. This ornament we speake of is giuen
to it by figures and figuratiue speaches, which be the flowers,
as it were, and coulours that a Poet setteth vpon his language
of arte, as the embroderer doth his stone and perle or passements
of gold vpon the stuffe of a Princely garment, or as th'excellent
painter bestoweth the rich Orient coulours vpon his table of
pourtraite: so neuerthelesse as if the same coulours in our arte
of Poesie (as well as in those other mechanicall artes) be not
well tempered, or not well layd, or be vsed in excesse, or neuer
so litle disordered or misplaced, they not onely giue it no maner
of grace at all, but rather do disfigure the stuffe and spill the
whole workmanship, taking away all bewtie and good liking from
it, no lesse then if the crimson tainte, which should be laid
vpon a Ladies lips, or right in the center of her cheekes, should
by some ouersight or mishap be applied to her forhead or chinne,
it would make (ye would say) but a very ridiculous bewtie;
wherfore the chief prayse and cunning of our Poet is in the
discreet vsing of his figures, as the skilfull painters is in the
good conueyance of his coulours and shadowing traits of his
pensill, with a delectable varietie, by all measure and iust proportion, and in places most aptly to be bestowed.

CHAP. III.

HOW ORNAMENT POETICALL IS OF TWO SORTES ACCORDING TO THE DOUBLE VERTUE AND EFFICACIE OF FIGURES.

This ornament then is of two sortes, one to satisfie & delight
th'eare onely by a goodly outward shew set vpon the matter
with wordes and speaches smothly and tunably running, another
by certaine intendments or sence of such wordes & speaches
inwardly working a stirre to the mynde. That first qualitie the
Greeks called *Enargia*, of this word *argos*, because it geueth a
glorious lustre and light. This latter they called *Energia*, of
ergon, because it wrought with a strong and vertuous operation.
And figure breedeth them both, some seruing to giue glosse onely

to a language, some to geue it efficacie by sence; and so by that
meanes some of them serue th'eare onely, some serue the conceit
onely and not th'eare. There be of them also that serue both
turnes as common seruitours appointed for th'one and th'other
purpose, which shalbe hereafter spoken of in place; but because
we haue alleaged before that ornament is but the good or rather
bewtifull habite of language or stile, and figuratiue speaches the
instrument wherewith we burnish our language, fashioning it to
this or that measure and proportion, whence finally resulteth a
long and continuall phrase or maner of writing or speach, which
we call by the name of *stile*, we wil first speake of language,
then of stile, lastly of figure, and declare their vertue and differences, and also their vse and best application, & what portion
in exornation euery of them bringeth to the bewtifying of this
Arte.

CHAP. VI.

OF THE HIGH, LOW, AND MEANE SUBIECT.

The matters therefore that concerne the Gods and diuine
things are highest of all other to be couched in writing; next to
them the noble gests and great fortunes of Princes, and the notable accidents of time, as the greatest affaires of war & peace:
these be all high subiectes, and therefore are deliuered ouer to
the Poets *Hymnick* & historicall who be occupied either in diuine
laudes or in *heroicall* reports. The meane matters be those that
concerne meane men, their life and busines, as lawyers, gentlemen, and marchants, good housholders and honest Citizens,
and which sound neither to matters of state nor of warre, nor
leagues, nor great alliances, but smatch all the common conuersation, as of the ciuiller and better sort of men. The base and low
matters be the doings of the common artificer, seruingman, yeo-
man, groome, husbandman, day-labourer, sailer, shepheard,
swynard, and such like of homely calling, degree, and bringing
vp. So that in euery of the sayd three degrees not the selfe same
vertues be egally to be praysed nor the same vices egally to be
dispraised, nor their loues, mariages, quarels, contracts, and other
behauiours be like high nor do require to be set fourth with the
like stile, but euery one in his degree and decencie, which made

that all *hymnes* and histories and Tragedies were written in the high stile, all Comedies and Enterludes and other common Poesies of loues and such like in the meane stile, all *Eglogues* and pastorall poemes in the low and base stile; otherwise they had bene vtterly disproporcioned. Likewise for the same cause some phrases and figures be onely peculiar to the high stile, some to the base or meane, some common to all three, as shalbe declared more at large hereafter when we come to speake of figure and phrase: also some wordes and speaches and sentences doe become the high stile that do not become th'other two, and contrariwise, as shalbe said when we talke of words and sentences: finally, some kinde of measure and concord doe not beseeme the high stile, that well become the meane and low, as we haue said speaking of concord and measure. But generally the high stile is disgraced and made foolish and ridiculous by all wordes affected, counterfait, and puffed vp, as it were a windball carrying more countenance then matter, and can not be better resembled then to these midsommer pageants in London, where, to make the people wonder, are set forth great and vglie Gyants marching as if they were aliue, and armed at all points, but within they are stuffed full of browne paper and tow, which the shrewd boyes vnderpeering do guilefully discouer and turne to a great derision: also all darke and vnaccustomed wordes, or rusticall and homely, and sentences that hold too much of the mery & light, or infamous & unshamefast, are to be accounted of the same sort, for such speaches become not Princes, nor great estates, nor them that write of their doings to vtter or report and intermingle with the graue and weightie matters.

CHAP. VII.

OF FIGURES AND FIGURATIUE SPEACHES.

As figures be the instruments of ornament in euery language, so be they also in sorte abuses or rather trespasses in speach, because they passe the ordinary limits of common vtterance, and be occupied of purpose to deceiue the eare and also the minde, drawing it from plainnesse and simplicitie to a certain doublenesse, whereby our talke is the more guilefull & abusing. For what els is your *Metaphor* but an inuersion of sence by transport; your

allegorie by a duplicitie of meaning or dissimulation vnder couert
and darke intendments; one while speaking obscurely and in
riddle called *Ænigma*; another while by common prouerbe or
Adage called *Paremia*; then by merry skoffe called *Ironia*; then
by bitter tawnt called *Sarcasmus*; then by periphrase or circumlocution when all might be said in a word or two; then by incredible comparison giuing credit, as by your *Hyperbole*; and
many other waies seeking to inueigle and appassionate the mind:
which thing made the graue iudges *Areopagites* (as I find
written) to forbid all manner of figuratiue speaches to be vsed
before them in their consistorie of Iustice, as meere illusions to
the minde, and wresters of vpright iudgement, saying that to
allow such manner of forreine & coulored talke to make the iudges
affectioned were all one as if the carpenter before he began to
square his timber would make his squire crooked; in so much
as the straite and vpright mind of a Iudge is the very rule of
iustice till it be peruerted by affection. This no doubt is true and
was by them grauely considered; but in this case, because our
maker or Poet is appointed not for a iudge, but rather for a
pleader, and that of pleasant & louely causes and nothing peril-
lous, such as be those for the triall of life, limme, or liuelyhood,
and before iudges neither sower nor seuere, but in the eare of
princely dames, yong ladies, gentlewomen, and courtiers, beyng
all for the most part either meeke of nature, or of pleasant
humour, and that all his abuses tende but to dispose the hearers
to mirth and sollace by pleasant conueyance and efficacy of
speach, they are not in truth to be accompted vices but for
vertues in the poetical science very commendable. On the other
side, such trespasses in speach (whereof there be many) as geue
dolour and disliking to the eare & minde by any foule indecencie
or disproportion of sounde, situation, or sence, they be called
and not without cause the vicious parts or rather heresies of
language: wherefore the matter resteth much in the definition
and acceptance of this word *decorum,* for whatsoeuer is so cannot iustly be misliked. In which respect it may come to passe that
what the Grammarian setteth downe for a viciositee in speach
may become a vertue and no vice; contrariwise his commended
figure may fall into a reprochfull fault: the best and most assured
remedy whereof is generally to follow the saying of *Bias*: *ne*

quid nimis.[3] So as in keeping measure, and not exceeding nor shewing any defect in the vse of his figures, he cannot lightly do amisse, if he haue besides (as that must needes be) a speciall regard to all circumstances of the person, place, time, cause, and purpose he hath in hand; which being well obserued, it easily auoideth all the recited inconueniences, and maketh now and then very vice goe for a formall vertue in the exercise of this Arte.

CHAP. VIII.

SIXE POINTS SET DOWNE BY OUR LEARNED FOREFATHERS FOR A GENERALL REGIMENT OF ALL GOOD VTTERANCE, BE IT BY MOUTH OR BY WRITING.

But before there had bene yet any precise obseruation made of figuratiue speeches, the first learned artificers of language considered that the bewtie and good grace of vtterance rested in [s]o many pointes; and whatsoeuer transgressed those lymits, they counted it for vitious; and thereupon did set downe a manner of regiment in all speech generally to be obserued, consisting in sixe pointes. First, they said that there ought to be kept a decent proportion in our writings and speach, which they termed *Analogia*. Secondly, that it ought to be voluble vpon the tongue, and tunable to the eare, which they called *Tasis*. Thirdly, that it were not tediously long, but briefe and compendious, as the matter might beare, which they called *Syntomia*. Fourthly, that it should cary an orderly and good construction, which they called *Synthesis*. Fiftly, that it should be a sound, proper, and naturall speach, which they called *Ciriologia*. Sixtly, that it should be liuely & stirring, which they called *Tropus*. So as it appeareth by this order of theirs that no vice could be committed in speech, keeping within the bounds of that restraint. But, sir, all this being by them very well conceiued, there remayned a greater difficultie to know what this proportion, volubilitie, good construction, & the rest were, otherwise we could not be euer the more relieued. It was therefore of necessitie that a more curious and particular description should bee made of euery manner of speech, either transgressing or agreeing with their said generall

---

[3] "Nothing too much."

prescript. Whereupon it came to passe that all the commendable
parts of speech were set foorth by the name of figures, and all
the illaudable partes vnder the name of vices or viciosities, of
both which it shall bee spoken in their places.[4]

*   *   *   *

The Conclusion.

And with this (my most gratious soueraigne Lady) I make an
end, humbly beseeching your pardon in that I haue presumed to
hold your eares so long annoyed with a tedious trifle, so as,
vnlesse it proceede more of your owne Princely and naturall
mansuetude then of my merite, I feare greatly least you may
thinck of me as the Philosopher Plato did of *Aniceris,* an in-
habitant of the Citie *Cirene,* who, being in troth a very actiue and
artificiall man in driuing of a Princes Charriot or Coche (as your
Maiestie might be), and knowing it himselfe well enough, comming one day into Platos schoole, and hauing heard him largely
dispute in matters Philosophicall, 'I pray you' (quoth he) 'geue
me leaue also to say somewhat of myne arte,' and in deede
shewed so many trickes of his cunning, how to lanche forth, and
stay, and chaunge pace, and turne and winde his Coche, this way
and that way, vphill, downe hill, and also in euen or rough
ground, that he made the whole assemblie wonder at him. Quoth
Plato, being a graue personage, 'verely in myne opinion this man
should be vtterly vnfit for any seruice of greater importance then
to driue a Coche. It is a great pitie that so prettie a fellow had
not occupied his braynes in studies of more consequence.' Now
I pray God it be not thought so of me in describing the toyes of
this our vulgar art. But when I consider how euery thing hath his
estimation by oportunitie, and that it was but the studie of my
yonger yeares, in which vanitie raigned; also that I write to the
pleasure of a Lady and a most gratious Queene, and neither to
Priestes nor to Prophetes or Philosophers; besides finding by
experience that many times idlenesse is lesse harmefull then vn-

---

[4] Chapters ix–xx discuss and then list the principal rhetorical figures.
Chapters xxi–xxii treat 'vices of language'; chapters xii–xxiv treat decorum
of language and behavior; and the last chapter (xxv) advocates *ars celare
artem.*

profitable occupation, dayly seeing how these great aspiring mynds and ambitious heads of the world seriously searching to deale in matters of state be often times so busie and earnest that they were better be vnoccupied, and peraduenture altogether idle; I presume so much vpon your Maiesties most milde and gracious iudgement, howsoeuer you conceiue of myne abilitie to any better or greater seruice, that yet in this attempt ye wil allow of my loyall and good intent, alwayes endeuouring to do your Maiestie the best and greatest of those seruices I can.

Part III

PRACTICAL CRITICISM

Edmund Spenser

[1552?–1599]

_◆◆◆_

SPENSER'S _Shepheardes Calender_ was published in 1579. In it the young poet boldly compared himself to Virgil and hinted at plans for an English _Aeneid_. The _Faerie Queene_ fulfilled this promise. The first three books, together with the letter to Raleigh, appeared in 1590, followed in 1596 by the next three books, the last that Spenser completed. Troubles in Ireland, where Spenser had become Sheriff of Cork, apparently prevented further work on the poem before his death.

The preface to the _Shepheardes Calender_, the "October Eclogue," and the letter to Raleigh illustrate the practical influence of Renaissance critical theory on a major poet. The discussion of eclogue may be compared to that by Puttenham (above, p. 166). The plan for the work as a whole accurately reflects the way in which criticism, drawing on rhetorical ideas of 'disposition,' encouraged elaborately schematic arrangement. The "October Eclogue" is a poet's comment on his profession. Cuddie, "the perfecte patterne of a Poete," laments the lack of patronage, calls for a new Maecenas, and ends with a somewhat alcoholic version of _furor poeticus_. The notes by the enigmatic "E.K." illustrate accurately the mixture of scholarship and criticism which Elizabethans encountered in their annotated editions of the classics.

Like the preface to the _Shepheardes Calender_, the letter to Raleigh presents a highly schematic plan. Its relevance to the _Faerie Queene_ as written has been disputed, but its sincerity cannot be doubted. Homer, Xenophon, Virgil, Ariosto, and Tasso are all invoked as precedents which Spenser will imitate. His allegory will be especially elaborate because of his plan to concentrate on a particular knight and a particular virtue in each book, but he assumes the use of allegory to be standard epic practice. Reference to the comment by Chapman on Homer and Harington on Ariosto will show that his contemporaries agreed with him.

The present texts are based on the 1579 edition of the *Shepheardes Calender* and the 1590 edition of Books I–III of the *Faerie Queene*.

BIBLIOGRAPHY. J. Bennett, *The Evolution of the Faerie Queene* (1942); "Genre, Milieu, and the Epic Romance," *Eng. Inst. Essays* (1952); W. Bullock, "Spenser and Renaissance Criticism," *PMLA*, XLVI (1931); E. Greenlaw, *et al.*, Spenser *Variorum* (1933–49; the standard edition of the *Works*, with copious notes); A. Hamilton, "Spenser's *Letter to Raleigh*," *MLN*, LXXIII (1958); M. Hughes, *Virgil and Spenser* (1929); H. Jones, *A Spenser Handbook* (1930); I. Langdon, *Materials for a Study of Spenser's Theory of Fine Art* (1911); H. Maynadier, "The Areopagus of Sidney and Spenser," *MLR*, IV (1909); W Owen, "Spenser's Letter to Raleigh—A Reply," *MLN*, LXXV (1960); M. Parmenter, "Spenser's Twelve Aeglogues. . . .," *ELH*, III (1936); E. Pope, "Renaissance Criticism and the Diction of the *Faerie Queene*," *PMLA*, XLI (1926); W. Renwick, *Edmund Spenser* (1925; esp. good for critical influences); W. Webb, "Virgil in Spenser's Epic Theory," *ELH*, IV (1937).

Spenser became involved briefly in the attempt to create an English quantitative verse. For the earlier phase of the movement, the reader is referred to Ascham (above, pp. 70–73) and Stanyhurst (in G. Smith, *Elizabethan Critical Essays*, I, 135–47). In 1579–80 Spenser and Gabriel Harvey engaged in correspondence concerning reformed versifying according to the system of Thomas Drant. Their letters are available in de Selincourt's edition of Spenser (1912), and extracts are reprinted by G. Smith, I, 86–122. Of the scholarship relating to this phase of the controversy, see: R. Evans, "Spenser's Role in the Controversy Over Quantitative Verse," *NM*, LVII (1956); H. Maynadier (above); W. Ringler, "Master Drant's Rules," *PQ*, XXIX (1950); G. Willcock, "Passing Pitiful Hexameters: A Study of Quantity and Accent in English Renaissance Criticism," *MLR*, XXIX (1934). For later phases of the controversy, see: Campion and Daniel, both reprinted below.

Preface to

THE SHEPHEARDES CALENDER

[1579]

*The generall argument of
the whole booke.*

LITTLE I HOPE, needeth me at large to discourse the first Originall of Æglogues, hauing alreadie touched the same. But for the word Æglogues I know is vnknowen to most, and also mistaken of some the best learned (as they think) I wyll say somewhat thereof, being not at all impertinent to my present purpose.

They were first of the Greekes the inuentours of them called Æglogaj as it were αἴγων or αἰγονόμων. λόγοι. that is Goteheards tales. For although in Virgile and others the speakers be more shepheards, then Goteheards, yet Theocritus in whom is more ground of authoritie, then in Virgile, this specially from that deriuing, as from the first head and welspring the whole Inuencion of his Æglogues, maketh Goteheards the persons and authors of his tales. This being, who seeth not the grossenesse of such as by colour of learning would make vs beleeue that they are more rightly termed Eclogai, as they would say, extraordinary discourses of vnnecessarie matter, which definition albe in substaunce and meaning it agree with the nature of the thing, yet nowhit answereth with the ἀνάλυσις and interpretation of the word. For they be not termed Eclogues, but Æglogues. which sentence this authour very well obseruing, vpon good iudgement, though indeede few Goteheards haue to doe herein, nethelesse doubteth not to cal them by the vsed and best knowen name. Other curious discourses hereof I reserue to greater occasion. These xij. Æclogues euery where answering to the seasons of the twelue monthes may be well deuided into three formes or ranckes. For eyther they be Plaintiue, as the first, the sixt, the eleuenth, and the twelfth, or recreatiue, such as al those be, which conceiue matter of loue, or commendation of special personages, or Moral: which for the most part be mixed with some Satyrical bitternesse, namely the second of reuerence dewe to old age, the fift of coloured deceipt, the seuenth and ninth of dissolute shepheards and pastours, the tenth of contempt of Poetrie and pleasaunt wits. And to this diuision may euery thing herein be reasonably applyed: a few onely except, whose speciall purpose and meaning I am not priuie to. And thus much generally of these xij. Æclogues. Now will we speake particularly of all, and first of the first. which he calleth by the first monethes name Ianuarie: wherein to some he may seeme fowl to haue faulted, in that he erroniously beginneth with that moneth, which beginneth not the yeare. For it is wel known, and stoutely mainteyned with stronge reasons of the learned, that the yeare beginneth in March. for then the sonne reneweth his finished course, and the seasonable spring refresheth the earth, and the pleasaunce thereof being buried in the sadnesse of the dead winter now worne away, reliueth. This opinion maynteine the olde Astrologers and Philosophers, namely the reuerend Andalo, and Macrobius in his holydayes of Saturne, which accoumpt also was generally obserued both of Grecians and Romans. But sauing the leaue of such learned heads, we maytaine a custome of coumpting the seasons from the moneth Ianuary, vpon a more speciall cause, then the heathen Philosophers euer coulde conceiue, that is, for the incarnation of our mighty Sauiour and eternall redeemer the L. Christ, who as then renewing the state of the decayed world, and returning the compasse of expired yeres to theyr former date and first commencement, left to vs his heires a memoriall of his birth in the ende of the last yeere and beginning of the next. which reckoning, beside that eternall monument of our saluation, leaneth also vppon good proofe of special iudgement. For albeit that in elder times, when as yet the coumpt of the yere was not perfected, as afterwarde it was by Iulius Cæsar, they began to tel the monethes from Marches beginning, and according to the same God (as is sayd in Scripture) comaunded the people of the Iewes to count the moneth Abib, that which we call March, for the first moneth, in remembraunce that in that moneth he brought them out of the land of Ægipt: yet according to tradition of latter times it hath bene otherwise obserued, both in gouernment of the church, and rule of Mightiest Realmes. For from Iulius Cæsar who first obserued the leape yeere which he called Bissextilem Annum, and brought in to a more certain course the odde wandring dayes which of the Greekes were called ὑπερβαίνοντες. of the Romanes intercalares (for in such matter of learning I am forced to vse the termes of the learned) the monethes haue bene nombred xij. which in the first ordinaunce of Romulus were but tenne, counting but CCCiiij. dayes in euery yeare, and beginning with March. But Numa Pompilius, who was the father of al the Romain ceremonies and religion, seeing that reckoning to agree neither with the course of the sonne, nor of the Moone, therevnto added two monethes, Ianuary and February: wherein it seemeth, that wise king minded vpon good reason to begin the yeare at Ianuarie, of him therefore so called tanquam Ianua anni the gate and entraunce of the yere, or of the name of the god Ianus, to which god for that the old Paynims attributed the byrth and beginning of all creatures new comming into the worlde, it seemeth that he therefore to him assigned the beginning and first entraunce of the yeare. which account for the most part hath hetherto continued. Notwithstanding that the Ægiptians beginne theyre yeare at September, for that according to the opinion of the best Rabbins, and very purpose of the scripture selfe, God made the worlde in that Moneth, that is called of them Tisri. And therefore he commaunded them, to keepe the feast of Pauilions in the end of the yeare, in the xv. day of the seuenth moneth, which before that time was the first.

But our Authour respecting nether the subtiltie of thone parte, nor the antiquitie of thother, thinketh it fittest according to the simplicitie of commen vnderstanding, to begin with Ianuarie, wening it perhaps no decorum, that Shepheard should be seene in matter of so deepe insight, or canuase a case of so doubtful iudgment. So therefore beginneth he, and so continueth he throughout.

OCTOBER ECLOGUE

Ægloga decima.

ARGVMENT.

In Cuddie is set out the perfecte paterne of a Poete, which find-
ing no maintenaunce of his state and studies, complayneth of the
contempte of Poetrie, and the causes thereof: Specially hauing
bene in all ages, and euen amongst the most barbarous alwayes
of singular accounpt and honor, and being indede so worthy and
commendable an arte: or rather no arte, but a diuine gift and
heauenly instinct not to bee gotten by laboure and learning, but
adorned with both: and poured into the witte by a certaine
ἐνθουσιασμὸς.[1] *and celestiall inspiration, as the Author hereof els*
where at large discourseth, in his booke called the English Poete,[2]
which booke being lately come to my hands, I mynde also by
Gods grace vpon further aduisement to publish.

Pierce.   Cuddie.
Cvddie, for shame hold vp thy heauye head,
And let vs cast with what delight to chace,
And weary thys long lingring *Phœbus* race.
Whilome thou wont the shepheards laddes to leade,
In rymes, in ridles, and in bydding base:
Now they in thee, and thou in sleepe art dead.

Cuddye.
Piers, I haue pyped erst so long with payne,
That all mine Oten reedes bene rent and wore:
And my poore Muse hath spent her spared store,

---

[1] "Enthusiasm." Here, the word is synonymous with "inspiration." Later
it was used as a term of abuse to stigmatize subjective, highly emotional
utterances, especially sermons.

[2] The work was never published; its loss is particularly unfortunate.

Yet little good hath got, and much lesse gayne.
Such pleasaunce makes the Grashopper so poore,
And ligge so layd, when Winter doth her straine.

The dapper ditties, that I wont deuise,
To feede youthes fancie, and the flocking fry,
Delighten much: what I the bett for thy?
They han the pleasure, I a sclender prise.
I beate the bush, the byrds to them doe flye:
What good thereof to Cuddie can arise?

Piers.

Cuddie, the prayse is better, then the price,
The glory eke much greater then the gayne:
O what an honor is it, to restraine
The lust of lawlesse youth with good aduice:
Or pricke them forth with pleasaunce of thy vaine,
Whereto thou list their trayned willes entice.

Soone as thou gynst to sette thy notes in frame,
O how the rural routes to thee doe cleaue:
Seemeth thou dost their soule of sence bereaue,
All as the shepheard, that did fetch his dame
From *Plutoes* balefull bowre withouten leaue:
His musicks might the hellish hound did tame.

Cuddie.

So praysen babes the Peacoks spotted traine,
And wondren at bright *Argus* blazing eye:
But who rewards him ere the more for thy?
Or feedes him once the fuller by a graine?
Sike prayse is smoke, that sheddeth in the skye,
Sike words bene wynd, and wasten soone in vayne.

Piers.

Abandon then the base and viler clowne,
Lyft vp thy selfe out of the lowly dust:
And sing of bloody Mars, of wars, of giusts.
Turne thee to those, that weld the awful crowne,

To doubted Knights, whose woundlesse armour rusts,
And helmes vnbruzed wexen dayly browne.

There may thy Muse display her fluttrying wing,
And stretch her selfe at large from East to West:
Whither thou list in fayre *Elisa* rest,
Or if thee please in bigger notes to sing,
Aduaunce the worthy whome shee loueth best,
That first the white beare to the stake did bring.

And when the stubborne stroke of stronger stounds,
Has somewhat slackt the tenor of thy string:
Of loue and lustihead tho mayst thou sing,
And carrol lowde, and leade the Myllers rownde,
All were *Elisa* one of thilke same ring.
So mought our *Cuddies* name to Heauen sownde.

Cuddie.

Indeede the Romish *Tityrus*,[3] I heare,
Through his *Mecœnas* left his Oaten reede,
Whereon he earst had taught his flocks to feede,
And laboured lands to yield the timely eare,
And eft did sing of warres and deadly drede,
So as the Heauens did quake his verse to here.

But ah *Mecœnas* is yclad in claye,
And great *Augustus* long ygoe is dead:
And all the worthies liggen wrapt in leade,
That matter made for Poets on to play:
For euer, who in derring doe were dreade,
The loftie verse of hem was loued aye.

But after vertue gan for age to stoupe,
And mighty manhode brought a bedde of ease:
The vaunting Poets found nought worth a pease,
To put in preace among the learned troupe.
Tho gan the streames of flowing wittes to cease,
And sonnebright honour pend in shamefull coupe.

[3] I.e., Virgil.

And if that any buddes of Poesie,
Yet of the old stocke gan to shoote agayne:
Or it mens follies mote be forst to fayne,
And rolle with rest in rymes of rybaudrye:
Or as it sprong, it wither must agayne:
Tom Piper makes vs better melodie.

Piers.

O pierlesse Poesye, where is then thy place?
If nor in Princes pallace thou doe sitt:
(And yet is Princes pallace the most fitt)
Ne brest of baser birth doth thee embrace.
Then make thee winges of thine aspyring wit,
And, whence thou camst, flye backe to heauen apace.

Cuddie.

Ah *Percy* it is all to weake and wanne,
So high to sore, and make so large a flight:
Her peeced pyneons bene not so in plight,
For *Colin* fittes such famous flight to scanne:
He, were he not with loue so ill bedight,
Would mount as high, and sing as soote as Swanne.

Piers.

Ah fon, for loue does teach him climbe so hie,
And lyftes him vp out of the loathsome myre:
Such immortall mirrhor, as he doth admire,
Would rayse ones mynd aboue the starry skie.
And cause a caytiue corage to aspire,
For lofty loue doth loath a lowly eye.

Cuddie.

All otherwise the state of Poet stands,
For lordly loue is such a Tyranne fell:
That where he rules, all power he doth expell.
The vaunted verse a vacant head demaundes,
Ne wont with crabbed care the Muses dwell:
Unwisely weaues, that takes two webbes in hand.

Who euer casts to compasse weightye prise,
And thinks to throwe out thondring words of threate:
Let powre in lauish cups and thriftie bitts of meate,
For *Bacchus* fruite is frend to *Phœbus* wise.
And when with Wine the braine begins to sweate,
The nombers flowe as fast as spring doth ryse.

Thou knest not *Percie* howe the ryme should rage.
O if my temples were distaind with wine,
And girt in girlonds of wild Yuie twine,
How I could reare the Muse on stately stage,
And teache her tread aloft in buskin fine,
With queint *Bellona* in her equipage.

But ah my corage cooles ere it be warme,
For thy, content vs in thys humble shade:
Where no such troublous tydes han vs assayde,
Here we our slender pipes may safely charme.

Piers.
And when my Gates shall han their bellies layd:
Cuddie shall haue a Kidde to store his farme.

Cuddies Embleme.

Agitante caelescimus illo &c.[4]

GLOSSE.

This Æglogue is made in imitation of Theocritus his xvi. Idilion, wherein hee reproued the Tyranne Hiero of Syracuse for his nigardise towarde Poetes, in whome is the power to make men immortal for theyr good dedes, or shameful for their naughty lyfe. And the lyke also is in Mantuane, The style hereof as also that in Theocritus, is more loftye then the rest, and applyed to the heighte of Poeticall witte.

Cuddie) I doubte whether by Cuddie be specified the authour selfe, or some other. For in the eyght Æglogue the same person was brought in, singing a Cantion of Colins making, as he sayth. So

---

[4] Ovid, *Fasti*, VI, 5. The full quotation is, "There is a god in us; when he moves us, we grow hot with inspiration."

that some doubt, that the persons be different.

Whilome) sometime.   Oaten reedes) Auena.

Ligge so layde) lye so faynt and vnlustye.   Dapper) pretye.

Frye) is a bold Metaphore, forced from the spawning fishes, for the multitude of young fish be called the frye.[5]

To restraine.) This place seemeth to conspyre with Plato, who in his first booke de Legibus [6] sayth, that the first inuention of Poetry was of very vertuous intent. For at what time an infinite number of youth vsually came to theyr great solemne feastes called Panegyrica, which they vsed euery fiue yeere to hold, some learned man being more hable then the rest, for speciall gyftes of wytte and Musicke, would take vpon him to sing fine verses to the people, in prayse eyther of vertue or of victory or of immortality or such like. At whose wonderful gyft al men being astonied and as it were rauished, with delight, thinking (as it was indeed) that he was inspired from aboue, called him vatem: which kinde of men afterwarde framing their verses to lighter musick (as of musick be many kinds, some sadder, some lighter, some martiall, some heroicall: and so diuersely eke affect the mynds of men) found out lighter matter of Poesie also, some playing wyth loue, some scorning at mens fashions, some powred out in pleasures, and so were called Poetes or makers.

Sence bereaue) what the secrete working of Musick is in the myndes of men, aswell appeareth hereby, that some of the auncient Philosophers, and those the moste wise, as Plato and Pythagoras held for opinion, that the mynd was made of a certaine harmonie and musicall nombers, for the great compassion and likenes of affection in thone and in the other as also by that memorable history of Alexander: to whom when as Timotheus the great Musitian playd the Phrygian melodie, it is said, that he was distraught with such vnwonted fury, that streightway rysing from the table in great rage, he caused himselfe to be armed, as ready to goe to warre (for that musick is very war like:) And immediatly whenas the Musitian chaunged his stroke into the Lydian and Ionique harmony, he was so furr from warring, that he sat as styl, as if he had bene in matters of counsell. Such might is in musick. wherefore Plato and Aristotle forbid the Arabian Melodie from children and youth. for that being altogither on the fyft and vii, tone, it is of great force to molifie and quench the kindly courage, which vseth to burne in yong brests. So that it is not incredible which the Poete here sayth, that Musick can bereaue the soule of sence.

[5] Here and below, note "E.K.'s" interest in rhetorical figures.
[6] Most probably the reference is to *Laws*, VII, 801, rather than to Book I.

The shepheard that) Orpheus: of whom is sayd, that by his excellent
skil in Musick and Poetry, he recouered his wife Eurydice from
hell.

Argus eyes) of Argus is before said, that Iuno to him committed hir
husband Iupiter his Paragon Iô, bicause he had an hundred eyes:
but afterwarde Mercury wyth hys Musick lulling Argus aslepe, slew
him and brought Iô away, whose eyes it is sayd that Iuno for his
eternall memory placed in her byrd the Peacocks tayle. for those
coloured spots indeede resemble eyes.

Woundlesse armour) vnwounded in warre, doe rust through long
peace.

Display) A poeticall metaphore: whereof the meaning is, that if the
Poet list showe his skill in matter of more dignitie, then is the
homely Æglogue, good occasion is him offered of higher veyne and
more Heroicall argument, in the person of our most gratious
soueraign, whom (as before) he calleth Elisa. Or if mater of knight-
hoode and cheualrie please him better, that there be many Noble
and valiaunt men, that are both worthy of his payne in theyr deserued prayses, and also fauourers of hys skil and faculty.

The worthy) he meaneth (as I guesse) the most honorable and renowmed the Erle of Leycester, whom by his cognisance (although
the same be also proper to other) rather then by his name he be-
wrayeth, being not likely, that the names of noble princes be known
to country clowne.

Slack) that is when thou chaungest thy verse from stately discourse,
to matter of more pleasaunce and delight.

The Millers) a kind of daunce.　　　　Ring) company of dauncers.

The Romish Tityrus) wel knowen to be Virgile, who by Mecænas
means was brought into the fauor of the Emperor Augustus, and
by him moued to write in loftier kinde, then he erst had doen.

Whereon) in these three verses are the three seuerall workes of Virgile
intended. For in teaching his flocks to feede, is meant his Æglogues.
In labouring of lands, is hys Georgiques. In singing of wars and
deadly dreade, is his diuine Æneis figured.

For euer) He sheweth the cause, why Poetes were wont be had in
such honor of noble men; that is, that by them their worthines and
valor shold through theyr famous Posies be commended to al pos-
terities. wherfore it is sayd, that Achilles had neuer bene so famous,
as he is, but for Homeres immortal verses, which is the only
aduantage, which he had of Hector. And also that Alexander the
great comming to his tombe in Sigeus, with naturall teares blessed
him, that euer was his hap to be honoured with so excellent a Poets
work: as so renowmed and ennobled onely by hys meanes, which

being declared in a most eloquent Oration of Tullies, is of Petrarch
no lesse worthely sette forth in a sonet

> Giunto Alexandro a la famosa tomba
> Del fero Achille sospírando disse
> O fortunato che si chiara tromba. Trouasti &c.[7]

And that such account hath bene alwayes made of Poetes, aswell
sheweth this that the worthy Scipio in all his warres against Carthage
and Numantia had euermore in his company, and that in a most
familiar sort the good olde Poet Ennius: as also that Alexander
destroying Thebes, when he was enformed that the famous Lyrick
Poet Pindarus was borne in that citie, not onely commaunded
streightly, that no man should vpon payne of death do any violence
to that house by fire or otherwise: but also specially spared most,
and some highly rewarded, that were of hys kinne. So fauoured he
the only name of a Poete, whych prayse otherwise was in the same
man no lesse famous, that when he came to ransacking of king
Darius coffers, whom he lately had ouerthrowen, he founde in a
little coffer of siluer the two bookes of Homers works, as layd vp
there for speciall iewells and richesse, which he taking thence, put
one of them dayly in his bosome, and thother euery night layde
vnder his pillowe. Such honor haue Poetes alwayes found in the
sight of princes and noble men. which this author here very well
sheweth, as els where more notably.

In derring doe) In manhoode and cheualrie.

But after) he sheweth the cause of contempt of Poetry to be idlenesse
and basenesse of mynd.   Pent) shut vp in slouth, as in a coope
or cage.

Tom Piper) An Ironicall Sarcasmus, spoken in derision of these rude
wits, whych make more account of a ryming rybaud, then of skill
grounded vpon learning and iudgment.

Ne brest) the meaner sort of men.   Her peeced pineons) vnperfect skil. Spoken wyth humble modestie.

As soote as Swanne) The comparison seemeth to be strange: for the
swanne hath euer wonne small commendation for her swete singing:
but it is sayd of the learned that the swan a little before hir death,
singeth most pleasantly, as prophecying by a secrete instinct her
neere destinie. As well sayth the Poete elsewhere in one of his
sonetts.

---

[7] "When Alexander arrived at the tomb of fierce Achilles, he sighed and
said, 'O fortunate man who found so noble a clarion. . . .' " Sonnet 135 of
Petrarch's *Canzoniere*. The "clarion" is Homer, and the story is related in
Cicero's *Pro Archia Poeta*, X, 24.

The siluer swanne doth sing before her dying day
As shee that feeles the deepe delight that is in death &c.

Immortall myrrhour) Beauty, which is an excellent obiect of Poeticall spirites, as appeareth by the worthy Petrarchs saying.

> Fiorir faceua il mio debile ingegno
> A la sua ombra, et crescer ne gli affanni.[8]

A caytiue corage) a base and abiect minde.

For lofty loue) I think this playing with the letter to be rather a fault then a figure, aswel in our English tongue, as it hath bene alwayes in the Latine, called Cacozelon.

A vacant) imitateth Mantuanes saying. vacuum curis diuína cerebrum Poscit.[9]

Lauish cups) Resembleth that comen verse Fæcundi calices quem non fecere disertum.[10]

O if my) He seemeth here to be rauished with a Poetical furie. For (if one rightly mark) the numbers rise so ful, and the verse groweth so big, that it seemeth he hath forgot the meanenesse of shepheards state and stile.

Wild yuie) for it is dedicated to Bacchus and therefore it is sayd that the Mænades (that is Bacchus franticke priestes) vsed in theyr sacrifice to carry Thyrsos, which were pointed staues or Iauelins, wrapped about with yuie.

In buskin) it was the maner of Poetes and plaiers in tragedies to were buskins, as also in Comedies to vse stockes and light shoes. So that the buskin in Poetry is vsed for tragical matter, as it said in Virgile. Sola sophocleo tua carmina digna cothurno.[11] And the like in Horace, Magnum loqui, nitique cothurno.[12]

Queint) strange Bellona; the goddesse of battaile, that is Pallas, which may therefore wel be called queint for that (as Lucian saith) when Iupiter hir father was in traueile of her, he caused his sonne Vulcane with his axe to hew his head. Out of which leaped forth lustely a valiant damsell armed at all poyntes, whom Vulcane seeing so faire and comely, lightly leaping to her, proferred her some cortesie,

---

[8] "She made my weak talent flower in her shade and grow among hardships." Apparently, from Petrarch's *Canzoniere*, sonnet #38.

[9] "The divine [muse] demands a mind free of cares." Mantuan, *Eclogue* V, 70. Misquoted.

[10] "Who is not made learned by lavish cups?" Horace, *Epistles,* I, 5, 19.

[11] "Only your songs are worthy of the Sophoclean buskin." Virgil, *Eclogue* VIII, 10.

[12] "To speak grandly and wear the buskin." Horace, *Ars Poetica,* 280.

which the Lady disdeigning, shaked her speare at him, and
threatned his saucinesse. Therefore such straungenesse is well
applyed to her.

Æquipage.) order.   Tydes) seasons.

Charme) temper and order. for Charmes were wont to be made by
verses as Ouid sayth.   Aut si carminibus.[13]

Embleme.

Hereby is meant, as also in the whole course of this Æglogue, that
Poetry is a diuine instinct and vnnatural rage passing the reache of
comen reason. Whom Piers answereth Epiphonematicos [14] as admiring the excellencye of the skyll whereof in Cuddie hee hadde
alreadye hadde a taste.

LETTER TO SIR WALTER RALEIGH

[1590]

A
Letter of the Authors expounding his
whole intention in the course of this worke: which
for that it giueth great light to the Reader, for
the better vnderstanding is hereunto
annexed.

To the Right noble, and Valorous, Sir Walter Raleigh knight,
Lo. Wardein of the Stanneryes, and her Maiesties liefetenaunt
of the County of Cornewayll.

SIR KNOWING HOW DOUBTFULLY all Allegories may be construed,
and this booke of mine, which I haue entituled the Faery Queene,
being a continued Allegory, or darke conceit, I haue thought
good aswell for auoyding the gealous opinions and misconstruc-
tions, as also for your better light in reading thereof, (being so
by you commanded,) to discover vnto you the general intention
and meaning, which in the whole course thereof I haue fashioned,
without expressing of any particular purposes or by-accidents

13 "But if by songs. . . ." An allusion to *Ars Amatoria*, III, 7, 27–30.
14 "By way of summing up."

therein occasioned. The generall end therefore of all the booke
is to fashion a gentleman or noble person in vertuous and gentle
discipline. Which for that I conceiued shoulde be most plausible
and pleasing, being coloured with an historicall fiction, the which
the most part of men delight to read, rather for variety of matter,
then for profite of the ensample: I chose the historye of king
Arthure, as most fitte for the excellency of his person, being made
famous by many mens former workes, and also furthest from the
daunger of enuy, and suspicion of present time. In which I haue
followed all the antique Poets historicall, first Homere, who in
the Persons of Agamemnon and Vlysses hath ensampled a good
gouernour and a vertuous man, the one in his Ilias, the other in
his Odysseis: then Virgil, whose like intention was to doe in the
person of Aeneas: after him Ariosto comprised them both in his
Orlando: and lately Tasso disseuered them againe, and formed
both parts in two persons, namely that part which they in
Philosophy call Ethice, or vertues of a priuate man, coloured in
his Rinaldo: The other named Politice in his Godfredo. By ensample of which excellente Poets, I labour to pourtraict in Arthure,
before he was king, the image of a braue knight, perfected in
the twelue priuate morall vertues, as Aristotle hath deuised, the
which is the purpose of these first twelue bookes: which if I
finde to be well accepted, I may be perhaps encoraged, to frame
the other part of polliticke vertues in his person, after that hee
came to be king. To some I know this Methode will seeme dis-
pleasaunt, which had rather haue good discipline deliuered
plainly in way of precepts, or sermoned at large, as they vse,
then thus clowdily enwrapped in Allegoricall deuises. But such,
me seems, should be satisfide with the vse of these dayes, seeing
all things accounted by their showes, and nothing esteemed of,
that is not delightfull and pleasing to commune sence. For this
cause is Xenophon preferred before Plato, for that the one in
the exquisite depth of his iudgement, formed a Commune wealth
such as it should be, but the other in the person of Cyrus and
the Persians fashioned a gouernement such as might best be: So
much more profitable and gratious is doctrine by ensample,
then by rule. So haue I laboured to doe in the person of Arthure:
whome I conceiue after his long education by Timon, to whom
he was by Merlin deliuered to be brought vp, so soone as he

was borne of the Lady Igrayne, to haue seene in a dream or vision the Faery Queen, with whose excellent beauty rauished, he awaking resolued to seeke her out, and so being by Merlin armed, and by Timon thoroughly instructed, he went to seeke her forth in Faerye land. In that Faery Queene I meane glory in my generall intention, but in my particular I conceiue the most excellent and glorious person of our soueraine the Queene, and her kingdome in Faery land. And yet in some places els, I doe otherwise shadow her. For considering she beareth two persons, the one of a most royall Queene or Empresse, the other of a most vertuous and beautifull Lady, this latter part in some places I doe express in Belphœbe, fashioning her name according to your owne excellent conceipt of Cynthia, (Phœbe and Cynthia being both names of Diana.) So in the person of Prince Arthure I sette forth magnificence in particular, which vertue for that (according to Aristotle and the rest) it is the perfection of all the rest, and conteineth in it them all, therefore in the whole course I mention the deedes of Arthure applyable to that vertue, which I write of in that booke. But of the xii. other vertues, I make xii. other knights the patrones, for the more variety of the history: Of which these three bookes contayn three. The first of the knight of the Redcrosse, in whome I expresse Holynes: The seconde of Sir Guyon, in whome I sette forth Temperaunce: The third of Britomartis a Lady knight, in whome I picture Chastity. But because the beginning of the whole worke seemeth abrupte and as depending vpon other antecedents, it needs that ye know the occasion of these three knights seuerall aduentures. For the Methode of a Poet historical is not such, as of an Historiographer. For an Historiographer discourseth of affayres orderly as they were donne, accounting as well the times as the actions, but a Poet thrusteth into the middest, euen where it most concerneth him, and there recoursing to the thinges forepaste, and diuining of thinges to come, maketh a pleasing Analysis of all. The beginning therefore of my history, if it were to be told by an Historiographer, should be the twelfth booke, which is the last, where I deuise that the Faery Queene kept her Annuall feaste xii. dayes, vppon which xii. seuerall dayes, the occasions of the xii. seuerall aduentures hapned, which being vndertaken by xii. seuerall knights, are in these xii books seuerally handled and discoursed. The first was this. In the beginning of the feast, there presented him selfe a tall clownishe younge man, who falling before the Queen of Faries desired a boone (as the manner then was) which during that feast she might not refuse: which was that hee might haue the atchieuement of any aduenture, which during that feaste should happen, that being graunted, he rested him on the floore, vnfitte through his rusticity for a better place. Soone after entred a faire Ladye in mourning weedes, riding on a white Asse, with a dwarfe behind her leading a warlike steed, that bore the Armes of a knight, and his speare in the dwarfes hand. Shee falling before the Queene of Faeries, complayned that her father and mother an ancient King and Queene, had bene by a huge dragon many years shut vp in a brasen Castle, who thence suffred them not to yssew: and therefore besought the Faery Queene to assygne her some one of her knights to take on him that exployt. Presently that clownish person vpstarting, desired that aduenture: whereat the Queene much wondering, and the Lady much gainesaying, yet he earnestly importuned his desire. In the end the Lady told him that vnlesse that armour which she brought, would serue him (that is the armour of a Christian man specified by Saint Paul v. Ephes.) [15] that he could not succeed in that enterprise, which being forthwith put vpon him with dewe furnitures thereunto, he seemed the goodliest man in al that company, and was well liked of the Lady. And eftesoones taking on him knighthood, and mounting on that straunge Courser, he went forth with her on that aduenture: where beginneth the first booke, vz.

A gentle knight was pricking on the playne. &c.

The second day ther came in a Palmer bearing an Infant with bloody hands, whose Parents he complained to haue bene slayn by an Enchaunteresse called Acrasia: and therefore craued of the Faery Queene, to appoint him some knight, to performe that aduenture, which being assigned to Sir Guyon, he presently went forth with that same Palmer: which is the beginning of the second booke and the whole subiect thereof. The third day there came in, a Groome who complained before the Faery Queene, that a

[15] The *v* stands for *vide* (see), not five. The reference is to *Ephesians*, VI, 11.

vile Enchaunter called Busirane had in hand a most faire Lady called Amoretta, whom he kept in most grieuous torment, because she would not yield him the pleasure of her body. Whereupon Sir Scudamour the louer of that Lady presently tooke on him that aduenture. But being vnable to performe it by reason of the hard Enchauntments, after long sorrow, in the end met with Britomaris, who succoured him, and reskewed his loue.

But by occasion hereof, many other aduentures are intermedled, but rather as Accidents, then intendments. As the loue of Britomart, the ouerthrow of Marinell, the misery of Florimell, the vertuousnes of Belphœbe, the lasciuiousnes of Hellenora, and many the like.

Thus much Sir, I haue briefly ouerronne to direct your vnderstanding to the wel-head of the History, that from thence gathering the whole intention of the conceit, ye may as in a handfull gripe al the discourse, which otherwise may happily seeme tedious and confused. So humbly crauing the continuance of your honorable fauour towards me, and th' eternell establishment of your happines, I humbly take leaue.

23. Ianuary. 1589.
Yours most humbly affectionate.
Ed. Spenser.

George Chapman

[1559?–1634]

⊷§§⊷

CHAPMAN'S *Homer* is the culmination of the effort of Elizabethan translators to make the classics accessible to the English reading public. The work was issued in installments and finally, in 1616, as *The Whole Works of Homer*. Chapman's prefaces and introductory poems illustrate the light in which the classics were read during the sixteenth century and are heavily indebted to the Florentine Neoplatonists, especially Marsilio Ficino and Angelo Politian. As a proud representative of the new Greek scholarship of the sixteenth century, Chapman bitterly attacked Scaliger for preferring Virgil to Homer (*Poetices*, 1561, V, iii). The following excerpt from the prefatory matter to the *Odyssey* (1616 text) is particularly interesting for its defense of the fabulous elements of the Greek poem as a veil of allegory covering profound truths.

BIBLIOGRAPHY. A. Nicoll, *Chapman's Homer*, 2 vols. (1956). The prefaces to the earlier, partial editions are reprinted in G. Smith, *Elizabethan Critical Essays*, II, 295–307; and J. Spingarn, *Critical Essays of the Seventeenth Century*, I, 67–81. See also: E. Rees, *The Tragedies of George Chapman* (1949); F. Schoell, "George Chapman and the Neo-Latinists of the Quattrocento," *MP*, XIII (1915). For Elizabethan translations generally, see: H. Lathrop, *Translations from the Classics into English from Caxton to Chapman* (1933); and F. Matthiessen, *Translation: An Elizabethan Art* (1931).

Preface to

THE ODYSSEY

[1616]

. . . that your Lordship [1] may in his [Homer's] Face take view
of his Mind, the first word of his *Iliads* is μῆνιν, *wrath*; the first
word of his *Odysses*, ἄνδρα, *Man*—contracting in either word his
each worke's Proposition. In one, Predominant Pertubation; in the
other, over-ruling Wisedome; in one, the Bodie's fervour and
fashion of outward Fortitude to all possible height of Heroicall
Action; in the other, the Mind's inward, constant and unconquerd
Empire, unbroken, unaltered with any most insolent and tyrannous infliction. To many most sovereigne praises is this Poeme
entitled, but to that *Grace* in chiefe which sets on the Crowne
both of Poets and Orators, τὸ τὰ μικρὰ μεγάλως, καὶ τὰ κοινά
καινῶς—that is *Parva magnè dicere, pervulgata novè, jejuna
plenè*: To speake things litle, greatly; things commune, rarely;
things barren and emptie, fruitfully and fully. The returne of a
man into his Countrie is his whole scope and object, which in
itselfe, your Lordship may well say, is jejune and fruitlesse
enough, affoording nothing feastfull, nothing magnificent. And
yet even this doth the divine inspiration render vast, illustrous
and of miraculous composure. And for this, my Lord, is this
Poeme preferred to his *Iliads*; for therein much magnificence,
both of person and action, gives great aide to his industrie, but
in this are these helpes exceeding sparing or nothing; and yet is
the Structure so elaborate and pompous that the poore plaine
Groundworke (considered together) may seeme the naturally rich
wombe to it and produce it needfully. Much wonderd at, therefore, is the Censure of Dionysius Longinus (a man otherwise
affirmed, grave and of elegant judgement), comparing Homer in
his *Iliads* to the Sunne rising, in his *Odysses* to his descent or
setting, or to the Ocean robd of his aesture, many tributorie

---

[1] The "Preface" is addressed to the Earl of Somerset.

flouds and rivers of excellent ornament withheld from their observance [2]—when this his worke so farre exceeds the Ocean, with
all his Court and concourse, that all his Sea is onely a serviceable
streame to it. Nor can it be compared to any One power to be
named in nature, being an entirely wel-sorted and digested Confluence of all—where the most solide and grave is made as nimble
and fluent as the most airie and firie, the nimble and fluent as
firme and well-bounded as the most grave and solid. And (taking
all together) of so tender impression, and of such Command to
the voice of the Muse, that they knocke heaven with her breath
and discover their foundations as low as hell. Nor is this all-
comprising Poesie phantastique, or meere fictive, but the most
material and doctrinall illations of Truth, both for all manly information of Manners in the yong, all prescription of Justice,
and even Christian pietie, in the most grave and high-governd.
To illustrate both which in both kinds, with all height of expression, the Poet creates both a Bodie and a Soule in them—wherein,
if the Bodie (being the letter, or historie) seemes fictive and
beyond Possibilitie to bring into Act, the sence then and Allegorie
(which is the Soule) is to be sought—which intends a more
eminent expressure of Vertue, for her lovelinesse, and of Vice,
for her uglinesse, in their severall effects, going beyond the life
than any Art within life can possibly delineate. Why then is
Fiction to this end so hatefull to our true Ignorants? Or why
should a poore Chronicler of a Lord Maior's naked Truth (that
peradventure will last his yeare) include more worth with our
moderne wizerds than Homer for his naked Ulysses, clad in
eternall Fiction? But this Prozer Dionysius and the rest of these
grave and reputatively learned (that dare undertake for their
gravities the headstrong censure of all things, and challenge the
understanding of these Toyes in their childhoods, when even these
childish vanities retaine deepe and most necessarie learning
enough in them to make them children in their ages and teach
them while they live) are not in these absolutely divine Infusions
allowd either voice or relish—for *Qui Poeticas ad fores accedit,*
&c., sayes the Divine Philosopher, he that knocks at the Gates of

---

[2] *On the Sublime,* 21. One of the earliest references in English criticism
to Longinus.

the Muses, *sine Musarum furore*,[3] is neither to be admitted entrie nor a touch at their Thresholds, his opinion of entrie ridiculous and his presumption impious. Nor must Poets themselves (might I a litle insist on these contempts, not tempting too farre your Lordship's Ulyssean patience) presume to these doores without the truly genuine and peculiar induction—there being in Poesie a twofold rapture (or alienation of soule, as the abovesaid Teacher termes it), one *Insania*, a disease of the mind and a meere madnesse, by which the infected is thrust beneath all the degrees of humanitie, *et ex homine Brutum quodammodo redditur* [4] (for which poore Poesie in this diseasd and impostorous age is so barbarously vilified); the other is *Divinus furor*, by which the sound and divinely healthfull *supra hominis naturam erigitur, et in Deum transit*: [5] one a perfection directly infused from God, the other an infection obliquely and degenerately proceeding from man. Of the divine Furie, my Lord, your Homer hath ever bene both first and last Instance, being pronounced absolutely τὸν σοφώτατον καὶ τὸν θειότατον ποιητήν, the most wise and most divine Poet—against whom whosoever shall open his prophane mouth may worthily receive answer with this of his divine defender (Empedocles, Heraclitus, Protagoras, Epicharmus, &c. being of Homer's part) τίς οὖν, &c.,[6] who against such an Armie and Generall Homer dares attempt the assault but he must be reputed ridiculous? And yet against this hoast and this invincible Commander shall we have every Besogne and foole a Leader. . . .

[3] "Who comes to the portals of poetry . . . without the inspiration of the Muses. . . ." Quoted from Marsilio Ficino's introduction to the *Ion* in his *Opera Omnia Divini Platonis*.

[4] "A brute is somehow made from a man." Quoted from Ficino's introduction to the *Ion*.

[5] ". . . is lifted above the nature of a man and becomes God-like." Quoted from Ficino's introduction to the *Ion*.

[6] The allusion is obscure. Most probably the "divine defender" is Plato.

Sir John Harington

[1561-1612]

୰ఢఢ

HARINGTON'S *Ariosto* (1591) was undertaken at the request of his godmother, who was none other than Queen Elizabeth. Like the translation of Tasso's *Gerusalemme Liberata* by Edward Fairfax (1600), it illustrates the English taste for Italian romance. The preface is an elaborate defense of poetry in general and Ariosto in particular, and shows many debts to Sidney. Although it is hard today to read Ariosto as an allegorist, Harington's comments are no different from those of many Italian defenders of the *Orlando Furioso*. The distinction between types of allegory shows that the medieval methods of exegesis outlined by Dante in the *Convivo* and *Letter to Can Grande della Scala* persisted to the end of the sixteenth century. Harington's reference to Aristotelian 'rules' to justify Ariosto's highly unclassical performance deserves special attention, for it is a reminder that the *Poetics* could be (and was) used by humanists as well as Neoclassicists.

The present text is based on the edition of 1591.

BIBLIOGRAPHY. R. Elbrodt, "Sir John Harington and Leone Ebreo," *MLN*, LXV (1950); W. Raleigh, "Sir John Harington," in *Some Authors* (1923).

A PREFACE, OR RATHER A BRIEFE APOLOGIE OF POETRIE, AND OF THE AUTHOR

from

ARIOSTO

THE LEARNED *Plutarch* in his Laconicall Apothegmes tels of a Sophister that made a long and tedious Oration in praise of
208

Hercules, and expecting at the end thereof for some great thanks and applause of the hearers, a certaine Lacedemonian demanded him who had dispraised *Hercules.*[1] Me thinkes the like may be now said to me, taking vpon me the defence of Poesie, for surely if learning in generall were of that account among vs, as it ought to be among all men, and is among wise men, then should this my Apologie of Poesie (the verie first nurse and ancient grandmother of all learning) be as vaine and superfluous as was that Sophisters, because it might then be aunswered, and truly aunswered, that no man disgraced it. . . .

But briefly to answere to the chiefe objections: *Cornelius Agrippa,*[2] a man of learning & authoritie not to be despised, maketh a bitter inuectiue against Poets and Poesie, and the summe of his reproofe of it is this (which is al that can with any probability be said against it), that it is a nurse of lies, a pleaser of fooles, a breeder of dangerous errors, and an inticer to wantonnes. I might here warne those that wil vrge this mans authoritie to the disgrace of Poetrie, to take heed (of what calling so euer they be) least with the same weapon that they thinke to giue Poetrie a blow they giue themselues a maime. For *Agrippa* taketh his pleasure of greater matters then Poetrie; I maruel how he durst do it, saue that I see he hath done it; he hath spared neither myters nor scepters. The courts of Princes where vertue is rewarded, iustice maintained, oppressions relieued, he cals them a Colledge of Giants, of Tyrants, of oppressors, warriors: the most noble sort of noble men he termeth cursed, bloodie, wicked, and sacrilegious persons. Noble men (and vs poore Gentlemen) that thinke to borrow praise of our auncestors deserts and good fame, he affirmed to be a race of the sturdier sort of knaues and lycencious liuers. Treasurers & other great officers of the common welth, with graue counsellors whose wise heads are the pillers of the state, he affirmeth generally to be robbers and peelers of the realme, and priuie traitors that sell their princes fauours and rob weldeseruing seruitors of their reward. I omit, as his *pecca-*

---

[1] *Apophthegmata,* 192c.
[2] Agrippa's *De Vanitate et Incertitudine Omnium Scientiarum* was written about 1527 and was frequently reprinted both in Latin and in English translation. The work is an ill-tempered but learned blast at the pretensions of all branches of learning. Chapter IV deals with poetry.

dilia, how he nicknameth priests, saying for the most part they
are hypocrites, lawyers, saying they are all theeues, phisicians,
saying they are manie of them murtherers: so as I thinke it were
a good motion, and would easily passe by the consent of the
three estates, that this mans authoritie should be vtterly adnihi-
lated, that dealeth so hardly and vniustly with all sorts of professions. But for the reiecting of his writings, I refer it to others that
haue powre to do it, and to condemne him for a generall libeller;
but for that he writeth against Poetrie, I meane to speake a word
or two in refuting thereof.

And first for lying, I might if I list excuse it by the rule of
Poetica licentia, and claime a priuiledge giuen to Poet[s], whose
art is but an imitation (as *Aristotle* calleth it), & therefore are
allowed to faine what they list. . . .

Thus you see that Poets may lye if they list *Cum priuelegio.*
But what if they lye least of all other men? what if they lye not
at all? then I thinke that great slaunder is verie vniustly raised
upon them. For in my opinion they are said properly to lye that
affirme that to be true that is false: and how other arts can free
themselues from this blame, let them look that professe them:
but Poets neuer affirming any for true, but presenting them to vs
as fables and imitations, cannot lye though they would: and
because this obiection of lyes is the chief, and that vpon which
the rest be grounded, I wil stand the longer vpon the clearing
thereof.

The ancient Poets haue indeed wrapped as it were in their
writings diuers and sundry meanings, which they call the senses
or mysteries thereof. First of all for the literall sence (as it were
the vtmost barke or ryne) they set downe in manner of an
historie the acts and notable exploits of some persons worthy
memorie: then in the same fiction, as a second rine and somewhat
more fine, as it were nearer to the pith and marrow, they place
the Morall sence profitable for the active life of man, approuing
vertuous actions and condemning the contrarie. Manie times also
vnder the selfesame words they comprehend some true vnderstanding of naturall Philosophie, or sometimes of politike gouernement, and now and then of diuinitie: and these same sences that
comprehend so excellent knowledge we call the Allegorie, which
Plutarch defineth to be when one thing is told, and by that an-

other is vnderstood. Now let any man iudge if it be a matter of meane art or wit to containe in one historicall narration, either true or fained, so many, so diuerse, and so deepe conceits: but for making the matter more plaine I will alledge an example thereof.

Perseus sonne of Iupiter is fained by the Poets to hauc slaine *Gorgon,* and, after that conquest atchieued, to haue flown vp to heauen. The Historicall sence is this, *Perseus* the sonne of *Iupiter*, by the participation of *Iupiters* vertues which were in him, or rather comming of the stock of one of the kings of Creet, or Athens so called, slew *Gorgon,* a tryant in that countrey (*Gorgon* in Greeke signifieth earth), and was for his vertuous parts exalted by men vp vnto heauen. Morally it signifieth this much: *Perseus* a wise man, sonne of Iupiter, endowed with vertue from aboue, slayeth sinne and vice, a thing base & earthly signified by Gorgon, and so mounteth vp to the skie of vertue. It signifies in one kind of Allegorie thus much: the mind of man being gotten by God, and so the childe of God killing and vanquishing the earthlinesse of this Gorgonicall nature, ascendeth vp to the vnderstanding of heauenly things, of high things, of eternal things, in which contemplacion consisteth the perfection of man: this is the natural allegory, because man [is] one of the chiefe works of nature. It hath also a more high and heauenly Allegorie, that the heauenly nature, daughter of *Iupiter,* procuring with her continuall motion corruption and mortality in the inferiour bodies, seuered it selfe at last from these earthly bodies, and flew vp on high, and there remaineth for euer. It hath also another Theological Allegorie: that the angelicall nature, daughter of the most high God the creator of all things, killing & ouercomming all bodily substance, signified by *Gorgon,* ascended into heauen. The like infinite Allegories I could pike out of other Poeticall fictions, saue that I would auoid tediousnes. It sufficeth me therefore to note this, that the men of greatest learning and highest wit in the auncient times did of purpose conceale these deepe mysteries of learning, and, as it were, couer them with the vaile of fables and verse for sundrie causes: one cause was that they might not be rashly abused by prophane wits, in whom science is corrupted, like good wine in a bad vessell; another cause why they wrote in verse was conseruation of the memorie of their precepts, as we see yet the generall rules almost of euerie art, not so much as husbandrie, but they are oftner recited and better remembred in verse then in prose; another, and a principall cause of all, is to be able with one kinde of meate and one dish (as I may so call it) to feed diuers tastes. For the weaker capacities will feede themselues with the pleasantnes of the historie and sweetnes of the verse, some that haue stronger stomackes will as it were take a further taste of the Morall sence, a third sort, more high conceited then they, will digest the Allegorie: so as indeed it hath bene thought by men of verie good iudgement, such manner of Poeticall writing was an excellent way to preserue all kinde of learning from that corruption which now it is come to since they left that mysticall writing of verse. . . .

But to end this part of my Apologie, as I count and conclude Heroicall Poesie allowable and to be read and studied without all exception, so I may as boldly say that Tragedies well handled be a most worthy kinde of Poesie, that Comedies may make men see and shame at their owne faults, that the rest may be so written and so read as much pleasure and some profite may be gathered out of them. And for myne owne part, as *Scaliger* writeth of *Virgill*,[3] so I beleeue that the reading of a good Heroicall Poeme may make a man both wiser and honester. And for Tragedies, to omit other famous Tragedies, that that was played at S. *Iohns* in Cambridge, of *Richard the* 3,[4] would moue (I thinke) *Phalaris* the tyraunt, and terrifie all tyrannous minded men from following their foolish ambitious humors, seeing how his ambition made him kill his brother, his nephews, his wife, beside infinit others, and, last of all, after a short and troublesome raigne, to end his miserable life, and to haue his body harried after his death. Then, for Comedies, how full of harmeless myrth is our Cambridge *Pedantius*?[5] and the Oxford *Bellum Grammaticale*?[6] or, to speake of a London Comedie, how much good matter, yea and matter of state, is there in that Comedie cald the play of the Cards, in which it is showed how foure Parasiticall knaues robbe the foure

---

[3] *Poetices Libri Septem*, III, iv.
[4] A Neo-Latin tragedy by Thomas Legge.
[5] A Neo-Latin comedy by Edward Forsett.
[6] A Latin entertainment presented at Cambridge in 1592.

principall vocations of the Realme, *videl.* the vocation of Souldiers, Schollers, Marchants, and Husbandmen?⁷ Of which Comedie I cannot forget the saying of a notable wise counseller that is now dead, who when some (to sing *Placebo*) aduised that it should be forbidden, because it was somewhat too plaine, and indeed as the old saying is, *sooth boord is no boord,* yet he would haue it allowed, adding it was fit that *They which doe that they should not should heare that they would not.* Finally, if Comedies may be so made as the beholders may be bettered by them, without all doubt all other sortes of Poetrie may bring their profit as they do bring delight, and if all, then much more the chiefe of all, which by all mens consent is the Heroicall. And thus much be sayd for Poesie.

Now for this Pocme of *Orlando Furioso,* which, as I haue heard, hath been disliked by some (though by few of any wit or iudgement), it followes that I say somewhat in defence thereof, which I will do the more moderately and coldly; by how much the paynes I haue taken, it (rising as you may see to a good volume) may make me seeme a more partiall prayser. Wherefore I will make choise of some other Poeme that is allowed and approued by all men, and a litle compare them together. And what worke can serue this turne so fitly as *Virgils Æneados,* whom aboue all other it seemeth my authour doth follow, as appeares both by his beginning and ending? The tone begins,

> *Arma virumque cano.*⁸

The tother,

> *Le donne, i cauallier, l'arme, gli amori,*
> *Le cortesie, l'audaci imprese io canto.*⁹

Virgill endes with the death of *Turnus,*

> *Vitaque cum gemitu fugit indignata sub vmbras.*¹⁰

⁷ Unidentified.
⁸ "Arms and the man I sing." *Aeneid,* I, 1.
⁹ "I sing the ladies, the knights, the arms, the loves, the courtesies, the bold undertakings. . . ." *Orlando Furioso,* I, 1.
¹⁰ "And with a groan his life fled indignant among the shades." *Aeneid,* XII, 952.

Ariosto ends with the death of *Rodomont,*

> *Bestemmiando fuggì l'alma sdegnosa,*
> *Che fu sì altera al mondo, e sì orgogliosa.*[11]

Virgill extolled *Æneas* to please *Augustus,* of whose race he was thought to come; *Ariosto* prayseth *Rogero* to the honour of the house of *Este*: *Æneas* hath his *Dido* that retaineth him; *Rogero* hath his Alcina: finally, least I should note euery part, there is nothing of any speciall obseruation in *Virgill* but my author hath with great felicitie imitated it, so as whosoeuer wil allow *Virgil* must *ipso facto* (as they say) admit *Ariosto.* Now of what account *Virgil* is reckned, & worthily reckned, for auncient times witnesseth *August.* C. verse of him:

> *Ergone supremis potuit vox improba verbis*
> *Tam dirum mandare nefas?* &c.,[12]

concluding thus,

> *Laudetur, placeat, vigeat, relegatur, ametur.*[13]

This is a great prayse comming from so great a Prince. For later times, to omit *Scaliger,* whom I recited before, that affirmeth the reading of *Virgill* may make a man honest and vertuous, that excellent Italian Poet *Dant* professeth plainly that when he wandred out of the right way, meaning thereby when he liued fondly and looslie, *Virgill* was the first that made him looke into himselfe and reclaime himselfe from that same daungerous and lewd course. But what need we further witnes, do we not make our children read it commonly before they can vnderstand it, as a testimonie that we do generally approue it? And yet we see old men study it, as a proofe that they do specially admire it: so as one writes very pretily, that children do wade in *Virgill,* and yet strong men do swim in it.

Now to apply this to the prayse of myne author, as I sayd before so I say still, whatsoeuer is prayseworthy in *Virgill* is

[11] "The scornful spirit, cursing, fled, which was so haughty and proud toward the world." *Orlando Furioso,* XLVI, stanza 140.

[12] "And could a depraved voice recount such a dire crime in noble language?" Attributed to Caesar in the *Scholastica in Virgilium.*

[13] "May he be praised, may he please, may he flourish, be cherished and loved."

plentifully to be found in *Ariosto,* and some things that *Virgill* could not haue, for the ignoraunce of the age he liued in, you finde in my author, sprinckled ouer all his worke, as I will very briefly note and referre you for the rest to the booke it selfe. The deuout and Christen demeanor of Charlemayne in the 14 booke, with his prayer,

> *Non uoglia tua bontà per mio fallire,*
> *Che 'l tuo popol fedele habbia à patire.* &c.[14]

And in the beginning of the xvii booke, that would beseeme any pulpit,

> *Il giusto Dio, quando i peccati nostri.*[15]

But, aboue all, that in the xli. booke of the conuersion of *Rogero* to the Christen Religion, where the Hermit speaketh to him, contayning in effect a full instruction against presumption and dispaire, which I haue set downe thus in English,

> Now (as I sayd) this wise that Hermit spoke,
> And part doth comfort him, and part doth checke;
> He blameth him that in that pleasaunt yoke
> He had so long defer'd to put his necke,
> But did to wrath his maker still prouoke,
> And did not come at his first call and becke,
> But still did hide himselfe away from God
> Vntill he saw him comming with his rod;
> Then did he comfort him and make him know
> That grace is near denyde to such as aske,
> As do the workemen in the Gospell show
> Receauing pay alike for diuers taske.

And so after, concluding,

> How to Christ he must impute
> The pardon of his sinnes, yet near the later
> He told him he must be baptisde in water.

These and infinit places full of Christen exhortation, doctrine,

[14] "Your goodness does not wish that your faithful people should have to suffer for my error." *Orlando Furioso,* XIV, stanza 69.
[15] "The just God, when our sins. . . ." XVII, stanza 1.

& example, I could quote out of the booke, saue that I hasten to an ende, and it would be needles to those that will not read them in the booke it selfe, and superfluous to those that will: but most manifest it is & not to be denyed, that in this point my author is to be preferred before all the aunceint Poets, in which are mentioned so many false Gods, and of them so many fowle deeds, their contentions, their adulteries, their incest, as were both obscenous in recitall and hurtful in example: though indeed those whom they termed Gods were certaine great Princes that committed such enormous faults, as great Princes in late ages (that loue still to be cald Gods of the earth) do often commit. But now it may be & is by some obiected that although he write Christianly in some places, yet in other some he is too lasciuious, as in that of the baudy Frier, in *Alcina* and *Rogeros* copulation, in *Anselmus* his *Giptian,* in *Richardetto* his metamorphosis, in mine hosts tale of Astolfo, & some few places beside. Alas, if this be a fault, pardon him this one fault, though I doubt too many of you (gentle readers) wil be to exorable in this point: yea, me thinks, I see some of you searching already for these places of the booke, and you are halfe offended that I haue not made some directions that you might finde out and read them immediatly. But I beseech you stay a while, and as the Italian sayth *Pian piano,* fayre and softly, & take this caueat with you, to read them as my author ment them, to breed detestation and not delectation. . . .

As for Aristotles rules, I take it he hath followed them verie strictly.[16]

Briefly, *Aristotle* and the best censurers of Poesie would haue the *Epopeia,* that is the heroicall Poem, should ground on some historie, and take some short time in the same to bewtifie with his Poetrie: so doth mine Author take the storie of k. *Charls* the great, and doth not exceed a yeare or therabout in his whole work. Secondly, they hold that nothing should be fayned vtterly incredible. And sure *Ariosto* neither in his inchantments ex-

[16] This brief summary of rules owes more to Italian interpretations than to the *Poetics* proper. The argument that the *Orlando* has verisimilitude because its supernatural events can be considered Christian miracles was used by Tasso in his *Discourses* but became unpopular in the later seventeenth century. See Boileau, *Art of Poetry,* III, 620ff.

ceedeth credit (for who knowes not how strong the illusions of the deuill are?) neither in the miracles that *Altolfo* by the power of S. Iohn is fayned to do, since the Church holdeth that Prophetes both aliue and dead haue done mightie great miracles. Thirdly, they would haue an heroicall Poem (aswell as a Tragedie) to be full of *Peripet[e]ia*, which I interpret an agnition of some vnlooked for fortune either good or bad, and a sudden change thereof: of this what store there be the reader shall quickly find. As for apt similitudes, for passions well expressed of loue, of pitie, of hate, of wrath, a blind man may see, if he can but heare, that this worke is full of them.

There follows only two reproofs, which I rather interpret two peculiar praises of this writer aboue all that wrate before him in this kind. One, that he breaks off narrations verie abruptly, so as indeed a loose vnattentiue reader will hardly carrie away any part of the storie: but this doubtlesse is a point of great art, to draw a man with a continuall thirst to reade out the whole worke, and toward the end of the booke to close vp the diuerse matters briefly and clenly. If S. *Philip Sidney* had counted this a fault, he would not haue done so himselfe in his Arcadia. Another fault is, that he speaketh so much in his own person by digression, which they say also is against the rules of Poetrie, because neither *Homer* nor *Virgill* did it. Me thinks it is a sufficient defence to say, *Ariosto* doth it. Sure I am it is both delightfull and verie profitable, and an excellent breathing place for the reader, and euen as if a man walked in a faire long alley, to haue a seat or resting place here and there is easie and commodious: but if at the same seat were planted some excellent tree, that not onely with the shade shoulde keepe vs from the heat, but with some pleasant and right wholsom fruite should allay our thirst and comfort our stomacke, we would thinke it for the time a litle paradice. So are *Ariostos* morals and pretie digressions sprinkled through his long worke to the no lesse pleasure then profit of the reader. And thus much be spoken for defence of mine Author, which was the second part of my Apologie.

George Whetstone

[1544?–1587]

◈

ELIZABETHAN DRAMATIC THEORY was a blend of ideas derived (usually secondhand) from late classical critics, rhetoric, and home-grown didacticism. Not until the end of the century did Aristotelian ideas have any appreciable effect on popular dramatic practice. Whetstone's "Preface" to his two-part comedy *Promos and Cassandra* (pr. 1578) is a brief compendium of commonplaces. The purpose of comedy is moral—to show the rewards of virtue and the punishment of vice. The ancients are praised, and English authors are rebuked for disregarding the unities, mixing serious and low comic action, and violating decorum of character based on norms of age, sex, and social station. The preface is especially noteworthy since *Promos and Cassandra* is the source for Shakespeare's *Measure for Measure*.

The present text is based on the 1578 edition.

Preface to

PROMOS AND CASSANDRA

[1578]

TO HIS WORSHIPFVLL FRIENDE AND KINSEMAN, *WILLIAM FLEETEWOODE ESQUIER, RECORDER OF LONDON.*

SYR, (DESIROUS TO ACQUITE your tryed frendships with some token of good will) of late I perused diuers of my vnperfect workes, fully minded to bestowe on you the trauell of some of my fore-passed time. But (resolued to accompanye the aduenturous Captaine Syr *Humfrey Gylbert* in his honorable voiadge) I found

218

my leysure too littel to correct the errors in my sayd workes. So
that (inforced) I lefte them disparsed amonge my learned
freendes, at theyr leasure to polish, if I faild to returne: spoyling
(by this meanes) my studdy of his necessarye furnyture. Amonge
other vnregarded papers I fownde this Discource of *Promos* and
Cassandra; which for the rarenesse (and the needeful knowledge)
of the necessary matter contained therein (to make the actions
appeare more liuely) I deuided the whole history into two
Commedies, for that, *Decorum* vsed, it would not be conuayed
in one. The effects of both are good and bad: vertue intermyxt
with vice, vnlawfull desyres (yf it were posible) queancht with
chaste denyals: al needeful actions (I thinke) for publike vewe.
For by the rewarde of the good the good are encouraged in wel
doinge: and with the scowrge of the lewde the lewde are feared
from euill attempts: mainetayning this my oppinion with *Platoes*
auctority. *Nawghtinesse commes of the corruption of nature, and
not by reulinge or hearinge the liues of the good or lewde (for
such publication is necessarye), but goodnesse (sayth he) is
beawtifyed by either action.* And to these endes *Menander,
Plautus,* and *Terence,* them selues many yeares since intombed,
(by their Commedies) in honour liue at this daye. The auncient
Romanes heald these showes of such prise that not onely allowde
the publike exercise of them, but the graue Senators themselues
countenaunced the Actors with their presence: who from these
trifles wonne morallytye, as the Bee suckes honny from weedes.
But the aduised deuises of auncient Poets, disc[r]edited with
tryfels of yonge, vnaduised, and rashe witted wryters, hath
brought this commendable exercise in mislike. For at this daye
the *Italian* is so lasciuious in his commedies that honest hearers
are greeued at his actions: the *Frenchman* and *Spaniarde* folowes
the *Italians* humor: the *Germaine* is too holye, for he presentes
on euerye common Stage what Preachers should pronounce in
Pulpets. The *Englishman* in this quallitie is most vaine, indiscreete, and out of order: he fyrst groundes his worke on impossi-
bilities; then in three howers ronnes he throwe the worlde,
marryes, gets Children, makes Children men, men to conquer
kingdomes, murder Monsters, and bringeth Gods from Heauen,
and fetcheth Diuels from Hel. And (that which is worst) their
ground is not so vnperfect as their workinge indiscreete: not way-

ing, so the people laugh, though they laugh them (for theyr follyes) to scorne. Manye tymes (to make mirthe) they make a Clowne companion with a Kinge; in theyr graue Counsels they allow the aduise of fooles; yea, they vse one order of speach for all persons: a grose *Indecorum,* for a Crowe wyll yll counterfet the Nightingale's sweete voice; euen so affected speeche doth misbecome a Clowne. For, to worke a Commedie kindly, graue olde men should instruct, yonge men should showe the imperfections of youth, Strumpets should be lasciuious, Boyes vnhappy, and Clownes should speake disorderlye: entermingling all these actions in such sorte as the graue matter may instruct and the pleasant delight; for without this chaunge the attention would be small, and the likinge lesse.

But leaue I this rehearsall of the vse and abuse of Commedies, least that I checke that in others which I cannot amend in my selfe. But this I am assured, what actions so ever passeth in this History, either merry or morneful, graue or lasciuious, the conclusion showes the confusion of Vice and the cherising of Vertue. And sythe the end tends to this good, although the worke (because of euel handlinge) be vnworthy your learned Censure, allowe (I beseeche you) of my good wyll, vntyl leasure serues me to perfect some labour of more worthe. No more, but that almightye God be your protector, and preserue me from dainger in this voiadge, the xxix of July, 1578.

Your Kinsman to vse,

GEORGE WHETSTONE.

Thomas Heywood

[1570?–1641]

~~❦~~

HEYWOOD CLAIMED TO have written or collaborated in over two hundred and twenty plays during his dramatic career. His best work is *A Woman Killed With Kindness* (1603), which is both a pioneer domestic tragedy and a moving study of Puritan mores. *An Apology for Actors* (1612) is a professional playwright's defense of the theatre against Puritan opposition. Beneath its overlay of commonplace-book erudition it is a restatement of the didactic theory of drama advocated by Whetstone in 1578. Its explicit criticism is largely translated or paraphrased from the late classical essay on tragedy and comedy by Euanthius, which was conventionally included in Renaissance editions of Donatus' commentary on Terence and which Heywood doubtlessly read in grammar school.

The present text is based on the 1612 edition of the essay.

BIBLIOGRAPHY. *An Apology for Actors, Shakespeare Society Reprint* (1841); A. Clark, *Thomas Heywood* (1931). See also the items on the stage controversy under Gosson (above, pp. 85–6).

from

AN APOLOGY FOR ACTORS

[1612]

MOOVED BY THE SUNDRY exclamations of many seditious sectists in this age, who, in the fatnes and ranknes of a peacable commonwealth, grow up like unsavery tufts of grasse, which, though outwardly greene and fresh to the eye, yet are they both unpleasant and unprofitable, beeing too sower for food, and too ranke for

fodder; these men, like the ancient Germans, affecting no fashion
but their owne, would draw other nations to bee slovens like
them-selves, and, undertaking to purifie and reforme the sacred
bodies of the church and common-weale (in the trew use of both
which they are altogether ignorant), would but like artlesse
phisitions, for experiment sake, rather minister pils to poyson the
whole body, then cordials to preserve any, or the least part.
Amongst many other thinges tollerated in this peaceable and
florishing state, it hath pleased the high and mighty princes of
this land to limit the use of certain publicke theaters, which, since
many of these over-curious heads have lavishly and violently slan-
dered, I hold it not amisse to lay open some few antiquities to
approve the true use of them, with arguments (not of the least
moment) which, according to the weaknes of my spirit and in-
fancy of my iudgment, I will (by God's grace) commit to the
eyes of all favorable and iudiciall readers, as well to satisfie the
requests of some of our well qualified favorers, as to stop the
envious acclamations of those who chalenge to themselves a
priveledge[d] invective, and against all free estates a railing
liberty. . . .

[A Defense of tragedy by Melpomene, Muse of Tragedy]

Grande sonant tragici, tragicos decet ira cothurnos.[1]

Am I Melpomene, the buskened Muse,
That held in awe the tyrants of the world,
And playde their lives in publicke theaters,
Making them feare to sinne, since fearelesse I
Prepar'd to write their lives in crimson inke,
And act their shames in eye of all the world?
Have not I whipt Vice with a scourge of steele,
Unmaskt sterne Murther, sham'd lascivious Lust,
Pluckt off the visar from grimme Treason's face,
And made the sunne point at their ugly sinnes?
Hath not this powerful hand tam'd fiery Rage,
Kild poysonous Envy with her owne keene darts,
Choak't up the covetous mouth with moulten gold,

---

[1] "The tragedians speak grandly, and wrath befits the tragic buskins."
Ovid, *Remedia Amoris*, 375.

Burst the vast wombe of eating Gluttony,
And drown'd the Drunkard's gall in juice of grapes?
I have showed Pryde his picture on a stage,
Layde ope the ugly shapes his steele-glasse hid,
And made him passe thence meekely. In those daies
When emperours with their presence grac't my sceanes,
And thought none worthy to present themselves
Save emperours, to delight embassadours,
Then did this garland florish, then my roabe
Was of the deepest crimson, the best dye:

Cura ducum fuerant olim regumque poetæ,
Præmiaque antiqui magna tulere chori.[2]

Who lodge then in the bosome of great kings,
Save he that had a grave cothurnate Muse?
A stately verse in an Iambick stile
Became a Kesar's mouth. Oh! these were times
Fit for you bards to vent your golden rymes.
Then did I tread on arras; cloth of tissues
Hung round the fore-front of my stage; the pillers
That did support the roofe of my large frame
Double appareld in pure Ophir gold,
Whilst the round circle of my spacious orbe
Was throng'd with princes, dukes, and senators.
Nunc hedaræ sine honore jacent.[3]
But now's the iron age, and black-mouth'd curres
Barke at the vertues of the former world.
Such with their breath have blasted my fresh roabe,
Pluckt at my flowry chaplet, towsed my tresses;
Nay, some who, for their basenesse hist and skorn'd,
The stage, as loathsome, hath long-since spued out,
Have watcht their time to cast invenom'd inke
To stayne my garments with. Oh! Seneca,
Thou tragicke poet, hadst thou liv'd to see
This outrage done to sad Melpomene,
With such sharpe lynes thou wouldst revenge my blot,
As armed Ovid against Ibis wrot.

[2] "Poets were once the concern of leaders and kings; and the ancient choruses received great rewards." Ovid, *Ars Amatoria*, III, 405–6.
[3] "Now ivies lie dishonored in the dust." *Ars Amatoria*, III, 411.

With that in rage shee left the place, and I my dreame, for at the instant I awaked; when, having perused this vision over and over againe in my remembrance, I suddenly bethought mee, how many ancient poets, tragicke and comicke, dying many ages agoe, live still amongst us in their works: as, amongst the Greekes, Euripides, Menander, Sophocles, Eupolis, Æschylus, Aristophanes, Apollodorus, Anaxandrides, Nicomachus, Alexis, Tereus, and others; so, among the Latins, Attilius, Actius, Melithus, Plautus, Terens, and others, whome for brevity sake I omit.

> *Hos ediscit, et hos arcto stipata theatro*
> *Spectat Roma potens; habet hos, numeratque poëtas.*[4]

These potent Rome acquires and holdeth deare,
And in their round theatres flocks to heare.

These, or any of these, had they lived in the afternoone of the world, as they dyed even in the morning, I assure my selfe would have left more memorable tropheys of that learned Muse, whome, in their golden numbers, they so richly adorned. And, amongst our moderne poets, who have bene industrious in many an elaborate and ingenious poem, even they whose pennes have had the greatest trafficke with the stage, have bene in the excuse of these Muses most forgetfull. But, leaving these, lest I make too large a head to a small body, and so mishape my subject, I will begin with the antiquity of acting comedies, tragedies, and hystories. . . .

OF ACTORS, AND

the true use of their quality.

THE THIRD BOOKE.

Tragedies and comedies, saith Donatus, had their beginning *a rebus divinis*, from divine sacrifices. They differ thus: in comedies *turbulenta prima, tranquilla ultima;* in tragedyes, *tranquilla prima, turbulenta ultima:* comedies begin in trouble and end in peace; tragedies begin in calmes, and end in tempest. Of comedies there be three kindes—moving comedies,

---

[4] Horace, *Epistles*, II, 1, 60–1. Misquoted.

called *motariæ;* standing comedies, called *stataricæ,* or mixt betwixt both, called *mistæ:* they are distributed into foure parts, the *prologue,* that is, the preface; the *protasis,* that is the proposition, which includes the first act, and presents the actors; the *epitasis,* which is the businesse and body of the comedy; the last, the *catastrophe,* and conclusion.[5] The deffinition of the comedy, according to the Latins: a discourse, consisting of divers institutions, comprehending civill and domesticke things, in which is taught what in our lives and manner is to be followed, what to bee avoyded. The Greekes define it thus: Κωμῳδία ἔστιν ἰδιωτικῶν καὶ πολιτικῶν πραγμάτων ἀχιν δονος ποροιχην.[6] Cicero saith a comedy is the imitation of life, the glasse of custome, and the image of truth.[7] In Athens they had their first originall. The ancient comedians used to attire their actors thus: the old men in white, as the most ancient of all, the yong men in party-coloured garments, to note their diversity of thoughts, their slaves and servants in thin and bare vesture, either to note their poverty, or that they might run the more lighter about their affaires: their parasites wore robes that were turned in, and intricatcly wrapped about them; the fortunate in white, the discontented in decayed vesture, or garments growne out of fashion; the rich in purple, the poore in crimson; souldiers wore purple jackets, hand-maids the habits of strange virgins, bawds pide coates, and curtezans garments of the colour of mud, to denote their covetousnesse: the stages were hung with rich arras, which was first brought from King Attalus into Rome; his state hangings were so costly, that from him all tapestries and rich arras were called *Attalia.* This being a thing antient, as I have proved it, next of dignity. As many arguments have confirmed it, and now even in these dayes by the best, without exception, favourably tollerated, why should I yeeld my censure, grounded on such firm and establisht

---

[5] Here and frequently below, Heywood is paraphrasing Euanthius, *De Comoedia et Tragoedia,* a fragmentary essay usually included at the beginning of editions of the commentaries on Terence of Donatus, and ascribed to him.

[6] "Comedy is [a representation of] a portion of the actions of average men and citizens, which involves no danger." Attributed to Theophrastus and repeated by Diomedes, *Ars Grammatica,* III.

[7] This frequently-quoted definition is not by Cicero but is attributed to him by Euanthius.

sufficiency, to any tower founded on sand, any castle built in the aire, or any triviall upstart, and mere imaginary opinion? . . .

To proceed to the matter. First, playing is an ornament to the citty, which strangers of all nations repairing hither report of in their countries, beholding them here with some admiration; for what variety of entertainment can there be in any citty of christendome more then in London? But some will say, this dish might be very well spared out of the banquet: to him I answere, Diogenes, that used to feede on rootes, cannot relish a marchpane. Secondly, our English tongue, which hath ben the most harsh, uneven, and broken language of the world, part Dutch, part Irish, Saxon, Scotch, Welsh, and indeed a gallimaffry of many, but perfect in none, is now by this secondary meanes of playing continually refined, every writer striving in himselfe to adde a new florish unto it; so that in processes, from the most rude and unpolisht tongue, it is growne to a most perfect and composed language, and many excellent workes and elaborate poems writ in the same, that many nations grow inamored of our tongue (before despised.) Neither Saphicke, Ionicke, Iambicke, Phaleuticke, Adonicke, Gliconicke, Hexamiter, Tetramiter, Pentamiter, Asclepediacke, Choriambicke, nor any other measured verse used among the Greekes, Latins, Italians, French, Dutch, or Spanish writers, but may be exprest in English, be it blanke verse or meeter, in distichon, or hexastichon, or in what forme or feet, or what number you can desire. Thus you see to what excellency our refined English is brought, that in these daies we are ashamed of that euphony and eloquence, which within these 60 yeares the best tongues in the land were proud to pronounce. Thirdly, playes have made the ignorant more apprehensive, taught the unlearned the knowledge of many famous histories, instructed such as cannot reade in the discovery of all our English chronicles; and what man have you now of that weake capacity that cannot discourse of any notable thing recorded even from William the Conquerour, nay, from the landing of Brute, untill this day? beeing possest of their true use, for or because playes are writ with this ayme, and carryed with this methode, to teach their subjects obedience to their king, to shew the people the untimely ends of such as have moved tumults, commotions, and insurrections, to present them with the flourishing estate of such as live in obedience, exhorting them to allegeance, dehorting them from all trayterous and fellonious stratagems.

Omne genus scripti gravitate tragedia vincit.[8]

If we present a tragedy, we include the fatall and abortive ends of such as commit notorious murders, which is aggravated and acted with all the art that may be to terrifie men from the like abhorred practises. If wee present a forreigne history, the subject is so intended, that in the lives of Romans, Grecians, or others, either the vertues of our countrymen are extolled, or their vices reproved; as thus, by the example of Cæsar to stir souldiers to valour and magnanimity; by the fall of Pompey that no man trust in his owne strength: we present Alexander killing his friend in his rage, to reprove rashnesse; Mydas, choked with his gold, to taxe covetousnesse; Nero against tyranny; Sardanapalus against luxury; Ninus against ambition, with infinite others, by sundry instances either animating men to noble attempts, or attacking the consciences of the spectators, finding themselves toucht in presenting the vices of others. If a morall,[9] it is to perswade men to humanity and good life, to instruct them in civility and good manners, shewing them the fruits of honesty, and the end of villany.

Versibus exponi tragicis res comica non vult.[10]

Againe Horace, *Arte Poeticâ,*

At vestri proavi Plautinos et numeros et
Laudavere sales.[11]

If a comedy, it is pleasantly contrived with merry accidents, and intermixt with apt and witty jests, to present before the prince at certain times of solemnity, or else merily fitted to the stage. And what is then the subject of this harmlesse mirth? either in the shape of a clowne to shew others their slovenly and un-handsome behaviour, that they may reforme that simplicity in themselves which others make their sport, lest they happen to

---

[8] "Tragedy surpasses every other kind of writing in gravity." Ovid, *Tristia*, II, 381.

[9] I.e., a morality play.

[10] "Comic subject-matter should not be set forth in tragic meters." *Ars Poetica*, 89.

[11] "Your forefathers praised Plautine meter and satire." *Ars Poetica*, 270–1.

become the like subject of generall scorne to an auditory; else it intreates of love, deriding foolish inamorates, who spend their ages, their spirits, nay themselves, in the servile and ridiculous imployments of their mistresses: and these are mingled with sportfull accidents, to recreate such as of themselves are wholly devoted to melancholly, which corrupts the bloud, or to refresh such weary spirits as are tired with labour or study, to moderate the cares and heavinesse of the minde, that they may returne to their trades and faculties with more zeale and earnestnesse, after some small, soft, and pleasant retirement. Sometimes they discourse of pantaloones, usurers that have unthrifty sonnes, which both the fathers and sonnes may behold to their instructions: sometimes of curtezans, to divulge their subtelties and snares in which young men may be intangled, shewing them the meanes to avoyd them. If we present a pastorall, we shew the harmlesse love of sheepheards diversely moralized, distinguishing betwixt the craft of the citty, and the innocency of the sheep-coat. Briefly, there is neither tragedy, history, comedy, morrall, or pastorall, from which an infinite use cannot be gathered. I speake not in the defence of any lascivious shewes, scurrelous jeasts, or scandalous invectives. If there be any such I banish them quite from my patronage; yet Horace, Sermon I., satyr iv., thus writes:—

> *Eupolis atque Cratinus Aristophanesque poetæ,*
> *Atque alii quorum comœdia prisca virorum est,*
> *Si quis erat dignus describi, quòd malus, aut fur,*
> *Quòd mæchus foret, aut sicarius, aut alioqui*
> *Famosus, multâ cum libertate notabant.*[12]

Eupolis, Cratinus, Aristophanes, and other comike poets in the time of Horace, with large scope and unbridled liberty, boldly and plainly scourged all abuses, as in their ages were generally practised, to the staining and blemishing of a faire and beautifull common-weale. Likewise a learned gentleman in his Apology for

---

[12] "The poets Eupolis, Cratinus, and Aristophanes, and other writers of the early comedy stigmatized with great freedom anyone who was worthy of [such] description because he was evil or a thief, an adulterer or a cutthroat, or infamous in any other way." The reference is to the "old comedy" as distinguished from the less bitter and more impersonal "new comedy" of Menander, Plautus, and Terence.

Poetry [13] speakes thus: Tragedies well handled be a most worthy kind of poesie. Comedies make men see and shame at their faults: and, proceeding further, amongst other University-playes he remembers the Tragedy of Richard the third,[14] acted in St. Johns, in Cambridge, so essentially, that had the tyrant Phalaris beheld his bloudy proceedings, it had mollified his heart, and made him relent at sight of his inhuman massacres. Further, he commends of comedies, the Cambridge *Pedantius*,[15] and the Oxford *Bellum Grammaticale;* [16] and, leaving them, passes on to our publicke playes, speaking liberally in their praise, and what commendable use may be gathered of them. If you peruse *Margarita Poetica*,[17] you may see what excellent uses and sentences he hath gathered out of *Terence* his *Andrea, Eunuchus,* and the rest: likewise out of *Plautus,* his *Amphytryo, Asinaria;* and, moreover, *ex Comediis Philodoxis, Caroli Acretini: De falsâ Hypocritâ, et tristi Mercurio, Ronsii Versellensis: ex Comœdiâ Philanirâ, Ugolini Parmensis,*[18] all reverend schollers, and comicke poets. Reade elce the 4 tragedies, *Philunica, Petrus, Aman, Katherina, Claudii Roiletti Belvensis.*[19] But I should tire my selfe to reckon the names of all French, Roman, German, Spanish, Italian, and English poets, being in number infinite, and their labours extant to approve their worthinesse.

Is thy minde noble, and wouldst thou be further stir'd up to magnanimity? Behold upon the stage thou maist see Hercules, Achilles, Alexander, Cæsar, Alcibiades, Lysander, Sertorius, Hannibal, Antigonus, Philip of Macedon, Mithridates of Pontus, Pyrrhus of Epirus: Agesilaus among the Lacedemonians; Epaminondas amongst the Thebans: Sævola alone entring the armed tents of Porsenna: Horatius Cocles alone withstanding the whole army of the Hetrurians: Leonidas of Sparta choosing a lyon to

[13] The reference is to Sir John Harington (above, pp. 212–13).

[14] A Neo-Latin tragedy by Thomas Legge.

[15] A Neo-Latin comedy by Edward Forsett.

[16] A dramatic entertainment in Latin, acted at Cambridge in 1592.

[17] An anthology compiled in the fifteenth century by Albertus de Eyb.

[18] "from the comedies, the *Philodoxis* by Carolus Acretinus, *The False Hypocrite* and *Sad Mercury* by Ronsius Versellensis, and the *Philanira* by Ugolinus Parmensis."

[19] "the *Philunica, Peter, Hamann,* and *Catherine* by Claudius Roilettus Belvensis."

leade a band of deere, rather then one deere to conduct an army
of lyons, with infinite others, in their own persones, qualities,
and shapes, animating thee with courage, deterring thee from
cowardise. Hast thou of thy country well deserved? and art thou
of thy labour evil requited? To associate thee thou mayst see the
valiant Roman Marcellus pursue Hannibal at Nola, conquering
Syracusa, vanquishing the Gauls at Padua, and presently (for his
reward) banisht his country into Greece. There thou mayest see
Scipio Africanus, now triumphing for the conquest of all Africa,
and immediately exil'd the confines of Romania. Art thou inclined
to lust? behold the falles of the Tarquins in the rape of Lucrece;
the guerdon of luxury in the death of Sardanapalus; Appius destroyed in the ravishing of Virginia, and the destruction of Troy
in the lust of Helena. Art thou proud? our scene presents thee
with the fall of Phaeton; Narcissus pining in the love of his
shadow; ambitious Hamon, now calling himselfe a God, and by
and by thrust headlong among the divels. We present men with
the uglinesse of their vices to make them the more to abhorre
them; as the Persians use, who, above all sinnes loathing drunken-
nesse, accustomed in their solemne feasts to make their servants
and captives extremely overcome with wine, and then call their
children to view their nasty and lothsome behaviour, making
them hate that sinne in themselves, which shewed so grosse and
abhominable in others. The like use may be gathered of the
drunkards, so naturally imitated in our playes, to the applause
of the actor, content of the auditory, and reproving of the vice.
Art thou covetous? go no further then Plautus, his comedy called
Euclio.

> *Dum fallax servus, durus pater, improba lena*
> *Vixerit, et meretrix blanda, Menandros erit.*[20]

> While ther's false servant, or obdurate sire,
> Sly baud, smooth whore, Menandros wee'l admire.

To end in a word, art thou addicted to prodigallity, envy,
cruelty, perjury, flattery, or rage? our scenes affoord thee store of
men to shape your lives by, who be frugall, loving, gentle, trusty,
without soothing, and in all things temperate. Wouldst thou be

[20] Ovid, *Amores*, I, 15, 17–8.

honourable, just, friendly, moderate, devout, mercifull, and loving
concord? thou mayest see many of their fates and ruines who
have beene dishonourable, injust, false, gluttenous, sacrilegious,
bloudy-minded, and brochers of dissention. Women, likewise,
that are chaste are by us extolled and encouraged in their vertues,
being instanced by Diana, Belphœbe, Matilda, Lucrece, and the
Countess of Salisbury. The unchaste are by us shewed their errors
in the persons of Phryne, Lais, Thais, Flora; and amongst us
Rosamond and Mistresse Shore. What can sooner print modesty
in the soules of the wanton, then by discovering unto them the
monstrousnesse of their sin? It followes, that we prove these exercises to have beene the discoverers of many notorious murders,
long concealed from the eyes of the world. . . .[21]

---

[21] Heywood relates several allegedly true anecdotes to illustrate the power
of dramas to awaken the consciences of criminals and sinners. His stories
recall Hamlet's belief that his 'play within a play' will cause Claudius to
make a public confession of his murder (*Hamlet*, II, ii, 596 606). They are
also a reminder that one seriously held and widespread Renaissance definition of tragic catharsis was "a purging of the desire to sin of members of
the audience."

Thomas Campion

[1567–1620]

❧❦❧

THOMAS CAMPION IS ONE of the most charming poets of the turn of the century. A physician by profession, he excelled in graceful lyrics in the Horatian manner, which he then set to faultless lute accompaniments. His four *Books of Airs* (1613, 1617) are an English musical classic. The much-maligned *Observations in the Art of English Poesie* (1602) should be read with this fact in mind. On the one hand, the essay is the last important Renaissance contribution to the English debate over quantitative verse, and a distinct anachronism in view of the achievements of the Elizabethan poets. On the other, it is a musician's attempt to express truths about the sound value of poetry in the critical language of his age. The attempt seems clumsy because Campion's vocabulary was inadequate; however, its measure of truth is at least suggested by the beautiful "Rose-Cheekt Lawra."

Not until the twentieth century, and against a background of some fifty years of experiment with free verse, were critics able to discuss the prosody of unrhymed, non-metrical verse in terms more adequate than Campion's. Campion and his fellow classicists failed in their immediate aim, but they helped to make English poets aware of the subtle music of the language. The grandest poetic experiment of the seventeenth century, *Paradise Lost*, consistently reveals Milton's awareness of the twin claims of quantity and accent.

The present text of the *Observations* is based on the 1602 edition.

BIBLIOGRAPHY. *Works*, ed. P. Vivian (1909); M. Kastendieck, *England's Musical Poet: Thomas Campion* (1938); T. MacDonagh, *Campion and the Art of English Poetry* (1913); R. Short, "The Metrical Theory and Practice of Thomas Campion," *PMLA*, LIX (1944). More generally, see A. Clark, "Milton and the Renaissance Revolt Against Rhyme," in *Studies in Literary Modes* (1946); V. Rubel, *Poetic Diction in the English Renaissance* (1941); G. Saintsbury, *A History of English Prosody*, 3 vols. (1906–10); and the second section of the bibliography following the headnote on Spenser (above, p. 186).

from

OBSERVATIONS IN THE ART OF ENGLISH POESIE

[1602]

THE FIRST CHAPTER, INTREATING OF NUMBERS IN GENERALL.

THERE IS NO WRITING too breefe that, without obscuritie, comprehends the intent of the writer. These my late obseruations in English Poesy I haue thus briefely gathered, that they might proue the lesse troublesome in perusing, and the more apt to be rctayn'd in memorie. And I will first generally handle the nature of Numbers. Number is *discreta quantitas*: [1] so that when we speake simply of number, we intend only the disseruer'd quantity; but when we speake of a Poeme written in number, we consider not only the distinct number of the sillables, but also their value, which is contained in the length or shortnes of their sound. As in Musick we do not say a straine of so many notes, but so many sem'briefes (though sometimes there are no more notes then sem'briefes), so in a verse the numeration of the sillables is not so much to be obserued as their waite and due proportion. In ioyning of words to harmony there is nothing more offensiue to the eare then to place a long sillable with a short note, or a short sillable with a long note, though in the last the vowell often beares it out. The world is made by Simmetry and proportion, and is in that respect compared to Musick, and Musick to Poetry: for *Terence* saith, speaking of Poets, *artem qui tractant musicam*,[2] confounding Music and Poesy together. What musick can there be where there is no proportion obserued? Learning first flourished in *Greece*; from thence it was deriued vnto the *Romaines*, both diligent obseruers of the number and quantity of

---

[1] "Measured quantity."
[2] "Who deal with the art of music." Reference to Terence, *Phormio*, Prologue, 18.

sillables, not in their verses only but likewise in their prose. Learning, after the declining of the *Romaine* Empire and the pollution of their language through the conquest of the *Barbarians*, lay most pitifully deformed till the time of *Erasmus, Rewcline,* Sir *Thomas More,* and other learned men of that age, who brought the Latine toong again to light, redeeming it with much labour out of the hands of the illiterate Monks and Friers: as a scoffing booke, entituled *Epistolae obscurorum virorum*,[3] may sufficiently testifie. In those lack-learning times, and in barbarized Italy, began that vulgar and easie kind of Poesie which is now in vse throughout most parts of Christendome, which we abusively call Rime and Meeter, of *Rithmus* and *Metrum,* of which I will now discourse.

THE SECOND CHAPTER, DECLARING THE VNAPTNESSE OF RIME IN POESIE.

I am not ignorant that whosoeuer shall by way of reprehension examine the imperfections of Rime must encounter with many glorious enemies, and those very expert and ready at their weapon, that can if neede be extempore (as they say) rime a man to death. Besides there is growne a kind of prescription in the vse of Rime, to forestall the right of true numbers, as also the consent of many nations, against all which it may seeme a thing almost impossible and vaine to contend. All this and more can not yet deterre me from a lawful defence of perfection, or make me any whit the sooner adheare to that which is lame and vnbeseeming. For custome I allege that ill vses are to be abolisht, and that things naturally imperfect can not be perfected by vse. Old customes, if they be better, why should they not be recald, as the yet florishing custome of numerous poesy vsed among the *Romanes* and *Grecians*? But the vnaptnes of our toongs and the difficultie of imitation dishartens vs: againe, the facilitie and popularitie of Rime creates as many Poets as a hot sommer flies.

But let me now examine the nature of that which we call Rime. By Rime is vnderstoode that which ends in the like sound, so that verses in such maner composed yeeld but a continual repetition of that Rhetoricall figure which we terme *similiter desinentia*,[4]

---

[3] *Letters of Obscure Men* (1515). A famous satirical work of the early humanistic period in Germany, mainly by Ulrich von Hutten.

[4] "Similar ending." I.e., rhyme.

and that, being but *figura verbi*,[5] ought (as *Tully* and all other
Rhetoritians have iudicially obseru'd) sparingly to be vs'd, least
it should offend the eare with tedious affectation. Such was that
absurd following of the letter amongst our English so much of
late affected, but now hist out of Paules Churchyard: which
foolish figuratiue repetition crept also into the Latine toong, as
it is manifest in the booke of P[s] called *praelia porcorum*,[6] and
another pamphlet all of F[s] which I haue seene imprinted; but
I will leaue these follies to their owne ruine, and returne to the
matter intended. The eare is a rationall sence and a chief iudge
of proportion; but in our kind of riming what proportion is there
kept where there remaines such a confused inequalitie of sillables? *Iambick* and *Trochaick* feete, which are opposed by nature,
are by all Rimers confounded; nay, oftentimes they place instead
of an *Iambick* the foot *Pyrrychius*, consisting of two short sillables, curtalling their verse, which they supply in reading with a
ridiculous and vnapt drawing of their speech. As for example:

Was it my desteny, or dismall chaunce?

In this verse the two last sillables of the word *Desteny*, being
both short, and standing for a whole foote in the verse, cause the
line to fall out shorter then it ought by nature. The like impure
errors haue in time of rudenesse bene vsed in the Latine toong,
as the *Carmina prouerbialia*[7] can witnesse, and many other such
reuerened bables. But the noble *Grecians* and *Romaines*, whose
skilfull monuments outliue barbarisme, tyed themselues to the
strict obseruation of poeticall numbers, so abandoning the childish titillation of riming that it was imputed a great error to *Ouid*
for setting forth this one riming verse,

Quot caelum stellas tot habet tua Roma puellas.[8]

For the establishing of this argument, what better confirmation
can be had then that Sir *Thomas Moore* in his booke of Epigrams,

[5] "A figure of language." A figure resulting from the manipulation of
word patterns, and distinguished from a 'figure of thought' where ideas are
manipulated, as in metaphor.
[6] *The Pigs' Wars. The Pugna Porcorum* (1530) by Joannes Placentius,
was a burelesque in which every word began with *P*. The book of *F*'s has
not been identified.
[7] *The Proverb-Poems*—a commonplace book often reprinted in the sixteenth century; e.g., London, 1588.
[8] "Your Rome has as many girls as the sky has stars." *Ars Amatoria*, I, 59.

where he makes two sundry Epitaphs vpon the death of a singing-man at *Westminster,* the one in learned numbers and dislik't, the other in rude rime and highly extold: so that he concludes, *tales lactucas talia labra petunt,*[9] like lips like lettuce.

But there is yet another fault in Rime altogether intollerable, which is, that it inforceth a man oftentimes to abiure his matter and extend a short conceit beyond all bounds of arte; for in Quatorzens, methinks, the poet handles his subiect as tyrannically as *Procrustes* the thiefe his prisoners, whom, when he had taken, he vsed to cast vpon a bed, which if they were to short to fill, he would stretch them longer, if too long, he would cut them shorter. Bring before me now any the most self-lou'd Rimer, and let me see if without blushing he be able to reade his lame halting rimes. Is there not a curse of Nature laid vpon such rude Poesie, when the Writer is himself asham'd of it, and the hearers in contempt call it Riming and Ballating? What Deuine in his Sermon, or graue Counsellor in his Oration, will alleage the testimonie of a rime? But the deuinity of the *Romaines* and *Gretians* was all written in verse; and *Aristotle, Galene,* and the bookes of all the excellent Philosophers are full of the testimonies of the old Poets. By them was laid the foundation of all humane wisdome, and from them the knowledge of all antiquitie is deriued. I will propound but one question, and so conclude this point. If the *Italians, Frenchmen,* and *Spanyards,* that with commendation have written in Rime, were demaunded whether they had rather the bookes they haue publisht (if their toong would beare it) should remaine as they are in Rime or be translated into the auncient numbers of the Greekes and Romaines, would they not answere into numbers? What honour were it then for our English language to be the first that after so many yeares of barbarisme could second the perfection of the industrious *Greekes* and *Romaines?* which how it may be effected I will now proceede to demonstrate.

THE THIRD CHAPTER: OF OUR ENGLISH NUMBERS IN GENERALL.

There are but three feete which generally distinguish the Greeke and Latine verses, the *Dactil,* consisting of one long

---

[9] Literally, "Such lips seek such lettuce." From More's epigram on Henry Abyngdon, Master of the Children of the Royal Chapel at Westminster.

sillable and two short, as *vĭuĕrĕ*; the *Trochy*, of one long and one
short, as *vĭtă*; and the *Iambick* of one short and one long, as
ămōr. The *Spondee* of two long, the *Tribrach* of three short, the
Anapæstick of two short and a long, are but as seruants to the
first. Diuers other feete I know are by the Grammarians cited,
but to little purpose. The *Heroicall* verse that is distinguisht by
the *Dactile* hath bene oftentimes attempted in our English toong,
but with passing pitifull successe; and no wonder, seeing it is an
attempt altogether against the nature of our language. For both
the concurse of our monasillables make our verses vnapt to slide,
and also, if we examine our polysillables, we shall finde few of
them, by reason of their heauinesse, willing to serue in place of
a *Dactile*. Thence it is that the writers of English heroicks do so
often repeate *Amyntas, Olympus, Auernus, Erinnis,* and suchlike
borrowed words, to supply the defect of our hardly intreated
Dactile. I could in this place set downe many ridiculous kinds of
Dactils which they vse, but that it is not my purpose here to incite
men to laughter. If we therefore reiect the *Dactil* as vnfit for our
vse (which of necessity we are enforst to do), there remayne
only the *Iambick* foote, of which the *Iambick* verse is fram'd,
and the *Trochee*, from which the *Trochaick* numbers haue their
originall. Let vs now then examine the property of these two
feete, and try if they consent with the nature of our English
sillables. And first for the *Iambicks*, they fall out so naturally in
our toong, that, if we examine our owne writers, we shall find
they vnawares hit oftentimes vpon the true *Iambick* numbers,
but alwayes ayme at them as far as their eare without the guid-
ance of arte can attain vnto, as it shall hereafter more euidently
appeare. The *Trochaick* foote, which is but an *Iambick* turn'd
ouer and ouer, must of force in like manner accord in proportion
with our Brittish sillables, and so produce an English *Trochaicall*
verse. Then hauing these two principall kinds of verses, we may
easily out of them deriue other formes, as the Latines and Greekes
before vs haue done: whereof I will make plaine demonstration,
beginning at the *Iambick* verse.

THE FOURTH CHAPTER: OF THE IAMBICK VERSE.

I haue obserued, and so may any one that is either practis'd
in singing, or hath a naturall eare able to time a song, that the

Latine verses of sixe feete, as the *Heroick* and *Iambick*, or of
fiue feete, as the *Trochaick*, are in nature all of the same length
of sound with our English verses of fiue feet; for either of them
being tim'd with the hand, *quinque perficiunt tempora*, they fill
vp the quantity (as it were) of fiue sem'briefs; as for example, if
any man will proue to time these verses with his hand.

A pure *Iambick*.

Suis et ipsa Roma viribus ruit.[10]

A licentiate *Iambick*.

Ducunt volentes fata, nolentes trahunt.[11]

An *Heroick* verse.

Tityre, tu patulae recubans sub tegmine fagi.[12]

A *Trochaick* verse.

Nox est perpetua vna dormienda.[13]

English *Iambicks* pure.

The more secure, the more the stroke we feele
Of vnpreuented harms; so gloomy stormes
Appeare the sterner, if the day be cleere.

Th' English *Iambick* licentiate.

Harke how these winds do murmur at thy flight.

The English *Trochee*.

Still where Envy leaues, remorse doth enter.

The cause why these verses differing in feete yeeld the same
length of sound, is by reason of some rests which either the
necessity of the numbers or the heauiness of the sillables do beget.
For we find in musick that oftentimes the straines of a song cannot
be reduct to true number without some rests prefixt in the beginning and middle, as also at the close if need requires. Besides,
our English monasillables enforce many breathings which no
doubt greatly lengthen a verse, so that it is no wonder if for these
reasons our English verses of fiue feete hold pace with the *Latines*
of sixe. The pure *Iambick* in English needes small demonstration,

[10] "And Rome herself fell through her own strength."
[11] "The fates lead those who are willing; they drag those who are not."
Seneca, *Epistles*, 107.
[12] "Tityrus, you, lying under the shade of the spreading beech. . . ."
Virgil, *Eclogues*, I, 1.
[13] "Night is one endless sleep." Catullus, "To Lesbia."

because it consists simply of *Iambick* feete; but our *Iambick* licentiate offers itselfe to a farther consideration, for in the third and fift place we must of force hold the *Iambick* foote, in the first, second, and fourth place we may vse a *Spondee* or *Iambick* and sometime a *Tribrack* or *Dactile*, but rarely an *Anapestick* foote, and that in the second or fourth place. But why an *Iambick* in the third place? I answere, that the forepart of the verse may the gentlier slide into his *Dimeter*, as, for example sake, deuide this verse:

Harke how these winds do murmure at thy flight.

Harke how these winds, there the voice naturally affects a rest; then *murmur at thy flight*, that is of itselfe a perfect number, as I will declare in the next Chapter; and therefore the other odde sillable betweene them ought to be short, least the verse should hang too much betweene the naturall pause of the verse and the *Dimeter* following; the which *Dimeter* though it be naturally *Trochaical*, yet it seemes to haue his originall out of the *Iambick* verse. But the better to confirme and expresse these rules, I will set downe a short Poeme in *Licentiate Iambicks*, which may giue more light to them that shall hereafter imitate these numbers.

Goe, numbers, boldly passe, stay not for ayde
Of shifting rime, that easie flatterer,
Whose witchcraft can the ruder eares beguile.
Let your smooth feete, enur'd to purer arte,
True measures tread. What if your pace be slow,
And hops not like the Grecian elegies? . . .

Though, as I said before, the naturall breathing-place of our English *Iambick* verse is in the last sillable of the second foote, as our *Trochy* after the manner of the Latine *Heroick* and *Iambick* rests naturally in the first of the third foote, yet no man is tyed altogether to obserue this rule, but he may alter it, after the iudgment of his eare, which Poets, Orators, and Musitions of all men ought to haue most excellent. Againe, though I said peremtorily before that the third and fift place of our licentiate *Iambick* must alwayes hold an *Iambick* foote, yet I will shew you example in both places where a *Tribrack* may be very formally taken, and first in the third place:

Some trade in *Barbary,* some in *Turky* trade.

An other example:

Men that do fall to misery, quickly fall.

If you doubt whether the first of *misery* be naturally short or no, you may iudge it by the easy sliding of these two verses following:

The first:

Whome misery cannot alter, time devours.

The second:

What more vnhappy life, what misery more?

Example of the *Tribrack* in the fift place, as you may perceiue in the last foote of the fourth verse:

Some from the starry throne his fame deriues,
Some from the mynes beneath, from trees or herbs:
Each hath his glory, each his sundry gift,
Renown'd in eu'ry art there liues not any.

To proceede farther, I see no reason why the English *Iambick* in his first place may not as well borrow a foote of the *Trochy* as our *Trochy,* or the Latine *Hendicasillable,* may in the like case make bold with the *Iambick*: but it must be done euer with this caueat, which is, that a *Sponde, Dactile,* or *Tribrack* do supply the next place; for an *Iambick* beginning with a single short sillable, and the other ending before with the like, would too much drinke vp the verse if they came immediatly together.

The example of the *Sponde* after the *Trochy*:

As the faire sonne the lightsome heau'n adorns.

The example of the *Dactil*:

Noble, ingenious, and discreetly wise.

The example of the *Tribrack*:

Beauty to ielousie brings ioy, sorrow, feare.

Though I haue set downe these second licenses as good and agreable enough, yet for the most part my first rules are generall.

These are those numbers which Nature in our English destinates to the Tragick and Heroik Poeme: for the subiect of them both being all one, I see no impediment why one verse may not serue for them both, as it appeares more plainly in the old comparison of the two Greeke writers, when they say, *Homerus est Sophocles heroicus*,[14] and againe *Sophocles est Homerus tragicus*,[15] intimating that both Sophocles and Homer are the same in height and subiect, and differ onely in the kinde of their numbers.

The Iambick verse in like manner being yet made a little more licentiate, that it may thereby the neerer imitate our common talke, will excellently serue for Comedics; and then may we vse a *Sponde* in the fift place, and in the third place any foote except a *Trochy*, which neuer enters into our Iambick verse but in the first place, and then with his caueat of the other feete which must of necessitie follow.

THE EIGHT CHAPTER: OF DITTIES AND ODES.

To descend orderly from the more simple numbers to them that are more compounded, it is now time to handle such verses as are fit for *Ditties* or *Odes*; which we may call *Lyricall*, because they arc apt to be soong to an instrument, if they were adorn'd with conuenient notes. Of that kind I will demonstrate three in this Chapter, and in the first we will proceede after the manner of the *Saphick,* which is a *Trochaicall* verse as well as the *Hendicasillable* in Latine. The first three verses therefore in our English *Saphick* are meerely those *Trochaicks* which I handled in the sixt Chapter, excepting only that the first foote of either of them must euer of necessity be a *Spondee,* to make the number more graue. The fourth and last closing verse is compounded of three *Trochyes* together, to giue a more smooth farewell, as you may easily obserue in this Poeme made vpon a Triumph at Whitehall, whose glory was dasht with an vnwelcome showre, hindring the people from the desired sight of her Majestie.

The English *Sapphick*.

Faiths pure shield, the Christian *Diana,*
Englands glory crownd with all deuinenesse,
Liue long with triumphs to blesse thy people
    At thy sight triumphing.

[14] "Homer is an epic Sophocles."
[15] "Sophocles is a tragic Homer."

Loe, they sound; the Knights in order armed
Entring threat the list, adrest to combat
For their courtly loues; he, hees the wonder
    Whome *Eliza* graceth.

Their plum'd pomp the vulgar heaps detaineth,
And rough steeds; let vs the still deuices
Close obserue, the speeches and the musicks
    Peacefull arms adorning.

But whence showres so fast this angry tempest,
Clowding dimme the place? Behold, *Eliza*
This day shines not here; this heard, the launces
    And thick heads do vanish.

The second kinde consists of *Dimeter*, whose first foote may
either be a *Sponde* or a *Trochy*. The two verses following are
both of them *Trochaical*, and consist of foure feete, the first of
either of them being a *Spondee* or *Trochy*, the other three only
Trochyes. The fourth and last verse is made of two *Trochyes*.
The number is voluble, and fit to expresse any amorous conceit.

The Example.

Rose-cheekt *Lawra*, come
Sing thou smoothly with thy beawtie's
Silent musick, either other
    Sweetely gracing.

Louely formes do flowe
From concent deuinely framed;
Heau'n is musick, and thy beawtie's
    Birth is heauenly.

These dull notes we sing
Discords neede for helps to grace them;
Only beawty purely louing
    Knowes no discord,

But still moues delight,
Like cleare springs renu'd by flowing,
Euer perfet, euer in them-
    selues eternall.

The third kind begins as the second kind ended, with a verse consisting of two *Trochy* feete, and then as the second kind had in the middle two *Trochaick* verses of foure feete, so this hath three of the same nature, and ende in a *Dimeter* as the second began. The *Dimeter* may allow in the first place a *Trochy* or a *Spondee*, but no *Iambick*.

The Example.

Iust beguiler,
Kindest loue, yet only chastest,
Royall in thy smooth denyals,
Frowning or demurely smiling,
Still my pure delight.

Let me view thee
With thoughts and with eyes affected,
And if then the flames do murmur,
Quench them with thy vertue, charme them
With thy stormy browes.

Heau'n so cheerefull
Laughs not euer, hory winter
Knowes his season, euen the freshest
Sommer mornes from angry thunder
Iet not still secure.[16]

[16] Chapter IX treats Anacreontic verse; Chapter X, the concluding chapter, is a technical discussion "Of the Quantity of English Sillables."

Samuel Daniel

[1562–1619]

❧❧❧

DANIEL's *Defence of Ryme* (1603?) was written expressly to refute Campion, who is referred to in the pamphlet as "the detractor" and "the adversary." It was a decisive refutation, and no serious effort to 'classicize' English prosody was made after its appearance. Unlike many controversial works of the period, it is tolerant and restrained. It reveals a flexible, witty, and incisive mind. Daniel appeals to nature and custom for his defense. His arguments often anticipate twentieth-century attacks on the Latin terminology of traditional English grammar. Equally notable is Daniel's praise of the Middle Ages, which humanists from Petrarch to Milton had vied with one another in abusing.

The present text is based on the 1603 edition.

BIBLIOGRAPHY. *Poems and A Defence of Ryme*, ed. A. Sprague (1930); J. Stewart, "Montaigne and the *Defence of Ryme*," *RES*, IX (1933).

from

A DEFENCE OF RYME

[1603]

TO WILLIAM HERBERT, ERLE OF PEMBROOKE.

THE GENERALL CUSTOME and vse of Ryme in this kingdome, Noble Lord, hauing beene so long (as if from a Graunt of Nature) held vnquestionable, made me to imagine that it lay alto-

gither out of the way of contradiction, and was become so natural, as we should neuer haue had a thought to cast it off into
reproch, or be made to thinke that it ill-became our language.
But now I see, when there is opposition made to all things in the
world by wordes, wee must nowe at length likewise fall to contend for words themselues, and make a question whether they be
right or not. For we are tolde how that our measures goe wrong,
all Ryming is grosse, vulgare, barbarous; which if it be so, we
haue lost much labour to no purpose; and, for mine owne particular, I cannot but blame the fortune of the times and mine owne
Genius, that cast me vppon so wrong a course, drawne with the
current of custome and an vnexamined example. Hauing beene
first incourag'd or fram'd thereunto by your most Worthy and
Honorable Mother, and receiuing the first notion for the formall
ordering of those compositions at Wilton, which I must euer
acknowledge to haue beene my best Schoole, and thereof alwayes
am to hold a feeling and gratefull Memory; afterward drawne
farther on by the well liking and approbation of my worthy
Lord, the fosterer of mee and my *Muse*; I aduentured to bestow
all my whole powers therein, perceiuing it agreed so well, both
with the complexion of the times and mine owne constitution, as
I found not wherein I might better imploy me. But yet now, vpon
the great discouery of these new measures, threatning to ouerthrow the whole state of Ryme in this kingdom, I must either
stand out to defend, or els be forced to forsake my selfe and
giue ouer all. And though irresolution and a selfe distrust be the
most apparent faults of my nature, and that the least checke of
reprehension, if it sauor of reason, will as easily shake my resolution as any man's liuing, yet in this case I know not how I am
growne more resolued, and, before I sinke, willing to examine
what those powers of iudgement are that must beare me downe
and beat me off from the station of my profession, which by the
law of Nature I am set to defend: and the rather for that this
detractor (whose commendable Rymes, albeit now himselfe an
enemy to ryme, haue giuen heretofore to the world the best notice
of his worth) is a man of faire parts and good reputation; and
therefore the reproach forcibly cast from such a hand may throw
downe more at once then the labors of many shall in long time
build vp againe, specially vpon the slippery foundation of opin-

ion, and the world's inconstancy, which knowes not well what it would haue, and

> *Discit enim citius meminitque libentius illud*
> *Quod quis deridet, quam quod probat et veneratur.*[1]

And he who is thus become our vnkinde aduersarie must pardon vs if we be as iealous of our fame and reputation as hee is desirous of credite by his new-old arte, and must consider that we cannot, in a thing that concernes vs so neere, but haue a feeling of the wrong done, wherein euery Rymer in this vniuersall Iland, as well as myselfe, stands interressed. So that if his charitie had equally drawne with his learning, hee would haue forborne to procure the enuie of so powerfull a number vpon him, from whom he can not but expect the returne of a like measure of blame, and onely haue made way to his owne grace by the proofe of his abilitie, without the disparaging of vs, who would haue bin glad to haue stood quietly by him, and perhaps commended his aduenture, seeing that euermore of one science an other may be borne, and that these Salies made out of the quarter of our set knowledges are the gallant proffers onely of attemptiue spirits, and commendable, though they worke no other effect than make a Brauado: and I know it were *Indecens et morosum nimis alienae industriae modum ponere.*[2]

We could well haue allowed of his numbers, had he not disgraced our Ryme, which both Custome and Nature doth most powerfully defend: Custome that is before all Law, Nature that is aboue all Arte. Euery language hath her proper number or measure fitted to vse and delight, which Custome, intertaininge by the allowance of the Eare, doth indenize and make naturall. All verse is but a frame of wordes confined within certaine measure, differing from the ordinarie speach, and introduced, the better to expresse mens conceipts, both for delight and memorie. Which frame of words consisting of Rithmus or Metrum, Number or measure, are disposed into diuers fashions, according to the humour of the Composer and the set of the time. And these

---

[1] "It sooner learns and more willingly remembers what someone derides than what he approves and admires." Horace, *Epistles*, II, i, 262–3.

[2] "It is improper and extremely ill-tempered to set limits on another man's work."

Rhythms, as *Aristotle* saith, are familiar amongst all Nations, and
e naturali et sponte fusa compositione: [3] and they fall as naturally already in our language as euer Art can make them, being
such as the Eare of it selfe doth marshall in their proper roomes;
and they of themselues will not willingly be put out of their ranke,
and that in such a verse as best comports with the nature of our
language. And for our Ryme (which is an excellencie added to
this worke of measure, and a Harmonie farre happier than any
proportion Antiquitie could euer shew vs) dooth adde more
grace, and hath more of delight then euer bare numbers, howsoeuer they can be forced to runne in our slow language, can
possibly yeeld. Which, whether it be deriu'd of *Rhythmus* or of
Romance, which were songs the *Bards* and *Druydes* about Rymes
vsed, and therof were called *Remensi,* as some Italians holde, or
howsoeuer, it is likewise number and harmonie of words, consisting of an agreeing sound in the last sillables of seuerall verses,
giuing both to the Eare an Echo of a delightful report, and to the
Memorie a deeper impression of what is deliuered therein. For
as Greeke and Latine verse consists of the number and quantitie
of sillables, so doth the English verse of measure and accent. And
though it doth not strictly obserue long and short sillables, yet it
most religiously respects the accent; and as the short and the long
make number, so the acute and graue accent yeelde harmonie.
And harmonie is likewise number; so that the English verse then
hath number, measure, and harmonie in the best proportion of
Musicke. Which, being more certain and more resounding, works
that effect of motion with as happy successe as either the Greek
or Latin. And so naturall a melody is it, and so vniuersall, as it
seems to be generally borne with al the Nations of the world as an
hereditary eloquence proper to all mankind. . . .

'Ill customes are to be left.' I graunt it; but I see not howe that
can be taken for an ill custome which nature hath thus ratified,
all nations receiued, time so long confirmed, the effects such as
it performes those offices of motion for which it is imployed;
delighting the eare, stirring the heart, and satisfying the iudgement in such sort as I doubt whether euer single numbers will
doe in our Climate, if they shew no more worke of wonder than

[3] "From a natural and spontaneous composition." *Poetics,* IV, 6.

yet we see. And if euer they prooue to become anything, it must be by the approbation of many ages that must giue them their strength for any operation, as before the world will feele where the pulse, life, and enargie lies; which now we are sure where to haue in our Rymes, whose knowne frame hath those due staies for the minde, those incounters of touch, as makes the motion certaine, though the varietie be infinite.

Nor will the Generall sorte for whom we write (the wise being aboue books) taste these laboured measures but as an orderly prose when wee haue all done. For this kinde acquaintance and continuall familiaritie euer had betwixt our eare and this cadence is growne to so intimate a friendship, as it will nowe hardly euer be brought to misse it. For be the verse neuer so good, neuer so full, it seemes not to satisfie nor breede that delight, as when it is met and combined with a like sounding accent: which seemes as the iointure without which it hangs loose, and cannot subsist, but runnes wildely on, like a tedious fancie without a close. Suffer then the world to inioy that which it knowes, and what it likes: Seeing that whatsoeuer force of words doth mooue, delight, and sway the affections of men, in what Scythian sorte soeuer it be disposed or vttered, that is true number, measure, eloquence, and the perfection of speach: which I said hath as many shapes as there be tongues or nations in the world, nor can withall the tyrannicall Rules of idle Rhetorique be gouerned otherwise then custome and present obseruation will allow. And being now the trym and fashion of the times, to sute a man otherwise cannot but giue a touch of singularity; for when hee hath all done, hee hath but found other clothes to the same body, and peraduenture not so fitting as the former. But could our Aduersary hereby set vp the musicke of our times to a higher note of iudgement and discretion, or could these new lawes of words better our imperfections, it were a happy attempt; but when hereby we shall but as it were change prison, and put off these fetters to receiue others, what haue we gained? As good still to vse ryme and a little reason as neither ryme nor reason, for no doubt, as idle wits will write in that kinde, as do now in this, imitation wil after, though it breake her necke. . . .

But such affliction doth laboursome curiositie still lay vpon our best delights (which euer must be made strange and variable), as if Art were ordained to afflict Nature, and that we could not goe but in fetters. Euery science, euery profession, must be so wrapt vp in unnecessary intrications, as if it were not to fashion but to confound the vnderstanding: which makes me much to distrust man, and feare that our presumption goes beyond our abilitie, and our Curiositie is more then our Iudgement; laboring euer to seeme to be more then we are, or laying greater burthens vpon our mindes then they are well able to beare, because we would not appeare like other men.

And indeed I haue wished that there were not that multiplicitie of Rymes as is vsed by many in Sonets, which yet we see in some so happily to succeed, and hath beene so farre from hindering their inuentions, as it hath begot conceit beyond expectation, and comparable to the best inuentions of the world: for sure in an eminent spirit, whome Nature hath fitted for that mysterie, Ryme is no impediment to his conceit, but rather giues him wings to mount, and carries him, not out of his course, but as it were beyond his power to a farre happier flight. Al excellencies being sold vs at the hard price of labour, it followes, where we bestow most thereof we buy the best successe: and Ryme, being farre more laborious than loose measures (whatsoeuer is obiected), must needs, meeting with wit and industry, breed greater and worthier effects in our language. So that if our labours haue wrought out a manumission from bondage, and that wee goe at libertie, notwithstanding these ties, wee are no longer the slaues of Ryme, but we make it a most excellent instrument to serue vs. Nor is this certaine limit obscrued in Sonnets, any tyrannicall bounding of the conceit, but rather reducing it in *girum* and a iust forme, neither too long for the shortest proiect, nor too short for the longest, being but onely imployed for a present passion. For the body of our imagination being as an vnformed *Chaos* without fashion, without day, if by the diuine power of the spirit it be wrought into an Orbe of order and forme, is it not more pleasing to Nature, that desires a certaintie and comports not with that which is infinite, to haue these clozes, rather than not to know where to end, or how farre to goe, especially seeing our passions are often without measure? and wee finde the best of the Latines many times either not concluding or els otherwise in the end then they began. Besides, is it not most delightfull to see

much excellentlie ordred in a small roome, or little gallantly disposed and made to fill vp a space of like capacitie, in such sort
that the one would not appeare so beautifull in a larger circuite,
nor the other do well in a lesse? which often we find to be so,
according to the powers of nature in the workman. And these
limited proportions and rests of stanzes, consisting of six, seuen,
or eight lines, are of that happines both for the disposition of the
matter, the apt planting the sentence where it may best stand to
hit, the certaine close of delight with the full bodie of a iust
period well carried, is such as neither the Greekes or Latines euer
attained vnto. For their boundlesse running on often so con-
founds the Reader, that, hauing once lost himselfe, must either
giue off vnsatisfied, or vncertainely cast backe to retriue the
escaped sence, and to find way againe into this matter.

Me thinkes we should not so soone yeeld our consents captiue
to the authoritie of Antiquitie, vnlesse we saw more reason; all
our vnderstandings are not to be built by the square of *Greece*
and *Italie*. We are the children of nature as well as they; we are
not so placed out of the way of iudgement but that the same
Sunne of Discretion shineth vppon vs; we haue our portion of
the same virtues as well as of the same vices. . . .

Will not experience confute vs, if wee shoulde say the state of
China, which neuer heard of Anapestiques, Trochies, and Tri-
bracques, were grosse, barbarous, and vnciuille? And is it not a
most apparent ignorance, both of the succession of learning in
Europe and the generall course of things, to say 'that all lay pittifully deformed in those lacke-learning times from the declining
of the Romane Empire till the light of the Latin tongue was reuiued by Rewcline, Erasmus, and Moore'? when for three hundred
yeeres before them, about the comming downe of *Tamburlaine*
into *Europe*, *Franciscus Petrarcha* (who then no doubt likewise found whom to imitate) shewed all the best notions of learning, in that degree of excellencies both in Latine, Prose and Verse,
and in the vulgare Italian, as all the wittes of posteritie haue not
yet much ouer-matched him in all kindes to this day: his great
Volumes in Moral Philosophie shew his infinite reading and most
happy power of disposition: his twelue *Æglogues*, his *Africa*,
containing nine Bookes of the last Punicke warre, with his three
bookes of Epistles in Latine verse shew all the transformations of

wit and inuention that a Spirite naturally borne to the inheritance
of Poetrie and iudiciall knowledge could expresse: all which notwithstanding wrought him not that glory and fame with his owne
Nation as did his Poems in Italian, which they esteeme aboue al
whatsoeuer wit could haue inuented in any other forme then
wherein it is: which questionles they wil not change with the best
measures Greeks or Latins can shew them, howsoeuer our Aduersary imagines. Nor could this very same innouation in Verse,
begun amongst them by C. Tolomœi,[4] but die in the attempt, and
was buried as soone as it came borne, neglected as a prodigious
and vnnaturall issue amongst them: nor could it neuer induce
Tasso, the wonder of Italy, to write that admirable Poem of
Ierusalem, comparable to the best of the ancients, in any other
forme than the accustomed verse. And with *Petrarch* liued his
scholar *Boccacius,* and neere about the same time *Iohannis
Rauenensis,* and from these, *tanquam ex equo Troiano,*[5] seemes
to haue issued all those famous Italian Writers, *Leonardus
Aretinus, Laurentius Valla, Poggius, Biondus,* and many others.
Then *Emanuel Chrysolaras,* a Constantinopolitan gentleman,
renowmed for his learning and vertue, being imployed by *Iohn
Paleologus,* Emperour of the East, to implore the ayde of Christian Princes for the succouring of perishing *Greece,* and vnder-
standing in the meane time how *Baiazeth* was taken prisoner by
Tamburlan, and his country freed from danger, stayed still at
Venice, and there taught the Greeke tongue, discontinued before
in these parts the space of seauen hundred yeeres. Him followed
Bessarion, George Trapezuntius, Theodorus Gaza, and others,
transporting Philosophie, beaten by the Turke out of *Greece,*
into christendome. Hereupon came that mightie confluence of
Learning in these parts, which, returning as it were *per post-
liminium,*[6] and heere meeting then with the new inuented stampe
of Printing, spread it selfe indeed in a more vniuersall sorte
then the world euer heeretofore had it; when *Pomponius Laetus,
Aeneas Syluius, Angelus Politanus, Hermolaus Barbarus, Iohannes
Picus de Mirandula,* the miracle and Phœnix of the world,

[4] Claudio Tolomei's *Versi et Regole della Nuova Poesia Toscana* (1539)
was a notorious example of attempts to classicize Italian.

[5] "As though from the Trojan horse."

[6] "Through a restoration of rights." A legal term.

adorned *Italie,* and wakened other Nations likewise with this desire of glory, long before it brought foorth *Rewclen, Erasmus,* and *Moore,* worthy men, I confesse, and the last a great ornament to this land, and a Rymer.[7]

And yet long before all these, and likewise with these, was not our Nation behinde in her portion of spirite and worthinesse, but concurrent with the best of all this lettered world; witnesse venerable *Bede,* that flourished aboue a thousand yeeres since; *Aldelmus Durotelmus,* that liued in the yeere 739, of whom we finde this commendation registered: *Omnium Poetarum sui temporis facile primus, tantae eloquentiae, maiestatis, et eruditionis homo fuit, vt nunquam satis admirari possim vnde illi in tam barbara ac rudi aetate facundia accreuerit, vsque adeo omnibus numeris tersa, elegans, et rotunda, versus edidit cum antiquitate de palma contendentes.*[8] Witnesse *Iosephus Deuonius,* who wrote *de bello Troiano* in so excellent manner, and so neere resembling Antiquitie, as Printing his Worke beyond the seas they haue ascribed it to *Cornelius Nepos,* one of the Ancients. What should I name *Walterus Mape, Gulielmus Nigellus, Geruasius Tilburiensis, Bracton, Bacon, Ockam,* and an infinite Catalogue of excellent men, most of them liuing about foure hundred yeeres since, and haue left behinde them monuments of most profound iudgement and learning in all sciences! So that it is but the clowds gathered about our owne iudgement that makes vs thinke all other ages wrapt vp in mists, and the great distance betwixt vs that causes vs to imagine men so farre off to be so little in respect of our selues.

We must not looke vpon the immense course of times past as men ouer-looke spacious and wide countries from off high Mountaines, and are neuer the neere to iudge of the true Nature of the soyle or the particular syte and face of those territories they see. Nor must we thinke, viewing the superficiall figure of a region in a Mappe, that wee know strait the fashion and

---

[7] This role-call of humanists reproduces in little the history of the humanistic movement. See appendix for brief notices.

[8] "Of all the poets of his time, easily the first. He was a man of such eloquence, majesty, and erudition that I cannot cease admiring how he gained his eloquence in such a barbarous and rude time—an eloquence neat in its prosody, elegant, and well-rounded. He wrote verses rivaling antiquity for the prize."

place as it is. Or reading an Historie (which is but a Mappe
of Men, and dooth no otherwise acquaint vs with the true
Substance of Circumstances then a superficiall Card dooth the
Seaman with a Coast neuer seene, which alwayes prooues other
to the eye than the imagination forecast it), that presently wee
know all the world, and can distinctly iudge of times, men, and
maners, iust as they were: When the best measure of man is to
be taken by his owne foote bearing euer the neerest proportion
to himselfe, and is neuer so farre different and vnequall in his
powers, that he hath all in perfection at one time, and nothing
at another. The distribution of giftes are vniuersall, and all seasons haue them in some sort. We must not thinke but that there
were *Scipioes, Cæsars, Catoes,* and *Pompeies* borne elsewhere
then at *Rome;* the rest of the world hath euer had them in the
same degree of nature, though not of state. And it is our weak-
nesse that makes vs mistake or misconscieue in these deliniations
of men the true figure of their worth. And our passion and
beliefe is so apt to leade vs beyond truth, that vnlesse we try
them by the iust compasse of humanities, and as they were
men, we shall cast their figures in the ayre, when we should make
their models vpon Earth. It is not the contexture of words, but
the effects of Action, that giues glory to the times: we find they
had *mercurium in pectore,* though not in *lingua;* [9] and in all ages,
though they were not Ciceronians, they knew the Art of men,
which onely is *Ars Artium,*[10] the great gift of heauen, and the
chiefe grace and glory on earth; they had the learning of Gouernement, and ordring their State; Eloquence inough to shew their
iudgements. And it seemes the best times followed *Lycurgus*
councell; *Literas ad vsum saltem discebant, reliqua omnis dis-
ciplina erat vt pulche pararent vt labores preferrent, &c.*[11] Had
not vnlearned *Rome* laide the better foundation, and built the
stronger frame of an admirable state, eloquent *Rome* had confounded it vtterly, which we saw ranne the way of all confusion,
the plaine course of dissolution, in her greatest skill: and though
she had not power to vndoe herselfe, yet wrought she so that she

9 "Eloquence in the heart, though not in the tongue."
10 "The art of arts."
11 "They learned letters for use; all the rest of their learning was to pre-
pare them beautifully to prefer labors. . . ."

cast herselfe quite away from the glory of a commonwealth, and fell vpon the forme of state she euer most feared and abhorred of all other: and then scarse was there seene any shadowe of pollicie vnder her first Emperours, but the most horrible and grosse confusion that could be conceued; notwithstanding it still indured, preseruing not onely a Monarchie, locked vp in her own limits, but therewithall held vnder her obedience so many Nations so farre distant, so ill affected, so disorderly commanded and vniustly conquered, as it is not to be attributed to any other fate but to the first frame of that commonwealth; which was so strongly ioynted, and with such infinite combinations interlinckt as one naile or other euer held vp the Maiestie thereof. There is but one learning, which *omnes gentes habent scriptum in cordibus suis*,[12] one and the selfe-same spirit that worketh in all. We haue but one bodie of Iustice, one bodie of Wisdome thorowout the whole world; which is but apparelled according to the fashion of euery nation.

Eloquence and gay wordes are not of the substance of wit; it is but the garnish of a nice time, the Ornaments that doe but decke the house of a State, and *imitatur publicos mores*:[13] Hunger is as well satisfied with meat serued in pewter as siluer. Discretion is the best measure, the rightest foote in what habit soeuer it runne. *Erasmus, Rewcline,* and *More* brought no more wisdome into the world with all their new reuiued wordes then we finde was before; it bred not a profounder Diuine then S. *Thomas,* a greater Lawyer then *Bartolus,* a more acute Logician then *Scotus*; nor are the effects of all this great amasse of eloquence so admirable or of that consequence, but that *impexa illa antiquitas* [14] can yet compare with them. . . .

[Against Campion's 'Kinds' of Verse]

. . . what adoe haue we heere? what strange precepts of Arte about the framing of an Iambique verse in our language? which, when all is done, reaches not by a foote, but falleth out to be the plaine ancient verse, consisting of ten sillables or fiue feete, which hath euer beene vsed amongst vs time out of minde, and,

---

[12] "All people have written in their hearts."
[13] "Imitate public customs."
[14] "That rude antiquity."

for all this cunning and counterfeit name, can or will [not] be any other in nature then it hath been euer heretofore: and this new *Dimeter* is but the halfe of this verse diuided in two, and no other then the *Caesura* or breathing place in the middest thereof, and therefore it had bene as good to haue put two lines in one, but only to make them seeme diuerse. Nay, it had beene much better for the true English reading and pronouncing thereof, without violating the accent, which now our Aduersarie hath heerein most vnkindly doone: for, being as wee are to sound it, according to our English March, we must make a rest, and raise the last sillable, which falles out very vnnaturall in *Desolate, Funerall, Elizabeth, Prodigall,* and in all the rest, sauing the Monosillables. Then followes the English *Trochaicke,* which is saide to bee a simple verse, and so indeede it is, being without Ryme: hauing here no other grace then that in sound it runnes like the knowne measure of our former ancient Verse, ending (as we terme it according to the French) in a feminine foote, sauing that it is shorter by one sillable at the beginning, which is not much missed, by reason it falles full at the last. Next comes the *Elegiacke,* being the fourth kinde, and that like-wise is no other then our old accustomed measure of fiue feet: if there be any difference, it must be made in the reading, and therein wee must stand bound to stay where often we would not, and sometimes either breake the accent or the due course of the word. And now for the other foure kinds of numbers, which are to be employed for *Odes,* they are either of the same measure, or such as haue euer beene familiarly vsed amongst vs.

So that of all these eight seuerall kindes of new promised numbers, you see what we haue: Onely what was our owne before, and the same but apparelled in forraine Titles; which had they come in their kinde and naturall attire of Ryme, we should neuer haue suspected that they had affected to be other, or sought to degenerate into strange manners, which now we see was the cause why they were turnd out of their proper habite, and brought in as Aliens, onely to induce men to admire them as farre-commers. But see the power of Nature; it is not all the artificiall couerings of wit that can hide their natiue and originall condition, which breakes out thorow the strongest bandes of affectation, and will be it selfe, doe Singularitie what it can.

And as for those imagined quantities of sillables, which haue bin euer held free and indifferent in our language, who can inforce vs to take knowledge of them, being *in nullius verba iurati,*[15] and owing fealty to no forraine inuention? especially in such a case where there is no necessitie in Nature, or that it imports either the matter or forme, whether it be so or otherwise. But euery Versifier that wel obserues his worke findes in our language, without all these vnnecessary precepts, what numbers best fitte the Nature of her Idiome, and the proper places destined to such accents as she will not let in to any other roomes then in those for which they were borne. As for example, you cannot make this fall into the right sound of a verse—

None thinkes reward rendred worthy his worth,

vnlesse you thus misplace the accent vpon *Rendrèd* and *Worthìe,* contrary to the nature of these wordes: which sheweth that two feminine numbers (or Trochies, if so you wil call them) will not succeede in the third and fourth place of the Verse. And so likewise in this case,

Though Death doth consume, yet Vertue preserues.

it wil not be a Verse, though it hath the iust sillables, without the same number in the second, and the altering of the fourth place in this sorte,

Though Death doth ruine, Virtue yet preserues.

Againe, who knowes not that we can not kindely answere a feminine number with a masculine Ryme, or (if you will so terme it) a *Trochei* with a *Sponde,* as *Weaknes* with *Confesse, Nature* and *Indure,* onely for that thereby wee shall wrong the accent, the chiefe Lord and graue Gouernour of Numbers? Also you cannot in a verse of foure feet place a *Trochei* in the first, without the like offence, as, *Yearely out of his watry Cell;* for so you shall sound it Yearleliè, which is vnnaturall. And other such like obseruations vsually occurre, which Nature and a iudiciall eare of themselues teach vs readily to auoyde. . . .

[Needed Reforms]

15 "Pledged to no one."

But yet notwithstanding all this which I haue heare deliuered in the defence of Ryme, I am not so farre in loue with mine owne mysterie, or will seeme so froward, as to bee against the reformation and the better setling these measures of ours. Wherein there be many things I could wish were more certaine and better ordered, though my selfe dare not take vpon me to be a teacher therein, hauing so much neede to learne of others. And I must confesse that to mine owne eare those continuall cadences of couplets vsed in long and continued Poemes are verie tyresome and vnpleasing, by reason that still, me thinks, they run on with a sound of one nature, and a kinde of certaintie which stuffs the delight rather then intertaines it. But yet, notwithstanding, I must not out of mine owne daintinesse condemne this kinde of writing, which peraduenture to another may seeme most delight-full; and many worthy compositions we see to haue passed with commendation in that kinde. Besides, me thinkes, sometimes to beguile the eare with a running out, and passing ouer the Ryme, as no bound to stay vs in the line where the violence of the matter will breake thorow, is rather gracefull then otherwise. Wherein I finde my Homer-Lucan, as if he gloried to seeme to haue no bounds, albeit hee were confined within his measures, to be in my conceipt most happy. For so thereby they who care not for Verse or Ryme may passe it ouer with taking notice thereof, and please themselues with a well measured Prose. And I must confesse my Aduersary hath wrought this much vpon me, that I thinke a Tragedie would indeede best comporte with a blank Verse and dispence with Ryme, sauing in the *Chorus*, or where a sentence shall require a couplet. And to auoyde this ouer-glutting the eare with that alwayes certaine and full incounter of Ryme, I haue assaid in some of my Epistles to alter the vsuall place of meeting, and to sette it further off by one Verse, to trie how I could disuse mine owne eare and to ease it of this continuall burthen which indeede seemes to surcharge it a little too much: but as yet I cannot come to please my selfe therein, this alternate or crosse Ryme holding still the best place in my affection.

Besides, to me this change of number in a Poem of one nature fits not so wel as to mixe vncertainly feminine Rymes with masculine, which euer since I was warned of that deformitie

by my kinde friend and countri-man Maister Hugh Samford,
I haue alwayes so auoyded it, as there are not aboue two
couplettes in that kinde in all my Poem of the Ciuill warres: [16]
and I would willingly if I coulde haue altered it in all the rest,
holding feminine Rymes to be fittest for Ditties, and either to be
set for certaine, or els by themselues. But in these things, I say,
I dare not take vpon mee to teach that they ought to be so, in
respect my selfe holds them to be so, or that I thinke it right:
for indeed there is no right in these things that are continually
in a wandring motion, carried with the violence of vncertaine
likings, being but onely the time that giues them their power.
For if this right or truth should be no other thing then that wee
make it, we shall shape it into a thousand figures, seeing this
excellent painter, Man, can so well lay the colours which himselfe
grindes in his owne affections, as that hee will make them serue
for any shadow and any counterfeit. But the greatest hinderer
to our proceedings and the reformation of our errours is this
Selfe-loue, whereunto we Versifiers are euer noted to bee specially
subiect; a disease of all other the most dangerous and incur-
able, being once seated in the spirits, for which there is no
cure but onely by a spirituall remedie. *Multos puto ad sapientiam
potuisse peruenire, nisi putassent se peruenisse*: [17] and this opinion of our sufficiencie makes so great a cracke in our iudgement,
as it wil hardly euer holde any thing of worth. *Caecus amor sui*; [18]
and though it would seeme to see all without it, yet certainely
it discernes but little within. For there is not the simplest writer
that will euer tell himselfe he doth ill, but, as if he were the
parasite onely to sooth his owne doings, perswades him that his
lines can not but please others which so much delight himselfe:
Suffenus est quisque sibi

—neque idem vnquam
Aeque est beatus, ac poema cum scribit.
Tam gaudet in se tamque se ipse miratur.[19]

[16] A reference to Daniel's own major poem, the *Civil Wars* (1595–1609).
[17] "I think that many could have gained wisdom if they had not thought
that they had already gained it."
[18] "Blind love of self." Horace, *Odes*, I, 18, 14.
[19] "Each man is a Suffenus to himself . . . Nor is one ever so happy as
when he writes a poem, so heartily does he rejoice in himself and admire
himself." Catullus, XXII.

And the more to shew that he is so, we shall see him euermore in all places, and to all persons repeating his owne compositions; and

Quem vero arripuit, tenet, occiditque legendo.[20]

Next to this deformitie stands our affectation, wherein we alwayes bewray our selues to be both vnkinde and vnnaturall to our owne natiue language, in disguising or forging strange or vnusuall wordes, as if it were to make our verse seeme another kind of speach out of the course of our vsuall practise, displacing our wordes, or inuenting new, onely vpon a singularitie, when our owne accustomed phrase, set in the due place, would expresse vs more familiarly and to better delight than all this idle affectation of antiquitie or noueltie can euer doe. And I cannot but wonder at the strange presumption of some men, that dare so audaciously aduenture to introduce any whatsoeuer forraine wordes, be they neuer so strange, and of themselues, as it were, without a Parliament, without any consent or allowance, establish them as Free-denizens in our language. But this is but a Character of that perpetuall reuolution which wee see to be in all things that neuer remaine the same: and we must heerein be content to submit our selues to the law of time, which in few yeeres wil make al that for which we now contend *Nothing.*

[20] "Whom he has seized, he holds, and kills by reading." *Ars Poetica,* 474.

Part IV

SEVENTEENTH CENTURY
CROSS CURRENTS

Francis Bacon

[1561–1626]

❧᳐᳐᳐

ALTHOUGH HE HAS BEEN blamed (and praised) for most of the significant developments of later seventeenth-century poetry, Bacon produced little formal criticism. His longest 'literary' work is his *Wisdom of the Ancients* (1625), an allegorical interpretation of such classical myths as Pan, Orpheus, and Proserpine. This work is quite consistent with Elizabethan taste and in a tradition which goes back through Comes and Pico della Mirandola to Boccaccio's *Genealogy of the Gods* (c. 1365). It was greatly overshadowed by the two brief discussions of poetry in *The Advancement of Learning* (1605) and the *De Argumentis Scientiarum* (1623), II, xiii. Bacon's subordination of poetry to 'imagination' (*cf.* 'phantasy' in Sidney and Puttenham, above, pp. 129, 155) contributed to the view that poetry is inherently trivial or that the 'poetic' part of poetry is separable from its more important 'rational' element.

His slighting remarks about modern 'parabolicall' poetry encouraged many later poets to concentrate on men and manners while pruning their work of the marvelous episodes, digressions, and gorgeous ornament so admired by the Elizabethans. Bacon's view was challenged by Henry Reynolds (*Mythomystes*, 1632), who denied that fabulous poems were "amusements for fooles and children," and scornfully pointed out Bacon's own inconsistency: "What shall we make of such willing contradictions, when a man to vent a few fancies of his owne shall tell us first, they are the wisdome of the Auncients, and next, that those Auncient fables were but meere fables, and without wisdom or meaning . . . and then scornefully and contemptuously (as if all Poetry were but Play-vanity) shut up that discourse of his of Poetry with 'It is not good to stay too long in the Theater.'"

The habit of 'placing' poetry in a system of sciences and basing its definition on the position assigned goes back to scholasticism. Originally the 'placing' was based on the Aristotelian division of learning into rational science (the works comprising the *Organon*), theoretical science (metaphysics, the physical sciences), and moral science (poli-

263

tics, economics, and ethics). Poetry was most commonly considered
a part of logic or ethics. (See Domenicus Gundissalinus, *De Divisione
Philosophiae,* ed. Bauer, *Beiträge zur Geschichte der Philosophie des
Mittelalters,* IV, ii–iii.) Bacon's 'psychological' scheme was less common than the scholastic one, but was adopted before him by such
scholars as Juan Huarte and Pierre Charron.

The present text is based on the 1605 edition of *The Advancement
of Learning.*

BIBLIOGRAPHY. Bacon, *Works,* ed. Spedding *et al.*, 7 vols. (1857–9).
For comment see: D. Bond, "Distrust of Imagination in English Neo-
Classicism," *SP,* XXX (1933); W. Bundy, "Bacon's True Opinion of
Poetry," *SP,* XXVII (1930); J. Harrison, "Bacon's View of Rhetoric,
Poetry, and the Imagination," *HLQ,* XX (1957); L. Knights, "Bacon
and the Seventeenth Century Dissociation of Sensibility," *Scrutiny,* XI
(1943); C. Lemmi, *The Classical Deities in Bacon* (1933); K. Wallace,
Francis Bacon on Communication and Rhetoric (1943). The complex
history of Renaissance classifications of poetry among the other
sciences is discussed in the introductory chapters of B. Weinberg, *A
History of Italian Literary Criticism in the Renaissance,* 2 vols. (1961).

Sections on Poetry from

THE ADVANCEMENT OF LEARNING

[1605]

THE PARTS OF HUMANE learning haue reference to the three partes
of Mans vnderstanding, which is the seate of Learning: HISTORY
to his MEMORY, POESIE to his IMAGINATION, and PHILOSOPHIE to his
REASON. Diuine learning receiueth the same distribution, for the
Spirit of Man is the same, though the Reuelation of Oracle and
Sense be diuerse: So as Theologie consisteth also of HISTORIE
of the Church, of PARABLES, which is Diuine *Poesie,* and of holie
DOCTRINE or *Precept.* For as for that part which seemeth super-
numerarie, which is *Prophecie,* it is but Diuine Historie, which
hath that prerogatiue ouer humane as the Narration may bee
before the fact aswell as after.

HISTORY is NATVRALL, CIVILE, ECCLESIASTICALL, & LITERARY, whereof the three first I allow as extant, the fourth I note as deficient. For no man hath propounded to himselfe the generall state of learning to bee described and represented from age to age, as many haue done the works of Nature & the State ciuile and Ecclesiastical, without which the History of the world seemeth to me to be as the *Statua* of *Polyphemus* with his eye out, that part being wanting which doth most shew the spirit and life of the person. And yet I am not ignorant that in diuers particular sciences, as of the Iurisconsults, the Mathematicians, the Rhetoricians, the Philosophers, there are set down some smal memorials of the Schooles, Authors, and Bookes; and so likewise some barren relations touching the Inuention of Arts or vsages. But a iust story of learning, containing the Antiquities & Orig-inalls of Knowledges & their Sects, their Inuentions, their Tradi-tions, their diuerse Administrations and Managings, their Flour-ishings, their Oppositions, Decayes, Depressions, Obliuions, Remoues, with the causes and occasions of them, and all other euents concerning learning throughout the ages of the world, I may truly affirme to be wanting. The vse and end of which worke I doe not so much designe for curiositie or satisfaction of those that are the louers of learning, but chiefely for a more serious & graue purpose, which is this in fewe wordes, that it will make learned men wise in the vse and administration of learning. For it is not Saint *Augustines* nor Saint *Ambrose* workes that will make so wise a Diuine as Ecclesiasticall His-torie thoroughly read and obserued, and the same reason is of Learning.

* * * *

POESIE is a part of Learning in measure of words for the most part restrained, but in all other points extreamely licensed, and doth truly referre to the Imagination, which, beeing not tyed to the Lawes of Matter, may at pleasure ioyne that which Nature hath seuered, & seuer that which Nature hath ioyned, and so make vnlawfull Matches & diuorses of things: *Pictoribus atque Poetis &c.*[1] It is taken in two senses in respect of Wordes

---

[1] "To painters and poets. . . ." *Ars Poetica*, 9.

or Matter. In the first sense it is but a *Character* of stile, and belongeth to Arts of speeche, and is not pertinent for the present. In the later, it is, as hath beene saide, one of the principall Portions of learning, and is nothing else but FAINED HISTORY, which may be stiled as well in Prose as in Verse.

The vse of this FAINED HISTORIE hath beene to giue some shadowe of satisfaction to the minde of Man in those points wherein the Nature of things doth denie it, the world being in proportion inferiour to the soule; by reason whereof there is agreeable to the spirit of Man a more ample Greatnesse, a more exact Goodnesse, and a more absolute varietie then can bee found in the Nature of things. Therefore, because the Acts or Euents of *true Historie* haue not that Magnitude which satisfieth the minde of Man, *Poesie* faineth Acts and Euents Greater and more Heroicall; because *true Historie* propoundeth the successes and issues of actions not so agreable to the merits of Vertue and Vice, therefore *Poesie* faines them more iust in Retribution and more according to Reuealed Prouidence; because *true Historie* representeth Actions and Euents more ordinarie and lesse interchanged, therefore *Poesie* endueth them with more Rarenesse and more vnexpected and alternatiue Variations: So as it appeareth that *Poesie* serueth and conferreth to Magnanimitie, Moralitie, and to delectation. And therefore it was euer thought to haue some participation of diuinesse, because it doth raise and erect the Minde, by submitting the shewes of things to the desires of the Mind, whereas reason doth buckle and bowe the Mind vnto the Nature of things. And we see that by these insinuations and congruities with mans Nature and pleasure, ioyned also with the agreement and consort it hath with Musicke, it hath had accesse and estimation in rude times and barbarous Regions, where other learning stoode excluded.

The diuision of Poesie which is aptest in the proprietie therof (besides those diuisions which are common vnto it with history, as fained Chronicles, fained liues, & the Appendices of History, as fained Epistles, fained Orations, and the rest) is into POESIE NARRATIVE, REPRESENTATIVE, and ALLVSIVE. The NARRATIVE is a meere imitation of History with the excesses before remembred, Choosing for subiect commonly Warrs and Loue, rarely State, and sometimes Pleasure or Mirth. REPRESENTA-

TIVE is as a visible History, and is an Image of Actions as if they were present, as History is of actions in nature as they are, that is past; ALLVSIVE, or PARABOLICALL, is a NARRATION applied onely to expresse some speciall purpose or conceit: Which later kind of Parabolical wisedome was much more in vse in the ancient times, as by the Fables of *Aesope,* and the briefe sentences of the seuen, and the *vse* of *Hieroglyphikes* may appeare. And the cause was for that it was then of necessitie to expresse any point of reason which was more sharpe or subtile then the vulgar in that maner, because men in those times wanted both varietie of examples and subtiltie of conceit: And as *Hierogliphikes* were before Letters, so parables were before arguments: And neuerthelesse now and at all times they doe retaine much life and vigor, because reason cannot bee so sensible, nor examples so fit.

But there remaincth yet another vse of POESY PARABOLI-CAL, opposite to that which we last mentioned; for that tendeth to demonstrate and illustrate that which is taught or deliucred, and this other to retire and obscure it: That is, when the Secrets and Misteries of Religion, Pollicy, or Philosophy, are inuolued in Fables or Parables. Of this in diuine Poesie wee see the vse is authorised. In Heathen Poesie wee see the exposition of Fables doth fall out sometimes with great felicitie, as in the Fable that the Gyants beeing ouerthrowne in their warre against the Gods, the Earth their mother in reuenge thereof brought forth Fame:

> *Illam terra Parens ira irritata Deorum,*
> *Extremam, vt perhibent, Cæo Enceladoque Sororem*
> *Progenuit:* [2]

expounded that when Princes & Monarches haue suppressed actuall and open Rebels, then the malignitie of people, which is the mother of Rebellion, doth bring forth Libels & slanders, and taxations of the states, which is of the same kind with Rebellion, but more Feminine: So in the Fable that the rest of the Gods hauing conspired to binde *Iupiter, Pallas* called *Briareus* with his hundreth hands to his aide, expounded, that Mon-

[2] "The earth, the mother of the gods, enraged that they should frustrate her, brought forth that last sister of Coeus and Enceladus." *Aeneid,* IV, 178.

archies neede not feare any courbing of their absolutenesse by
Mightie Subiects, as long as by wisedome they keepe the hearts
of the people, who will be sure to come in on their side: So in
the fable that *Achilles* was brought vp vnder *Chyron* the *Cen-
taure,* who was part a man & part a beast, expounded Ingenuously,
but corruptly by Machiauell,[3] that it belongeth to the education
and discipline of Princes to knowe as well how to play the part
of the Lyon in violence and the Foxe in guile, as of the Man
in vertue and Iustice. Neuerthelesse in many the like incounters,
I doe rather think that the fable was first and the exposition
deuised then that the Morall was first & thereupon the fable
framed. For I finde it was an auncient vanitie in *Chrisippus* that
troubled himselfe with great contention to fasten the assertions
of the *Stoicks* vpon the fictions of the ancient Poets: But yet that
all the Fables and fictions of the Poets were but pleasure and
not figure, I interpose no opinion. Surely of those Poets which
are now extant, euen *Homer* himselfe (notwithstanding he was
made a kinde of Scripture by the later Schooles of the Grecians)
yet I should without any difficultie pronounce, that his Fables
had no such inwardnesse in his owne meaning: But what
they might haue, vpon a more originall tradition, is not easie
to affirme, for he was not the inuentor of many of them. In
this third part of Learning which is Poesie, I can report no
deficience. For being as a plant that commeth of the lust of the
earth, without a formall seede, it hath sprung vp and spread
abroad, more then any other kinde: But to ascribe vnto it that
which is due for the expressing of affections, passions, corrup-
tions and customes, we are beholding to Poets more then to the
Philosophers workes, and for wit and eloquence not much lesse
then to Orators harangues. But it is not good to stay too long in
the Theater: let vs now passe on to the iudicial Place or Pallace
of the Mind, which we are to approach and view, with more
reuerence and attention. . . .

[3] *The Prince,* XVIII.

Ben Jonson

[1572–1637]

◦§§◦

BEN JONSON WAS A self-made man and he never let the world forget it. The stepson of a bricklayer, he acquired an education which made him the foremost man of letters in England. He is best known for his comedies, but he was also proficient in lyric poetry and struggled manfully to surpass Shakespeare in tragedy. His criticism stamps him as the first true English Neoclassicist. His masters are Scaliger and Heinsius, from whose *De Tragoediae Constitutione* (1611) he paraphrased many passages of his *Discoveries*. Other sources, classical and Renaissance, are innumerable.

Jonson's "Dialogue" on Horace, which he mentioned to William Drummond in 1619, was either never completed or burned in the fire which destroyed his manuscripts in 1623. In lieu of this synthesis, his critical ideas must be pieced together from prefaces, 'inductions' to plays, occasional poems such as his elegy to Shakespeare and "A Fit of Rime Against Rime," his conversations with Drummond, and his *Timber, or Discoveries*. The latter work is Jonson's most complete critical statement. In its present form it appears to be a series of notes for a projected essay or series of essays, probably made between 1620 and 1625. Depite its fragmentary nature it is a manifesto of the movement which was to triumph after the Restoration and one of the most significant literary documents of its time.

The present text is based on the edition of 1641.

BIBLIOGRAPHY. *Works*, ed. Herford and Simpson (1925 ff.; excellent notes). The most important criticism is collected in G. Smith, *Elizabethan Critical Essays*, II, 387–97; and J. Spingarn, *Seventeenth Century Critical Essays*, I, 10–64, and 210–217 (extracts from the *Conversations With Drummond*). For comment see: J. Bryant, "The Significance of Ben Jonson's First Requirement for Tragedy: Truth of Argument," *SP*, XLIX (1952); "*Catiline* and the Nature of Jonson's Tragic Fable," *PMLA*, LXIX (1954); D. Clark, "The Requirements of a Poet," *MP*, XVI (1918); W. McKennen, *Critical Theory and*

Poetic Practice in Jonson (1937); P. Simpson, *"Tanquam Explorator:* Jonson's Method in the *Discoveries," MLR,* II (1907); H. Snuggs, "The Source of Jonson's Definition of Comedy," *MLN,* LXV (1950); J. Spingarn, "The Source of Jonson's *Discoveries," MP,* II (1905); E. Talbert, "The Interpretation of Jonson's Courtly Spectacles," *PMLA,* LXI (1946); "The Purpose and Technique of Jonson's *Poetaster," SP,* XLII (1945); R. Walker, "Literary Criticism in Jonson's Conversations With Drummond," *English,* VIII (1951); "Jonson's *Discoveries:* A New Analysis," *Essays and Studies,* V (1952).

from

TIMBER, OR DISCOVERIES

[1620–1625]

[Judgments of Poets]

Poetry, IN THIS LATTER AGE, hath prov'd but a meane *Mistresse* to such as have wholly addicted themselves to her, or given their names up to her family. They who have but saluted her on the by, and now and then tendred their visits, shee hath done much for, and advanced in the way of their owne professions (both the *Law* and the *Gospel*) beyond all they could have hoped or done for themselves without her favour. Wherein she doth emulate the judicious but preposterous bounty of the times *Grandes,* who accumulate all they can upon the *Parasite* or *Freshman* in their friendship, but thinke an old Client or honest servant bound by his place to write and starve.

Indeed, the multitude commend Writers as they doe Fencers or Wrastlers, who, if they come in robustiously and put for it with a deale of violence, are received for the *braver-fellowes*; when many times their owne rudenesse is a cause of their disgrace, and a slight touch of their Adversary gives all that boisterous force the foyle. But in these things the unskilfull are naturally deceiv'd, and judging wholly by the bulke, thinke rude things greater then polish'd, and scatter'd more numerous then composed. Nor thinke this only to be true in the sordid multitude, but the neater sort of our *Gallants*; for all are the multitude, only they differ in cloaths, not in judgement or understanding.

I remember the Players have often mentioned it as an honour to *Shakespeare*, that in his writing, whatsoever he penn'd, hee never blotted out [a] line. My answer hath beene, would he had blotted a thousand: Which they thought a malevolent speech. I had not told posterity this, but for their ignorance who choose that circumstance to commend their friend by wherein he most faulted; And to justifie mine owne candor, for I lov'd the man, and doe honour his memory, on this side Idolatry, as much as any. He was indeed honest, and of an open and free nature, had an excellent *Phantsie*, brave notions, and gentle expressions, wherein hee flow'd with that facility that sometime it was necessary he should be stop'd: *Sufflaminandus erat*, as *Augustus* said of *Haterius*.[1] His wit was in his owne power; would the rule of it had been so too. Many times hee fell into those things, could not escape laughter; As when hee said in the person of *Cæsar*, one speaking to him: *Cæsar, thou does me wrong*. Hee replyed: *Cæsar did never wrong but with just cause*;[2] and such like, which were ridiculous. But hee redeemed his vices with his vertues. There was ever more in him to be praysed then to be pardoned.

In the difference of wits, I have observ'd there are many notes: And it is a little *Maistry* to know them, to discerne what every nature, every disposition will beare: For before wee sow our land, we should plough it. There are no fewer formes of minds then of bodies amongst us. The variety is incredible, and therefore wee must search. Some are fit to make *Divines*, some *Poets*, some *Lawyers*, some *Physicians*, some to be sent to the plough and trades.[3]

There is no doctrine will doe good where nature is wanting. Some wits are swelling and high, others low and still: Some hot and fiery, others cold and dull: One must have a bridle, the other a spurre.

---

[1] "He should hae been slowed down with a drag." Seneca, *Controversiae*, IV.

[2] Cf. *Julius Caesar*, III, i, 47.

[3] Paraphrased from Quintilian, *Inst. Orat.*, II, 8, 1.

There be some that are forward and bold, and these will doe every little thing easily: I meane that is hard by, and next them, which they will utter unretarded without any shamefast-nesse. These never performe much, but quickly. They are what they are on the sudden; they shew presently like *Graine* that, scatter'd on the top of the ground, shoots up, but takes no root, has a yellow blade, but the eare empty. They are wits of good promise at first, but there is an *Ingeni-stitium*: [4] They stand still at sixteene, they get no higher.

You have others that labour onely to ostentation, and are ever more busie about the colours and surface of a worke then in the matter and foundation: For that is hid, the other is seene.

Others that in composition are nothing but what is rough and broken: *Quæ per salebras altaque saxa cadunt.*[4a] And if it would come gently, they trouble it of purpose. They would not have it run without rubs, as if that stile were more strong and manly, that stroke the eare with a kind of unevenesse. These men erre not by chance, but knowingly and willingly; they are like men that affect a fashion by themselves, have some singularity in a Ruffe, Cloake, or Hat-band; or their beards specially cut to pro-voke beholders, and set a marke upon themselves. They would be reprehended while they are look'd on. And this vice, one that is in authority with the rest, loving, delivers over to them to bee imitated: so that oft-times the faults which he fell into, the others seeke for. This is the danger, when vice becomes a *Precedent*.

Others there are that have no composition at all, but a kind of tuneing and riming fall in what they write. It runs and slides, and onely makes a sound. Womens-*Poets* they are call'd, as you have womens-*Taylors*.

> *They write a verse as smooth, as soft as creame,*
> *In which there is no torrent, nor scarce streame.*

You may sound these wits and find the depth of them with your middle finger. They are *Cream-bowle* or but puddle deepe.

Some that turne over all bookes, and are equally searching in all papers; that write out of what they presently find or meet, without choice; by which meanes it happens that what they have descredited and impugned in one worke, they have before

[4] An arresting of the wit.
[4a] See below, note 44.

or after extolled the same in another. Such are all the *Essayists*, even their Master *Mountaigne*. These in all they write confesse still what bookes they have read last, and therein their owne folly so much that they bring it to the *Stake* raw and undigested; not that the place did need it neither, but that they thought themselves furnished and would vent it.

Some againe, who, after they have got authority, or, which is lesse, opinion, by their writings, to have read much, dare presently to faine whole bookes and Authors, and lye safely. For what never was will not easily be found, not by the most *curious*.

And some, by a cunning protestation against all reading, and false vendition of their owne *naturals*, thinke to divert the *sagacity* of their Readers from themselves, and coole the sent of their owne *fox-like* thefts, when yet they are so ranke as a man may find whole pages together usurp'd from one Author: Their necessities compelling them to read for present use, which could not be in many books, and so come forth more ridiculously and palpably guilty then those who, because they cannot trace, they yet would slander their industry.

But the Wretcheder are the obstinate contemners of all helpes and Arts, such as presuming on their owne *Naturals*, which perhaps are excellent, dare deride all diligence, and seeme to mock at the termes when they understand not the things, thinking that way to get off wittily with their Ignorance. These are imitated often by such as are their Peeres in negligence, though they cannot be in nature: And they utter all they can thinke with a kind of violence and *indisposition*, unexamin'd, without relation either to person, place, or any fitnesse else; and the more wilfull and stubborne they are in it, the more learned they are esteem'd of the *multitude*, through their excellent vice of Judgement: Who thinke those things the stronger that have no Art; as if to breake were better then to open, or to rent asunder gentler then to loose.

It cannot but come to passe that these men who commonly seeke to doe more then enough may sometimes happen on some thing that is good and great; but very seldome: And when it comes, it doth not recompence the rest of their ill. For their jests and their sentences, which they onely and ambitiously seeke for, sticke out and are more eminent, because all is sordid and vile about them; as lights are more discern'd in a thick darknesse then a faint shadow. Now because they speake all they can, how

ever unfitly they are thought to have the greater copy. Where
the learned use ever election and a meane, they looke back to
what they intended at first, and make all an even and proportion'd body. The true Artificer will not run away from nature,
as hee were afraid of her, or depart from life and the likenesse
of Truth, but speake to the capacity of his hearers. And though
his language differ from the vulgar somewhat, it shall not fly
from all humanity, with the *Tamerlanes* [5] and *Tamer-Chams* of
the late Age, which had nothing in them but the *scenicall* strut-
ting and furious vociferation to warrant them to the ignorant
gapers. Hee knowes it is his onely Art so to carry it, as none
but Artificers perceive it. In the meane time perhaps hee is call'd
barren, dull, leane, a poore Writer, or by what contumelious
word can come in their cheeks, by these men who, without labour,
judgement, knowledge, or almost sense, are received or preferr'd
before him. He gratulates them and their fortune. An other Age,
or juster men, will acknowledge the vertues of his studies, his
wisdome in dividing, his subtilty in arguing, with what strength
hee doth inspire his Readers, with what sweetnesse hee strokes
them; in inveighing, what sharpnesse; in Jest, what urbanity hee
uses; How he doth raigne in mens affections; how invade and
breake in upon them, and makes their minds like the thing he
writes. Then in his Elocution to behold what word is proper,
which hath ornament, which height, what is beautifully translated,[6] where figures are fit, which gentle, which strong to shew
the composition *Manly*: and how hee hath avoyded faint, obscure,
obscene, sordid, humble, improper, or effeminate *Phrase*, which
is not only prais'd of the most, but commended, which is worse,
especially for that it is naught.

[Ut Pictura Poesis]

Poetry and *Picture* are Arts of a like nature, and both are busie
about imitation. It was excellently said of *Plutarch*, *Poetry* was
a speaking Picture, and *Picture* a mute Poesie.[7] For they both

---

[5] Marlowe's *Tamburlaine*, Part I, was acted in 1588; a play called *Tamer-
cam* was acted in 1592.

[6] "Translated." That is, expressed metaphorically. *Translatio* is the Latin
term for figurative expression, esp. metaphor.

[7] Plutarch, *De Audiendis Poetis*, 3.

invent, faine, and devise many things, and accommodate all
they invent to the use and service of nature. Yet of the two the
Pen is more noble then the Pencill: For that can speake to the
Understanding, the other but to the Sense. They both behold
pleasure and profit as their common Object; but should abstaine
from all base pleasures, lest they should erre from their end,
and, while they seeke to better mens minds, destroy their manners. They both are borne *Artificers*, not made. Nature is more
powerfull in them then study.

Whosoever loves not *Picture* is injurious to Truth and all the
wisdome of *Poetry*. Picture is the invention of Heaven, the most
ancient and most a kinne to Nature. It is it selfe a silent worke,
and always of one and the same habit: Yet it doth so enter
and penetrate the inmost affection (being done by an excellent
Artificer) as sometimes it orecomes the power of speech and
oratory. There are diverse graces in it, so are there in the
Artificers. One excels in care, another in reason, a third in easi-
nesse, a fourth in nature and grace. Some have diligence and
comelinesse, but they want Majesty. They can expresse a humane
forme in all the graces, sweetnesse, and elegancy, but they misse
the Authority. They can hit nothing but smooth cheeks; they
cannot expresse roughnesse or gravity. Others aspire to Truth
so much as they are rather Lovers of likenesse then beauty.
Zeuxsis and *Parrhasius* are said to be contemporaries. The first
found out the reason of lights and shadowes in Picture; the other
more subtily examined the lines.

In Picture, light is requir'd no lesse then shadow; so in stile,
height as well as humblenesse. But beware they be not too
humble, as *Pliny* pronounc'd of *Regulus* writings: [8] You would
thinke them written, not on a child, but by a child. Many, out of
their owne obscene Apprehensions, refuse proper and fit words,
as *occupie, nature*, and the like: So the curious industry in some,
of having all alike good, hath come neerer a vice then a vertue.

[Rules and Precepts]

I take this labour in teaching others, that they should not be
always to bee taught, and I would bring my Precepts into prac-

[8] Pliny, *Epistles*, IV, 7.

tise. For rules are ever of lesse force and valew then experiments: Yet with this purpose, rather to shew the right way to those that come after, then to detect any that have slipt before by errour; and I hope it will bee more profitable: For men doe more willingly listen, and with more favour, to precept then reprehension. Among diverse opinions of an Art, and most of them contrary in themselves, it is hard to make election; and therefore, though a man cannot invent new things after so many, he may doe a welcome worke yet to helpe posterity to judge rightly of the old. But Arts and Precepts availe nothing, except nature be beneficiall and ayding. And therefore these things are no more written to a dull disposition then rules of husbandry to a barren Soyle. No precepts will profit a Foole, no more then beauty will the blind, or musicke the deafe. As wee should take care that our style in writing be neither dry nor empty, wee should looke againe it be not winding, or wanton with far-fetcht descriptions: Either is a vice. But that is worse which proceeds out of want then that which riots out of plenty. The remedy of fruitfulnesse is easie, but no labour will helpe the contrary. I will like and praise some things in a young Writer which yet, if hee continue in, I cannot but justly hate him for the same. There is a time to bee given all things for maturity, and that even your Countrey-husband-man can teach, who to a young plant will not put the proyning knife, because it seemes to feare the iron, as not able to admit the scarre. No more would I tell a greene Writer all his faults, lest I should make him grieve and faint, and at last despaire. For nothing doth more hurt then to make him so afraid of all things as hee can endeavour nothing. Therefore youth ought to be instructed betimes, and in the best things; for we hold those longest wee take soonest: As the first sent of a Vessell lasts, and that tinct the wooll first receives. Therefore a Master should temper his owne powers, and descend to the others infirmity. If you powre a glut of water upon a Bottle, it receives little of it; but with a Funnell, and by degrees, you shall fill many of them, and spill little of your owne; to their capacity they will all receive and be full. And as it is fit to reade the best Authors to youth first, so let them be of the openest and clearest: As *Livy* before *Salust*, *Sydney* before *Donne*; and beware of letting them taste *Gower* or *Chaucer* at first, lest falling too much in love with Antiquity, and not apprehending the weight, they grow rough and barren in language onely. When their judgements are firme and out of danger, let them reade both the old and the new; but no lesse take heed that their new flowers and sweetnesse doe not as much corrupt as the others drinesse and squallor, if they choose not carefully. *Spencer*, in affecting the Ancients, writ no Language: Yet I would have him read for his matter, but as *Virgil* read *Ennius*. The reading of *Homer* and *Virgil* is counsell'd by *Quintilian*[9] as the best way of informing youth and confirming man. For, besides that the mind is rais'd with the height and sublimity of such a verse, it takes spirit from the greatnesse of the matter, and is tincted with the best things. *Tragicke* and *Liricke* Poetry is good too; and *Comicke* with the best, if the manners of the Reader be once in safety. In the *Greeke* Poets, as also in *Plautus*, wee shall see the Oeconomy and disposition of *Poems* better observed then in *Terence* and the later, who thought the sole grace and vertue of their *Fable* the sticking in of sentences, as ours doe the forcing in of jests.

[Language, Metaphor, Allegory]

It is not the passing through these Learnings that hurts us, but the dwelling and sticking about them. To descend to those extreame anxieties and foolish cavils of *Grammarians* is able to breake a wit in pieces; being a worke of manifold misery and vainnesse to bee *Elementarij senes*.[10] Yet even Letters are, as it were, the Banke of words, and restore themselves to an Author as the pawnes of Language. But talking and Eloquence are not the same: to speake, and to speake well, are two things. A foole may talke, but a wise man speakes, and out of the observation, knowledge, and use of things. Many Writers perplexe their Readers and Hearers with meere *Non-sense*. Their writings need sunshine. Pure and neat Language I love, yet plaine and customary. A barbarous Phrase hath often made mee out of love with a good sense, and doubtfull writing hath wrackt mee beyond my patience. The reason why a *Poet* is said that hee ought to have all knowledges, is that hee should not be ignorant of the most, espe-

---

[9] *Inst. Orat.*, I, 8, 5–9.
[10] "Old men occupied with elementary knowledge." Cf. Seneca, *Epistles*, 36.

cially of those hee will handle. And indeed, when the attaining
of them is possible, it were a sluggish and base thing to despaire.
For frequent imitation of any thing becomes a habit quickly. If
a man should prosecute as much as could be said of every thing,
his worke would find no end.

   Speech is the only benefit man hath to expresse his excellencie
of mind above other creatures. It is the Instrument of *Society*.
Therefore *Mercury*, who is the President of Language, is called
Deorum hominumque interpres. In all speech, words and sense
are as the body and the soule. The sense is as the life and soule of
Language, without which all words are dead. Sense is wrought
out of experience, the knowledge of humane life and actions, or
of the liberall Arts, which the *Greeks* call'd Ἐγκυκλοπαιδείαν.[11]
Words are the Peoples, yet there is a choise of them to be made.
For *Verborum delectus origo est eloquentiæ*.[12] They are to be
chose according to the persons wee make speake, or the things
wee speake of. Some are of the Campe, some of the Councell-
board, some of the Shop, some of the Sheepe-coat, some of the
Pulpit, some of the Barre, &c. And herein is seene their Elegance
and Propriety, when wee use them fitly, and draw them forth to
their just strength and nature by way of Translation or *Metaphore*. But in this Translation wee must only serve necessity
(*Nam temerè nihil transfertur à prudenti*),[13] or commodity,
which is a kind of necessity; that is, when wee either absolutely
want a word to expresse by, and that is necessity; or when wee
have not so fit a word, and that is commodity. As when wee
avoid losse by it, and escape obscenenesse, and gaine in the grace
and property which helpes significance. *Metaphors* farfet hinder
to be understood; and affected, lose their grace. Or when the
person fetcheth his translations from a wrong place: As if a
Privie-Counsellor should at the Table take his *Metaphore* from
a Dicing-house, or Ordinary, or a Vintners Vault; or a Justice of
Peace draw his similitudes from the *Mathematicks*; or a *Divine*
from a Bawdy-house, or Tavernes; or a Gentleman of *Northamp-
ton-shire*, *Warwick-shire*, or the *Mid-land*, should fetch all his

---

[11] "General education." Cf. Quintilian, *Inst. Orat.*, I, 10, 1.
[12] "Delight in words is the origin of eloquence." Cicero, *Brutus*, 72.
[13] "Nothing is rashly made into a metaphor by a prudent man."

Illustrations to his countrey neighbours from shipping, and tell them of the maine *sheat* and the Boulin. *Metaphors* are thus many times deform'd, as in him that said, *Castratam morte Aphricani Rempublicam.*[14] . . . All attempts that are new in this kind are dangerous, and somewhat hard, before they be softned with use. A man coynes not a new word without some perill and lesse fruit; for if it happen to be received, the praise is but moderate; if refus'd, the scorne is assur'd. Yet wee must adventure; for things at first hard and rough are by use made tender and gentle. . . .

. . . wee must consider in every tongue what is us'd, what receiv'd. *Quintilian* [15] warnes us that in no kind of Translation, or *Metaphore,* or *Allegory,* wee make a turne from what wee began; As, if wee fetch the originall of our *Metaphore* from sea and billowes, wee end not in flames and ashes: It is a most fowle inconsequence. Neither must wee draw out our *Allegory* too long, lest either wee make our selves obscure, or fall into affectation, which is childish. But why doe men depart at all from the right and naturall wayes of speaking? Sometimes for necessity, when wee are driven, or thinke it fitter, to speake that in obscure words, or by circumstance, which utter'd plainely would offend the hearers: Or to avoid obscenenesse, or sometimes for pleasure and variety, as Travailers turne out of the high way, drawne either by the commodity of a footpath, or the delicacy or freshnesse of the fields. And all this is call'd ἐσχηματισμένη, or figur'd Language.

What is a Poet?

A *Poet* is that which by the *Greeks* is call'd κατ᾽ ἐξοχήν, ὁ Ποιητής,[16] a Maker, or a fainer: His Art, an Art of imitation or faining, expressing the life of man in fit measure, numbers, and harmony, according to *Aristotle*: From the word ποιεῖν, which signifies to make or fayne. Hence hee is call'd a *Poet*, not hee which writeth in measure only, but that fayneth and formeth a fable, and writes things like the Truth. For the Fable and Fiction

---

[14] "The republic has been castrated by the death of Africanus." Quintilian, *Inst. Orat.*, VIII, 6, 15.

[15] *Inst. Orat.*, VIII, 6.

[16] "The chief men, the Poets."

is, as it were, the forme and Soule of any Poeticall worke or
Poeme.

What meane you by a Poeme?

A *Poeme* is not alone any worke or composition of the Poets
in many or few verses; but even one alone verse sometimes makes
a perfect *Poeme*. As when *Aeneas* hangs up and consecrates the
Armes of *Abas* with this Inscription:

> *Aeneas hæc de Danais victoribus arma,*[17]

And calls it a *Poeme*, or *Carmen*. Such are those in *Martiall*:

> *Omnia, Castor, emis: sic fiet, ut omnia vendas,*[18]

And:

> *Pauper videri Cinna vult, & est pauper.*[19]

So were *Horace* his *Odes* call'd *Carmina*, his *Lirik* Songs. And
Lucretius designes a whole booke in his sixt:

> *Quod in primo quoque carmine claret.*[20]

And anciently all the Oracles were call'd *Carmina*; or what ever
Sentence was express'd, were it much or little, it was call'd an
Epick, Dramatick, Lirike, Elegiake, or *Epigrammatike Poeme*.

But how differs a Poeme from what wee call Poesy?

A *Poeme*, as I have told you, is the worke of the Poet, the end
and fruit of his labour and studye. *Poesy* is his skill or Crafte of
making; the very Fiction it selfe, the reason or forme of the
worke. And these three voices differ, as the thing done, the doing,
and the doer; the thing fain'd, the faining, and the fainer: so the
Poeme, the *Poesy*, and the *Poet*. Now, the *Poesy* is the habit or

[17] "Aeneas [dedicates] these arms [won] from the victorious Greeks."
Aeneid, III, 288.
[18] "You buy everything Castor; so it may be that you will sell everything." Martial, *Epigrams*, VII, 98.
[19] "Cinna wishes to seem a pauper: He is a pauper." *Ibid.*, VIII, 19.
[20] "Which is also in the first book." *De Rerum Natura*, VI, 937. Jonson
calls attention to the fact that Lucretius refers to a whole book of his work
as a *carmina*.

the Art; nay, rather the Queene of Arts, which had her Originall from heaven, received thence from the *'Ebrewes,* and had in prime estimation with the *Greeks,* transmitted to the *Latines* and all Nations that profess'd Civility. The Study of it, if wee will trust *Aristotle,* offers to mankinde a certaine rule and Patterne of living well and happily, disposing us to all Civill offices of Society. If wee will beleive *Tully,*[21] it nourisheth and instructeth our Youth, delights our Age, adornes our prosperity, comforts our Adversity, entertaines us at home, keepes us company abroad, travailes with us, watches, devides the times of our earnest and sports, shares in our Country recesses and recreations; insomuch as the wisest and best learned have thought her the absolute Mistresse of manners and neerest of kin to Vertue. And wheras they entitle *Philosophy* to bee a rigid and austere *Poesie,* they have, on the contrary, stiled *Poesy* a dulcet and gentle *Philosophy,* which leades on and guides us by the hand to Action with a ravishing delight and incredible Sweetnes. But before wee handle the kindes of *Poems,* with their speciall differences, or make court to the Art it selfe as a Mistresse, I would leade you to the knowledge of our *Poet* by a perfect Information, what he is or should bee by nature, by exercise, by imitation, by Studie, and so bring him downe through the disciplines of *Grammar, Logicke, Rhetorticke,* and the *Ethicks,* adding somewhat out of all, peculiar to himselfe, and worthy of your Admittance or reception.

First, wee require in our *Poet* or maker (for that Title our Language affordes him elegantly with the *Greeke*) a goodnes of naturall wit. For wheras all other Arts consist of Doctrine and Precepts, the *Poet* must bee able by nature and instinct to powre out the Treasure of his minde, and as *Seneca* saith, *Aliquando secundum Anacreontem insanire jucundum esse;* [22] by which hee understands the *Poeticall Rapture.* And according to that of *Plato, Frustrà Poeticas fores sui compos pulsavit:* [23] And of *Aristotle, Nullum magnum ingenium sine mixturâ dementiæ fuit. Nec potest grande aliquid, & supra cæteros loqui, nisi mota*

---

[21] *Pro Archia,* 7.

[22] "According to Anacreon, it is sometimes pleasant to be a bit mad." Seneca, *De Tranquillitate Animi,* 15. Misquoted.

[23] "In vain the composed man knocked on the doors of poetry." Also misquoted from Seneca. The reference is to the *Ion.*

mens.[24] Then it riseth higher, as by a divine Instinct, when it contemnes common and knowne conceptions. It utters somewhat above a mortall mouth. Then it gets a loft and flies away with his Ryder, whether before it was doubtfull to ascend. This the *Poets* understood by their *Helicon, Pegasus,* or *Parnassus*; and this made *Ovid* to boast:

> *Est Deus in nobis, agitante calescimus illo:*
> *Sedibus æthereis spiritus ille venit.*[25]

And *Lipsius* to affirme, *Scio Poetam neminem præstantem fuisse, sine parte quadam uberiore divinæ auræ.*[26] An hence it is that the comming up of good Poets (for I minde not *mediocres* or *imos*) is so thinne and rare among us. Every beggerly Corporation affoords the State a *Major* or two *Bailiffs* yearly; but *solus Rex, aut Poeta, non quantannis nascitur.*[27] To this perfection of Nature in our *Poet* wee require Exercise of those parts, and frequent. If his wit will not arrive soddainly at the dignitie of the Ancients, let him not yet fall out with it, quarrell, or be over hastily Angry, offer to turne it away from Study in a humor; but come to it againe upon better cogitation, try an other time with labour. If then it succeed not, cast not away the Quills yet, nor scratch the Wainescott, beate not the poore Deske, but bring all to the forge and file againe; torne it a newe. There is no Statute *Law* of the Kingdome bidds you bee a Poet against your will or the first Quarter. If it come in a yeare or two, it is well. The common Rymers powre forth Verses, such as they are, *ex tempore*; but there never come[s] from them one Sense worth the life of a Day. A Rymer and a *Poet* are two things. It is said of the incomparable *Virgil* that he brought forth his verses like a Beare, and after form'd them with licking. *Scaliger* the Father writes it of him, that he made a quantitie of verses in the morning, which a fore night hee reduced to a lesse number. But that which *Valerius*

[24] "There was never a great genius untinged by madness. Nor can anyone say anything great and above the commonplace unless his mind is moved." Again, misquoted from the Seneca essay. The reference is to *Poetics*, XVII.
[25] "There is a god in us; when he moves us we grow hot. That spirit comes from the heavens." Ovid, *Fasti*, VI, 5; *Ars Amatoria*, III, 550.
[26] "I know there has never been an outstanding poet who did not have an extremely rich share of divine spirit." Justus Lipsius, *Electorum Liber*, I, 5.
[27] "Only a king and a poet are not born yearly." Petronius, *Fragments*.

Maximus hath left recorded of *Euripides,* the *tragicke Poet,* his
answer to *Alcestis,* an other *Poet,* is as memorable as modest; who
when it was told to *Alcestis* that *Euripides* had in three daies
brought forth but three verses, and those with some difficultie
and throwes, *Alcestis* glorying hee could with ease have sent forth
a hundred in the space, *Euripides,* roundly repl[y]'d: like enough;
But here is the difference: Thy verses will not last those three
daies, mine will to all time.[28] Which was as to tell him he could
not write a verse. I have met many of these Rattles that made a
noyse and buz'de. They had their humme, and no more. Indeed,
things wrote with labour deserve to be so read, and will last their
Age. The third requisite in our *Poet* or Maker is *Imitation,* to bee
able to convert the substance or Riches of an other *Poet* to his
owne use. To make choise of one excellent man above the rest,
and so to follow him till he grow very *Hee,* or so like him as the
Copie may be mistaken for the Principall. Not as a Creature that
swallowes what it takes in, crude, raw, or indigested, but that
feedes with an Appetite, and hath a Stomacke to concoct, devide,
and turne all into nourishment. Not to imitate servilely, as *Horace*
saith, and catch at vices for vertue, but to draw forth out of the
best and choisest flowers with the Bee, and turne all into Honey,
worke it into one relish and savour; make our *Imitation* sweet;
observe how the best writers have imitated, and follow them:
How *Virgil* and *Statius* have imitated *Homer;* how *Horace,*
Archilochus, how *Alcæus* and the other *Liricks;* and so of the
rest. But that which wee especially require in him is an exactnesse
of Studie and multiplicity of reading, which maketh a full man,
not alone enabling him to know the *History* or Argument of a
Poeme and to report it, but so to master the matter and Stile, as
to shew hee knowes how to handle, place, or dispose of either
with *elegancie* when need shall bee: And not thinke hee can
leape forth suddainely a *Poet* by dreaming hee hath been in
Parnassus, or having washt his lipps, as they say, in *Helicon.*
There goes more to his making then so: For to Nature, Exercise,
Imitation, and Studie, *Art* must bee added to make all these
perfect. And though these challenge to themselves much in the
making up of our Maker, it is Art only can lead him to perfection,

---

[28] Valerius Maximus, *Memorabilia,* III, 7.

and leave him there in possession, as planted by her hand. It is the assertion of *Tully*,[29] If to an excellent nature there happen an accession or confirmation of Learning and Discipline, there will then remaine somewhat noble and singular. For, as *Simylus* saith in *Stobæus*, Οὔτε φύσις ἱκανὴ γίνεται τέχνης ἄτερ, οὔτε πᾶν τέχνη μὴ φύσιν κεκτημένη,[30] without Art Nature can nere bee perfect, & without Nature Art can clayme no being. But our Poet must beware that his Studie bee not only to learne of himself; for hee that shall affect to doe that confesseth his ever having a Foole to his master. Hee must read many, but ever the best and choisest; those that can teach him any thing hee must ever account his masters, and reverence: among whom *Horace* and hee that taught him, *Aristotle*, deserv'd to bee the first in estimation. *Aristotle* was the first accurate *Criticke* and truest Judge, nay, the greatest *Philosopher* the world ever had; for hee noted the vices of all knowledges in all creatures, and out of many mens perfections in a Science hee formed still one Art. So hee taught us two Offices together, how we ought to judge rightly of others, and what wee ought to imitate specially in our selves: But all this in vaine without a naturall wit and a Poeticall nature in chiefe. For no man, so soone as hee knowes this or reades it, shall be able to write the better; but as he is adapted to it by Nature, he shall grow the perfecter Writer. Hee must have Civil *prudence* and *Eloquence*, & that whole, not taken up by snatches or peeces, in Sentences or remnants, when he will handle businesse or carry Counsells, as if he came then out of the Declamors Gallerie, or Shadowe, but furnish'd out of the body of the State, which commonly is the Schoole of men.[31] The *Poet* is the neerest Borderer upon the Orator, and expresseth all his vertues, though he be tyed more to numbers, is his equall in ornament, and above him in his strengths.[32] And of the kind the *Comicke* comes neerest: Because in moving the minds of men, and stirring of affections, in which Oratory shewes, and especially approves her eminence, hee chiefly excells. What figure of a Body was *Lysippus* ever able to

[29] *Pro Archia*, 7.
[30] Strobaeus, *Florilegium*, ii. Translated in text.
[31] The preceding passage, beginning with "Aristotle was the first. . . ." is taken from Heinsius, *De Tragoediae Constitutione* (1611).
[32] Cf. Cicero, *De Oratore*, III, 48.

forme with his Graver, or *Apelles* to paint wih his Pencill, as the Comedy to life expresseth so many and various affections of the minde? There shall the Spectator see some insulting with Joy, others fretting with Melancholy, raging with Anger, mad with Love, boiling with Avarice, undone with Riot, tortur'd with expectation, consum'd with feare: no perturbation in common life but the Orator findes an example of it in the Scene. And then for the Elegancy of Language, read but this Inscription on the *Grave* of a *Comicke Poet*:

> *Immortales mortales si fas esset flere,*
> *Flerent divæ Camænæ Nævium Poetam;*
> *Itaque postquam est Orcino traditus thesauro,*
> *Obliti sunt Romæ linguâ loqui Latinâ.*[33]

Or that modester Testimonie given by *Lucius Aelius Stilo* upon *Plautus*, who affirmed, *Musas, si latinè loqui voluissent, Plautino sermone fuisse loquuturas.*[34] And that illustrious judgement by the most learned *M. Varro* of him,[35] who pronounced him the *Prince of Letters* and *Elegancie* in the Roman Language.

I am not of that opinion to conclude a *Poets* liberty within the narrowe limits of lawes which either the *Grammarians* or *Philosophers* prescribe. For before they found out those Lawes there were many excellent Poets that fulfill'd them: Amongst whome none more perfect then *Sophocles*, who liv'd a little before *Aristotle*.

Which of the *Greekelings* durst ever give precepts to *Demosthenes?* or to *Pericles*, whom the Age surnam'd *heavenly*, because he seem'd to thunder and lighten with his Language? or to *Alcibiades*, who had rather Nature for his guide then Art for his master?

But whatsoever Nature at any time dictated to the most happie, or long exercise to the most laborious, that the wisdome and

---

[33] "If immortal gods can weep for mortals, they wept for Naevius, the poet of rich Camoena. Since he was carried to the treasure-house of Orcus [i.e., Hades] the Romans have forgotten how to speak the Latin language." Aulus Gellius, *Noctes Atticae*, I, 24.

[34] "The Muses, if they had wished to speak in Latin, would have spoken in the language of Plautus." Quintilian, *Inst. Orat.*, X, 1, 99.

[35] Cited in Aulus Gellius, I, 24.

Learning of *Aristotle* hath brought into an Art, because he understood the Causes of things; and what other men did by chance
or custome he doth by reason; and not only found out the way
not to erre, but the short way we should take not to erre.

Many things in *Euripides* hath *Aristophanes* wittily reprehended, not out of Art, but out of Truth. For *Euripides* is sometimes peccant, as he is most times perfect. But Judgement when
it is greatest, if reason doth not accompany it, is not ever absolute.[36]

To judge of Poets is only the facultie of Poets; and not of all
Poets, but the best. *Nemo infælicùs de Poetis judicavit, quam qui
de Poetis scripsit.*[37] But some will say, *Criticks* are a kind of
Tinkers, that make more faults then they mend ordinarily. See
their diseases and those of *Grammarians*. It is true, many bodies
are the worse for the medling with: And the multitude of *Physicians* hath destroyed many sound patients with their wrong practise. But the office of a true *Critick* or *Censor* is not to throw by
a letter any where, or damne an innocent Syllabe, but lay the
words together, and amend them; judge sincerely of the Author
and his matter, which is the signe of solid and perfect learning in
a man. Such was *Horace,* an Author of much Civilitie, and, if
any one among the heathen can be, the best master both of vertue
and wisdome; an excellent and true judge upon cause and reason,
not because he thought so, but because he knew so out of use
and experience.

Cato the *Grammarian,* a defender of *Lucilius.*

> *Cato Grammaticus, Latina Syren,*
> *Qui solus legit, & facit Poetas.*[38]

Quintilian of the same heresie, but rejected.
Horace his judgement of *Chærillus* defended against *Ioseph
Scaliger*: And of *Laberius* against *Julius.*

---

[36] The preceding passage, beginning with "I am not of that opinion. . . ."
is translated from Heinsius' essay on tragedy.
[37] "No one judged the poets more poorly than the man who wrote a book
On Poets." The idea that only poets are qualified to judge poets is perhaps
ultimately derived from *Rhetorica ad Herennium,* IV, 2. It was often repeated during the Neoclassic period.
[38] "Cato the Grammarian, the Latin siren, who alone selects and makes
poets." Suetonius, *De Illust. Gram.,* XI, apparently derived from the essay
De Satyra Horatiana appended to Heinsius' *Horace* (1612).

But chiefly his opinion of *Plautus* vindicated against many that are offended, and say it is a hard Censure upon the parent of all conceipt and sharpnesse. And they wish it had not fallen from so great a master and Censor in the Art, whose bondmen knew better how to judge of *Plautus* then any that dare patronize the family of learning in this Age; who could not bee ignorant of the judgement of the times in which hee liv'd, when *Poetrie* and the *Latin* language were at the height; especially being a man so conversant and inwardly familiar with the censures of great men that did discourse of these things daily amongst themselves. Againe, a man so gratious and in high favour with the Emperour, as *Augustus* often called him his wittie *Manling*, for the littlenes of his stature; and, if wee may trust Antiquity, had design'd him for a Secretary of Estate, and invited him to the place, which he modestly praid off and refus'd.

Horace did so highly esteeme *Terence* his Comedies, as he ascribes the Art in Comedie to him alone among the *Latines*, and joynes him with *Menander*.

Now, let us see what may be said for either, to defend *Horace* his judgement to posterity, and not wholly to condemne *Plautus*.

The parts of a Comedie are the same with a *Tragedie*, and the end is partly the same: For they both delight and teach; the *Comicks* are call'd διδάσκαλοι [39] of the *Greekes* no lesse then the *Tragicks*.

Nor is the moving of laughter alwaies the end of *Comedy*; that is rather a fowling for the peoples delight, or their fooling. For, as *Aristotle* saies rightly, the moving of laughter is a fault in Comedie, a kind of turpitude that depraves some part of a mans nature without a disease: [40] As a wry face without paine moves laughter, or a deformed vizard, or a rude Clowne drest in a Ladies habit and using her actions; wee dislike and scorne such representations, which made the ancient Philosophers ever thinke laughter unfitting in a wise man. And this induc'd *Plato* to esteeme of *Homer* as a sacrilegious Person, because he presented

[39] "Teachers." Originally, because the authors 'taught' the actors; but here used with didactic overtones.

[40] The idea that comedies should not always 'move to laughter' is based on a misunderstanding of *Poetics*, V, 1, and was often reiterated in order to emphasize the serious moral purpose of comedy. The reference to Aristotle at the end of the paragraph is to *Nichomachean Ethics*, IV, 9.

the *Gods* sometimes laughing. As also it is divinely said of *Aristotle*, that to seeme ridiculous is a part of dishonesty, and foolish.

So that what either in the words or Sense of an Author, or in the language or Actions of men, is awry or depraved doth strangely stirre meane affections, and provoke for the most part to laughter. And therefore it was cleare that all insolent and ob-scene speaches, jest upon the best men, injuries to particular persons, perverse and sinister Sayings, and the rather unexpected, in the old Comedy did move laughter, especially where it did imitate any dishonesty; and scurrility came forth in the place of wit; which, who understands the nature and *Genius* of laughter cannot but perfectly know.

Of which *Aristophanes* affords an ample harvest, having not only out gone *Plautus* or any other in that kinde, but express'd all the moods and figures of what is ridiculous oddly. In short, as Vinegar is not accounted good untill the wine be corrupted, so jests that are true and naturall seldome raise laughter with the beast, the multitude. They love nothing that is right and proper. The farther it runs from reason or possibility with them the better it is.

What could have made them laugh, like to see *Socrates* pre-sented, that Example of all good life, honesty, and vertue, to have him hoisted up with a Pullie, and there play the Philosopher in a basquet: Measure how many foote a Flea could skip *Geometri-cally*, by a just Scale, and edifie the people from the ingine.[41] This was *Theatricall* wit, right Stage-jesting, and relishing a Play-house, invented for scorne and laughter; whereas, if it had savour'd of equity, truth, perspicuity, and Candor, to have tasten a wise or a learned Palate, spit it out presantly! this is bitter and profitable, this instructs, and would informe us; what neede wee know any thing, that are nobly borne, more then a Horse-race or a hunting-match, our day to breake with Citizens, and such innate mysteries?

This is truly leaping from the Stage to the Tumbrell againe, reducing all witt to the Originall Dungcart.

[41] The preceding passage, beginning with "But chiefly his opinion of Plautus. . . ." is translated from the notes to Heinsius' edition of Horace (1612), pp. 78ff. Socrates is ridiculed in Aristophanes, *Clouds*, 217ff.

Of the magnitude and compasse of any Fable, Epicke or Dramatick.[42]

To the resolving of this *Question* wee must first agree in the definition of the Fable. The Fable is call'd the *Imitation* of one intire and perfect Action, whose parts are so joyned and knitt together, as nothing in the structure can be chang'd or taken away without impairing or troubling the whole, of which there is a proportionable magnitude in the members. As, for example, if a man would build a house, he would first appoint a place to build it in, which he would define within certaine bounds: So in the Constitution of a *Poeme*, the Action is aym'd at by the *Poet*, which answers Place in a building, and that Action hath his largenesse, compasse, and proportion. But as a Court or Kings Palace requires other dimensions then a private house: So the *Epick* askes a magnitude from other Poëms: Since what is Place in the one is Action in the other; the difference is in space. So that by this definition wee conclude the fable to be the *imitation* of one perfect and intire Action, as one perfect and intire place is requir'd to a building. By perfect, wee understand that to which nothing is wanting, as Place to the building that is rais'd, and Action to the fable that is form'd. It is perfect, perhaps not for a Court or Kings Palace, which requires a greater ground, but for the structure wee would raise; so the space of the Action may not prove large enough for the *Epick Fable*, yet bee perfect for the *Dramatick*, and whole.

Whole wee call that, and perfect, which hath a *beginning*, a *mid'st*, and an *end*. So the place of any building may be whole and intire for that worke, though too little for a palace. As to a *Tragedy* or a *Comedy*, the Action may be convenient and perfect that would not fit an *Epicke Poeme* in Magnitude. So a Lion is a perfect creature in himself, though it bee lesse then that of a *Buffalo* or a *Rhinocerote*. They differ but in *specie*: either in the kinde is absolute. Both have their parts, and either the whole. Therefore, as in every body, so in every Action, which is the subject of a just worke, there is requir'd a certaine proportionable greatnesse, neither too vast nor too minute. For that which hap-

---

[42] From here to the end with the exception of the last five lines, Jonson translates from Heinsius, *De Tragoediae Constitutione*, Chapter IV.

pens to the Eyes when wee behold a body, the same happens to the Memorie when wee contemplate an action. I looke upon a monstrous Giant, as *Tityus,* whose body cover'd nine Acres of Land, and mine eye stickes upon every part; the whole that consists of those parts will never be taken in at one intire view. So in a *Fable,* if the Action be too great, wee can never comprehend the whole together in our Imagination. Againe, if it be too little, there ariseth no pleasure out of the object; it affords the view no stay: It is beheld, and vanisheth at once. As if wee should looke upon an Ant or Pismyre, the parts fly the sight, and the whole considered is almost nothing. The same happens in Action, which is the object of Memory, as the body is of sight. Too vast oppresseth the Eyes, and exceeds the Memory; too little scarce admits either.

Now, in every Action it behooves the *Poet* to know which is his utmost bound, how farre with fitnesse and a necessary proportion he may produce and determine it: That is, till either good fortune change into the worse, or the worse into the better. For as a body without proportion cannot be goodly, no more can the Action, either in Comedy or Tragedy, without his fit bounds. And every bound, for the nature of the Subject, is esteem'd the best that is largest, till it can increase no more; so it behooves the Action in *Tragedy* or *Comedy* to be let grow till the necessity aske a Conclusion; wherin two things are to be considered: First, that it exceed not the compasse of one Day; Next, that there be place left for digression and Art. For the *Episodes* and digressions in a Fable are the same that houshold stuffe and other furniture are in a house. And so farre for the measure and extent of a *Fable Dramaticke.*

Now, that it should be one and intire. One is considerable two waies; either as it is only separate, and by it self, or as being compos'd of many parts, it beginnes to be one as those parts grow or are wrought together. That it should be one the first way alone, and by it self, no man that hath tasted letters ever would say, especially having required before a just Magnitude and equall Proportion of the parts in themselves. Neither of which can possibly bee, if the Action be single and separate, not compos'd of parts, which laid together in themselves, with an equall and fitting proportion, tend to the same end; which thing out of

Antiquitie it selfe hath deceiv'd many, and more this Day it doth deceive.

So many there be of old that have thought the Action of one man to be one: As of *Hercules, Theseus, Achilles, Ulysses,* and other *Heroes*; which is both foolish and false, since by one and the same person many things may be severally done which cannot fitly be referred or joyned to the same end: which not only the excellent *Tragick-Poets,* but the best Masters of the *Epick, Homer* and *Virgil,* saw. For though the Argument of an *Epick-Poeme* be farre more diffus'd & powr'd out then that of *Tragedy,* yet *Virgil,* writing of *Aeneas,* hath pretermitted many things. He neither tells how he was borne, how brought up, how he fought with *Achilles,* how he was snatch'd out of the battaile by *Venus*; but that one thing, how *he came into Italie,* he prosecutes in twelve bookes. The rest of his journey, his error by Sea, the Sacke of *Troy,* are put not as the Argument of the worke, but *Episodes* of the Argument. So *Homer* lai'd by many things of *Ulysses,* and handled no more then he saw tended to one and the same end.

Contrarie to which, and foolishly, those *Poets* did, whom the *Philosopher* taxeth: Of whom one gather'd all the Actions of *Theseus,* another put all the Labours of *Hercules* in one worke. So did he whom *Juvenal* [43] mentions in the begining, *hoarse Codrus,* that recited a volume compil'd, which he call'd his *Theseide,* not yet finish'd, to the great trouble both of his hearers and himself: Amongst which there were many parts had no coherence nor kindred one with other, so farre they were from being one Action, one *Fable.* For as a house, consisting of diverse materialls, becomes one structure and one dwelling, so an Action, compos'd of diverse parts, may become one *Fable, Epicke* or *Dramaticke.* For *example,* in a *Tragedy,* looke upon *Sophocles* his *Ajax: Ajax,* depriv'd of *Achilles's* Armour, which he hop'd from the suffrage of the *Greekes,* disdaines, and, growing impatient of the Injurie, rageth and turnes mad. In that humour he doth many senselesse things, and at last falls upon the *Grecian* flocke, and kills a great Ramme for *Ulysses*: Returning to his Sense, he growes asham'd of the scorne, and kills himself; and is by the *Chiefes* of the *Greekes* forbidden buriall. These things

[43] *Satires,* I, 2, III, 203.

agree and hang together, not as they were done, but as seeming to be done, which made the Action whole, intire, and absolute.

For the *whole,* as it consisteth of parts, so without all the parts it is not the whole; and to make it absolute is requir'd not only the parts, but such parts as are true. For a part of the whole was true, which, if you take away, you either change the whole or it is not the whole. For if it be such a part, as, being present or absent, nothing concernes the whole, it cannot be call'd a part of the whole; and such are the *Episodes,* of which hereafter. For the present, here is one example: The single Combat of *Ajax* with *Hector,* as it is at large describ'd in *Homer,* nothing belongs to this *Ajax* of *Sophocles.*

You admire no *Poems* but such as run like a Brewers-cart upon the stones, hobling:

> *Et quæ per salebras altaque saxa cadunt,*
> *Actius & quidquid Pacuviusque vomunt.*
> *Attonitusque legis,* terrai frugiferai.[44]

---

[44] ". . . things which jolt over rough crags and high rocks, and whatever Actius and Pacuvius vomit forth. And you ecstatically read, 'Ye fruit-bearinge londes'." Martial, *Epigrams,* II, 90.

Thomas Hobbes

[1588–1679]

⋖⋛⋗

BY 1650 THE ENGLISH critical climate was strongly affected by Neo-classical and Baconian influences. Both elements are prominent in the "Preface" addressed to Hobbes which William Davenant wrote in 1650 for his epic *Gondibert*. 'Probability' and moral instruction are the keynotes of the preface. Tasso is criticized for his fantastic episodes since he was "a Christian Poet, whose Religion little needs the aids of Invention . . . ." Hobbes' "Answer to Davenant" (1650) is still more interesting than the original preface. The comments on judgment and fancy echo Bacon's on reason and imagination and anticipate the prominence of the terms "wit" and "fancy" in eighteenth-century criticism. The praise of Davenant's adherence to 'probability' carries forward the cause of Neoclassic 'verisimilitude'; and the remarks on the elegance of the language of *Gondibert* anticipate later efforts to purge English of its vestigal crudities.

The present text is based on the edition of 1651.

BIBLIOGRAPHY. *Works*, ed. W. Molesworth, 16 vols. (1839–45). For comment see: C. Dowlin, *Davenant's Gondibert, its Preface,* and *Hobbes' Answer: A Study in Neo-classicism* (1934); M. Kallich, "The Association of Ideas and Critical Theory: Hobbes, Locke, and Addison," *ELH*, XII (1945); R. Perkinson, "The Epic in Five Acts," *SP*, XLIII (1946); R. Sharpe, *From Donne to Dryden* (1940); C. Thorpe, *The Aesthetic Theory of Thomas Hobbes* (1940); G. Watson, "Hobbes and the Metaphysical Conceit," *JHI*, XVI (1955).

ANSWER TO DAVENANT'S

Preface to "Gondibert"

[1650]

Sir,

If to commend your Poem I should onely say, in general Termes, that in the choice of your Argument, the disposition of the parts, the maintenance of the Characters of your Persons, the dignity and vigor of your expression, you have performed all the parts of various experience, ready memory, clear judgement, swift and well govern'd fancy, though it were enough for the truth, it were too little for the weight and credit of my testimony. For I lie open to two Exceptions, one of an incompetent, the other of a corrupted Witness. Incompetent, because I am not a Poet; and corrupted with the Honor done me by your Preface. The former obliges me to say something, by the way, of the Nature and differences of Poesy.

As Philosophers have divided the Universe, their subject, into three Regions, *Celestiall, Aëriall,* and *Terrestriall,* so the Poets (whose worke it is, by imitating humane life in delightful and measur'd lines, to avert men from vice and incline them to vertuous and honorable actions) have lodg'd themselves in the three Regions of mankinde, *Court, City,* and *Country,* correspondent in some proportion to those three Regions of the World. For there is in Princes and men of conspicuous power, anciently called *Heroes,* a lustre and influence upon the rest of men resembling that of the Heavens, and an insincereness, inconstancy, and troublesome humor of those that dwell in populous Cities, like the mobility, blustring, and impurity of the Aire; and a plainness, and though dull, yet a nutritive faculty in rurall people, that endures a comparison with the Earth they labour.

From hence have proceeded three sorts of Poesy, *Heroique, Scommatique,* and *Pastorall.* Every one of these is distinguished again in the manner of *Representation,* which sometimes is *Narra-*

tive, wherein the Poet himself relateth, and sometimes *Dramatique,* as when the persons are every one adorned and brought upon the Theater to speak and act their own parts. There is therefore neither more nor less than six sorts of Poesy. For the Heroique Poem narrative, such as is yours, is called an *Epique Poem.* The Heroique Poem Dramatique is *Tragedy.* The Scommatique Narrative is *Satyre,* Dramatique is *Comedy.* The Pastorall narrative is called simply *Pastorall,* anciently *Bucolique*; the same Dramatique, *Pastorall Comedy.* The Figure therefore of an Epique Poem and of a Tragedy ought to be the same, for they differ no more but in that they are pronounced by one or many Persons. Which I insert to justifie the figure of yours, consisting of five books divided into Songs, or Cantoes, as five Acts divided into Scenes has ever been the approved figure of a Tragedy.

They that take for Poesy whatsoever is writ in Verse will think this Division imperfect, and call in Sonets, Epigrams, Eclogues, and the like pecces, which are but Essayes and parts of an entire Poem, and reckon *Empedocles* and *Lucretius* (natural Philosophers) for Poets, and the moral precepts of *Phocylides, Theognis,* and the Quatraines of *Pybrach* and the History of *Lucan,* and others of that kind amongst Poems, bestowing on such Writers for honor the name of Poets rather then of Historians or Philosophers. But the subject of a Poem is the manners of men, not natural causes; manners presented, not dictated; and manners feigned, as the name of Poesy imports, not found in men. They that give entrance to Fictions writ in Prose err not so much, but they err: For Prose requireth delightfulness, not onely of fiction, but of stile, in which, if Prose contend with Verse, it is with disadvantage and, as it were, on foot against the strength and wings of *Pegasus.*

For Verse amongst the *Greeks* was appropriated anciently to the service of their Gods, and was the Holy stile, the stile of the Oracles, the stile of the Laws, and the stile of men that publiquely recommended to their Gods the vowes and thanks of the people, which was done in their holy songs called Hymnes, and the Composers of them were called Prophets and Priests before the name of Poet was known. When afterwards the majestie of that stile was observed, the Poets chose it as best becoming their high invention. And for the Antiquity of Verse, it is greater then the antiquity of Letters. For it is certain *Cadmus* was the first that from *Phœnecia,* a country that neighboureth *Judea,* brought the use of Letters into *Greece.* But the service of the Gods and the Laws, which by measured Sounds were easily committed to the memory, had been long time in use before the arrivall of *Cadmus* there.

There is, besides the grace of stile, another cause why the ancient Poets chose to write in measured language, which is this. Their Poems were made at first with intention to have them sung, as well Epique as Dramatique,—which custom hath been long time laid aside, but began to be revived, in part, of late years in *Italy,*—and could not be made commensurable to the Voyce or Instruments in Prose, the ways and motions whereof are so uncertain and undistinguished, like the way and motion of a Ship in the Sea, as not onely to discompose the best Composers, but also to disappoint some times the most attentive Reader and put him to hunt counter for the sense. It was therefore necessary for Poets in those times to write in Verse.

The verse which the *Greeks* and *Latines,* considering the nature of their own Languages, found by experience most grave, and for an Epique Poem most decent, was their *Hexameter,* a Verse limited not onely in the length of the line, but also in the quantity of the syllables. In stead of which we use the line of ten Syllables, recompencing the neglect of their quantity with the diligence of Rime. And this measure is so proper for an Heroique Poem as without some losse of gravity and dignity it was never changed. A longer is not far from ill Prose, and a shorter is a kinde of whisking, you know, like the unlacing rather then the singing of a Muse. In an Epigram or a Sonnet a man may vary his measures, and seek glory from a needlesse difficulty, as he that contrived Verses into the formes of an Organ, a Hatchet, an Egg, an Altar, and a paire of Wings; but in so great and noble a worke as is an Epique Poem, for a man to obstruct his own way with unprofitable difficulties is great imprudence. So likewise to chuse a needlesse and difficult correspondence of Rime is but a difficult toy, and forces a man sometimes for the stoping of a chink to say somewhat he did never think; I cannot therefore but very much approve your *Stanza,* wherein the syllables in every Verse are ten, and the Rime Alternate.

For the choyce of your subject, you have sufficiently justified your self in your Preface. But because I have observed in *Virgil,* that the Honor done to *Æneas* and his companions has so bright a reflection upon *Augustus Cæsar* and other great *Romans* of that time as a man may suspect him not constantly possessed with the noble spirit of those his *Heroes,* and beleeve you are not acquainted with any great man of the Race of *Gondibert,* I add to your justification the purity of your purpose, in having no other motive of your labour but to adorn vertue and procure her Lovers, then which there cannot be a worthier designe, and more becoming noble Poesy.

In that you make so small account of the example of almost all the approved Poets, ancient and modern, who thought fit in the beginning, and sometimes also in the progress of their Poems, to invoke a Muse or some other Deity that should dictate to them or assist them in their writings, they that take not the laws of Art from any reason of their own but from the fashion of precedent times will perhaps accuse your singularity. For my part, I neither subscribe to their accusation, nor yet condemn that Heathen custom otherwise then as accessary to their false Religion. For their Poets were their Divines, had the name of Prophets; Exercised amongst the People a kinde of spiritual Authority, would be thought to speak by a divine spirit, have their works which they writ in Verse (the divine stile) pass for the word of God and not of man, and to be hearkened to with reverence. Do not our Divines (excepting the stile) do the same, and by us that are of the same Religion cannot justly be reprehended for it? Besides, in the use of the spiritual calling of Divines, there is danger sometimes to be feared from want of skill, such as is reported of unskilful Conjurers, that mistaking the rites and cerimonious points of their art, call up such spirits as they cannot at their pleasure allay again, by whom storms are raised that overthrow buildings and are the cause of miserable wracks at sea. Unskilful Divines do often times the like: For when they call unseasonably for *Zeal* there appears a Spirit of *Cruelty*; and by the like error, instead of *Truth* they raise *Discord*; instead of *Wisdom, Fraud*; instead of *Reformation, Tumult*; and *Controversie* instead of *Religion.* Whereas in the Heathen Poets, at least in those whose works have lasted to the time we are in, there are none of those indiscretions to be found that tended to subversion or disturbance of the Common-wealths wherein they lived. But why a Christian should think it an ornament to his Poem, either to profane the true God or invoke a false one, I can imagin no cause but a reasonless imitation of Custom, of a foolish custome, by which a man, enabled to speak wisely from the principles of nature and his own meditation, loves rather to be thought to speak by inspiration, like a Bagpipe.

Time and Education begets experience; Experience begets memory; Memory begets Judgement and Fancy: Judgment begets the strength and structure, and Fancy begets the ornaments of a Poem. The Ancients therefore fabled not absurdly in making memory the Mother of the Muses. For memory is the World (though not really, yet so as in a looking glass) in which the Judgment, the severer Sister, busieth her self in a grave and rigid examination of all the parts of Nature, and in registring by Letters their order, causes, uses, differences, and resemblances; Whereby the Fancy, when any work of Art is to be performed, findes her materials at hand and prepared for use, and needs no more then a swift motion over them, that what she wants, and is there to be had, may not lie too long unespied. So that when she seemeth to fly from one *Indies* to the other, and from Heaven to Earth, and to penetrate into the hardest matter and obscurest places, into the future and into her self, and all this in a point of time, the voyage is not very great, her self being all she seeks; and her wonderful celerity consisteth not so much in motion as in copious Imagery discreetly ordered & perfectly registred in the memory, which most men under the name of Philosophy have a glimpse of, and is pretended to by many that, grosly mistaking her, embrace contention in her place. But so far forth as the Fancy of man has traced the ways of true Philosophy, so far it hath produced very marvellous effects to the benefit of mankinde. All that is beautiful or defensible in building, or marvellous in Engines and Instruments of motion, whatsoever commodity men receive from the observations of the Heavens, from the description of the Earth, from the account of Time, from walking on the Seas, and whatsoever distinguisheth the civility of *Europe* from the Barbarity of the *American* savages, is the workmanship of Fancy but guided by the Precepts of true Philosophy. But where these precepts fail, as they have hitherto failed in the doctrine of Moral vertue, there the Architect, *Fancy,* must take the Philosophers part upon her self. He therefore that undertakes an Heroick Poem, which is to exhibit a venerable & amiable Image of Heroick vertue, must not only be the Poet, to place & connect, but also the Philosopher, to furnish and square his matter, that is, to make both Body and Soul, colour and shadow of his Poem out of his own Store: Which how well you have performed I am now considering.

Observing how few the Persons be you introduce in the beginning, and how in the course of the actions of these (the number increasing) after several confluences they run all at last into the two principal streams of your Poem, *Gondibert* and *Oswald,* methinks the Fable is not much unlike the Theater. For so, from several and far distant Sources, do the lesser Brooks of *Lombardy,* flowing into one another, fall all at last into the two main Rivers, the *Po* and the *Adice.* It hath the same resemblance also with a mans veins, which, proceeding from different parts, after the like concourse insert themselves at last into the two principal veins of the Body. But when I considered that also the actions of men, which singly are inconsiderable, after many conjunctures grow at last either into one great protecting power or into two destroying factions, I could not but approve the structure of your Poem, which ought to be no other then such as an imitation of humane life requireth.

In the Streams themselves I finde nothing but setled Valor, cleane Honor, calm Counsel, learned diversion, and pure Love, save onely a torrent or two of Ambition, which, though a fault, has somewhat Heroick in it, and therefore must have place in an Heroick Poem. To shew the reader in what place he shall finde every excellent picture of vertue you have drawn is too long. And to shew him one is to prejudice the rest; yet I cannot forbear to point him to the Description of Love in the person of *Birtha,* in the seventh *Canto* of the second Book. There has nothing been said of that Subject neither by the Ancient nor Modern Poets comparable to it. Poets are Painters: I would fain see another Painter draw so true, perfect, and natural a Love to the Life, and make use of nothing but pure Lines, without the help of any the least uncomely shadow, as you have done. But let it be read as a piece by it self, for in the almost equal height of the whole the eminence of parts is Lost.

There are some that are not pleased with fiction, unless it be bold, not onely to exceed the *work*, but also the *possibility* of nature: they would have impenetrable Armors, Inchanted Castles, invulnerable bodies, Iron Men, flying Horses, and a thousand other such things, which are easily feigned by them that dare. Against such I defend you (without assenting to those that condemn either *Homer* or *Virgil*) by dissenting onely from those that think the Beauty of a Poem consisteth in the exorbitancy of the fiction. For as truth is the bound of Historical, so the Resemblance of truth is the utmost limit of Poeticall Liberty. In old time amongst the Heathen such strange fictions and Metamorphoses were not so remote from the Articles of their Faith as they are now from ours, and therefore were not so unpleasant. Beyond the actual works of nature a Poet may now go; but beyond the conceived possibility of nature, never. I can allow a Geographer to make in the Sea a Fish or a Ship which by the scale of his Mapp would be two or three hundred mile long, and think it done for ornament, because it is done without the precincts of his undertaking; but when he paints an *Elephant* so, I presently apprehend it as ignorance, and a plain confession of *Terra incognita*.

As the description of Great Men and Great Actions is the constant designe of a Poet, so the descriptions of worthy circumstances are necessary accessions to a Poem, and being well performed are the Jewels and most precious ornaments of Poesy. Such in *Virgil* are the Funeral games of *Anchises,* The duel of *Æneas* and *Turnus, &c.*; and such in yours are *The Hunting, The Bataile, The City Mourning, The Funeral, The House of Astragon, The Library, and the Temple,* equal to his, or those of *Homer* whom he imitated.

There remains now no more to be considered but the Expression, in which consisteth the countenance and colour of a beautiful Muse, and is given her by the Poet out of his own provision, or is borrowed from others. That which he hath of his own is nothing but experience and knowledge of Nature, and specially humane nature, and is the true and natural Colour. But that which is taken out of Books (the ordinary boxes of Counterfeit

Complexion) shews well or ill, as it hath more or less resemblance with the natural, and are not to be used without examination unadvisedly. For in him that professes the imitation of Nature, as all Poets do, what greater fault can there be then to bewray an ignorance of nature in his Poem,—especially having a liberty allowed him, if he meet with any thing he cannot master, to leave it out?

That which giveth a Poem the true and natural Colour consisteth in two things, which are, *To know well,* that is, to have images of nature in the memory distinct and clear, and *To know much.* A signe of the first is perspicuity, property, and decency, which delight all sorts of men, either by instructing the ignorant or soothing the learned in their knowledge. A signe of the latter is novelty of expression, and pleaseth by excitation of the minde; for novelty causeth admiration, and admiration curiosity, which is a delightful appetite of knowledge.

There be so many words in use at this day in the English Tongue, that though of magnifique sound, yet (like the windy blisters of a troubled water) have no sense at all, and so many others that lose their meaning by being ill coupled, that it is a hard matter to avoid them; for having been obtruded upon youth in the Schools by such as make it, I think, their business there (as 'tis exprest by the best Poet)

With terms to charm the weak and pose the wise.[1]

they grow up with them, and, gaining reputation with the ignorant, are not easily shaken off.

To this palpable darkness I may also add the ambitious obscurity of expressing more then is perfectly conceived, or perfect conception in fewer words then it requires. Which Expressions, though they have had the honor to be called strong lines, are indeed no better then Riddles, and, not onely to the Reader but also after a little time to the Writer himself, dark and troublesome.

To the property of Expression I referr that clearness of memory by which a Poet, when he hath once introduced any person

---

[1] *Gondibert,* Bk. I, Canto 5.

whatsoever speaking in his Poem, maintaineth in him to the end
the same character he gave him in the beginning. The variation
whereof is a change of pace that argues the Poet tired.

Of the Indecencies of an Heroick Poem the most remarkable
are those that shew disproportion either between the persons and
their actions, or between the manners of the Poet and the Poem.
Of the first kinde is the uncomliness of representing in great persons the inhumane vice of Cruelty or the sordid vice of Lust and
Drunkenness. To such parts as those the Ancient approved Poets
thought it fit to suborn, not the persons of men, but of monsters
and beastly Giants, such as *Polyphemus, Cacus,* and the *Cen-
taures.* For it is supposed a Muse, when she is invoked to sing a
song of that nature, should maidenly advise the Poet to set such
persons to sing their own vices upon the Stage, for it is not so
unseemly in a *Tragedy.* Of the same kinde it is to represent scurrility or any action or language that moveth much laughter. The
delight of an *Epique* Poem consisteth not in mirth, but admiration. Mirth and Laughter is proper to *Comedy* and *Satyre.* Great
persons that have their mindes employed on great designes have
not leasure enough to laugh, and are pleased with the contemplation of their own power and vertues, so as they need not the in-
firmities and vices of other men to recommend themselves to their
own favour by comparison, as all men do when they laugh. Of
the second kinde, where the disproportion is between the Poet
and the Persons of his Poem, one is in the Dialect of the Inferior
sort of People, which is always different from the language of
the Court. Another is to derive the Illustration of any thing from
such Metaphors or Comparisons as cannot come into mens
thoughts but by mean conversation and experience of humble or
evil Arts, which the Person of an *Epique* Poem cannot be thought
acquainted with.

From *Knowing much,* proceedeth the admirable variety and
novelty of Metaphors and Similitudes, which are not possible to
be lighted on in the compass of a narrow knowledge. And the
want whereof compelleth a Writer to expressions that are either
defac'd by time or sullied with vulgar or long use. For the Phrases
of Poesy, as the airs of musick, with often hearing become in-
sipide, the Reader having no more sense of their force then our
Flesh is sensible of the bones that sustain it. As the sense we have

of bodies consisteth in change and variety of impression, so also does the sense of language in the variety and changeable use of words. I mean not in the affectation of words newly brought home from travail, but in new and with all significant translation to our purposes of those that be already received, and in far fetch't but withall apt, instructive, and comly similitudes.

Having thus, I hope, avoided the first Exception against the incompetency of my Judgement, I am but little moved with the second, which is of being bribed by the honor you have done me by attributing in your Preface somewhat to my Judgment. For I have used your Judgment no less in many things of mine, which coming to light will thereby appear the better. And so you have your bribe again.

Having thus made way for the admission of my Testimony, I give it briefly thus: I never yet saw Poem that had so much shape of Art, health of Morality, and vigour and beauty of Expression as this of yours. And but for the clamour of the multitude, that hide their Envy of the present under a Reverence of Antiquity, I should say further that it would last as long as either the *Æneid* or *Iliad*, but for one Disadvantage; and the Disadvantage is this: The languages of the *Greeks* and *Romans*, by their Colonies and Conquests, have put off flesh and blood, and are becom immutable, which none of the modern tongues are like to be. I honor Antiquity, but that which is commonly called *old time* is *young time*. The glory of Antiquity is due, not to the Dead, but to the Aged.

And now, whilst I think on't, give me leave with a short discord to sweeten the Harmony of the approaching close. I have nothing to object against your Poem, but dissent onely from something in your Preface sounding to the prejudice of Age. 'Tis commonly said that old Age is a return to childhood: Which methinks you insist on so long, as if you desired it should be believed. That's the note I mean to shake a little. That saying, meant onely of the weakness of body, was wrested to the weakness of minde by froward children, weary of the controulment of their parents, masters, and other admonitors. Secondly, the dotage and childishness they ascribe to Age is never the effect of Time, but sometimes of the excesses of youth, and not a returning to, but a continual stay with, childhood. For they that, wanting the

curiosity of furnishing their memories with the rarities of nature
in their youth, and pass their time in making provision onely for
their ease and sensual delight, are children still at what years
soever, as they that coming into a populous City, never going out
of their Inn, are strangers still, how longsoever they have bin
there. Thirdly, there is no reason for any man to think himself
wiser to day then yesterday, which does not equally convince
he shall be wiser to morrow then to day.

Fourthly, you will be forced to change your opinion hereafter
when you are old; and in the mean time you discredit all I
have said before in your commendation, because I am old already. But no more of this.

I beleeve, Sir, you have seen a curious kinde of perspective,
where he that looks through a short hollow pipe upon a picture
containing divers figures sees none of those that are there painted,
but some one person made up of their parts, conveyed to the eie by
the artificial cutting of a glass. I finde in my imagination an effect
not unlike it from your Poem. The vertues you distribute there
amongst so many noble Persons represent in the reading the
image but of one mans vertue to my fancy, which is your own,
and that so deeply imprinted as to stay for ever there, and govern
all the rest of my thoughts and affections in the way of honouring
and serving you to the utmost of my power, that am,

 Sir,

    Your most humble and obedient Servant,

        Thomas Hobbes.

Paris, Ian. 10, 1650.

John Milton

[1608–1674]

◈

MILTON IDENTIFIED THE PRINCIPAL sources for his critical ideas in his treatise *Of Education* (1644). They are Aristotle's *Poetics,* Horace's *Ars Poetica,* and "the Italian commentaries of Castelvetro, Tasso, Mazzoni, and others . . . ." The list accurately shows that Milton's allegiance was to the Italian humanists of the sixteenth century rather than to the French and English Neoclassicists of his own age. His early Ovidian elegy to Diodati (1629) indicates that, while remarkably tolerant of the poetry of the Good Life, he was determined to follow the ascetic discipline which would fit him for the role of *vates.* In the introduction to Book II of *The Reason of Church Government* (1641) he repeats the point with great seriousness and in characteristically gorgeous rhetoric.

His comments on epic and tragedy contrast distinctly with those of Davenant and Hobbes, although he agrees with them (and Renaissance tradition) that one of poetry's functions is "teaching over the whole book of sanctity and vertu, through all the instances of example." The brief note on the verse of *Paradise Lost* (1667) and the preface to *Samson Agonistes* (1671) say more in a few pages than most of his contemporaries were able to say in whole books. A careful reading of Milton's critical observations in the light of his literary practice will do much to illuminate the distinction between humanistic and Neoclassic 'classicism'.

The present texts are based on William Cowper's translation of Elegy VI, and the 1642, 67, and 71 editions of the respective works.

BIBLIOGRAPHY. *Works,* Columbia Edition, 18 vols. (1931–8); *The Student's Milton,* ed. Patterson (1933). Among the innumerable books and articles, see especially: A. Clark, "Milton and the Renaissance Revolt Against Rhyme," in *Studies in Literary Modes* (1946); H. Grierson, "John Milton and the Renaissance Theory of Poetry," in *Milton and Wordsworth* (1937); J. Hanford, "Milton and the Return to Humanism," *SP,* XV (1919); *A Milton Handbook* (1946); M.

Hughes, "The Christ of *Paradise Regained* and the Renaissance Heroic
Tradition," *SP*, XXXV (1938); I. Langdon, *Milton's Theory of Poetry
and Fine Art* (1924); M. Nicolson, "Milton and Hobbes," *SP*, XXIII
(1926); W. Parker, *Milton's Debt to Greek Tragedy in Samson
Agonistes* (1937); B. Rajan, "Simple, Sensuous, and Passionate," *RES*,
XX (1945); B. Willey, *Seventeenth Century Background* (1934);
D. Wolfe, "Milton and Hobbes," *SP*, XLI (1944).

ELEGY VI

[1629]

TO CHARLES DIODATI

WHO, WHILE HE SPENT his Christmas in the country, sent the
Author a poetical Epistle, in which he requested that his verses,
if not so good as usual, might be excused on account of the many
feasts to which his friends had invited him, and which would not
allow him leisure to finish them as he wished.

With no rich viands overcharged, I send
Health, which perchance you want, my pampered friend;
But wherefore should thy muse tempt mine away
From what she loves, from darkness into day?
Art thou desirous to be told how well
I love thee, and in verse? verse cannot tell,
For verse has bounds, and must in measure move
But neither bounds nor measure knows my love.
How pleasant, in thy lines described, appear
December's harmless sports, and rural cheer!
French spirits kindling with cærulean fires,
And all such gambols as the time inspires!
　　Think not that wine against good verse offends;
The Muse and Bacchus have been always friends,
Nor Phœbus blushes sometimes to be found
With ivy, rather than with laurel, crowned.
The Nine themselves ofttimes have joined the song
And revels of the Bacchanalian throng;

Not even Ovid could in Scythian air
Sing sweetly—why? no vine would flourish there.
What in brief numbers sung Anacreon's muse?
Wine, and the rose, that sparkling wine bedews.
Pindar with Bacchus glows—his every line
Breathes the rich fragrance of inspiring wine,
While, with loud crash o'erturned, the chariot lies
And brown with dust the fiery courser flies.
The Roman lyrist steeped in wine his lays,
So sweet in Glycera's and Chloe's praise.
Now too the plenteous feast and mantling bowl
Nourish the vigour of thy sprightly soul;
The flowing goblet makes thy numbers flow,
And casks not wine alone, but verse bestow.
Thus Phœbus favours, and the arts attend,
Whom Bacchus, and whom Ceres, both befriend:
What wonder, then, thy verses are so sweet,
In which these triple powers so kindly meet?
The lute now also sounds, with gold inwrought,
And touched with flying fingers, nicely taught;
In tapestried halls, high-roofed, the sprightly lyre
Directs the dancers of the virgin choir.
If dull repletion fright the muse away,
Sights, gay as these, may more invite her stay:
And, trust me, while the ivory keys resound,
Fair damsels sport, and perfumes steam around,
Appollo's influence, like ethereal flame,
Shall animate, at once, thy glowing frame,
And all the Muse shall rush into thy breast,
By love and music's blended powers possest.
For numerous powers light Elegy befriend,
Hear her sweet voice, and at her call attend;
Her Bacchus, Ceres, Venus, all approve,
And, with his blushing mother, gentle Love.
Hence to such bards we grant the copious use
Of banquets, and the vine's delicious juice.

But they, who demi-gods and heroes praise,
And feats performed in Jove's more youthful days,

Who now the counsels of high heaven explore,
Now shades, that echo the Cerberean roar,
Simply let these, like him of Samos, live;
Let herbs to them a bloodless banquet give;
In beechen goblets let their beverage shine,
Cool from the crystal spring, their sober wine!
Their youth should pass in innocence, secure
From stain licentious, and in manners pure,
Pure as the priest, when robed in white he stands,
The fresh lustration ready in his hands.
Thus Linus lived, and thus, as poets write,
Tiresias, wiser for his loss of sight;
Thus exiled Chalcas, thus the bard of Thrace,[1]
Melodious tamer of the savage race;
Thus, trained by temperance, Homer led, of yore,
His chief of Ithaca from shore to shore.
Through magic Circe's monster-peopled reign,
And shoals insidious with the Siren train;
And through the realms where grizly spectres dwell,
Whose tribes he fettered in a gory spell:
For these are sacred bards, and, from above,
Drink large infusions from the mind of Jove.
   Wouldst thou, (perhaps 'tis hardly worth thine ear)
Wouldst thou be told my occupation here?
The promised King of peace employs my pen,
The eternal covenant made for guilty men,
The new-born Deity with infant cries
Filling the sordid hovel, where he lies;
The hymning Angels, and the herald star,
That led the Wise, who sought him from afar,
And idols on their own unhallowed shore
Dashed, at his birth, to be revered no more!
   This theme on reeds of Albion I rehearse: [2]
The dawn of that blest day inspired the verse;
Verse that, reserved in secret, shall attend
Thy candid voice, my critic, and my friend!

[1] Orpheus.
[2] An allusion to Milton's "Hymn on the Morning of Christ's Nativity."

Comments on Poetry from

THE REASON OF CHURCH GOVERNEMENT URG'D AGAINST PRELATY

[1641–1642]

(From the introduction to Book II)

. . . ALTHOUGH A POET, soaring in the high region of his fancies, with his garland and singing robes about him, might without apology speak more of himself then I mean to do, yet for me sitting here below in the cool element of prose, a mortall thing among many readers of Empyreall conceit, to venture and divulge unusual things of my selfe, I shall petition to the gentler sort, it may not be envy to me. I must say therefore that after I had from my first yeeres by the ceaselesse diligence and care of my father, whom God recompence, bin exercis'd to the tongues, and some sciences, as my age would suffer, by sundry masters and teachers both at home and at the schools, it was found that whether ought was impos'd me by them that had the overlooking, or betak'n to of mine own choise, in English or other tongue, prosing or versing, but chiefly this latter the stile, by certain vital signes it had, was likely to live. But much latelier in the privat Academies of *Italy*, whither I was favor'd to resort, perceiving that some trifles which I had in memory, compos'd at under twenty or thereabout (for the manner is that every one must give some proof of his wit and reading there) met with acceptance above what was lookt for, and other things which I had shifted in scarsity of books and conveniences to patch up amongst them were receiv'd with written Encomiums, which the Italian is not forward to bestow on men of this side the *Alps*, I began thus farre to assent both to them and divers of my friends here at home, and not lesse to an inward prompting which now grew daily upon me, that by labour and intent study (which I take to be my portion in this life), joyn'd with the strong propensity of nature, I might perhaps leave something so written to aftertimes as they should not willingly let it die. These thoughts at once possest me, and these other: That if *I* were certain to write as men buy Leases, for three lives and downward, there ought no regard be sooner had then to God's glory by the honour and instruction of my country. For which cause, and not only for that I knew it would be hard to arrive at the second rank among the Latines, *I* apply'd my selfe to that resolution which *Ariosto* follow'd against the perswasions of *Bembo,* to fix all the industry and art I could unite to the adorning of my native tongue: not to make verbal curiosities the end (that were a toylsom vanity), but to be an interpreter & relater of the best and sagest things among mine own Citizens throughout this Iland in the mother dialect: That what the greatest and choycest wits of *Athens, Rome,* or modern *Italy,* and those Hebrews of old, did for their country, I in my proportion, with this over and above of being a Christian, might doe for mine; not caring to be once nam'd abroad, though perhaps I could attaine to that, but content with these British Ilands as my world, whose fortune hath hitherto bin, that if the Athenians, as some say, made their small deeds great and renowned by their eloquent writers, *England* hath had her noble atchievments made small by the unskilfull handling of monks and mechanicks.

Time servs not now, and perhaps I might seem too profuse, to give any certain account of what the mind at home in the spacious circuits of her musing hath liberty to propose to her self, though of highest hope and hardest attempting: whether that Epick form whereof the two poems of *Homer,* and those other two of *Virgil* and *Tasso* are a diffuse, and the book of *Iob* a brief, model: or whether the rules of *Aristotle* herein are strictly to be kept, or nature to be follow'd, which, in them that know art and use judgement, is no transgression, but an inriching of art: And, lastly, what K [ing] or Knight before the conquest might be chosen in whom to lay the pattern of a Christian *Heroe.* And as *Tasso* gave to a prince of *Italy* his chois whether he would command him to write of *Godfreys* expedition against the infidels, or *Belisarius* against the Gothes, or *Charlemain* against the Lombards, if to the instinct of nature and the imboldning of art ought may be trusted, and that there be nothing advers in our climat or the fate of this age, it haply would be no rashnesse from an equal diligence and inclination to present the like offer in our own ancient stories. Or whether those Dramatick constitutions,

wherein *Sophocles* and *Euripides* raigne, shall be found more
doctrinal and exemplary to a nation: the Scripture also affords us
a divine pastoral Drama in the Song of *Salomon,* consisting of
two persons and a double *Chorus,* as *Origen* rightly judges: And
the Apocalyps of Saint *Iohn* is the majestick image of a high and
stately Tragedy, shutting up and intermingling her solemn Scenes
and Acts with a sevenfold *Chorus* of halleluja's and harpes, sym-
phonics; and this my opinion the grave autority of *Pareus,* commenting that booke, is sufficient to confirm. Or if occasion shall
lead to imitat those magnifick Odes and Hymns wherein *Pindarus*
and *Callimachus* are in all things worthy, some others in their
frame judicious, in their matter most an[d] end faulty: But
those frequent songs throughout the law and prophets beyond all
these, not in their divine argument alone, but in the very critical
art of composition, may be easily made appear over all the kinds
of Lyrick poesy to be incomparable. These abilities, wheresoever
they be found, are the inspired guift of God rarely bestow'd, but
yet to some (though most abuse) in every Nation; and are of
power, beside the office of a pulpit, to inbreed and cherish in a
great people the seeds of vertu and publick civility, to allay the
perturbations of the mind, and set the affections in right tune,
to celebrate in glorious and lofty Hymns the throne and equipage
of Gods Almightinesse, and what he works, and what he suffers
to be wrought with high providence in his Church, to sing the
victorious agonies of Martyrs and Saints, the deeds and triumphs
of just and pious Nations, doing valiantly through faith against
the enemies of Christ; to deplore the general relapses of King-
doms and States from justice and Gods true worship. Lastly,
whatsoever in religion is holy and sublime, in vertu amiable or
grave, whatsoever hath passion or admiration in all the changes
of that which is call'd fortune from without, or the wily suttleties
and refluxes of mans thoughts from within, all these things with
a solid and treatable smoothnesse to paint out and describe:
Teaching over the whole book of sanctity and vertu, through all
the instances of example, with such delight to those especially
of soft and delicious temper, who will not so much as look upon
Truth herselfe unlesse they see her elegantly drest, that whereas
the paths of honesty and good life appear now rugged and difficult, though they be indeed easy and pleasant, they would then
appeare to all men both easy and pleasant, though they were

rugged and difficult indeed. And what a benefit this would be to
our youth and gentry may be soon guest by what we know of
the corruption and bane which they suck in dayly from the
writings and interludes of libidinous and ignorant Poetasters,
who, having scars ever heard of that which is the main con-
sistence of a true poem, the choys of such persons as they ought
to introduce, and what is morall and decent to each one, doe for
the most part lap up vitious principles in sweet pils to be swallow'd down, and make the tast of vertuous documents harsh and
sowr. . . .

Comments on Poetry from

AN APOLOGY AGAINST . . . SMECTYMNUUS

[1642]

I HAD MY TIME, Readers, as others have, who have good learning
bestow'd upon them, to be sent to those places where, the
opinion was, it might be soonest attain'd; and as the manner is,
was not unstudied in those authors which are most commended;
whereof some were grave Orators & Historians, whose matter me
thought I lov'd indeed, but as my age then was, so I understood
them; others were the smooth Elegiack Poets, whereof the
Schooles are not scarce: Whom, both for the pleasing sound of
their numerous writing, which in imitation I found most easie,
and most agreeable to natures part in me, and for their matter,
which what it is there be few who know not, I was so allur'd
to read, that no recreation came to me better welcome. For that
it was then those years with me which are excus'd, though they
be least severe, I may be sav'd the labour to remember ye.
Whence having observ'd them to account it the chief glory of
their wit, in that they were ablest to judge, to praise, and by
that could esteeme themselves worthiest to love those high perfections which under one or other name they took to celebrate;
I thought with my selfe by every instinct and presage of nature
which is not wont to be false, that what imboldn'd them to this
task might with such diligence as they us'd imbolden me; and

that what judgement, wit, or elegance was my share would herein best appeare, and best value it selfe, by how much more wisely and with more love of vertue I should choose (let rude eares be absent) the object of not unlike praises. For albeit these thoughts to some will seeme vertuous and commendable, to others only pardonable, to a third sort perhaps idle, yet the mentioning of them now will end in serious. Nor blame it, Readers, in those years to propose to themselves such a reward as the noblest dispositions above other things in this life have sometimes preferr'd: Whereof not to be sensible, when good and faire in one person meet, argues both a grosse and shallow judgement, and withall an ungentle and swainish brest. For by the firme setling of these perswasions, I became, to my best memory, so much a proficient, that if I found those authors any where speaking unworthy things of themselves, or unchaste of those names which before they had extoll'd, this effect it wrought with me, from that time forward their art I still applauded, but the men I deplor'd; and above them all, preferr'd the two famous renowners of *Beatrice* and *Laura,* who never write but honour of them to whom they devote their verse, displaying sublime and pure thoughts, without transgression. And long it was not after when I was confirm'd in this opinion, that he who would not be frustrate of his hope to write well hereafter in laudable things, ought him self to bee a true Poem; that is, a composition and patterne of the best and honourablest things; not presuming to sing high praises of heroick men or famous Cities, unlesse he have in himselfe the experience and the practice of all that which is praise-worthy. . . .

A Note on the Verse of

PARADISE LOST

[1667]

The Measure is *English* Heroic Verse without Rime, as that of *Homer* in *Greek,* and of *Virgil* in *Latin,*—Rime being no necessary Adjunct or true Ornament of Poem or good Verse, in longer Works especially, but the Invention of a barbarous Age, to set

off wretched matter and lame Meeter; grac't indeed since by
the use of some famous modern Poets, carried away by Custom,
but much to their own vexation, hindrance, and constraint to
express many things otherwise, and for the most part worse, then
else they would have exprest them. Not without cause therefore
some both *Italian* and *Spanish* Poets of prime note have rejected Rime both in longer and shorter Works, as have also long
since our best *English* Tragedies, as a thing of it self, to all judicious eares, triveal and of no true musical delight; which consists only in apt Numbers, fit quantity of Syllables, and the sense
variously drawn out from one Verse into another, not in the
jingling sound of like endings, a fault avoyded by the learned
Ancients both in Poetry and all good Oratory. This neglect then
of Rime so little is to be taken for a defect, though it may seem
so perhaps to vulgar Readers, that it rather is to be esteem'd
an example set, the first in *English*, of ancient liberty recover'd
to Heroic Poem from the troublesom and modern bondage of
Rimeing.

Preface to

SAMSON AGONISTES

[1671]

Of that sort of Dramtic Poem which is call'd Tragedy

TRAGEDY, as it was antiently compos'd, hath been ever held the
gravest, moralest, and most profitable of all other Poems; therefore said by *Aristotle* to be of power, by raising pity and fear, or
terror, to purge the mind of those and such like passions, that is,
to temper and reduce them to just measure with a kind of delight,
stirr'd up by reading or seeing those passions well imitated.[3] Nor
is Nature wanting in her own effects to make good his assertion;
for so, in Physic, things of melancholic hue and quality are us'd
against melancholy, sowr against sowr, salt to remove salt hu-

---

[3] *Poetics*, VI.

mours. Hence Philosophers and other gravest Writers, as *Cicero*, *Plutarch*, and others, frequently cite out of Tragic Poets, both to adorn and illustrate their discourse. The Apostle *Paul* himself thought it not unworthy to insert a verse of *Euripides* into the Text of Holy Scripture, 1 *Cor.* 15. 33; and *Paræus*, commenting on the *Revelation*, divides the whole Book, as a Tragedy, into Acts, distinguisht each by a Chorus of Heavenly Harpings and Song between. Heretofore Men in highest dignity have labour'd not a little to be thought able to compose a Tragedy. Of that honour *Dionysius* the elder was no less ambitious then before of his attaining to the Tyranny. *Augustus Cæsar* also had begun his *Ajax*, but, unable to please his own judgment with what he had begun, left it unfinisht. *Seneca* the Philosopher is by some thought the Author of those Tragedies (at lest the best of them) that go under that name. *Gregory Nazianzen*, a Father of the Church, thought it not unbeseeming the sanctity of his person to write a Tragedy, which he entitl'd *Christ suffering*. This is mention'd to vindicate Tragedy from the small esteem, or rather infamy, which in the account of many it undergoes at this day, with other common Interludes; hap'ning through the Poets error of intermixing Comic stuff with Tragic sadness and gravity, or introducing trivial and vulgar persons: which by all judicious hath bin counted absurd, and brought in without discretion, corruptly to gratifie the people. And though antient Tragedy use no Prologue, yet using sometimes, in case of self defence or explanation, that which *Martial* calls an Epistle, in behalf of this Tragedy, coming forth after the antient manner, much different from what among us passes for best, thus much before-hand may be Epistl'd: that *Chorus* is here introduc'd after the Greek manner, not antient only, but modern, and still in use among the *Italians*. In the modelling therefore of this Poem, with good reason, the Antients and *Italians* are rather follow'd, as of much more authority and fame. The measure of Verse us'd in the Chorus is of all sorts, call'd by the Greeks *Monostrophic*, or rather *Apolelymenon*, without regard had to *Strophe*, *Antistrophe*, or *Epod*; which were a kind of Stanza's fram'd only for the Music, then us'd with the Chorus that sung, not essential to the Poem, and therefore not material; or being divided into Stanza's or Pauses, they may be call'd *Allæostropha*. Division into Act and Scene, referring chiefly to the Stage (to which this work never was intended), is here omitted.

It suffices if the whole Drama be found not produc't beyond the fift Act; of the style and uniformitie, and that commonly call'd the Plot, whether intricate or explicit,—which is nothing indeed but such œconomy or disposition of the fable as may stand best with verisimilitude and decorum,—they only will best judge who are not unacquainted with *Æschulus, Sophocles,* and *Euripides,* the three Tragic Poets unequall'd yet by any, and the best rule to all who endeavor to write Tragedy. The circumscription of time, wherein the whole Drama begins and ends, is, according to antient rule and best example, within the space of 24 hours.

Abraham Cowley

[1618–1667]

ABRAHAM COWLEY BALANCED precariously on the line separating the Restoration from the preceding age. In his own day he was extravagantly admired, but by the time of Dr. Johnson's famous *Life of Cowley* in *The Lives of the Poets* (1779), he was considered obscure and 'metaphysical' or simply disregarded. His early poetry (*The Mistress*, 1647) is in the tradition of Donne. Later he turned to Christian epic (*Davideis*, 1656), the ode, and the informal essay. His *Pindarique Odes* are an attempt to domesticate an intractable and misunderstood form to the English language. While no more successful than earlier efforts in Italian and French by men like Gabriello Chiabrera and Ronsard, they were acclaimed and imitated by poets of the Restoration.

The introductory section of Cowley's "Preface" to his *Poems* (1656) is a lament for an age which has passed. The comments on ode and epic anticipate the future. Cowlely defends the extravagance of the Pindaric as an exception, sanctioned by the ancients, to the general rules of poetry. The discussion of epic echoes Renaissance thought but is much closer in tone to Davenant's preface to *Gondibert* and Dryden's essay *Of Heroic Poetry* than to Milton's impassioned comments.

The present text is from the 1656 edition of the *Poems*.

BIBLIOGRAPHY. *English Works*, ed. A. Waller, 2 vols. (1905–6). For comment see: A. Nethercot, *Abraham Cowley* (1931); "Abraham Cowley's [Lost] Discourse Concerning Style," *RES*, II (1926); G. Schuster, *The English Ode from Milton to Keats* (1940); R. Shafer, *The English Ode to 1660* (1918); R. Wallerstein, "Cowley as a Man of Letters," *Trans. of Wisc. Academy*, XXVII (1932); G. Walton, "Cowley and the Decline of Metaphysical Poetry," *Scrutiny*, VI (1937).

Preface to

POEMS

[1656]

AT MY RETURN lately into *England,* I met by great accident (for
such I account it to be, that any Copy of it should be extant any
where so long, unless at his house who printed it) a *Book* entituled, *The Iron Age,*[1] and published under *my name* during the
time of my absence. I wondred very much how one who could be
so *foolish* to write so ill Verses, should yet be so *Wise* to set them
forth as another *Mans* rather than his *own;* though perhaps he
might have made a better choice, and not fathered the *Bastard*
upon such a person, whose stock of Reputation is, I fear, little
enough for maitnenance of his own numerous *Legitimate Off-
spring* of that kinde. It would have been much less injurious, if
it had pleased the *Author* to put forth some of my Writings under
his *own name,* rather then his own under *mine.* He had been in
that a more pardonable Plagiary, and had done less wrong by
Robbery then he does by such a *Bounty;* for no body can be
justified by the *Imputation* even of anothers *Merit,* and our own
course *Cloathes* are like to become us better then those of another mans, though never so *rich:* but these, to say the truth,
were so *beggarly,* that I my self was ashamed to *wear* them.
It was in vain for me that I avoided censure by the concealment
of my own writings, if my reputation could be thus *Executed in
Effigie;* and impossible it is for any good *Name* to be in safety, if
the malice of *Witches* have the power to consume and destroy it
in an *Image* of their own making. This indeed was so ill made,
and so *unlike,* that I hope the *Charm* took no effect. So that I
esteem my self less prejudiced by it then by that which has been
done to me since, almost in the same kinde, which is the publication of some things of mine without my consent or knowledge,

---

[1] The reference is to *The Foure Ages of England, or The Iron Age*
(1648).

and those so mangled and imperfect that I could neither with honor acknowledge nor with honesty quite disavow them. Of which sort was a *Comedy* called *The Guardian,* printed in the year 1650, but made and acted before the *Prince,* in his passage through *Cambridge* towards *York,* at the beginning of the late unhappy War; or rather neither *made* nor *acted,* but *rough-drawn* onely, and *repeated*; for the haste was so great that it could neither be *revised* or *perfected* by the *Author,* nor learnt *without-Book* by the *Actors,* nor set forth in any measure tolerably by the *Officers* of the *College.* After the *Representation* (which, I confess, was somewhat of the *latest*) I began to look it over, and changed it very much, striking out some whole parts, as that of the *Poet* and the *Souldier*; but I have lost the *Copy,* and dare not think it deserves the pains to write it again, which makes me omit it in this publication, though there be some things in it which I am not ashamed of, taking in the excuse of my age and small experience in humane conversation when I made it. But as it is, it is onely the hasty *first-sitting* of a *Picture,* and therefore like to resemble me accordingly. From this which had hapned to my self, I began to reflect upon the fortune of almost all *Writers,* and especially *Poets,* whose *Works* (commonly printed after their deaths) we finde stuffed out, either with *counterfeit pieces,* like *false Money* put in to fill up the *Bag,* though it adde nothing to the *sum,* or with such, which though of their own *Coyn,* they would have called in themselves for the baseness of the *Alloy*: whether this proceed from the indiscretion of their *Friends,* who think a vast *heap* of Stones or Rubbish a better *Monument* then a little *Tomb* of *Marble,* or by the unworthy avarice of some *Stationers,* who are content to diminish the value of the *Author,* so they may encrease the price of the *Book,* and like *Vintners* with sophisticate mixtures, spoil the whole vessel of wine, to make it yield more *profit.* This has been the case with *Shakespear, Fletcher, Johnson,* and many others, part of whose *Poems* I should take the boldness to prune and lop away, if the care of replanting them in print did belong to me; neither would I make any scruple to cut off from some the unnecessary yong *Suckars,* and from others the old withered *Branches*; for *a great Wit* is no more tyed to live in a *Vast Volume* then in a *Gigantic Body*; on the contrary, it is commonly more

vigorous, the less space it animates. And as *Statius* says of little
Tydeus,

——*Totos infusa per artus*
Major in exiguo regnabat corpore virtus.[2]

I am not ignorant that, by saying this of others, I expose my selfe
to some *Raillery*, for not using the same severe discretion in my
own case, where it concerns me nearer. But though I publish
here more then in strict wisdom I ought to have done, yet I have
supprest and cast away more than I *publish*; and for the ease
of my selfe and others, have *lost*, I believe, too, more then *both*.
And upon these considerations I have been perswaded to overcome all the just repugnances of my own *modesty*, and to produce these *Poems* to the light and view of the World; not as a
thing that I approved of in it self, but as a lesser evil, which I
chose rather then to stay till it were done for me by some body
else, either surreptitiously before, or avowedly after, my death;
and this will be the more excusable, when the *Reader* shall know
in what respects he may look upon me as a *Dead*, or at least a
Dying Person, and upon my *Muse* in this action, as appearing,
like the *Emperor Charles the Fifth*, and *assisting* at her own
Funeral.

For to make myself absolutely dead in a *Poetical* capacity, my
resolution at present is never to exercise any more that faculty.
It is, I confess, but seldom seen that the *Poet* dyes before the
man; for when we once fall in love with that bewitching *Art*,
we do not use to court it as a *Mistress*, but marry it as a *Wife*,
and take it for better or worse, as an *Inseparable Companion* of
our whole life. But as the *Mariages* of *Infants* do but rarely
prosper, so no man ought to wonder at the diminution or decay
of my affection to *Poesie*, to which I had contracted my self so
much under *Age*, and so much to my own prejudice in regard of
those more profitable matches which I might have made among
the *richer Sciences*. As for the *Portion* which this brings of *Fame*,
it is an *Estate* (if it be any, for men are not oftner deceived in
their hopes of *Widows* then in their opinion of *Exegi monu-*

---

[2] "Infused through all his limbs, a greater virtue ruled in a little body."
Statius, *Thebiad*, I, 416–7.

mentum ære perennius [3]) that hardly ever comes in whilst we are *Living* to enjoy it, but is a *fantastical kind of Reversion to our own selves*; neither ought any man to envy *Poets* this posthumous and imaginary happiness, since they finde commonly so little in present, that it may be truly applyed to them, which S. *Paul* speaks of the first *Christians, If their reward be in this life, they are of all men the most miserable.*

And if in quict and flourishing times they meet with so small encouragement, what are they to expect in rough and troubled ones? if *wit* be such a *Plant* that it scarce receives heat enough to preserve it alive even in the *Summer* of our cold *Clymate*, how can it choose but wither in a long and a sharp *winter?*—a warlike, various, and a tragical age is best to *write of*, but worst to *write in*. And I may, though in a very unequal proportion, assume that to my self which was spoken by *Tully* to a much better person, upon occasion of the *Civil Wars* and Revolutions in his time, *Sed in te intuens, Brute, doleo, cvjus in adolescentiam per medias laudes quasi quadrigis vehentem transversa incurrit misera fortuna Reipublicæ.* [4]

Neither is the present constitution of my *Mind* more proper then that of the *Times* for this exercise, or rather divertisement. There is nothing that requires so much serenity and chearfulness of *Spirit*; it must not be either overwhelmed with the cares of *Life*, or overcast with the *Clouds* of *Melancholy* and *Sorrow*, or shaken and disturbed with the storms of injurious *Fortune*; it must, like the *Halcyon*, have *fair weather* to breed in. The *Soul* must be filled with bright and delightful *Idæa's*, when it undertakes to communicate delight to others, which is the main end of *Poesie*. One may see, through the stile of *Ovid de Trist.*,[5] the humbled and dejected condition of *Spirit* with which he wrote it; there scarce remains any footsteps of that *Genius*,

Quem nec Iovis ira, nec ignes, &c.[6]

[3] "I have built a monument more enduring than bronze." Horace, *Odes*, III, 30.

[4] "But considering you, Brutus, I am sorrowful. The sad fate of the republic cut across your youth when it was being carried forward, as though in a triumphal chariot, in the midst of honors." Cicero, *Brutus*, XCVII.

[5] Cowley's lament frequently echoes *Tristia*, I, 1, 39ff.

[6] "Whom not the anger of Jove, nor fire. . . ." Ovid, *Metamorphoses*, XV, 871.

The *cold* of the Countrey had strucken through all his faculties, and benummed the very *feet* of his *Verses*. He is himself, methinks, like one of the *Stories* of his *own Metamorphosis*; and though there remain some weak *resemblances* of *Ovid* at *Rome*, It is but as he says of *Niobe*,

> *In vultu color est sine sanguine, lumina mœstis*
> *Stant immota genis; nihil est in Imagine vivum;—*
> *Flet tamen.—*[7]

The truth is, for a man to write well it is necessary to be in good humor; neither is *Wit* less eclypsed with the unquietness of *Mind* then *Beauty* with the *Indisposition* of *Body*. So that 'tis almost as hard a thing to be a *Poet* in despight of *Fortune*, as it is in despight of *Nature*. For my own part, neither my obligations to the *Muses*, nor expectations from them are so great, as that I should suffer my self upon no considerations to be *divorced*, or that I should say, like *Horace*,

> *Quisquis erit vitæ, Scribam, color.*[8]

I shall rather use his words in another place,

> *Vixi Camœnis nuper idoneus,*
> *Et militavi non sine gloriá,*
> *Nunc arma defunctumque bello*
> *Barbiton hic paries habebit.*[9]

And this resolution of mine does the more befit me, because my desire has been for some years past (though the execution has been accidentally diverted) and does stil vehemently continue, to retire my self to some of our *American Plantations*, not to seek for *Gold* or inrich my self with the traffique of those parts (which is the end of most men that travel thither, so that of *these Indies* it is truer then it was of the former,

---

[7] "The face is bloodless, the eyes motionless in the sad features; there is nothing living in the image; yet it weeps." *Metamorphoses*, VI, 304–5, 310.

[8] "Whatever coloration life has, I will write about it." Horace, *Satires*, II, 1, 60.

[9] "I lived of late suitable to the Muses, and I struggled not without glory. Now this wall will hold my arms and my lyre, finished with war." Horace, *Odes*, III, 26.

> *Improbus extremos currit Mercator ad Indos*
> *Pauperiem fugiens—*) [10]

But to forsake this world for ever, with all the *vanities* and *Vexations* of it, and to bury my self in some obscure retreat there (but not without the consolation of *Letters* and *Philosophy*),

> *Oblitúsque meorum, obliviscendus & illis,*[11]

As my former *Author* speaks too, who has inticed me here, I know not how, into the *Pedantry* of this heap of *Latine Sentences*. And I think *Doctor Donnes Sun Dyal in a grave* [12] is not more useless and ridiculous then *Poetry* would be in that *retirement*. As this therefore is in a true sense a kind of *Death* to the *Muses*, and a real *literal quitting* of this *World*: So, methinks, I may make a just claim to the undoubted priviledge of *Deceased Poets*, which is to be read with more *favor* then the *Living*:

> *Tanti est ut placeam tibi, Perire.*[13]

Having been forced for my own necessary justification to trouble the *Reader* with this long Discourse of the *Reasons* why I trouble him also with all the rest of the *Book*, I shall onely add some what concerning the several parts of it and some other pieces which I have thought fit to reject in this publication: As first, all those which I wrote at *School* from the age of ten years till after fifteen, for even so far backward there remains yet some *traces* of me in the little *foosteps* of a *childe*; which though they were then looked upon as *commendable extravagances* in a *Boy* (men setting a value upon *any kind* of *fruit* before the usual *season* of it), yet I would be loth to be bound now to read them all over *my self*, and therefore should do ill to expect that patience from *others*. Besides, they have already past through several *Editions*, which is a longer *Life* then uses to be enjoyed by *Infants* that are born before the ordinary *terms*. They had the good fortune then to find the world so *indulgent* (for consid-

[10] "The guilty merchant runs to the ends of India fleeing poverty." Horace, *Epistles*, I, 1, 45.

[11] "Forgetting my friends and to be forgotten by them." *Ibid.*, I, 11, 9.

[12] The reference is to Donne's "The Will."

[13] "In order to please you, I must die." Martial, *Epigrams*, VIII, 69. Misquoted, since the original reads "tanti non est."

ering the time of their production, who could be so hard-hearted
to be *severe*?) that I scarce yet apprehend so much to be cen-
sured for *them* as for not having made *advances* afterwards
proportionable to the speed of my *setting out*, and am obliged
too in a maner by Discretion to conceal and suppress them, as
Promises and *Instruments* under my own hand, whereby I stood
engaged for more then I have been able to *perform*; in which
truly, if I have failed, I have the real excuse of the *honestest*
sort of *Bankrupts*, which is to have been made *Unsolvable*, not
so much by their own *negligence* and ill-husbandry, as by some
notorious accidents and publike disasters. In the next place, I
have cast away all such pieces as I wrote during the time of
the late troubles, with any relation to the differences that caused
them, as among others, *three Books of the Civil War it self*, reaching as far as the first *Battel* of *Newbury*, where the succeeding
misfortunes of the *party* stopt the *work;* for it is so uncustomary
as to become almost *ridiculous*, to make *Lawrels* for the *Conquered*. Now, though in all *Civil Dissentions*, when they break
into open hostilities, the *War* of the *Pen* is allowed to accompany
that of the *Sword*, and every one is in a maner obliged with his
Tongue as well as *Hand* to serve and assist the side which he
engages in; yet when the event of battel and the unaccountable
Will of *God* has determined the controversie, and that we have
submitted to the conditions of the *Conquerer*, we must lay down
our *Pens* as well as *Arms*, we must *march* out of our *Cause* it
self, and *dismantle* that, as well as our *Towns* and *Castles*, of all
the *Works* and *Fortifications* of *Wit* and *Reason* by which we
defended it. *We* ought not, sure, to begin our selves to revive the
remembrance of those times and actions for which we have received a *General Amnestie* as a *favor* from the *Victor*. The truth
is, neither *We* nor *They* ought by the *Representation* of *Places*
and *Images* to make a kind of *Artificial Memory* of those things
wherein we are all bound to desire, like *Themistocles*, the *Art*
of *Oblivion*. The *enmities* of *Fellow-Citizens* should be, like that
of *Lovers*, the *Redintegration* of their *Amity*. The Names of *Party*
and *Titles* of *Division*, which are sometimes in effect the whole
quarrel, should be extinguished and forbidden in peace under
the notion of *Acts* of *Hostility*. And I would have it accounted no
less unlawful to *rip up old wounds* then to *give new ones*; which

has made me not onely abstain from printing any things of this kinde, but to burn the very copies, and inflict a severer punishment on them my self then perhaps the most rigid Officer of *State* would have thought that they deserved.

As for the ensuing Book, it consists of four parts: The first is a *Miscellanie* of several Subjects, and some of them made when I was very young, which it is perhaps *superfluous* to tell the *Reader*; I know not by what chance I have kept *Copies* of them, for they are but a very few in comparison of those which I have lost, and I think they have no extraordinary virtue in them, to deserve more care in preservation then was bestowed upon their *Brethren*, for which I am so little concerned that I am ashamed of the *arrogancy* of the *word*, when I said *I had lost them*.

The *Second* is called, *The Mistress*, or *Love-Verses*; for so it is that *Poets* are scarce thought *Free-men* of their *Company*, without paying some duties and obliging themselves to be true to *Love*. Sooner or later they must all pass through that *Tryal*, like some *Mahumetan Monks*, that are bound by their *Order*, once at least in their life, to make a *Pilgrimage* to *Meca*,—

In furias ignémque ruunt; Amor omnibus idem.[14]

But we must not always make a judgement of their *manners* from their *writings* of this kind, as the *Romanists* uncharitably do of *Beza* for a few lascivious *Sonnets* composed by him in his youth.[15] It is not in this sense that *Poesie* is said to be a kind of *Painting*; it is not the *Picture* of the *Poet*, but of *things* and *persons* imagined by him. He may be in his own practice and disposition a *Philosopher*, nay a *Stoick*, and yet speak sometimes with the softness of an amorous *Sappho*.

Feret & rubus asper Amomum.[16]

He professes too much the use of *Fables* (though without the malice of deceiving) to have his testimony taken even against himself. Neither would I here be misunderstood, as if I affected

[14] "They rush among furies and fire; love is the same for everyone." Virgil, *Georgics*, III, 244.
[15] Beza's youthful love poems *Juvenalia* were published in 1548.
[16] "The rough bramble may bear spices." Virgil, *Eclogues*, III, 89.

so much gravity as to be ashamed to be thought really in *Love*. On the contrary, I cannot have a good opinion of any man who is not at least capable of being so. But I speak it to excuse some expressions (if such there be) which may happen to offend the severity of supercilious *Readers*; for much *Excess* is to be allowed in *Love*, and even more in *Poetry*, so we avoid the two unpardonable vices in both, which are *Obscenity* and *Prophaneness*, of which I am sure, if my *words* be ever guilty, they have ill-represented my *thoughts* and *intentions*. And if, notwithstanding all this, the lightness of the matter here displease any body, he may finde wherewithal to content his more serious inclinations in the weight and height of the ensuing Arguments.

For as for the *Pindarick Odes* (which is the third part) I am in great doubt whether they will be understood by most *Readers*; nay, even by very many who are well enough acquainted with the common Roads and ordinary Tracks of *Poesie*. They either are, or at least were meant to be, of that kinde of *Stile* which *Dion. Halicarnasseus* calls, Μεγαλοφυὲς καὶ ἡδὺ μετὰ δεινότητος,[17] and which he attributes to *Alcæus*. The digressions are many and sudden, and sometimes long, according to the fashion of all *Lyriques*, and of *Pindar* above all men living. The *Figures* are unusual and *bold*, even to *Temeritie*, and such as I durst not have to do withal in any other kinde of *Poetry*. The *Numbers* are various and irregular, and sometimes (especially some of the long ones) seem harsh and uncouth, if the just measures and cadencies be not observed in the *Pronunciation*. So that almost all their *Sweetness* and *Numerosity* (which is to be found, if I mistake not, in the roughest, if rightly repeated) lies in a maner wholly at the *Mercy* of the *Reader*. I have briefly described the nature of these Verses in the *Ode* entituled, *The Resurrection*: And though the *Liberty* of them may incline a man to believe them easie to be composed, yet the undertaker will finde it otherwise.

> —*Vt sibi quivis*
> *Speret idem, multum sudet frustráque laboret*
> *Ausus idem.*—[18]

[17] "Grand-natured and having sweetness along with awesome elevation." *De Veterum Scriptorum Censura*, II, 8.

[18] "So that someone trying to do the same for himself, having tried it, may sweat a great deal and labor in vain." *Ars Poetica*, 240–2.

I come now to the last Part, which is, *Davideis,* or an *Heroical Poem* of the *Troubles of David,* which I designed into *Twelve Books,* not for the *Tribes* sake but after the *Patern* of our Master *Virgil,* and intended to close all with that most Poetical and excellent *Elegie* of *Davids* upon the death of *Saul* and *Jonathan.* For I had no mind to carry him quite on to his *Anointing* at *Hebron,* because it is the custom of *Heroick Poets* (as we see by the examples of *Homer* and *Virgil,* whom we should do ill to forsake to imitate others) never to come to the full end of their *Story,* but onely so near that every one may see it; as men commonly play not out the game, when it is evident that they can win it, but lay down their *Cards* and take up what they have won. This, I say, was the *whole Designe,* in which there are many noble and fertile Arguments behinde; as, The barbarous cruelty of *Saul* to the *Priests* at *Nob,* the several flights and escapes of *David,* with the maner of his living in the *Wilderness,* the *Funeral* of *Samuel,* the love of *Abigal,* the sacking of *Ziglag,* the loss and recovery of *Davids* wives from the *Amalekites,* the *Witch* of *Endor,* the war with the *Philistines,* and the *Battel* of *Gilboa;* all which I meant to interweave upon several occasions with most of the illustrious *Stories* of the *Old Testament,* and to embellish with the most remarkable *Antiquities* of the *Jews* and of other Nations before or at that *Age.* But I have had neither *Leisure* hither to nor have *Appetite* at present to finish the work, or so much as to revise that part which is done with that care which I resolved to bestow upon it, and which the *Dignity* of the *Matter* well deserves. For what worthier *subject* could have been chosen among all the *Treasuries* of past times then the Life of this young *Prince,* who from so small beginnings, through such infinite troubles and oppositions, by such miraculous virtues and excellencies, and with such incomparable variety of wonderful actions and accidents, became the greatest *Monarch* that ever sat upon the most *famous* Throne of the whole Earth? whom should a *Poet* more justly seek to *honor* then the highest person who ever *honored* his Profession? whom a *Christian Poet,* rather then *the man after Gods own heart,* and the man who had that sacred pre-eminence above all other *Princes,* to be the best and mightiest of that Royal Race from whence *Christ* himself according to the flesh disdained not to descend? When I consider this, and how many other bright and magnificent subjects of the like nature the

Holy Scripture affords and *proffers,* as it were, to *Poesie,* in the wise managing and illustrating whereof the *Glory* of *God Almighty* might be joyned with the singular utility and noblest delight of *Mankinde*: It is not without grief and indignation that I behold that *Divine Science* employing all her inexhaustable riches of *Wit* and *Eloquence,* either in the wicked and beggarly *Flattery* of great persons, or the unmanly *Idolizing* of *Foolish Women,* or the wretched affectation of scurril *Laughter,* or at best on the confused antiquated *Dreams* of senseless *Fables* and *Metamorphoses.* Amongst all holy and consecrated things which the *Devil* ever stole and alienated from the service of the *Deity,* as *Altars, Temples, Sacrifices, Prayers,* and the like, there is none that he so universally and so long usurpt as *Poetry.* It is time to recover it out of the *Tyrants* hands, and to restore it to the *Kingdom* of *God,* who is the *Father* of it. It is time to *Baptize* it in *Jordan,* for it will never become clean by bathing in the *Waters* of *Damascus.* There wants, methinks, but the *Conversion* of *That* and the *Jews,* for the accomplishing of the *Kingdom of Christ.* And as men before them receiving of the *Faith* do not without some carnal reluctancies apprehend the *bonds* and *fetters* of it, but finde it afterwards to be the truest and greatest *Liberty*: It will fare no otherwise with this *Art,* after the *Regeneration* of it; it will meet with wonderful variety of new, more beautiful, and more delightful *Objects;* neither will it want *Room,* by being *confined to Heaven.* There is not so great a *Lye* to be found in any *Poet* as the vulgar conceit of men that *Lying* is *Essential* to good *Poetry.* Where there never so wholesome *Nourishment* to be had (but, alas, it breeds nothing but *Diseases*) out of these boasted *Feasts* of *Love* and *Fables,* yet, methinks, the unalterable continuance of the *Diet* should make us *Nauseate* it: For it is almost impossible to serve up any *new Dish* of that kinde. They are all but the *Cold-meats* of the *Antients,* new-heated, and new set forth. I do not at all wonder that the old Poets made some rich crops out of these grounds; the heart of the *Soil* was not then wrought out with continual *Tillage.* But what can we expect now, who come a *Gleaning,* not after the first *Reapers,* but after the very *Beggars*? Besides, though those mad stories of the *Gods* and *Heroes* seem in themselves so ridiculous, yet they were then the *whole Body* (or rather *Chaos*) of the *Theologie* of those times.

They were believed by all but a few *Philosophers* and perhaps some *Atheists,* and served to good purpose among the *vulgar* (as pitiful things as they are) in strengthening the authority of *Law* with the terrors of *Conscience,* and expectation of certain rewards and unavoidable punishments. There was no other *Religion* and therefore *that* was better then *none at all.* But to us who have no need of them, to us who deride their *folly* and are wearied with their *impertinencies,* they ought to appear no better arguments for *Verse* then those of their worthy *Successors,* the *Knights Errant.* What can we imagine more proper for the ornaments of *Wit* or *Learning* in the story of *Deucalion* then in that of *Noah?* why will not the actions of *Sampson* afford as plentiful matter as the *Labors* of *Hercules?* why is not *Jeptha's Daughter* as *good a woman* as *Iphigenia,* and the friendship of *David* and *Jonathan* more worthy celebration then that of *Theseus* and *Perithous?* Does not the passage of *Moses* and the *Israelites* into the *Holy Land* yield incomparably more *Poetical* variety then the voyages of *Ulysses* or *Æneas?* Are the obsolete threadbare tales of *Thebes* and *Troy* half so stored with great, heroical, and supernatural actions (since *Verse* will needs *finde* or *make* such) as the wars of *Joshua,* of the *Judges,* of *David,* and many others? Can all the *Transformations* of the *Gods* give such copious hints to flourish and expatiate on as the true *Miracles of Christ,* or of his *Prophets* and *Apostles?* What do I instance in these few particulars? All the *Books* of the *Bible* are either already most admirable and exalted pieces of Poesie, or are the best *Materials* in the world for it. Yet, though they be in themselves so proper to be made use of for this purpose, none but a good *Artist* will know how to do it; neither must we think to cut and polish *Diamonds* with so little pains and skill as we do *Marble.* For if any man design to compose a *Sacred Poem* by onely turning a story of the *Scripture,* like Mr. *Quarles's,* or some other godly matter, like Mr. *Heywood of Angels,* into *Rhyme,*[19] he is so far from elevating of *Poesie* that he onely *abases Divinity.* In brief, he who can write a *prophane Poem well* may write a *Divine one better;* but he who can do that but ill will do this much worse. The same fertility of *Invention,* the same wisdom of *Disposition,*

[19] Francis Quarles' *Job Militant* was published in 1624; Thomas Heywood's *The Hierarchy of the Blessed Angels,* in 1635.

the same *Judgement* in observance of *Decencies,* the same lustre and vigor of *Elocution,* the same modesty and majestie of *Number,* briefly, the same kinde of *Habit,* is required to both; only this latter allows better *stuff,* and therefore would look more deformedly, if *ill drest* in it. I am farre from assuming to my self to have fulfilled the duty of this weighty undertaking: But sure I am that there is nothing yet in our *Language* (nor perhaps in *any*) that is in any degree answerable to the *Idea* that I conceive of it. And I shall be ambitious of no other fruit from this weak and imperfect attempt of mine but the opening of a way to the courage and industry of some other persons, who may be better able to perform it throughly and successfully.

APPENDIX

A Glossary of Continental Humanists

Referred to by English Critics

AGRIPPA VON NETTESHEIM, Henricus Cornelius (1486–1535). German physician, soldier, scholar, and (by reputation) magician. In 1510 he went to England and met John Colet. His *De Occulta Philosophia* (1530) was condemned by the Inquisition. His *De Incertitudine et Vantiate Omnium Scientiarum* (wr. *c.* 1527) was a notorious and often-reprinted attack on the pretensions of learning, and contains a violent chapter against the poets.

ARETINO, Leonardo Bruni (1374?–1444). A close friend of Coluccio Salutati (*q.v.*) and a standard-bearer of Petrarchan humanism. Translator of works by Plato, Aristotle, Xenophon, Plutarch, etc., and author of lives of Aristotle, Cicero, and Dante. His *History of his Own Times* and his letters are valuable records of the age.

ARETINO, Pietro (1492–1556). Notorious during the sixteenth century for his obscene verses written to accompany equally obscene drawings by Giulio Romano. Author of comedies, satires, and letters which are often witty and frequently off-color. His life was a series of scandalous episodes which fascinated Renaissance authors.

ARIOSTO, Ludovico (1474–1533). Italian epic and lyric poet and dramatist. His *Orlando Furioso* (1532) is the best of the Italian epic-romances before Tasso (*q.v.*). Crowded with digressions, marvels, and ornaments, and often tending to satire, it much influenced Books III and IV of Spenser's *Faerie Queene*. It was translated into English in 1591 by Sir John Harington. Ariosto's comedy *I Supposti* was translated in 1563 by George Gascoigne, becoming the first regular comedy in English prose.

BARBARUS, Hermolaus (Ermolao Barbaro, 1454–95). Italian humanist and student of Pomponius Lactus (*q.v.*). He is best known for his scholarship (*Castigationes Plinianae*, 1492) and his commentaries on Aristotle's philosophical works.

BEMBO, Pietro (1470–1547). Papal Secretary under Leo X, made Cardinal by Paul III. Among his works are *Gli Asolani* (1505), a Platonic dialogue on love, elegant Neo-Latin pastorals, and a dialogue on vernacular grammar and style, *Prose della Volgare Lingua* (1525). Bembo is a representative of the pagan and Ciceronian tendencies of Renaissance humanism; it is said that he disliked reading the Vulgate Bible because of its poor style. His speech on Platonic love is a high point in Castiglione's *Courtier*.

BESSARION, Johannes (1395?–1472). Byzantine humanist influential in spreading Greek learning in Florence in the mid-fifteenth century. His Greek manuscripts became the nucleus of the Library of St. Mark's in Venice; and his enthusiasm for Plato and the Neoplatonists encouraged this element among the Italians. Among his works are translations of Aristotle's *Metaphysics* and Xenophon's *Memorabilia*. His violent quarrel with George Trapezuntius (*q.v.*) resulted in his defense of Plato against the Aristotelians, *In Calumniatorem Platonis*.

BEZA, Theodore (1519–1605). French Calvinist and successor to Calvin in the Chair of Theology at Geneva in 1564. His theological treatises and editorial work on the Greek and Latin versions of the New Testament gave him a European reputation. His metrical versions of the Psalms were also highly regarded.

BIBBIENA (Bernardo Dovizi da Bibbiena, 1470–1520). Author of an early Neoclassic comedy, *La Calandria* (1513), modeled on the *Menaechmi* and enlivened by off-color dialogue. One of the speakers in Castiglione's *Courtier*.

BIONDUS (Flavio Biondo, 1388–1463). One of the great Italian scholars of the fifteenth century, especially active in antiquarian and archeological research. E.g., *Roma Instaurata, Roma Triumphans, Italia Illustrata*. His *Historiarum ab Inclinatione Romanorum*, a history of the decline and fall of Rome, remained incomplete at his death.

BOCCACCIO, Giovanni (1313–75). Best known today for his Italian

Decameron (1353), he was internationally famous as the compiler of the fifteen books of the *Genealogy of the Gods,* a compilation of classical mythology with allegorical explanations, ending with two books in defense of poetry. Other works include *De Casibus Virorum Illustrium,* a collection of non-dramatic 'tragedies,' and a *Life of Dante.*

BRACCIOLINI, Poggio (1380–1459). Italian humanist particularly famous for his discoveries of manuscripts of Lucretius' *De Rerum Natura* and Quintilian's *Institute of Oratory.* His *Facetiae* (pr. 1474), a collection of witty anecdotes, was very popular during the sixteenth century. His sensational quarrels with Lorenzo Valla and Francesco Filelfo (*q.q.v.*) illustrate the bitter invective which characterized Renaissance scholarly controversies.

BUCHANAN, George (1506–82). A Scotsman who spent his early career in France and became the best of the English Neo-Latin authors of the sixteenth century. His Latin tragedies (e.g., *Jephtha,* 1552) were written at this time. He also tutored Montaigne. In 1560 he returned to Scotland with Queen Mary and from 1570–78 was tutor to the future James I of England. His major work is his history of Scotland, *Rerum Scoticorum Historia* (publ. 1582).

CASTELVETRO, Lodovico (1505?–1571). Italian dramatist (*Gli Ingannati,* 1531) and critic best known for his dispute with Annibale Caro in the '50's over the canzone "Venite all'ombra. . . ." and for his *Poetica D'Aristotele Vulgarizzata* (1570), in which he formulated the idea of the three unities in something like its Neoclassic form.

CHRYSOLORAS, Manuel (1355?–1415). Byzantine scholar who introduced Greek to Florence, wrote a Greek grammar, and translated from Homer and Plato.

CLAUSERUS, Conrad (1520–1611). German humanist; translator of "On the Natures of the Gods" of Annaeus Cornutus from Greek into Latin in 1543.

EOBANUS. See HESSUS.

ERASMUS, Desiderius (1469?–1536). The greatest Dutch humanist and a major figure of world literature. Friend of Sir Thomas More, John Colet, and Henry VIII. He edited Jerome, Athanasius, and the New Testament. Among his original compositions are *Institutio Principis Christiani,* on the education of princes, the *Colloquies,* charming Latin dialogues illustrating Latin usage, and the *Adagia,* a collection of commonplaces much used by his successors. His best-known work is his *Moriae Encomium* (*The Praise of Folly,* with a pun on the name More, 1509). Erasmus protested against slavish Ciceronianism in his *Ciceronianus.* His later life was embittered by the Reformation, since he had criticized the Catholic church but resisted Luther's efforts to enlist him on the side of the Protestant cause.

FICINO, Marsilio (1433–99). Italian Platonic philosopher chosen by Cosimo de'Medici to head the Platonic Academy of Florence. His Latin *Works of Plato* (1482), with introductory commentaries, became the standard Renaissance text of the dialogues. His *Theologia Platonica* (*c.* 1485) is an ambitious attempt to reconcile Christianity with Plato and has been accused of rationalism, syncretism, and deism.

FIGLIUCCI, Felice. Sienese humanist, translator of Demosthenes' *Philippics*, and author of a commentary on Aristotle's *Ethics-Della Filosofia morale* (1551).

FILELFO, Francesco (1398–1481). A transition figure between Petrarch and the sixteenth century. He studied Greek and collected manuscripts in Constantinople, and returned to Italy as a lecturer, writer, and poet. Among his works are translations, orations, odes, panegyrics, and an unfinished *Sforziad* celebrating the ruling house of Milan.

FRACASTORO, Girolamo (1483–1553). Physician, philosopher, and poet of considerable merit. He is remembered today for his *Syphilidis sive De Morbo Gallico* (1530), an elegant Virgilian account of the origin and spread of syphilis, often reprinted. His *Naugerius* is a dialogue on poetry which uses Aristotelian ideas but remains emphatically Platonic.

GAZA, Theodorus (1400–75). After 1457, Professor of Greek at Ferrara, later Rome and Naples. Author of a Greek grammar and translations of Aristotle, Dionysius of Halicarnassus, and Cicero (into Greek).

GEMISTUS PLETHO, George (1355–1452). Greek Platonic philosopher and inventor of a mystic religion based on Neoplatonic lore which he believed would replace all existing theologies. During his visit to Florence he popularized Plato and was influential in persuading Cosimo de'Medici to found the Platonic Academy.

HEINSIUS, Daniel (1580–1655). Dutch historian, legalist, and student of political science important to criticism for his annotated edition of Horace (1612) and his *De Tragoediae Constitutione* (1611), both paraphrased in Jonson's *Timber, or Discoveries*.

HESSUS, Eobanus (1488–1540). German humanist. Editor of Theocritus, Virgil, the *Iliad*, etc. An associate of Reuchlin and supporter of Luther in reformation controversies. His original works include metrical versions of the Psalms and a Christian *Heroides* consisting of epistles from famous female saints, including the Blessed Virgin.

JOHANNIS RAVENNENSIS. Either Giovanni de'Malpaglini, d. 1420; or Giovanni da Ravenna, fl. 1400, author of an *Apologia* and a *Historia Elisiae*.

JUNIUS, Franciscus (or Franz, 1545–1602). French Protestant educator. With Emanuel Tremellius (*q.v.*) he produced a Latin Bible (1590, 1624), in which the *Psalms, Proverbs, Song of Solomon*, etc., are referred to as 'poetical parts.' As Librarian for the Earl of Arundel, his son made important contributions to early Anglo-Saxon studies.

LAETUS, Pomponius (1428–98). The leader of the Roman Academy, which was briefly discontinued by Paul II in 1468 for alleged paganism. His reputation as a teacher is great, but his chief literary work is an autobiography written during his brief imprisonment after the closing of the Roman Academy.

LANDINO, Cristoforo (1424–1504). Italian humanist whose most important work is the *Disputationes Camaldulenses* (*c.* 1475), a dialogue the first book of which is a debate on the active *vs.* the contemplative life. The third and fourth books contain an allegorical exegesis of the *Aeneid*.

LIPSIUS, Justus (1547–1606). An important figure in the Renaissance revival of stoicism and an anti-Ciceronian stylist. His critical reputation is established by his *Variae Lectiones*.

MANTUAN (Baptista Spagnolo, 1448–1516). Famous and much imitated during the Renaissance for his *Eclogues* in imitation of Virgil.

MAZZONI, Iacopo (1548–98). Professor of philosophy at Pisa and Rome. His *Defense of Dante* (1572, 1587) attempts to defend the *Divine Comedy* against Aristotelian and other critics. It is particularly interesting for its classification of poetry under Sophistic rather than Dialectic, a classification which implies that poetry and truth are separate.

MELANCHTHON, Philip (1497–1560). Luther's great disciple and a distinguished writer on educational theory. Late in his life he showed a desire to reconcile the Lutheran and Catholic churches, but the project proved impractical.

MINTURNO, Sabestian. Author of two critical works (*De Poeta*, 1559; *L'Arte Poetica*, 1563) which were highly regarded, especially by Sir Philip Sidney. Although recognizing Aristotle's importance, Minturo remained essentially Platonic.

MURETUS, Marc-Antonius (1526–85). French humanist who had to flee to Italy because of charges of immorality. Among his French students was Montaigne. At Rome he was patronized by Gregory

XIII. His writings include works of scholarship (*Variae Lectiones*), commentaries on Cicero, Plato, Aristotle, etc., and Neo-Latin poetry highly regarded by his contemporaries.

MIRANDOLA. See PICO DELLA MIRANDOLA.

PALENGENIUS, Marcellus (Pietro Angelo Manzolli). Author of the *Zodiacus Vitae* (1543), translated by Barnabe Googe as *The Zodiake of Life* (1565).

PAREUS, David (1548–1622). German biblical scholar, popular among Calvinists. His commentaries were published in 1628 and were frequently cited. They are notable for their restatement of the ancient tradition that certain books of the Bible use regular literary forms; e.g., *Revelation* is in the form of a tragedy.

PERIZ, Consalvo. A friend of Ascham and translator of the *Odyssey* into experimental unrhymed Spanish verses: *La Ulyxea de Homero* (1553).

PETRARCH, Francesco (1304–74). The first true humanist. Admired throughout Europe during the Renaissance for his sonnets to Laura (*Canzoniere*), his letters, his discovery of Cicero's *Letters*, and his Neo-Latin verse, especially his epic *Africa*. The *Secretum*, a dialogue between himself and St. Augustine, is a repudiation of his earlier secularism.

PICO DELLA MIRANDOLA, Giovanni (1463–94). The most brilliant of the associates of Marsilio Ficino (*q.v.*). His enthusiasms led him to study the Neoplatonists and the Hebrew and Arabic theological and mystical authors in a search for a 'natural religion' which would reconcile ancient wisdom with Christianity. Today he is remembered for his *Oration on the Dignity of Man,* an expression of Renaissance faith in the significance of the human condition, composed as a preamble to the 900 theses which he offered to defend publicly in Florence. Pico also encouraged the allegorical interpretation of classical mythology. A *Life* by Sir Thomas More is extant.

PICCOLOMINI, Aeneas Silvius (Pius II, 1405–64). The author of a remarkable series of *Memoirs* of his travels throughout Europe as a diplomat and Church official, also known as a humanist and poet. In 1445 he experienced a 'conversion,' turned to God, and rose rapidly in the Church, becoming Pius II in 1458.

POGGIO. See BRACCIOLINI.

POLITIAN (Angelo Ambrogini, 1454–94). After translating several books of Homer at 16, Politian embarked on a dazzling career which made him the foremost poet of his age in Florence, equally skilled in Latin and Italian verse. His *Sylvae* contains poems celebrating poetry as the nurse of mankind (*Nutricia*), Homer, and Virgil. His

Orfeo is a beautiful vernacular retelling of the Orpheus myth in lyric-dramatic form.

PONTANO, Giovanni Gioviano (1426–1503). Neapolitan humanist, historian, and statesman. His *Dialogues*—esp. *Actius*—treat rhetoric, versification, and history. He re-discovered Tiberius Claudius Donatus' commentary on Virgil and produced excellent Neo-Latin verse, including a moving series of poems celebrating his love for his wife.

REUCHLIN, Johann (1455–1522). German humanist and student of Greek and Hebrew. His *Rudimenta Hebraica* (1506) was the first Hebrew grammar written by a Christian. His defense of Hebrew literature and his suggestion that chairs of Hebrew be established at each German university gave rise to the violent controversy between the humanists and the traditionalists which begot the *Epistolae Obscurorum Virorum*, satiric letters largely by Crotus Rubianus and Ulrich von Hutten (*q.v.*).

RICCI, Bartolommeo. Patronized by Ercole d'Este, Duke of Ferrara, author of a Latin lexicon and a work on imitation (*De Imitatione Libri Tres*, 1545).

SALUTATI, Coluccio (1331–1406). The foremost disciple of Petrarch and friend of Boccaccio and Leonardo Bruni (*q.q.v.*). Although primarily a man of affairs, he was responsible for bringing Manuel Chrysoloras (*q.v.*) to Florence, and was the author of orations, letters, and an elaborate allegorical interpretation of the myth of Hercules (*De Laboribus Hercules, c.* 1406).

SANNAZARO, Iacopo (1458–1530). The most brilliant of the Neapolitan poets. His vernacular pastoral-romance *Arcadia* (1504) was widely read and imitated. His Neo-Latin piscatory eclogues were also admired, as was his Christian epic *De Partu Virginis*, in which the theme is embellished with Virgilian epic machinery.

SCALIGER, Julius Caesar (1484–1558). Italian physician, scholar, and humanist who spent most of his life in France. Scaliger's most important literary work is his *Poetice*, a survey in seven books of the major critical topics, published in 1561. Among the many influences evident in the work Aristotle is especially important. The *Poetice* has marked Neoclassic tendencies and was extremely influential throughout Eureope. Scaliger's defense of Virgil at the expense of Homer was often debated *pro* or *con* during the seventeenth century.

SILVIUS. See PICCOLOMINI.

STURMIUS, Johannes (1507–89). German humanist, close friend of Ascham, and ardent Ciceronian. Among his works are a nine-volume edition of Cicero (1557) and a dialogue *De Imitatione Oratoria* (1574). Ascham discussed the question of imitation with Sturmius in a long letter written in 1568 and reprinted in Giles' edition of Ascham, ii, 174–91.

TASSO, Torquato (1544–95). Author of the finest of the Italian epic-romances, the *Gerusalemme Liberata,* and two series of *Discorsi* explaining and defending his critical views. Like many humanists Tasso absorbed Aristotelian ideas but remained a Platonist at heart. His later life was clouded by periods of insanity and persecution by the Inquisition. The *Gerusalemme* influenced Spenser and was translated into English by Fairfax (1600).

TRAPEZUNTIUS, George (1395–1484). Byzantine scholar who taught Greek in several Italian cities and translated Greek authors including Aristotle. His attack on Plato (*Comparatio Aristotelis et Platonis*) led to a controversy with Bessarion (*q.v.*). Poor scholarship and equally poor judgment led to the loss of his once considerable reputation and he died in poverty.

TREMELLIUS, Emanuel (1510–80). A Jewish convert and student of oriental languages. See JUNIUS.

ULRICH VON HUTTEN (1488–1523). Perhaps the most violent of the early German reformationists. Author of poems, letters, and of a major part of the *Epistolae Obscurorum Virorum.* See REUCHLIN.

VALLA, Lorenzo (1407–57). Brilliant scholar and ardent Ciceronian. His demonstration that the *Donation of Constantine* is a forgery was his most sensational achievement. Despite the blow which it dealt the Church, he was patronized by Nicholas V for his knowledge of Greek and Latin and his abilities as a stylist. His *De Voluptate* illustrates his paganism, and his translation of the *Poetics* give him a place in the history of criticism, despite its inadequacy.